MW01592365

125 Years of
Adath Jeshurun Congregation

From Generation
to Generation

Etta Fay Orkin

and Deborah Tolmach Sugerman

ADATH
JESHURUN
CONGREGATION

עדת ישורון

Design and layout: John Toren

Bibliography for first 100 years available through Etta Fay Orkin and the Jewish Historical Society of the Upper Midwest.

Photo Credits: Many individuals and families contributed the photographs that appear in this book. They are too numerous to thank individually, although the contributions of Sam Bender, who served as an unofficial Adath photo archivist until his death, deserves a special note. We would like to thank Richard Sennott for generously contributing the photos of artworks in the color section, and the architectural firm of Finegold Alexander and Associates for providing the architectural photographs in the same section.
Other sources of imagery to whom we are indebted are:

The Minnesota Historical Society
8, Washington Avenue from First Avenue South toward Hennepin Avenue, Minneapolis, ca. 1890; Photographer: William H. Jacoby
9, John H. Stevens house being moved across the Milwaukee tracks, Minneapolis, 5/28/1896.
17, Samuel Deinard, rabbi, Minneapolis. ca. 1905
52, Adath Jeshurun Temple, 3400 Dupont Avenue South, Minneapolis, ca. 1930; Photographer: Lee Brothers
135, Fanny Fligelman Brin (Mrs. Arthur) ca. 1925; Photographer: Eugene G. Garrett

The Jewish Historical Society of the Upper Midwest
25, The Brin Family
74, Womens' League costume party

The St. Louis Park Sun
225, Thomas Friedman

The Star-Tribune, Newspaper of the Twin Cities
208, Moving the Window, Photographer: Richard Sennott

Produced by:
IGI Publishing
A division of Lerner Publishing Group, Inc.
241 First Avenue North
Minneapolis, MN 55401 U.S.A.

Website address: www.igigraphics.com

Library of Congress Cataloging-in-Publication Data
Orkin, Etta Fay.
125 years of Adath Jeshurun Congregation : from generation to generation / by Etta Fay Orkin and Deborah Tolmach Sugerman.
p. cm.
ISBN 978-0-9820870-3-9 (alk. paper)
1. Adath Jeshurun Congregation (Minneapolis, Minn.) 2. Jews--Minnesota--Minneapolis--History. 3. Conservative Judaism--Minnesota--Minneapolis--History. 4. Rabbis--Minnesota--Minneapolis. 5. Minneapolis (Minn.)--Ethnic relations. I. Sugerman, Deborah Tolmach. II. Title. III. Title: One hundred and twenty-five years of Adath Jeshurun Congregation.
BM225.M562A336 2009 296'.09776579--dc22

2009014472

Manufactured in the United States of America
1 2 3 4 5 6 __ 14 13 12 11 10 09

A WORD OF THANKS

Our congregation owes a debt of gratitude to Etta Fay Orkin for more than 30 years of work in lovingly researching, collecting and writing the history of the Adath's first 100 years. It would be impossible to calculate the hours that Etta has spent on this project. This book draws upon just a small part of the material she has assembled.

My sincerest appreciation to Deborah Tolmach Sugerman. In only 12 months she has been able to tirelessly research, organize and capture in writing our history, covering the past 25 years. Without her firm commitment to this project, we would not have been able to meet our publication schedule.

In every project there must be an individual that keeps the program on track. Joni Sussman is the person responsible for answering all our questions, setting our schedule, solving our technical challenges, keeping our spirits high and working almost daily as a liaison with our editor. We are deeply indebted to Joni for her contributions.

John Toren, our editor, must be thanked for his outstanding work. He was quick to master the complexity of this project and organize the hundreds of papers, articles, photos, Hebrew phrases, and interviews. His patience, ability and willingness to work with our committee is sincerely appreciated.

Thank you to the Adath Book Committee that helped interview congregants, collected, sorted and scanned photos, and helped with the numerous other tasks that were required to produce a book of this magnitude. Without the help of Barb Fishman, Jeanne Kagin, Sue Kane, Sherri Lear, David Pink, Glenn Sherling, Dianne Silverman and Norton Stillman, this beautiful book would not be a reality today.

There are so many congregants who have contributed to the success of the Adath Jeshurun that it would be impossible to list every name and accomplishment. For this reason we have listed all of our congregants as of December 31, 2008 in the back of the book. Whatever your involvement in our synagogue life, know that you all have contributed to our congregation's past successes and our future growth.

– Norman Pink
Book Committee Chair

Author's Dedication

To my husband, Dr. Milton Orkin, of Blessed Memory, 1929-1999;
to our children, Dr. Bruce & Ethel Seltzer Orkin, Craig and Catherine Orkin Oskow,
Martin Lee Abramson, of Blessed Memory, Michael & Aimee Orkin (Abramson) Raymond;
our grandchildren, Roxanne, Daniel, David, Kevin, Noah, Aviva, Rachel, Abe, Ora & Leila.
And to all of those who are no longer with us who contributed their impressions between 1981 and 2009
when this project was in progress, I am grateful that I had the opportunity to meet,
talk, interview, and to gain from them their wealth of memories.

– Etta Fay Orkin

Adath Jeshurun Congregation gratefully acknowledges the

Leo and Lillian Gross Family Philanthropic Fund

for making possible the publication of this book

in honor of the 125th anniversary of our congregation.

Contents

3   The Early Years (1884 – 1903)

15   The New Century (1903 – 1912)

29   The Rabbi Matt Years (1912 – 1927)

53   The Rabbi Schwartz Years (1927 – 1929)

61   The Rabbi Albert Gordon Years (1930 – 1946)

97   The Rabbi Morris Gordon Years (1947 – 1952)

121   The Rabbi Rabinowitz Years (1953 – 1960)

139   The Rabbi Lipnick Years (1960 – 1965)

151   The Rabbi Goodman Years (1966 – 1982)

181   The Rabbi Cytron Years (1983 – 1996)

219   The Rabbi Kravitz Years (1996 –)

233   Adath Jeshurun Today

Preface and Acknowledgements

by Etta Fay Orkin

This is the story of the Adath Jeshurun Congregation (Adath) which was founded in Minneapolis, Minnesota, in 1884. It also tells about the beginnings of the Jews in Minnesota, because the history of the Adath Jeshurun is an integral part of the story of the entire community.

I have drawn the story from the recollections of members, past presidents, and people whose families were connected with the synagogue. More than 70 oral histories were recorded and many more people were interviewed or helped to identify people in photos. Other information came from newspaper clippings, tapes, personal memoirs and letters sent by former associates of the congregation, their descendants and other members of the community.

I started the book more than 25 years ago for the synagogue's Centennial, in 1983/1984, and a very short version of this history was printed then.

Articles in the *American Jewish World* have been an invaluable resource and deserve a special note. The *AJW* has chronicled the happenings of local, national and international Jewry since 1915. The articles were about Minnesotans, their social and communal events, where they travelled, who was born, (Bar/Bat) B'nai Mitzvah, engaged, married, organizational and educational involvement, accomplishments, and obituaries. From birth to death the *AJW* for many years was the Minnesota Jew's best friend, telling all that the friend wished to tell. And each Rosh Hashanah an article appeared giving a summary of what had taken place in the Jewish world the previous year.

Information also came from synagogue files and the congregation's newsletter, the *Clarion* (1930-2008). Minneapolis City Directories, 1884-1914, local newspapers and previously published histories were also useful.

Some of the most valuable information came from the Joseph Schanfeld papers, Rabbi Albert I. Gordon's book, *Jews In Transition*, Rabbi Gunther Plaut's book, *The Jews of Minnesota*, and from the personal collection of Dorothy Davis Gordon. Anna K. Schwartz, a former Adath Religious School principal, past president of both the Adath's and the Midwest Regional Women's League, and wife of Adath president, Louis B. Schwartz, had planned to write a book on the life of Rabbi Albert Gordon. The materials she had accumulated would have made a fascinating book but death put an end to her pursuits.

Last, but a very vital source are the visual images: pictures of the people who founded the congregation, their families, the men, women and children, who were members, the buildings that housed the synagogue and the rabbis, cantors, teachers and dedicated staff.

MY VERY SPECIAL THANKS TO:

Rabbi Arnold M. Goodman – who formed a committee to plan the Adath's Centennial in 1981. It was his suggestion that we write a book, and so we began with an oral history project and began taping the older members of the congregation. Thus began a process of plus 25 years in which a new generation was born, a new synagogue building was built in Miinnetonka and sadly - many of those that were involved are now gone. But, happily, we have their wonderful memories!

Rabbi David Younger – for his friendship and expertise in many areas.

Dr. Rhoda Green Lewin – for her generous help in editing an earlier version of this book and for being my ally.

Ruth Firestone Brin – for her insight and assistance for the Rabbi Jerome Lipnick Years, and to her husband, Howard , of blessed memory, for his encouragement.

Judith Brin Ingber – for her help with the Brin Family's lineage as the Adath's longest continuous family with her cousins, Doris Kirschner, Sally Minsberg, Barbara Hoffman and Buddy Brin.

Joyce Dechter Orbuch – Adath Past President, and co-chair with Cantor Morton Kula of the Centennial Year's Programing, 1983-84, and **Melissa Cohen Silberman**, Public Relations Chair for help in writing the centennial year.

Deborah Sugerman – for writing the sections about the last 25 years.

Norman Pink....Norton Stillman...Rabbi Kravitz...... Because you cared...

And most especially to my editor **John H. Toren**, who pulled this book together and made my years of research a printed reality!

I hope you will enjoy reading and learning about, and remembering our collective past. Every person connected with the Adath Jeshurun has a memory that could be told and I wish that we could have recorded each and every one of them.

לדור ודור

Todah Rabah!!!

December 22, 2008
25 Kislev 5769

Rabbi Harold Kravitz
Moe and Esther Sabes Campus
Adath Jeshurun Congregation
10500 Hillside Lane West
Minnetonka, MN 55305

Dear Rabbi Kravitz,

It is an honor to send greetings on the occasion of the 125th anniversary of Adath Jeshurun Congregation, the oldest Conservative synagogue west of Chicago.

My visit to you last January remains with me: your beautiful facility, the *yiddishkeit* and warmth of the community of Israel that dwells within are all models to be emulated.

Adath Jeshurun's heritage of spirituality and inclusion that began with fifteen members in 1884 is alive and thriving, as is evident from the diversity of your membership and the nurturing of Jewish prayer through music and movement. Both the strength of your history and the promise of your future are evident in programming that includes Jewish learning, international cooking, family *kallot*, and groundbreaking efforts to reach out to Christian and Muslim neighbors through the Interfaith Conversations Project.

May Adath Jeshurun Congregation have another 125 years of learning, praying, and building community together. May you go from strength to strength, and may you celebrate many milestones yet to come.

Yours,

Arnold Eisen

Arnold Eisen

Office of the Chancellor
www.jtsa.edu

RABBINICAL ASSEMBLY   כנסת הרבנים

The International Association of Conservative/Masorti Rabbis, established 1901

0 Broadway   New York, NY 10027   phone 212.280.6000   fax 212.749.9166   info@rabbinicalassembly.org   www.rabbinicalassembly.org

December 3, 2008
6 Kislev 5769

Mrs. Heidi Schneider
President
Adath Jeshurun Congregation
10500 Hillside Ln., West
Minnetonka, MN 55305

Dear Mrs. Schneider:

On behalf of the Rabbinical Assembly, we extend to the Adath Jeshurun Congregation family our greetings and good wishes as the Congregation celebrates its 125th anniversary. As one of the most senior Conservative congregations in our movement, indeed, as one of the oldest congregations in our country, Adath Jeshurun has been an ongoing source of leadership and strength in its dedication to learning and mitzvot, its commitment to community, in providing strength to our movement, and in its involvement and ardent support of our People everywhere. The Congregation has also provided exceptional leadership to the civic life of the community through its commitment to social activism, and with its dedication to put into practice the ideals of our tradition.

Throughout its distinguished history Adath Jeshurun has been blessed with learning, caring and creative rabbinic leadership, and we applaud, at this time of celebration, the religious leadership of our colleagues who today so ably serve the congregation. You have also had the good fortune of generations of extraordinary leadership and voluntary commitment on the part of so many individuals from within the congregational family whose dedication and efforts have built a vibrant synagogue community. We extend not only a mazal tov to the Congregation at this happy time, but offer as well our prayers for continuing success and strength in the Congregation's commitment to ever be a vibrant kehillah kedosha dedicated to emunah, Torah and gemilut hassadim.

May the Congregation continue to be blessed in all that it does.

Sincerely yours,

Rabbi Jeffrey A. Wohlberg
President

Rabbi Joel H. Meyers
Executive Vice President

Magen Avraham Congregation   קהילת מגן אברהם, עומר
ע.ר. 580085538
20 Marganit Street, P. O. B. 63, Omer, Israel 84965   מרגנית 20, ת.ד. 63, עומר, מיקוד 84965
טלפון: 08-6460424   פקס: 08-6467321
Telephone: +972-8-6460424   Fax: +972-8-6467321
website: www.magenavraham.org   *   e-mail: efrat@magenav.org

December 1, 2008 - 4 Kislev, 5769

Dear Congregants of Adath Jeshurun,

Congratulations to you all as you celebrate 125 years that Adath Jeshurun has been in existence. What a wonderful and strong congregation you are. Adath Jeshurun is one of the leading Jewish congregations in North America. It has been groundbreaking in many ways, not the least of which is the wonderful commitment to Jewish life that membership and participation in Adath Jeshurun engenders in so many people. Your commitment to the growth of the Conservative/Masorti Movement here in Israel is pioneering and outstanding among US Conservative Congregations. We are proud to be connected to you as your sister congregation in Israel (a relationship first formed by our first rabbi Michael Graetz, when he would visit the Twin Cities in the 1970's).

Our ties have been strengthened through the years as Rabbis Goodman, Kravitz and Brusso have brought groups from Adath to visit Magen Avraham in Omer. Rabbi Graetz has served as a scholar-in-residence at Adath and Rabbi Gil Nativ will be visiting again in March, 2009 as a scholar-in-residence. Our teens visited you in the summer of 2005 and then again last summer. Members of your congregation have found a home away from home in Omer and strong friendships have developed.

Your commitment to the safety of Jews living in Israel is expressed by the security room at the Activity Center at Kehillat Magen Avraham which was built through your generosity. This Center houses our after-school and summer day camp programs as well as serving as a community center for adults.

In addition, you have recognized the importance of a unique program at Magen Avraham that trains rabbinical students to be congregational rabbis and you have helped make it the success that it is.

The members of Kehillat Magen Avraham have great admiration for your congregation. We deeply appreciate your ongoing support.

Mazal Tov on your accomplishments. We wish that your next 125 years are as vibrant and important for the Jewish people as your first.
Sincerely,

Rabbi Dr. Gil Nativ

Eyal Sabatani,
Chairman of the Board

Rabbi Dr. Gil Nativ, Phone: 08-6467205   רב ד"ר גיל נתיב, טל. 08-6467205

A Message from Rabbi Kravitz

Isaac Leib Peretz, one of the great writers in Yiddish, wrote in 1890, "A people's memory is history; and as a man without a memory, so a people without a history cannot grow wiser, better." Peretz's statement is in keeping with the tone set in the book of Genesis, as it recalls the stories of the founding families of our people. The Bible records the past not simply as an academic exercise, but rather as a record of our people's covenant with God. We preserve the memory of previous generations to guide our people to grow wiser and better.

This volume, which seeks to capture the first 125 years of the Adath Jeshurun Congregation, represents one more chapter in the long history of the Jewish people. It preserves memories of our congregation and describes how each generation contributed to making us the flourishing Jewish community we are today.

Last Rosh Hashanah I recalled stories of our congregation's past, arguing that there was a common thread of commitment running through the history of Adath Jeshurun. At our best, each generation of our congregation was committed to the vitality of the Jewish people, maintaining tradition while seeking to live up to a high standard of ethical, human and Jewish conduct. These commitments are captured in two Yiddish words that convey what we should be about—*Yiddishkeit* and *Menschlichkeit*—people who are grounded in Judaism and people of integrity. I believe that these continue to be the most important tasks for those of us who inherit the legacy of the founders who established our synagogue and chose the name Adath Jeshurun, a gathering of the righteous.

Assembling this history has been an enormous task. Regretfully, there is no way that this volume could possibly record all of the acts of goodness, public and private, that have blessed our congregation and contributed to its ongoing vitality. We hope that people will be forgiving if they were not acknowledged adequately.

We offer profound thanks to Etta Fay Orkin for her incredible work over the last 30 years researching, preserving and recording our congregation's past. Our sincere thanks to Deborah Tolmach Sugerman who just a year ago accepted the challenge of writing the last 25 years. We are grateful to Norton Stillman who guided us when we first proposed getting this project done in time for the 125th Anniversary. As we sought to make this volume a reality, Joni Sussman played a crucial role in getting the project completed and we thank Harry Lerner and Lerner Publications for taking on this project. We thank John Toren, whose great skills as an editor have shaped this volume, and Norman Pink, who has stepped up whenever there has been a need for great leadership at Adath Jeshurun. Agreeing to chair the History Committee with his son David and shepherd this project was another example of their family's phenomenal contribution. We thank Jonathan Gross and the Gross family for their deep generosity in supporting the publication of this volume. We hope it will inspire a new generation to carry on the sacred work that has been done these last 125 years at Adath Jeshurun.

May God bless our efforts that we may continue to grow wiser and better.

Hazak, Hazak v'Nitchazek – Be strong, be strong and let us be strengthened together,

– Rabbi Harold J. Kravitz,
MAX NEWMAN FAMILY CHAIR IN RABBINICS

125 Years of

Adath Jeshurun Congregation

*From Generation
to Generation*

Three of the four men who signed the Articles of Incorporation of Adath Jeshurun, Simon Gittelson (above left), Akiba "Kive" Goldblum (left), and Abraham Louis Album (above right). Not pictured: David Cohen.

1

THE EARLY YEARS
1884 – 1903

On August 20, 1884, four members of the Minneapolis Jewish community met with Elijah Plum, Notary Public of Hennepin County, to file the Articles of Incorporation for a "society" to be known as A'Tas Yeshurun (Adath Jeshurun), a name for the people of Israel meaning "a gathering of the righteous." By one o'clock that afternoon they were finished with their day's task. Or better said, at one o'clock that afternoon they had begun. Where their efforts would ultimately lead was beyond anything they could possibly have envisioned.

The four men—Akiba (Kive) Goldblum, Abraham Louis Album, David Cohen and Simon Gittelson—were all from well-established East European merchant families. The question is, what were they doing in Minnesota at that early date in its history? What were the living conditions and level of civilization in the region at that time? And how did the new synagogue fit into the broader context of pioneer Jewish life? Most important of all, what were the motives prompting these men and women to start a new religious organization that would become the first Conservative synagogue west of the Mississippi, and a forerunner of a new ideological approach to Judaism in the United States?

PIONEERS

When European explorers arrived in the area that would later become the State of Minnesota, it was inhabited by Dakota and Ojibway tribes that were engaged in a fierce though intermittent conflict to secure control of its wild rice beds and hunting grounds. The first white visitor to record his experiences was Father Louis Hennepin, a Belgian and Franciscan priest and a member of LaSalle's expedition of 1678—though by that time French fur traders had already made contact with the natives of the region.

In 1819 a U.S. Army contingent arrived to build a fort overlooking the confluence of the Mississippi and Minnesota rivers. Its purpose was to protect the still-lucrative fur trade in the Upper Mississippi Valley from incursions by British and French traders, and to maintain peace between the Indian tribes. Fort Snelling was the first permanent white settlement in the region.

Before long the soldiers had built a sawmill and flour mill at the Falls of St. Anthony, a few miles upstream from the fort. (St. Anthony Falls later produced the first electricity generated by falling water in the Western Hemisphere.) Although most of the land in the vicinity still belonged to the Indians, a community of fur traders and frontiersmen developed, augmented by increasing numbers by settlers. When Wisconsin became a state in 1848, civic leaders hastily convened in the town of Stillwater, in the St. Croix River Valley, to form the new territory of Minnesota. Within a year their plan had become a reality.

As the territory developed, St. Paul became a commercial center and economic opportunities increased. By 1848 German and West European Jewish settlers had arrived to make new homes and establish businesses in the region.

The Jewish pioneers in Minnesota were as dissimilar in personality, fortune, character and purpose as human beings could be; yet at the same time, they were united by their common Jewish background and heritage. In the fluid, egalitarian society of the frontier, these Jews were not merely accepted but welcomed—an experience quite different from what Jews who arrived later often experienced.

Yet many of the Jews who arrived in Minnesota during the 1850's had several things in common. They were often from Germany and Central Europe, and most of them had already lived in other parts of the United States. They spoke English, were merchants, and many brought some capital with them. Like other settlers, many Jewish immigrants arrived in Minnesota in search of better opportunities, and they were a hardy crew. Most were in their twenties and thirties, and many, heeding the Biblical injunction to "be fruitful and multiply," brought large families with them.

MINNEAPOLIS

By 1853, St. Paul had grown into a sizable comunity, but Minneapolis, on the west side of the Mississippi across from St. Anthony, was still a tiny settlement, largely because the land still belonged to the Dakota Indians. One observer described the village at the time as "...a thriving little place, just sprung into existence, opposite St. Anthony, on land termed 'The Reserve,' which has not yet been brought into market, but which is rapidly becoming thickly populated."

On July 4, 1855, a suspension bridge was completed from St. Anthony across the Mississippi River to Minneapolis, and the first team of horses were driven across it. Minneapolis was incorporated in 1856 with a population of less than 200. By this time tourists had been journeying up the Mississippi River on steamboats to see the beauty of the area for years.

In that same year, 1856, Jewish residents purchased a burying ground in St. Paul and consecrated the first Jewish cemetery in Minnesota. The following year, the Jews of St. Paul, St. Anthony and surrounding settlements incorporated under the laws of the Territory of Minnesota as the Har Zion Association, later known as the Mount Zion Hebrew Association, the first Jewish congregation in Minnesota. There were approximately twenty Jewish families living in Minnesota when it became a state in 1858.

As the pine forests to the north were harvested and floated down the Mississippi, Minneapolis became a lumber milling center. As farmers settled the countryside, its flour mills brought even greater fame and prosperity to the area. Minneapolis soon became the milling capital of the world and Minnesota continued to attract a wide variety of people through its mining, milling, quarrying, logging, shipping and fishing industries.

The Jewish merchants of Minneapolis supplied thousands of these new arrivals with ready-made clothing, furnishings and supplies. Traders also arrived periodically from the Red River Valley to the northwest in long oxcart caravans to sell furs and purchase dry goods for trade of resale back home. In spring the lumberjacks would come to town with money in their pockets after a long winter felling trees, and in the fall it would be the farmhands. With all this commercial activity, poverty and want were almost unknown among the first Jewish settlers. (For those who arrived later with the great tide of East European Jewish emigration during the early 1880's, the story would be different.)

From the beginning Minneapolis and St. Paul developed in different directions. St. Paul became a railroad center with much of its economic success tied to its rail connections with the East. In 1858, it also became the capital of the new state of Minnesota. Minneapolis was more diversified in business and industry and more flexible. By June of 1862 trains were running between St. Anthony and St. Paul, and when the Civil War ended in 1865, there were five thousand people living in Minneapolis. St. Paul was still the larger of the two cities, with over 12,000 inhabitants, but Minneapolis was growing fast.

During the 1850's, 60's and 70's most immigrants to Minnesota were from the Scandinavian countries, Germany and the United Kingdom. In time various communities were established, and a network of separate yet highly interdependent businesses began to take shape.

Although many of the early Jewish settlers came from Germany, Austria, Hungary and Bohemia, they were usually referred to simply as "German" because of similar cultural traits. The first division in St. Paul's Jewish community arose when new settlers from Poland, Lithuania, Romania, and western Russia arrived. These newcomers, commonly referred to as "Polish," used Yiddish as their mother tongue, and they found the language and customs of the older "German" Jewish settlers unfamiliar. As for the established Jewish residents, they reacted to these new arrivals from a different culture with the age-old exclusiveness of an in-group becoming conscious of, and protective of, its own status. After all, (many of them reasoned) they had arrived when life was primitive and the frontier spirit was still alive. The new arrivals could have no idea what it was like in the "olden days." It was the very presence of these "Polish" Jews, rather than differing ritual practices, which encouraged the rise of the Reform Movement in Judaism and hastened it psychologically.

Due to dissension among the members of St. Paul's Mount Zion Congregation, another congregation arose known as Ahabath Achim, but it was short-lived, and Mount Zion, the bastion of the established Americanized Jews of St. Paul, remained the only synagogue in Minnesota until 1872, when a number of the new Eastern European families established the Congregation Sons of Jacob as a traditional synagogue. It was incorporated in 1875. Sons of Jacob later merged with another congregation into what is now the Conservative congregation of Beth Jacob in Mendota Heights.

In 1872, Minneapolis annexed St. Anthony, its neighbor across the river, and the *Minneapolis Tribune* noted that the Jewish population of the enlarged city consisted of nine heads of families plus several single men and women. By 1877, the Jewish population had risen to 172. Yet Minneapolis Jews had not formed any congregations. The *American Israelite* (a Jewish periodical founded by Isaac Mayer Wise in Cincinnati in 1854) chastised the Jews of Minneapolis for this lack of zeal.

In the early years Minneapolis Jews did not have a minyan, and when one of their number died, they would drive by horse and wagon across ten miles of rugged terrain to pray and bury the person at the Har Zion Cemetery in St. Paul. On one occasion a child in the community died and the funeral party became lost on the plains between the two cities in a blinding snow storm. It was night before they found their way into St. Paul, and by then it was too late to obtain a burial certificate or bury the body. They had to stay overnight in St. Paul.

Incidents like this one convinced the Minneapolis Jewish community that they needed a cemetery, and in 1876 they purchased land four miles from the center of the city, naming it the Montefiore Cemetery. It was unaffiliated with any congregation and all members of the Jewish community were permitted to bury their dead there. (In 1952 this cemetery merged with Temple Israel, becoming the Temple Israel Cemetery.)

SHAARAI TOV, THE FIRST MINNEAPOLIS SYNAGOGUE

On October 8, 1878, Minneapolis Jews organized their first congregation, Shaarai Tov ("Gates of Goodness"). Today it's known as Temple Israel. Because the community was so small, in the early years Shaarai Tov was traditional, and included both Germans and East Europeans. On September 8, 1880, the *Minneapolis Journal* described the new congregation as having a "Conservative-Reform Service, a union of orthodox and reform faiths leaning toward the liberal side." The first High Holiday Service was held in the newly built synagogue on Fifth Street South between First and Second Avenues.

To get some flavor of the times, in 1876 Alexander Graham Bell invented the telephone, and three years later Thomas Edison perfected his electric light. That same year there was a Yellow Fever epidemic in the South and many new Jewish citizens moved north to settle in "healthy" Minnesota. By 1880 Minneapolis had 103 Jewish families and the city had grown to nearly 50,000. There was a horse-drawn car line called the Minneapolis Lyndale and Lake Calhoun which went from the corner of 1st Avenue South and Washington out to Lake Calhoun, where people fished, picnicked, boated, and built summer cottages. The line was later extended to Lake Harriet and then to Lake Minnetonka at Excelsior. In 1882 the city's Grand Opera House was built and there were electric lights. By 1883, the famous Honeywell thermostat—a device that regulated furnace and boiler temperatures automatically—had been invented.

MASS MIGRATION

Minneapolis received its greatest spurt in population between 1880 and 1890, when the arrival of 120,000 new residents increased the population to 165,000. It was during this period, and extending on into the early 1920's, that the huge wave of East European Jews came to the United States and to Minnesota.

By the 1880's, conditions in Europe had changed drastically for the worse. New repressive laws were being enacted in Russia. There was social and political unrest in Romania, Russia, and the Austro-Hungarian Empire. In 1881 Czar Alexander II was assassinated in Russia. The blame was placed on the Jews. Pogroms flared. The May Laws, published in 1882, prohibited Jews from living in certain areas, and restricted the limits of their residence and opportunities to earn a living. The number of Jewish students in secondary and higher schools was also limited.

The governing body of the Russian Orthodox Church underscored government objectives when it formulated the policy for one third of Russia's Jews to convert, one third to die, and one third to flee the country. The pogroms, restrictive decrees, and administrative pressure caused the mass emigration of Jews from Russia.

In Romania the government also maintained an anti-Semitic atmosphere. The situation of the Jews continued to worsen through the end of the nineteenth century and into the twentieth. The inpouring of Russian and Romanian exiles began.

Early in 1882, two hundred East European Jewish refugees arrived in St. Paul. The city's well-established Jewish residents reacted with shock, dismay, and disbelief, but quickly rallied for them. This new influx put increasing strain on Jewish social welfare programs, however, and the growing diversity led in time to the creation of new institutions, as the newcomers formed communities of their own which developed alongside those of the original "German" group.

The pioneer German-Jewish community had been able to avoid the establishment of a voluntary ghetto because its members were already relatively prosperous and spoke English when they arrived. On the other hand, the newcomers from Eastern Europe arrived with little means of livelihood and scant command of the language. They settled in different sections of the city according to nationality, separated both from the older established Jews and from each other. Each group developed its own synagogues. The Romanians established themselves on the South Side around Franklin Avenue and 15th Street. Russians and Lithuanians who had come before the mass migration had also settled South. Another colony of Russian, Polish and Lithuanian Jews established itself on the near North Side of the city, west of the downtown area.

Thus Minneapolis, like most other communities, gradually saw the development of a form of self-segregation among Eastern European Jews. Variations in religious practices, though minor, were often regarded as of utmost importance. Memories associated with the "old home" required that persons who knew the places of which the immigrant spoke should be at hand or easily available. It was more comfortable to live near *landsmen* to stem homesickness. Jews from Eastern Europe generally were more meticulous in ritual observance than their German brethren and their services were held daily rather than weekly.

The Reform Movement in the 1880s

Reform Judaism was a trend advocating modifications of Orthodoxy to conform with the needs of contemporary life and thought. It asserted the legitimacy of several changes including making Kashrut an option rather than a necessity; no longer looking to the centrality of the Temple in Jerusalem as Diaspora Jews were building their own temples where they lived; eliminating the injunction for Jewish men to cover their heads when they prayed, and supplementing the traditional Hebrew prayers with German and then English prayers.

In the early 1880s, under the direction of Rabbi Henry Iliowizi (1880-1888), Shaarai Tov began to move in the direction of Reform Judaism. For example, congregants were given the option of wearing or not wearing a hat. In Minneapolis, the German group had preceded the East European Jew by only ten years, and the division between the two was based more on economics than on region or origin. The gap between old and new, Reform and Orthodoxy, was also narrower in Minneapolis than in St. Paul, and Shaarai Tov did not acquire the position of extreme self-segregation.

Jessie Bernard, a Minnesota Jew who became a renowned sociologist, arrived at the conclusion that the real difference between Eastern and Western European Jews consisted in neither degrees of wealth nor place of origin, but in degree of biculturalism. The German Jews had made the momentous decision to embrace the culture of the non-Jewish world a generation or two before the East European Jews. This placed them several rungs above the East European Jews in the social hierarchy of their new country. As soon as the children of the East European Jews became Americanized, they tended to become incorporated into the "German Jewish" community. The degree of acceptance of American culture, rather than national origin, was the real basis of differentiation.

It was clear to many observant Jews in Minneapolis that they needed an alternative to Shaarai Tov. Adath Jeshurun was established to meet that need.

THE FOUNDING OF ADATH JESHURUN

On Wednesday, August 20, 1884, the citizens of Minneapolis awoke to a bright sun. It was to be a mild day, with the temperature climbing only to 76 degrees. And the news on the front page of the *Minneapolis Journal* that day was fairly mild, too. The lead stories described a continuing conflict between France and China and Grover Cleveland's announcement of his candidacy for president. On that day four men gathered to incorporate Adath Jeshurun.

The founders, Akiba (Kive) Goldblum, Abraham Louis Album, David Cohen and Simon Gittelson, were all from East European merchant families. The Brin, Gittelson, and Cohen families had come originally from Poland and Lithuania, and had previously been members of Shaarai Tov.

The founders didn't leave much of a preamble, nor did they leave minutes of a meeting. We have no record of why they chose the name A'Tas Yeshurun (Adath Jeshurun) or even why they wanted to form their own congregation. We do know from brief early histories of the organization that the creation of the new congregation had been preceded by several attempts to hold a minyan on the High Holidays in halls in different sections of the city of Minneapolis, mainly near the old court house. A daily minyan had been meeting in various places and the need for a synagogue organization was felt.

It is clear that the society planned to follow strict Orthodox custom until such time as the membership decided otherwise. The *Minneapolis Journal* reported that the purpose of the society was the "worship of Jehovah according to the principles and precepts of the Jewish religion and in the mode prescribed by the Jewish Orthodox minhag." The newly formed congregation had 15 members (not including women and children).

Many questions remain about the early years of Adath Jeshurun, but by searching carefully though contemporary sources, we can begin to flesh out the story of this budding congregation.

In the 1880's half of Minneapolis's population lived within a mile of Washington Avenue, the city's Great White Way. This busy thoroughfare had seven banks, 29 clothing stores, 11 hotels, a music academy, and entertainment halls presenting the era's great actors. All four of Adath Jeshurun's founders operated businesses on Washington Avenue.

Abraham Louis Album and his wife were recent arrivals in Minneapolis from Lithuania. They owned a small

Fanny (Engler) Schanfield, Moses and Brana Schanfield, and baby Esther Schanfield, some of the Adath's early members.

clothing establishment at 623 Washington Avenue South and lived at 803 Eleventh Avenue South.

David Cohen operated another clothing business, known as D. Cohen and J. Rosenthal, two blocks north at 417. His home was at 228 Fifth Avenue South. Though there is no proof, it's possible that David Cohen was related to Jacob Cohen, one of Minnesota's pioneers. They both ran businesses on Fourth and Washington, and both were deeply interested in furthering the future of Judaism in their city. Jacob Cohen was born in Vilna, Lithuania, in 1843. He had emigrated to the United States in 1869, going first to Chicago and then in 1870 to Minneapolis, where he opened a dry goods and general merchandise store. He was considered the best Talmudic student in the community, and was interested in all things relating to Judaism.

Children of Isador Koval Cohen, Lillian, Benjamin, Josephine, Joseph and Edith

Isador Koval Cohen, one of the early presidents of Adath Jeshurun, was Jacob Cohen's brother-in-law, and had taken his name. Jacob's wife Celia and Isador's wife Josie (or Chana Golde) were sisters from the Blusten family.

A few doors down from the David Cohen establishment was Kive Goldblum's Dry Goods store at 425 Washington Avenue South. According to Kive's grandson, Kenneth Goldblum, and granddaughter, Genevieve Goldblum Barnett, the Goldblums were also from Lithuania and had come to the United States in the late 1860s, first to Chicago and then, in the late 1870s, to Minneapolis. By 1884 they and their five sons lived at 1219 South 7th Street.

Kive was considered a fine *chazan* (cantor), and later helped form the Kenesseth Israel Congregation on the North Side, becoming its first president. Kenesseth Israel, incorporated in 1894, was started by Russian and Lithuanian Jews. Kive had *landsmen* there. However, he always lived on the South Side and must have divided his time between Kenesseth Israel and Adath Jeshurun. The distance between the two neighborhoods was two-and-a-half miles.

Kenneth Goldblum recalled:

Life on Washington Avenue

Top: It was on this stretch of Washington Aveneue that the families who started Adath Jeshurun lived and ran their businesses.

Middle: Nathan Hershman, an early member of Adath Jeshurun, ran a grocery store on 3rd Street in downtown Minneapolis. In a photo from 1902 are his family (from left) Sophie, Frank, Rose, Faggie, Ruby (back) and Minnie.

Bottom Left: Faggie, Frank, Sophie, Minnie and Rose.

Many years ago I was at the Mincha minyan at Adath Jeshurun. David Bank said that as a chazan my grandfather Kive could make them all cry on Yom Kippur! My dad, David Goldblum, was born in a house on 8th Street and 12th Avenue South which the family lived in and rented. It was the Stevens' house, which was the first frame house built in Minneapolis. My uncle, George Goldblum, was born there. When the Stevens house was moved to Minnehaha Park, George was still a boy and rode on the roof!

(In July, 1985, the Stevens house was moved a second time under the auspices of the National Historical Society as a National Landmark. It now stands in Minnehaha Park.)

Moving the Stevens house. Note George Goldblum on the roof.

The fourth signatory on the A'Tas Yeshurun incorporation papers was Simon Gittelson. Simon's pawnbroker shop was next door to his friend Kive Goldblum's shop at 427 Washington Avenue. The Gittelson family had come to America from western Poland around 1874, settling first in Chicago. Simon arrived in Minneapolis about 1874, and was briefly employed by Jacob Cohen at his dry goods store before establishing his own business. The Gittelsons then lived at 823 Sixteenth Avenue South. Simon later went into the jewelry business.

Rachel Gittelson, Simon's sister, married Samuel Brin. The Gittelson/Brin family descendants have the oldest continuous family membership in the congregation.

Howard Brin, Rachel's grandson, recalled in 1983:

My father's mother, Rachel Gittelson, was Simon's younger sister. My dad, Arthur Brin, was born in Chicago in June of 1880 and came to Minneapolis in 1881 when he was 17 months old. My mother's family [Fligelman] was also associated with the Adath. They came from Romania.

Five generations have worshipped in [the Adath] building at 34th and Dupont; my grandfather, John Fligelman; my father and mother, Arthur Brin and Rachel Fligelman; myself and wife, Howard and Ruth Firestone Brin; our daughter, Judith Brin, and her husband, Jerry Ingber and their two boys, Shai and Noah.

According to the business directories, Kive Goldblum's wife Hannah operated a dressmaking shop where she also sold fabric. She was also in real estate, and built the Gold-

blum Building on Washington Avenue. The Goldblums' daughter-in-law, Anna, (Mrs. David Goldblum) was a sister to Moshe Bearman, the first president of the Talmud Torah of Minneapolis. The community was a small network strengthened by many family ties.

Also in business on Washington Avenue were Nathan Gumbiner, who became the first president of Adath Jeshurun, and John Gruenberg, of Wilzner and Gruenberg, who was one of the moving forces in the early days at the Adath. The dry goods firm of N. & J. Gumbiner was at 1313 North Washington Avenue. Gruenberg was from Botosani, Romania, and resided at 421 Seventh Avenue South, but moved East after the 1893 Depression. His descendants, like those of the four founders, still live in Minneapolis.

Although many of Adath's founders and early congregants came in search of new economic opportunities, they were also eager to leave the troubles they had faced in the Old World behind. A typical headline in a local newspaper at the time proclaimed:

"PERSECUTING JEWS - ISRAELITES FIND LIFE IN RUSSIA BURDENSOME"

The article reported from St. Petersburg: "There is another outbreak against the Jews at Dubrovitza near Kovno in Western Russia. An anti-Semitic mob pillaged 12 shops and 20 houses. Many of the Jews were wounded during the riot; one woman was killed. The police and clergy were powerless to quell the disturbance."

A half-century later, Louis Schwartz would describe the temper of the times in the following terms: "...there was a world-wide depression, rioting in Europe and anti-

Jewish demonstrations in Germany. Our ancestors, seeing that there was no hope in the Old World, came to this country and to Minneapolis and established this Synagogue, dedicated to their God and their children."

Among more encouraging events of 1884 was the discovery of the tetanus bacillus. The Equal Rights Party was formed and nominated the first women candidates for the highest offices in the nation. (Both major parties had refused to support woman suffrage in the national election.) A World's Fair was held in New Orleans, Mark Twain's *Adventures of Huckleberry Finn* was published, and Henrik Ibsen's *The Wild Duck* was first produced.

The million-dollar West Hotel opened in 1884 with rooms at $3 a day and was described as the most elegant hostelry between Chicago and San Francisco with a marble floor in the dining room and mahogany wainscoting.

A splendid new 9-room house (with barn) on Pleasant Avenue near 26th Street was renting for $20 a month, and a similar home could be purchased for $3,500 in the Blaisdell addition near Nicollet Avenue and 27th Street. Mayor George A. Pillsbury authorized a contract to pave both sides of 12th Avenue.

During its early years the new congregation of Adath Jeshurun gathered for minyan and High Holiday services in various halls. According to Joseph Schanfeld the first holiday minyan was held in Turner Hall at the corner of 6th Avenue North and Washington Avenue, (a building subsequently occupied by the Altman Implement Company). Next they met in buildings at the corner of Nicollet Avenue and 2nd Street (later torn down to make room for a city park); at the corner of 8th Avenue South and 4th Street (diagonally across from where the old courthouse stood); and on the second floor of a building at the corner of 15th Avenue South and Franklin. Minyans were also held in Schanfeld's home at 1207 South 1st Street.

These gatherings would usually take place in a spare room over somebody's store or in their homes. Schanfeld recalled, "The benches were hard, the accommodations poor, yet they were at least as good as those in their European village communities. The synagogues were centers of cultural life of the more learned East European Jews. The synagogue was used not only for prayer, but for study and social purposes as well. The first institution to be established was in every instance the synagogue."

In 1888 disaster struck, when a fire broke out after Kol Nidre services, destroying all ritual and other property. Reform Congregation Shaarai Tov came to the rescue by giving a Torah to the stricken group.

The October 12, 1888, issue of the *American Israelite* contained a detailed but condescending description of the accident::

The Sunday following Yom Kippur witnessed a novel and interesting event, the burial of the remains of the Sepher Torah, burned on 'Erev Yom Kippur.' The funeral train was composed of the members of the congregation Adath Yeshurun, headed by two rabbis, who pronounced the funeral prayers and sermon as if over a human corpse. Great fear exists among our Orthodox 'Yehudim' lest the destruction of the Sepher Torah augurs them great misfortune. The burial was somewhat like that of a human being, except that instead of a box or coffin being used to include the ashes, they were placed between two stones. Which were then cemented together and buried. To one not believing as they do, the affair has an appearance of the greatest superstition, and it seems as though a great deal of reform might be introduced into their religion with beneficial results.

By 1900 there were approximately 8,000 Jews living in Minneapolis out of a total population of 202,718. The Minneapolis School of Art had opened and the city had its first "skyscraper." William McKinley defeated William Jennings Bryan for the United States presidency in that year; Sigmund Freud published *The Interpretation of Dreams*; Anton Chekhov's *Uncle Vanya* received its first major staging, and the new popular dance was the Cake Walk.

RABBI AARON H. SINAI

Little is known about Rabbi Sinai's association with the newly formed Adath Jeshurun, though according to Minneapolis city directories of the time, he served as its rabbi from 1884 to 1893. In his obituary (September 9, 1903), which carried the title BELOVED RABBI, the *Minneapolis Journal* reported that he had lived in Minneapolis for 20 years and been associated with Congregation Kenesseth Israel. However, that congregation had only been in existence for ten years at the time of the rabbi's death. In any case, he was described as "one of the leading Orthodox rabbis of the country." The article went on to report:

Rabbi Sinai was one of the first rabbis to minister to the Orthodox Jews of Minneapolis and during the forty-five years he lived in America he was identified with every important Jewish movement in the country and

Early Adath Jeshurun Members

Rachel Gittelson, 1882

Arthur L. Brin, Ben, Sam, Sig, and Mamie

Noah and Fanny Schanfield on their wedding day, 1897

John and Antoinette Fligelman and baby Fanny.

held a place of the first order in the Orthodox Jewish church of America.

The Yiddish term for "Chief Rabbi" is *ShtadtRov* which literally means "city rabbi" or "chief rabbi" of the community. This was a European concept and in the early days of the community the settlers adhered to this practice. The chief rabbi rendered service in turn to the different segments of the Jewish community, and when issues would arise between them he would hand down decisions based on Jewish law. Rabbi Sinai must have served the traditional community in Minneapolis in that capacity until 1903.

Rabbi Aaron H. Sinai

Entries in the Minneapolis Directory offer clues to the early history of Adath Jeshurun. In 1885-86 it lists Rabbi Sinai as living at 422 6th Avenue North, and affiliated with the Hebrew Orthodox Church at 220 Nicollet. That must have been the Adath Jeshurun, which was at that time Minneapolis's only Orthodox congregation. In the next year the same home address is given but the synagogue address is now 529 North 2nd. Two years later, in 1888-89, the synagogue has moved to the corner of Nicollet and North 2nd and the rabbi has moved to 312 7th Avenue North. From 1890 to 1892 his home address is the same though the synagogue is listed at a hall in the south west corner of 2nd Street and Nicollet Avenue.

The Adath's first president and Sunday school principal was Nathan Gumbiner, who still has relatives in Minneapolis through the family of Edward and Gusty Rappaport, their daughter Mary Blaz, and her nephew Jon Rappaport.

EARLY WOMEN'S GROUPS

The Sisters of Peace was the first traditional women's group, started in 1882 by Mrs. Nathan Gumbiner, who was its first president. It was part of Adath Jeshurun Congregation. Twenty-five years later, in *The Jews in Minnesota*, Ruby Danenbaum described the Minnesota chapter as second in rank among the charitable societies in Minneapolis.

She gives greater attention to the Hebrew Ladies Benevolent Society, reporting that numerous families and individuals had been the recipients of its bounty, especially during the harsh winter months. It was founded in 1877, when Mrs. Baszion Rees invited to her home the 15 Jewish women living in the city to form the society. They were: Mmes. Malchen Deutch, Hannah Pflaum, Monasch, Jacob Cohen, S. Gittelson, J. Skoll, Dittenhoffer, Apt, Krutzkoff, Lewis Brin, K. Brin; and three young women, Miss Celia Rees (later Mrs. Sol Sulzberger), Anna Brin (who married David Burton), and Esther Konigsberger who became the wife of A. Brin of Chicago. Soon after organizing, the ladies gave an affair "netting the munificent sum of $60 ... to purchase a fence for the newly bought burial ground."

In her book Danenbaum highlights the organization's social impact on city life.

Through the necessity for raising funds, the Ladies Benevolent Society has been a factor in the society life in Minneapolis. The numerous parties and balls given under their auspices have in a measure held society together. The first charity ball was given by the society and proved such a success that for many years thereafter, it was repeated and was the society event of the season. It was at this affair that the debutantes made their first bow in the social world and the young men aired their first full dress suits.

In 1889, a Minneapolis correspondent of undisguised anti-Orthodox and anti-Eastern sentiments made special mention of the 4th Anniversary Ball of Adath Jeshurun, calling it a "brilliant" affair—a phrase he usually reserved for entertainments of his own social class. Ten years later the *Minneapolis Evening Edition* offered an equally glowing description of the annual event. It read, in part:

"The series of Hebrew charity balls are arranged in an ascending scale in the annuals of society life, and the fifteenth annual function, held last night, showed a marked advance in attendance, elegance and enthusiasm over last year. The great ballroom in Masonic Temple looked its best and the decorations were on a large scale... In the center of the stage a stand of handsome silk flags was placed between two large flags which hung from ceiling to floor...The stage was banked with palms and potted plants. Danz's orchestra furnished the music for the program."

The Annual Hebrew Charities included the Hebrew Ladies Benevolent Society and the Sisters of Peace in the early 1880's.

A valuable snapshot of social life at the turn of the

20th century has been given by Albert Gordon in his book *Jews in Transition*, which contains reminiscences of some of the earliest Jewish settlers:

"As I recall the scene in 1883 when I came here, there were not so very many Jews. There were three divisions of the community The most prominent Jews, who came in the early 70's, a group of about 25 or 30 families. They were engaged in various businesses. They were clothing merchants. Some had very fine businesses In the center of town, dry goods merchants, jewelers, and owners of pawn-shops and liquor stores, cigar merchant and makers and one lithographer. There was one very fine attorney with an excellent reputation. With a few exceptions, this group was all of German- Jewish origin, though most of them did not come here directly from Germany. They had lived in other sections of the U.S. before they came here. There were, among these families, a few Jews of 'Polish' origin. But their number was not very great proportionately."

"In those days, there were no pavements in Minneapolis. There were wooden sidewalks. The town had about 50,000 people. There was one car-line. The University of Minnesota had only one building.

"There was quite a colony of Romanian Jews. For the most part they lived on the South Side of town around Franklin Avenue and 15th. They had some nice people among them. Most of the people to whom I refer were not affluent. Only one family owned a horse and buggy. People lived in rather larger houses of seven to nine rooms, but their rent was very small. Most marriages took place in the homes. There were no intermarriages in those days, except for one case, that I can think of."

Many of the early Jewish settlers were eager to merge culturally with the non-Jewish community but they did not deny their Jewishness. On the social level, they generally associated only with each other.

Charles Shapera, born in 1888 in Minneapolis, reported that his father, Louis, came to St. Paul in 1879 from Lithuania and his mother, Sophia Benjamin Shapiro, arrived a few years later. They moved to Minneapolis in the mid-1880's. Sophia was a sister to Abraham Album's wife, Sadie.

"We didn't have any relatives out of town. It was a close-knit family. In fact, all of my mother's side of the family lived in Minneapolis and we were very close, living in one neighborhood. It was not a Jewish neighborhood at all. Within an area of one or two square miles there probably were about 20-25 Jewish families. None of them were

The first Bar Mitzvah at Adath Jeshurun was David Jeffrey in 1891. He is standing here between his two sisters.

Reform and all were members of the Adath. My mother's brothers were Moses, Nathan, Charles, Benjamin, and she had one sister, Sadie.

"There were Jews living in our area by the name of Goldman, Abraham Harris and his wife, Rachel, a lovely woman. There was the Brin family, the Sternbergs, Rosenfelds, Gittelsons, Maser and Joseph Cohen, the Goldblums, and there was a Mark Harris, brother of Abe, in the scrap iron business. The Blooms and Goldmans were in the scrap iron business too. My father was a traveling man for a Minneapolis hardware company. Some others were in insurance and real estate, such as there was. There was a Scandinavian section, another section of Catholics and we were in between. Most of the Protestants were English, Germans and Scandinavians and the Catholics were Irish."

Many of these families were the earliest members of Adath Jeshurun.

From upper left: Dora Freidman and her sister Lena, who married Rabbi Matt.
Jacob and Claire Halpern, with their children Bessie, Charles, Ben, Sam, Saul, Anna, Esther, Ruth, Blanche, Frances, Maurice, and Tobie, circa 1910
The Davis family: (From left) Glady Davis Miller, Dorothy Davis Gordon (Mrs.Albert I.), Ann Davis Orenstein, Rose Davis Zane, Bertha Davis Naftalin (standing), Mary Wolpert Davis ("Mama D." as she was called by her family), and her husband Max Davis, son Bob Davis, (standing), "Baubie" Baile Friedman Davis, and Davis sons Louis, Barney, James, and David.

2
THE NEW CENTURY (1903 – 1912)

In 1903 Adath Jeshurun got its first permanent synagogue building, but due to financial vicissitudes and natural calamities, it would move several more times before finding a long-term home in 1906. The arrival of M. D. Mirviss, who became the Adath's temporary "rabbi" in 1907, added further stability to the young but growing congregation.

In February of 1903 the Adath purchased its first permanent synagogue, a frame church building located on Seventh Street South between 11th and 12th Avenues. The building was secured making use of funds collected by "several affairs given by a committee of ladies, as well as by the loans advanced by several public spirited men, together with the proceeds from the *Minyan* on the Holy Days of 1900."

The *Minneapolis Journal* reported the sale as follows:

The Adath Jeshurun Congregation, the modern orthodox Jewish society, has bought the site, building and entire equipment of the First Swedish Methodist Church on 7th Street between 11th and 12th Avenues South....The price was $2,500...Adath Jeshurun Congregation was formed about 15 years ago [actually 19 years] but has had no regular place of meeting. It has used the Nazareth Church and other buildings. It numbers about seventeen [paying] members but expects an increase up to 200, as a great many of the Jewish race live in the neighborhood. The building will be remodeled and a school will be established. The congregation will secure a teacher and a rabbi. The business meeting of the members will be called by Chairman I. [Isador] Cohen as soon as convenient and the Ladies Aid Society which will cooperate in payment for the new church will meet also.

In early histories of Adath Jeshurun, we often read that a devastating tornado tore through Minneapolis in 1902 and destroyed the synagogue. But the disaster records of the era do not list any such tornado—though two years later Minneapolis did suffer from such a catastrophe. Further

doubt is cast on this date by the reminiscences of Charles Shapera, a long time resident of Minneapolis and early Adath member. He recalled that in 1903, when his father was terminally ill with heart trouble, Charles brought him to the first Adath Jeshurun Synagogue on 7th Street for the afternoon service on Yom Kippur. A discussion took place that day regarding the name of the synagogue. Charles recalled that it was his father who suggested that it be called "Adath Jeshurun" and not "A'tas." The two spellings had the same meaning—a gathering of the righteous—but he felt that the spelling "Adath Jeshurun" was more correct.

The elder Shapera died several months later, and Charles was sure that the year was 1903.

The date of purchase has been confirmned by a contemporary Minneapolis architect and Adath member, Peter Sussman, who researched the titles and deeds of the first two Adath buildings. Peter found that the structure called the Seventh Street Methodist Episcopal Church was completed at the cost of $7,000, and was located between 11th and 12th Avenues South. The First Swedish Methodist Episcopal Church purchased that building on August 9, 1882, for $5,000. On July 14, 1903, documents were filed attesting to the fact that the First Swedish Methodist Episocopal Church had, in turn, sold the property to Adath Jeshurun for $2,500.

In October of 1903, Rabbi Aaron Herman Sinai died. He had served as the rabbi at Adath from 1884 to 1893, but had moved in 1893 to Kenesseth Israel. Following his death, Rabbi S. Silber became the rabbi at Adath Jeshurun, and also at Kenesseth Israel and Anshei Tavrig. (Osias Kulberg is mentioned in early Adath histories as rabbi at the Rumanian Synagogue/Sons of Abraham.)

"Sons of Abraham" or B'nai Abraham Synagogue, referred to as the Rumanian Shul. Its members were all Romanian. A number of them had belonged to Adath Jeshurun but broke off following some disagreements in 1893.

With the death of Rabbi Sinai, Rabbi Silber became the new Chief Rabbi in Minneapolis, and was highly-respected throughout the local Jewish community. In a history of Kennesseth Israel written in 1945, we read that Silber "served not only as an arbiter in affairs that were strictly Jewish, but was an outstanding figure in the consideration of the oft-recurring problems of the community in general as related to its Jewish inhabitants."

Clearly Rabbi Silber's role at Adath Jeshurun was one of many he assumed. But during its early years, when a full time rabbi was unavailable, there were learned men that helped to conduct the services, instruct the children and run the affairs of the small congregation. Many of the East European Jews were well steeped in Judaism and could readily lead services. Among some of the names mentioned in the past are Moses Abramson, J. Joseph Frisch, Max B. Heiman, Osias Kulberg, and Zelik Shore.

There had been a Sunday School in the 1890s but after 1896, the Congregation seemed to have slipped and lost much of its membership, probably due to dissension among its members. It was at this time that Eastern Europeans were arriving in large numbers, and the Rumanian Shul/Sons of Abraham and other synagogues were started on the North Side, drawing members from several other synagogues, including the Adath.

Yet in 1903, the Ladies Aid Society (formerly the Sisters of Peace) was still actively raising funds both for the congregation and the needy. And the Adath's stature in the community might also be suggested by the fact that both Minnesota Governor Samuel Van Sant and Minneapolis Mayor Haynes spoke at the dedication ceremony at the synagogue's new building.

On September 17, 1903, the *Minneapolis Journal* reported on the event, noting the anticipated appearance of the governor and mayor and providing further details.

Addresses will be made by by Rev. M. F. Silber, Rev. S. N. Deinard and Rev. Jacob Aronsohn of St. Paul. The Journal Newsboys band will play and refreshments will be served by the Ladies' Aid Society. The receipts from the sale of seats Wednesday and Thursday next week and for the holidays will be devoted to the free school, the main purpose for the organization - being to establish this school.

A similar article appeared two days later in the same newspaper, and on the 21st, an article appeared with the headline:

NEW JEWISH SYNAGOGUE - ADATH YESHURIM
OCCUPIES NEW BUILDING ON SEVENTH ST.

The article described the event and the address given by Isador Cohen, the Master of Ceremonies, which detailed the congregation's long struggles to secure a synagogue of its own and establish a synagogue school.

Wedding of early Adath president Menashe H. Harris and Dora Freidman, 1904

In other addresses, Dr. Samuel N. Deinard of the "Reformed Jewish church" [Shaari Tov], congratulated the congregation and urged the cultivation of friendly relations between the Orthodox and the Reformed Jews, and Minneapolis Mayor Haynes spoke of the spirit of toleration, which he said "had done much to strengthen the American nation." Rabbi Silber, in a Yiddish address, also made a strong appeal for the proposed school. After the speeches, various "honorable privileges" connected with service of the synagogue were sold at auction. (There is some doubt about which Cohen actually spoke at this ceremony. Jacob Cohen, mentioned earlier, had a son by the name of Isaac Cohen. At that time Isaac would have been in his thirties. In previous histories of the Adath, both Isaac Cohen and Isador Cohen (brother-in-law of Jacob Cohen) were mentioned as early presidents but no firm years were given. However, Isador Cohen was the Adath president at the time the new building was purchased and it's likely that the paper, which referred to the speaker as Isaac, simply made a mistake.)

One of the rabbis who spoke at the ceremony, Dr. Samuel N. Deinard, had arrived in Minneapolis in 1901 as rabbi of Shaarai Tov, and soon became an important and beloved person not only to that congregation but to the entire Jewish community, including the Adath. He had an unusual background for a Reform rabbi. He was born in Lithuania in 1873. His father, a recognized Hebraic scholar and early Zionist, moved his family to Palestine before Samuel was ten years old, in 1882. At the age of 17, Samuel went to Berlin.

At the time, many Reform congregations associated Zionism with anarchy and radical socialism, but Rabbi Deinard vigorously advocated and worked for the creation of a Jewish state in Palestine on both the local and national levels. By the same token, although many Reform Jews were uncomfortable when they heard Yiddish being spoken, Deinard would often address Orthodox congregations in fluent Yiddish. These unusual traits notwithstanding, Rabbi Deinard was respected throughout the community on all levels. His admirable example helped to promote "modernism" and the English sermon into Adath Jeshurun.

Rabbi Deinard's espousal of Zionism helped him to win the respect and admiration of the Eastern European Jews. Within their community, Rabbi Deinard acted as a teacher while serving as a spokesman to his own temple. Through his efforts, congregants came to understand the strange "foreigners" from Eastern Europe. Deinard wanted more than just to explain one group to the other. He wanted to unify them.

Rabbi Deinard chose the press as the instrument to achieve this end. The first weekly newspaper he edited, *Jewish Progress*, was a failure, as were several subsequent efforts. Finally, with the *American Jewish World*, which first appeared in 1912, he succeeded in creating a durable outlet for his dream of bringing disparate groups of Jews together. The newspaper is still in print today.

Rabbi Deinard also believed in a strong Hebrew education for Jewish youth. His speaking at the dedication of the new Adath Jeshurun building in 1906 was one more effort on his part to unite the Orthodox and Reform. He was also recognized for the zeal with which he promoted organizations such as the YMHA, the Jewish Home and Free Dispensary Society, and the Hebrew Free Loan Society.

In anticipation of the school that the Adath was so eager to establish, an Adath Jeshurun Board of Education was organized. At the January 24, 2004, meeting, it was decided to hold Sunday School from 10 a.m. to 12 noon every Sunday. During the week, the Hebrew School would be held after the daily public school, from 4 to 6 p.m. And

Rabbi Samuel Deinard

every Friday Dr. Agat, who at the time was the rabbi and teacher in charge of the religious and Hebrew school, would deliver a sermon at 8 p.m.

At that same meeting, Dr. George J. Gordon was selected to replace Max Harris as a member of the Board of Education and a number of permanent committees were established. (The notes reveal that early in 1904, the Adath had only one woman among its 31 members, though it must be noted that only heads-of-households who had paid their dues were counted.)

Dr. Gordon was a strong advocate of Hebrew and Jewish education. In 1908, the Hebrew Free School of Knesset Israel that had been started in 1894 on the North Side was established as an independent school with a program of Jewish education for girls and boys. They later moved into their own quarters at 808 Bassett Place. In 1913, the name would be changed to Talmud Torah of Minneapolis.

This was a positive move to have one Hebrew school for the entire community instead of each synagogue sponsoring its own. The classes were held after the the public school classes ended. Dr. Gordon headed the Talmlud Torah Education Committee and later in 1928, became the Talmud Torah's Director.

On August 20, 1904, the plans for developing a new school were interrupted when a tornado swept across the northern plains. It touched down in the vicinity of Lake Calhoun and veered northeast up Hennepin Avenue. Many buildings were destroyed by the twister.

One local newspaper described the wreckage as follows:

The center of the storm seemed to hit the business district at the corner of Nicollet Avenue and Sixth Street. Here the immense front of the Glass Block was blown out and a huge skylight blown off, the rain doing damage to stock that cannot be estimated...Many of the fine residence districts of the city suffered terribly, but the greatest and irreparable damage was done to Minneapolis' beautiful shade trees. Thousands of them were broken off or twisted up by the roots and several streets, celebrated for their beautiful trees, are left bare of foliage and shade.

Among the buildings destroyed was the Adath Jeshurun Synagogue. The following High Holidays the congregation again had to resort to the use of a rented hall.

Hy Mendow in 1982

Hy Mendow, who was one of the first to attend the newly formed Adath Sunday School, said, "My recollection of Adath Jeshurun was a synagogue on 7th St. and 12th Ave. S. which was hit by a tornado about 1904. The synagogue was demolished, but rooms where they had the Sunday School were not, and I went to Sunday School there after delivering or selling papers on my way home. My first teacher was Fanny Fligelman."

And Maurice Selcer, the grandson of Mordecai Rivkin, who was an early employee who led services during that

Charles and Ida Selcer, parents of Rose Selcer Zimmerman, circa 1912

period, recalled: "In reference to the destruction of the 7th St. building, my mother told me that the roof caved in and they did not have the money to repair it; and, the carpenters could only work on Sundays!"

The next year a contract was drawn up under which various memebers of the congregation pledged to raise $15,000 to be used in construecting a new synagogue. It read, in part:

...Now, therefore, for the purposes as herein specified and in pursuance thereof the undersigned do each for themselves agree that they will become associated with and become charter members of the corporation by the purchase of two or more shares and assist in the organization and ... incorporation of a Religious Association for the establishment of an Orthodox Hebrew Synagogue and of the necessary building and edifice therefor,

The undersigned do further agree ... to meet the demands created in the constructions of the Synagogue which to be completed Sept.1, 1905, or as soon thereafter as possible....

IN TESTIMONY WHEREOF, The undersigned do hereunto subscribe their names at the date and for the amount as specified.

The legible names that appear on the document are:

M.Glassberg, A.M.Dimond, A.Goldman, S.Zalkind, J. Kosowitz, Simon Ravicz, M.Jeffery, M.Harris, Jos. H.Schanfeld, Phillip Resler, B.S.Harris, D. Jeffery, Arthur Harris, Isidore Weisman, William Weisman, David Ravitch, Michael Dockman, M. Sachs, John Fligelman, Henry Glassberg, Geo.J.Gordon, Jonas Rosenberg, H. Resler, J.H.Woolpy, E.Litowitz, Menashe H. Harris, Gross, Arthur Brin, James Samford[?], Martin Ginsberg, Chas. Juster, Joseph W. Cohen, H. Wolfson, S.Kronick, Sigmond Rauch, M.M.Benjamin, Harry Mitchell, Arthur Zekman, K. Goldlblum, A.Harris, I. Weisman, L. Joeslgorn [?], A. J. Weisman, Jos. Frudenfeld, L.I.Gold, Jacob Rosenberg, [Each man pledged $100.]

In 1906, after two years of holding services in various temporary locations, the congregation paid a deposit on a lot at the southeast corner of 9th Street and 11th Avenue. That deposit was forfeited when it was decided later that year to purchase something "ready-made," and the congregants paid $8,000 to purchase the building they were using as a temporary space on the corner of Ninth Street and Twelfth Avenue from the Free Christian Church of Minneapolis (also informally called the Nazareth Unitarian Church and the Norwegian Free Church). Joseph Schanfeld, who was president at the time, later recalled that during the next two years "appeals were made in the synagogue on High Holidays to raise funds for the remodeling and modernizing of the church into a synagogue." That building would house the synagogue for the next two decades.

RABBI MORDECAI RIVKIN

The Minneapolis Directory of 1907 lists Reverend Mordecai (Max) Rivkin as the rabbi of the Adath Jeshurun, and also lists its new quarters at 9th Street between 11th and 12th Avenues South. Rivkin's residence is given at 1206 South 9th Street. Rabbi Rivkin had been the sexton at the Adath during 1904 and 1905 but early in 1906 he had moved to the Sons of Jacob Synagogue in St. Paul.

Rivkin's granddaughter, Rose Selcer Zimmerman, described him as follows: "He had a short straight beard; he was tall, very handsome and very gentle. We all adored him. I think he must have been paid something because I don't ever remember hearing that he had any other outside jobs. He didn't do anything else. He was a very devout, a very religious man. He came from a little shtetl outside of Kiev."

Of the 8,000 Jews living in Minneapolis in 1907, more than half were Eastern Europeans and Russians who lived predominantly on the North Side. The Rumanians and a small number of Russians settled on the South Side with the more prosperous and established Jews living in the exclusive central residential districts. Twenty years earlier there had been barely 500 Jews in the entire city.

Reverend Mordecai (Max) Rivkin

On June 21, 1907, the Adath Jeshurun sold to Abraham Harris. "The property on 7th Street for $1,560, subject to a mortgage for $1,200 which (2nd party) assumes and agrees to pay as part of the consideration..." The following names signed the document as the Adath Jeshurun Board of Trustees: Menashe H. Harris, A.M. Harris, Abe Goldman, Simon Ravicz, J. H. Woolpy and Joseph Schanfeld.

From 1907, a new era began for the Adath Jeshurun—with a permanent structure of their own, and a new shamas/sexton named Meyer David Mirviss. "M.D.", as he affectionately was called, became the constant thread for the Adath Jeshurun Congregation from 1907 to 1955.

MEYER DAVID MIRVISS

Joseph Schanfeld, who served as president of the board of trustees at Adath for many years, once remarked:

The congregation then made its first lucky move which resulted to a very large extent in bringing the strength and the growth of the congregation to what it is today, and that was, we secured the services of M.D. Mirviss as our Sexton.

Having received his theological training in Kovno, Lithuania, where he studied for nine years and trained to be a rabbi, M.D. arrived in Minneapolis in 1906 and in 1907 became the temporary rabbi of the then traditional Adath Jeshurun. He was paid $10 per month and he and his family were given living quarters on the second floor of the synagogue on 9th Street. In this way he began a career of service to the Jewish community, which soon became a way of life for him. But Mirviss came to believe that the congregation should be led by an American-trained rabbi, and he voluntarily gave up his post when Rabbi C. David Matt came to the congregation in 1912.

THE SECOND SYNAGOGUE BUILDING

The building that the Adath chose to purchase in 1906 has an interesting history. The Nazareth Church was Unitarian and its first pastor, Kristofer Janson, had engaged Rabbi Iliowizi [from Shaari Tov Temple] to speak there on several occasions. The Adath Jeshurun Congregation had used the Nazareth Church to meet before it purchased its first building on 7th Street.

The Nazareth Unitarian Church's congregation was made up mostly of Norwegians (although a few Swedes and Danes also attended) and the Norwegian language was used in the services during the 1880s and 1890s. The building was erected in 1886.

The minister that succeeded Janson, Amandus Norman, moved to Hanska, Minnesota, in 1906. That was the year that the Adath took over the building. They had rented it for the preceding two years.

The plan agreed upon was to pay off the $8,000 purchase price in installments, with the final payment due on November 1, 1912. The papers were signed by various trustees of both congregations on July 28, 1906.

At that time M. D. became the sexton, cantor and fundraiser extraordinaire. He and his wife, Masha, became a steadfast link between the synagogue and the congregational family for the next forty-eight years.

M.D.'s son Jacob Mirviss, served as the Director of the Emanuel Cohen Center in Minneapolis, and the Hillel Foundation at the University of Ohio. When he retired, he made aliyah to Israel and lived on Kibbutz Urim. Jacob's daughter, Carmi Mirviss Pollack, taped him in Israel in 1983: "The Mirviss family consisted of my father, M.D., my mother, and the four children, Harold, Jacob, Rose and Herman, who came from Kovno, Lithuania, (now Kaunas). To us, Adath Jeshurun was home in every sense of the word, from the time we came to Minneapolis in 1906, until the synagogue moved to the West Side in 1927. M.D. had preceded us to Minneapolis. Subsequently, two more children were born in the United States—Samuel in 1908, and Sophia in 1910. The six of us, with our parents, lived in a five-room apartment on the second floor in back of the main chapel. It consisted of two bedrooms, a living room, dining room and kitchen.

"I don't recollect how the synagogue proper was heated during those early years, but in our apartment we had a potbelly coal stove and a cooking stove in the kitchen around which we huddled during the cold winters. A steam heat system was installed in the basement after Rabbi Matt became the first official rabbi, and the main auditorium was used for Shabbat evening and morning services. Until that time all services, except the High Holidays and Festivals, were held in the first floor vestry rooms, which were also heated in the earlier days by a potbelly stove. My older brother, Harold, and I had to carry the coal in buckets from an outside shed and empty the ashes from this stove and our house daily.

"The first floor of the building was divided into three rooms—a large assembly room and two smaller rooms. One was for daily minyans and the other was for classes. Harold and I did the janitorial work, sweeping and dusting. Father did the inspecting and made us go over the spots we missed. In the winter, of course, the sidewalks had to be cleared of snow and there was plenty of sidewalk to shovel!

The young M. D. Mirviss

"How did Father happen to become the 'Rabbi', cantor and shamas of Adath Jeshurun? In Kovno, he was a *yeshiva bachur* at the Yitzhak Elkana Yeshiva, but he didn't complete his studies of *s'micha*. He could read and write Yiddish and he knew Hebrew. He was qualified for the position. He didn't want to be drafted into the Czar's army so he came to Minneapolis, where his parents and some of his family had already settled.

"South Side Minneapolis had three synagogues at that time; the Adath Jeshurun, the Rumanishe Shul on 15th Avenue and the Agudath Achim on 17th near Franklin. The Jewish families lived in this area and up to Park and Portland to the west. The families of Dr. George Gordon, the Schanfelds, Harrises, Zimmermans, and Dockmans, all lived in this western area.

"In the early years of Adath Jeshurun, there were not enough members to support even a shamas and his family. So how did M. D. earn a livelihood? For the most part, he did it through contributions pledged for an *aliya l'Torah*, at weddings, Bar Mitzvahs, funerals and Yahrzeits. He also brought the lulav and esrog to some of the members' homes during Sukkot, so the women could perform the mitzvah of blessing the lulav.

"During Pesach, Father had another supplementary source of income. He was the distributor of Passover products of Manischewitz and other products, such as Carmel wine from Israel. After Yom Kippur and Pesach he was able to pay the grocer and the butcher for the purchases made on credit between these two periods. My mother was a very good and frugal homemaker. For Shabbas she always baked challahs and rolls—and they were delicious!

"In the earliest years there were Friday evening services but only a minyan, no sermon by the rabbi, no choir, no community singing. During the earlier years Father conducted all of the services, the three daily minyanim, the Friday nights, Saturday mornings, festivals, the holidays and later on he continued doing that. He was the *baal t'filah* or leader of prayers. His function was to conduct the services; to perform at the funerals, the weddings, when he was called upon to perform them; the Brit Milah (circumcision); and when the membership was organized, to go out and collect the dues. He was one of the experts in the city of Minneapolis in the collecting of funds for Jewish causes."

The June 7, 1907, edition of the *Minneapolis Journal* carried an article announcing that the Adath Jeshurun had obtained the services of the "eminent scholar and preacher" Reverend Dr. S. Roubin, who had formerly worked as a collaborator and reviser of the Jewish Encyclopedia, and before that had been pastor of the Congregation Sharrey Zedek at Winnipeg, Canada, for four years. The article continued:

This change is made in accordance with a recently adopted plan calling for the enlargement of the scope of the church, and the offering of inducements to the younger generation to attend the services. Dr. Roubin will conduct the services and lecture every Friday at 8:00 p.m.

The fact that services once again were being held at 8:00 p.m. and there were Sunday school classes shows that the Adath was attempting to modernize itself. In the strictly Orthodox congregations, there were no Sunday schools and more traditional services would have been held at sundown.

In a pamphlet that appeared in 1907, Ruby Danenbaum gives us the following description of the new rabbi:

...He was born in Suwalky, Russia, in 1854 and was educated in a rabbinical school/yeshiva there.... He is a scholarly man of broad learning attainments and his influence here should be of material benefit to Judaism. Besides ministering to the congregation, he will be the principal of the Talmud Torah.

Danenbaum went on to suggest that under Rabbi Roubin's guidance the Adath Jeshurun had become, next to Shaarai Tov, the most liberal synagogue in Minneapolis.

In his book, *The Jews of Minnesota*, Rabbi Gunther Plaut writes that Rabbi Roubin was:

a fifty-year-old man with distinguished features and keen eyes. He was the type of man who could symbolize the first departure from tradition. By learning and personal habit he belonged to the old school, but by experience and literally worldwide service, he was a far cry from the East European rabbis who had been transplanted from the forced ghettoes of Russia into a self-imposed seclusion in America.

One of the major differences between the Adath and the other Orthodox congregations of that period was that the men and women sat together, though some of the older women did choose to sit in the back of the synagogue.

"One of the reasons we joined the Adath Jeshurun," Hy Mendow later recalled, "was because my father's Rumanian synagogue was a segregated congregation. The

---

THE MINNEAPOLIS CITY DIRECTORY OF 1905-1906 GIVES AN OVERVIEW OF THE PROLIFERATION OF SYNAGOGUES IN THE CITY. ALL EXCEPT TEMPLE SHAARI TOV WERE ORTHODOX

1878: Temple Shaari Tov - 100 members - Rev. S. N. Deinard

1884: Adath Jeshurun - 7th St. between 11th & 12th Ave. S. - 40 members - Rev. S. M. Silber

1891: Rumanian Orthodox - 314 15th Ave. S. - 60 members - Rev. S. M. Silber

1895: Kennesseth Israel - Oak Lake Ave. S.E.cor.8th Ave.N. - 40 members - Rev. S. M. Silber

1895: Mikro Kodesh - Oak Lake Ave.S.E.cor.8th Ave. N.-1895-40 members - Rev. Israel Poses

1900: Anshei Tavrig - 601 N. 4th - 60 members - Rev. S. M. Silber

1902: Agidas Ackim - 1820 17th Ave. S. - 55 members - Rev.Samuel Josipowitz

1902: Nachlas Israel - Colfax Ave. N.W. cor. 35th Ave. N. - 104 members - Rev. A. S. Hurwitz

1902: Kennesseth Israel - Colfax Ave. N.W. cor. 35th Ave. - Rev. S. M. Silber

1904: B'nai Aaron - Aldrich Ave.N.-S.E.cor. 8th Ave. - 35 members - Rev. S. M. Silber

The members were dues-paying heads of households. The total number in the family was not counted. This accounts for the small totals, when one takes into account that by 1907 there were approximately 8,000 Jewish people living in Minneapolis. If one takes an average of 6 members to a family and multiply that by the total of 554 listed families, about 3,324 of the Jewish community belonged to a congregation. This is a very rough estimate, and doesn't include families who did not pay dues but did pay for seats to attend High Holiday Services and also sent their children to the Sunday Schools and Talmud Torah.

In the same dirctory, Rabbi Silber is listed as the rabbi for the Adath, the Rumanian Orthodox/Sons of Abraham, Kennesseth Israel, Anshei Tavrig, and B'nai Aaron. The synagogues in those days held a daily minyan and there were always lay leaders that would lead the services.

women had to sit upstairs. At the Adath the men and women were permitted to sit together."

In 1907 the Adath had a paid membership of forty, with dues at $6 a year. It had a free religious school which had about 125 pupils, many of whom were from other congregations and from homes where the parents did not affiliate with any religious organization.

The Bible, Jewish history, and literature were taught by a corps of teachers who worked as volunteers. Arthur Harris was the superintendent of the Free School but Miss Sarah Schanfeld was considered the real head of the institution. She was also a public school teacher. Others involved in helping to organize and conduct the school were Sarah's brother Joseph Schanfeld, David C. Jeffrey, J. H. Woolpy, and his daughter, Belle Woolpy. She married Charles Rauch. David Jeffrey was the son of Michael Jeffrey.

Joseph Schanfeld played a large role in the early history of Adath Jeshurun. His name first appears in the official records in the documents pertaining to the purchase of the Free Christian Church that were filed in 1906. He became the president of the Adath Jeshurun in 1909 and held that position until 1932. He had previously been secretary of the congregation, and by 1907 was president of the B'nai B'rith and chairman of the Jewish Aid Association.

Many of the facts included in this history are dervied from his extensive collection of papers. Among them we find his recollections of the evolution of B'nai B'rith:

In 1878, Mr. Ralph Rees, Isaac Weill, Henry Weiskopf and several others of our pioneers formed the Minneapolis B'nai B'rith Lodge 271, 10BB. At that time the B'nai B'rith was the fraternal insurance organization. In addition it was the clearing house for all Jewish activities, did social service work and was the mouthpiece of the Jewish people.

Gradually the insurance feature diminished until 1900, when Jonas Weil became the secretary of the Minneapolis Lodge. By that time, the insurance feature was entirely eliminated and the lodge confined itself entirely to the Jewish affairs.

Jonas Weil was very active and proceeded to enlist into the membership of the lodge some of the active young men at that time, including Schanfeld, Arthur Brin, Dr. Robitshek, Bernard Harris, George Monash, David Jeffrey and many others.

Joseph Schanfeld

In those days the usual manner of distributing financial aid to indigent people was through "handkerchief collections" during which a committee member would go around and ask for contributions for some needy person. The abuse of this system spawned the notorious Jewish tramp, who would work on the sympathies of the gullible while traveling from place to place. Recogizing the unsoundness of these hankerchief collections, the leaders of the Minneapolis Lodge, though a succession of meetings and fund-rasing events, developed what was then known as the Associated Jewish Charities and is known today as the Jewish Family & Children's Service.

"During all these years," Schanfeld recalled, "there was a great deal of social activity and an annual ball, an annual picnic, an annual boat excursion and similar activites."

Schanfeld was born in Port Neamte, Romania, in 1876. He arrived in Minneapolis with his parents in 1885 and while still in school, began to earn money for the family blacking shoes and selling newspapers. In an article devoted to his early years, the *Minneapolis Tribune* reported that "Joe's first stand was on the Hennepin side of the old Nicollet Hotel. He was so well-liked that pretty soon he became the official newsboy for the Boston Block. Then in 1889, he took a distinct step up in his profession; he became news carrier for the Guaranty Loan building. The Guaranty Loan was the last word in what a city office building should be. It even had a roof garden restaurant!"

Joe's big break came in 1889, when the *Tribune* staged

JOSEPH SCHANFELD DESCRIBES B'NAI B'RITH'S ROLE IN RESETTLING EASTERN EUROPEAN JEWRY

Most of you remember the Jewish pogroms in Russia, culminating in the horrible Kishinev Massacre! ... The result of these massacres was an increase in Jewish immigration into our country and the leaders decided ... to have them enter this country through Galveston and from there be distributed throughout the interior of the country.

Rabbi Kohn of Galveston came to Minneapolis and in a meeting with the leaders of B'nai B'rith, induced our organization to accept nineteen immigrants every month. Joe Schanfeld as chairman undertook this great task. A home was rented on 16th Avenue South near Seventh St., was furnished and a drive was made for used clothing. When we received word that immigrants were to arrive on a certain train, a committee of the B'nai B'rith met the train, took the immigrants to their new home, furnished them with new clothing. We also appointed Dr. Max Seham who at that time was a medical student at the University of Minnesota to become our employment agent.

He canvassed the city and secured jobs for these immigrants as fast as they came in. Committees would then call at the immigrants home at 5 or 6 in the morning and take him to his place of employment and meet him there after work hours and take him back to the home until the immigrant knew his own way about.

We then decided that these immigrants should be taught English and the American ways so a night school was started in the basement of the Adath Jeshurun on 12th Avenue South. We induced the Board of Education to give us a room at the Sumner School. Members of our lodge acted as teachers and we received a teacher or two from the public school system also. By the following year, the classes had so enlarged that we were also given additional space in the Adams School and by the third year (1906) the night school system had been so successful that the board of eucation took over the entire matter and that was the beginning of our night school system in the city of Minneapolis.

---

a contest to select the most popular newsboy. Joe won the contest and made good use of the prize—a six-month course at a business college.

Schanfeld's remarkable industry at the time was described by the *Tribune* as follows:

> *...paper route early in the morning, then business college, then relief to the cashier at the Guaranty Roof restaurant, back to business college, then office boy work for a firm in G.L., then carrying evening papers, a night job as cashier in the Roof restaurant, studying every available moment while on the job...*

Schanfeld's own comment was, "If I could keep my eyes open I would read the newspapers!"

Thinking back on those days, he added another detail. "Mr. Maurice Rothschild sent word to me that I could come down and pick out any suit in his store. And when I went, he wouldn't let any clerk wait on me. He helped me pick out that suit himself."

Eventually Schanfeld and a friend founded a real estate and insurance company, Chase and Schanfeld. In 1900, he married Pauline Bush, and the couple had four children. Following the Kishinev Massacre in Russia (1903), refugees began to arrive in greater numbers, and Schanfeld gathered a group of young men, all sons of immigrants, to help in the work of settling these newcomers into their new lives in America.

In his book *Jews in Transition*, Rabbi Albert Gordon writes that these men "...met immigrants coming in from Romania, Russia, Poland and other countries, found lodging and obtained subsistence loans for them, got up at 6 A.M. to take them to factories where they could obtain employment at $1.50 or $2 a day, set up classes to teach them English and did a thousand and one good deeds to mould new Americans who, in turn, would help Schanfeld and the others build a fine Jewish-American community. At that time there were 19 Jewish immigrants scheduled to arrive in Minneapolis from Europe each month." In reality many more were arriving daily.

By 1903 Schanfeld's work had attracted the attention of the Jewish Immigration Society of New York and he was invited to act as their representative in Minneapolis. This official recognition, coupled with an awareness of the work that he and his co-workers had already done, had an unexpected but important result. Schanfeld was invited to

The Brin Family: Fanny, Charles, Rachel, Howard, and Arthur, circa 1920.

become a member of the local B'nai B'rith Lodge, which had been established in 1877. By 1907, Joseph Schanfeld had become its president.

Also working on the committee were Arthur Brin and David C. Jeffrey.

Arthur was the grandnephew of Simon Gittelson, one of the four men who signed the Papers of Incorporation of the Adath Jeshurun Congregation. His parents had come from Lithuania to Chicago, where he was born. His father died when he was an infant and his mother, Rachel Gittelson, moved to be near her family in Minneapolis, where she married Samuel Brin and had three more children. Rachel G. Brin's progeny through her brother Simon Gittelson are the longest continous family—six generations—at the Adath Jeshurun.

Arthur Brin was another outstanding young leader with a strong interest in Jewish community affairs. Like Joseph Schanfeld, he was a selfless individual, devoted to the ideal of assisting his fellow man. Arthur also attracted the attention of B'nai B'rith and in 1905 was invited to join. Until this time Bnai B'rith had been made up of the older Jewish residents of Western European background.

Rabbi Albert Gordon later observed:

Neither Joe or Arthur cared much about the national origins that seemed so important to their elders. They paid little attention to the economic successes of certain members of the community and little more to the divisiveness resulting from different religious philosophies. They focused their attention and energy on the numerous problems that required solutions. There were the immigrants, arriving daily, who had

to be cared for and given a proper start in their new land. There were problems of adjustment of the residents to their new environment, as well as other vexing educational, religous, and social problems. Both men later distinguished themselves for their humanitarian efforts not only on behalf of the Jewish community but in the larger community as well.

An interview with Eddie Schwartz added information about this period. His father, Mayer Schwartz (who had married Daisy Gruenberg in 1896) taught English to newly arrived immigrants three nights a week. It wasn't long before this school was overflowing, so the men went to the Minneapolis School Board to argue for establishment of a night school in Adams School. The request was granted, and that was the beginning of the entire night school movement in this part of the country.

There was a tremendous amount of family networking. Many of the early families were interrelated, such as the Brins, Jeffreys, Schwartzs, Harris's and Schanfelds. A familiar saying in Minnesota is: "You don't talk about people disparagingly—you may be talking to someone's relative!"

Eddie Schwartz recalled Joe Schanfeld as "one of the nicest gentlemen that the town ever produced. He was the first Jew to be active in the Chamber of Commerce and the City Club which later became the Minneapolis Athletic Club."

Two other men who assumed early leadership roles in Adath community affairs were Dr. Moses Barron, a noted physician, and Dr. George J. Gordon, who rallied the more progressive Jewish members, and by sheer force of personality succeeded in establishing one of the outstanding consolidated Hebrew schools in the United States, the Talmud Torah of Minneapolis. In time, other young men also came forward to move Adath Jeshurun Synagogue in a more progressive direction. When Joe Schanfeld became president in 1912, the new management became insistent in demanding a type of synagogue which, while satisfying the old, would also have its appeal to the young.

One sign of this gradual shift, perhaps, was the amendment to the synagogue's articles of incorporation that took place on January 29, 1909, by which its name officially became Adath Jeshurun rather than A' Tas Jeshurun Congregation. The document went on to define the purpose of the congregation as "the worship of Jehovah accoarding to the manner designated by the Jewish Orthodox *minhag*: Provided, that changes in the *minhag* are not inconsistent with the principles and precepts of the Orthodox Jewish religion may be made from time to time."

It is not known how long Rabbi Roubin stayed with the congregation but a Reverend Paul Segall in 1908 and a Reverend S. A. Lass in 1911, are mentioned along with Meyer D. Mirviss as sexton in the Minneapolis Directories. Two other rabbis' names appeared briefly during this period.

In June of 1909, Rabbi Moses Farber joined the Adath as head of the congregation and as superintendent of the Free Hebrew School in South Minneapolis. The records suggest that his wife had died recently, and six months after his arrival Rabbi Farber himself contracted pneumonia and died rather suddenly at the age of fifty, leaving two children behind.

Two weeks later Reverend Joseph Silver was elected as Rabbi Farber's replacement. A graduate of the Schechter Seminary in New York, Silver had come west to assist Rabbi Farber during his wife's illness. He had been acting as rabbi for the congregation and principal of the Hebrew School since Rabbi Farber's death. Rabbi Silver was not only the first rabbi at Adath to have been educated at the Jewish Theological Seminary (JTS, often referred to as the Schechter Seminary in New York City) but also the first graduate of that institution to accept a position west of the Mississippi, which substantiates the claim that the Adath Jeshurun Congregation of Minneapolis is the oldest continuous Conservative synagogue between the Twin Cities and the West Coast. *

THE JEWISH THEOLOGICAL SEMINARY

What had happened to the JTS? In 1901 a group of prominent Jewish philanthropists, led by Jacob H. Schiff, Leonard Lewisohn and Daniel Guggenheim established a new corporation with a substantial endowment, The Jewish Theological Seminary of America, into which the older association merged. The revised Charter of 1902 eloquently acknowledged the broadening area over which

the seminary branches were beginning to spread. The seminary existed "...for the perpetuation of the tenets of the Jewish religion, the cultivation of Hebrew literature, the pursuit of biblical and archaeological research, the advancement of the Jewish scholarship, the establishment of a library and for the education and training of Jewish rabbis and teachers."

Dr. Schechter envisioned the seminary as a center of traditional yet scientific Jewish scholarship. He brought to the seminary a distinguished new faculty. The Rabbinical School was transformed into a graduate school, and in 1909 President Schechter established the Teachers Institute.

The seminary was interested in preserving and conserving historical Judaism in America. The policy Dr. Schechter projected for the JTS was to prepare rabbis and teachers to teach and preach and interpret Judaism to the American Jewish community. Schechter's vision was a theological center which would reconcile all parties and appeal to all sections of the community. He soon realized that reconciliation of all parties was not possible so he began to plan a union of traditional congregations.

Dr. Schechter was fully aware of the unprecedented role that the Jewish woman could contribute. He advocated seminary congregations to educate women and recognize their worth. He felt it was through women that children would be reached, the Sabbath saved, and dietary laws would be observed in the homes. He felt women should share in the synagogues' activities as they had far greater influence then their husbands.

In an interview in September 1983, Rabbi David Aronson, former rabbi of Beth El, Minneapolis, and past president of the Rabbinical Assembly, said: "The Jewish Theological Seminary was organized to create rabbis to Americanize the immigrant Jews. In the beginning they hadn't the slightest idea that they were forming a movement different from the Orthodox. It was the Orthodox that broke away from this movement officially."

A NEW ERA

By 1911, there was no longer any mention of Rabbi Silver. In past documentaries on the congregation, one account described the High Holidays of 1911 and mentioned that on the second day of Rosh Hashanah, Rabbi S. N. Deinard occupied the pulpit. His address was so well received that the movement for an American educated, English-speaking (rather than Yiddish speaking) rabbi became foremost in the minds of the new young leadership.

---

*Three other Conservative congregations west of Chicago date their beginnings to the last quarter of the nineteenth century. They are Beth Shalom of Kansas City, 1878; B'nai Amoona Congregation in St.Louis, which started approximately in 1882 but was not officially incorporated until 1886; and Congregation Shearith Israel of Dallas, which incorporated in 1884. However, these synagogues did not hire JTS graduates until 1912 or later. (It was not until 1913, however, when the United Synagogue of America was formed, that there could be said to be an official national Conservative organization other than the JTS, which was a seminary.)

Rabbi Deinard often spent the second day of Rosh Hashanah, when his own temple did not hold services, at the Adath Jeshurun or at the Kenesseth Israel. He was invited to deliver the sermon in Yiddish.

The younger members were dissatisfied, and they asserted themselves by electing a new group of officers including Joseph Schanfeld, president; Phillip Resler, vice president; Aaron L. Gruenberg, secretary; Michael S. Dockman, financial secretary; and M.N. Harris, treasurer.

(Former presidents of the Congregation had been: Nathan Gumbiner, 1884; Isador Cohen 1903; J. Frudenfield, 1904; Marx Harris; William Weisman, Charles Kronick, & Michael Jeffrey, 1890s-1911. Unfortunately, there are no exact dates for their presidencies.)

The younger men who took the helm were concerned with making the Adath Jeshurun more progressive. They had no desire to alienate the old congregants, but felt that the time had come for an English-speaking rabbi, more attractive services, and family pews where the men and women could sit together.

It has been said that the Jews in the Diaspora often take on the characteristics of the people they live with. And it seems that the makeup of Minnesotans in general was much the same as those of the Jewish people who settled here. Generally speaking, Minnesotans have exhibited an openness in government and a keen desire to become involved. There are both strong liberal and conservative traditions, but an enduring trait of Minnesota politics of both stripes has been a certain maverick tradition. Minnesotans have been willing to experiment and to pioneer new political movements and philosophies. They have been influenced by the past but are more interested in solving problems and shaping tomorrows.

The Jews who settled in Minnesota exhibited a similar array of qualities. In the early years, they grappled with becoming modern, while retaining the basic tenets of the Jewish religion. Over the years, Adath Jeshurun engaged a variety of rabbinic leaders with differing views. Some had very brief stays.

The lay leadership always exerted their opinions forcefully. Dissension played a part in the synagogue's molding. Even during periods of unusual harmony, there were always some who questioned and fought. This served the congregation in a positive way, but also had its negative effects. Going forward, whether becoming more progressive or returning to tradition, each movement, liberal or conservative, lost congregants and also gained new adherents.

Within the Romanian group the in-fighting was incessant. They'd fight about liturgy, who should conduct services, who should have honors, and who would be called up to the Torah.

Yet during its first quarter-century of life, the Adath Jeshurun had some remarkable achievements.

(Above left) Mr. J. H. Woolpy, an early officer of Adath Jeshurun, in the synagogue on 9th Street. (Above right), Rabbi Matt.
(Above), Rabbi Matt with the 1916 religious school class.

3
THE RABBI MATT YEARS (1912 – 1927)

Rabbi C. D. Matt brought modern Judaism to Adath Jeshurun by introducing new programs for youth and hiring a professional staff. He guided the congregation through a World War and the planning and construction of the building that would be the congregation's home for the next half-century. Yet Rabbi Matt himself was deeply rooted in tradition, and in his final years, the congregation that he had created began to outgrow him.

SOLOMON SCHECHTER

One man who had a profound impact on the shaping of Adath Jeshurun Congregation, though he never set foot in Minneapolis, was Solomon Schechter, the noted rabbinic scholar and president of the Jewish Theological Seminary (JTS). Schechter was born in Romania in 1847, where his father was a Habad Hasid and a *schochet* (a ritual slaughterer). In his teens Solomon studied with the rabbinic author Joseph Saul Nathanson in Lemberg, and then attended the Vienna Bet HaMidrash. He acquired a lifelong devotion to the scientific study of tradition and developed the central notion of the community of Israel as decisive for Jewish living and thinking. He was to call it "Catholic Israel." He also studied in Berlin and then went to London where he rose to prominence as a rabbinic scholar and spokesman for Jewish traditionalism. Following a decade of teaching at Cambridge University and at University College, London, in 1901 Schechter accepted the post of president of the Jewish Theological Seminary in New York. He was able to attract a distinguished faculty, including Louis Ginzberg, Alexander Marx, Israel Friedlander, Israel Davidson, and Mordecai M. Kaplan, and the seminary soon became one of the most important centers of both Jewish learning and Jewish intellectual and national revival.

As early as 1909, Dr. Schechter had obtained the cooperation of his JTS collaborators in developing a new organizational setup for American synagogues. He also recieved staunch support from the JTS Alumni Association (the forerunner of the Rabbinical Assembly of America.) In 1913 Dr. Schechter issued an official call for the organization of the United Synagogue of America, a union of Orthodox and

Solomon Schechter

Conservative forces. Before that time, Conservative Judaism had not been a distinctive movement. On February 23, backed by 80 seminary graduates, representative laymen of some 20 congregations and many of the outstanding Jewish scholars in America first met as the United Synagogue of America. It was composed of graduates of the Jewish Theological Seminary and the congregations of which they were rabbis. This included the Adath Jeshurun Congregation of Minneapolis and Rabbi C. D. Matt.

The binding procedures set out by Dr. Schechter for the new organization were:
- Order and decorum in the synagogue
- The English sermon
- Methodical instruction in religious schools
- The selection of rabbis and teachers scientifically trained and educated in institutions that fully utilize scientific methods and research

He also proposed and ecouraged other non-binding procedures:
- Religious instruction for women and their adequate participation in the work of the congregation and the Union
- The rejuvenation of the Jewish home through the introduction of observances and ceremonies
- The encouragement of study of Hebrew in the school

in order that it may be preserved in public worship

• A rounded religious education program, including the preparation of books, under expert supervision, for every member of the families enrolled in constituent congregations

• The retention of worship as the primary feature of the synagogue

• The dietary laws must be observed.

In setting out his program, Dr. Schechter made every effort to avoid theological controversy, hoping to minimize the differences between Conservative and Orthodox Jews and fashion an orderly union of congregations working together toward a common goal—the conservation of traditional Judaism in America. And during the initial years of Conservatism there was hope in some circles that all traditional American Jews would rally about Dr. Schechter's principles. Dr. Schechter had hoped to persuade Reform Jews to remain more firmly tied to Jewish tradition; and Orthodox Jews to embrace the American environment more wholeheartedly. This did not happen. The Orthodox faction rejected the leadership of the Jewish Theological Seminar and declined to affiliate itself with the United Synagogue.

RABBI C. D. MATT

Among the wholehearted supporter of the movement was Rabbi C. D. Matt, who had arrived from New York to become the rabbi at Adath Jeshurun in the autumn of 1912. When Dr. Schechter died in November, 1915, Rabbi Matt wrote admiringly of him in the *American Jewish World*:

In the death of Solomon Schechter who died last Friday, American Israel loses one of its most distinguished members, a profound and versatile scholar, a leader of Jewish thought, and a brilliant writer. Although a resident in this country only since 1901, his genius has made its imprint on American Judaism which time and circumstance will not so soon efface. Schechter was a type of the modern cosmopolitan Jew. Born and raised in Romania, he received his rabbinic and secular education in Vienna and Berlin, resided for 19 years in England...and spent the last 14 years of his life as a citizen of this country. No man of this generation has enriched Jewish literature with more valuable scholarly contributions written in a charming style than Schechter. But his great achievement for American Judaism has been his raising of the Jewish Theological Seminary of America to a high rank among seats of learning,

with a faculty of scholars of reputation, offering courses of instruction that make the modern rabbi as well-equipped for his calling as were any of his predecessors. The spirit of Solomon Schechter will be marching on in American Israel. The memory of the righteous is for a blessing.

On December 12, 1915, a service in memory of Dr. Solomon Schechter was held at the Adath Jeshurun.

Rabbi Matt was a true disciple of Schechter's philosophy, and in 1917, two years after Solomon Schechter's death, Rabbi Matt wrote about him: "Very often we would emerge from the classroom remembering less of what had been taught, but more of the refreshing views of our master, on the problems of life. Thus, we became imbued with the concept of catholic(universal)Israel."

Calman David Matt made his first official visit to the Adath in 1912 to officiate at the High Holy Days. At the time he was in his senior year of study at the Jewish Theological Seminary in New York. Upon conclusion of the holidays, he returned to New York. The congregants were clearly impressed with the young man. After a brief correspondence, he was elected rabbi of the Adath Jeshurun and returned to Minneapolis on November 1 to assume the pulpit. He had been given special permission from the seminary to leave early and would receive his degree with his class on June 6, 1913.

Rabbi Matt was born in Kovno, Lithuania, on June 24, 1887. He came to America with his parents in 1890, and they settled in Philadelphia, although his American upbringing was as strictly Orthodox and Jewish as if he had been reared in the Lithuanian town. As a boy he helped organize a Zionist group, the Aids of Zion. Ten of the young men in the group became rabbis.

In Philadelphia, he received his preliminary secular and Hebrew education, graduating from Gratz College and the University of Pennsylvania with a B.A. in 1909. He took graduate courses at Dropsie College, The Yeshivah Mishkan Israel and pursued his rabbinical studies at the Jewish Theological Seminary, where he received his rabbinical diploma. He also did graduate work at Columbia University. As a student, he occupied pulpits in Philadelphia, New York, and nearby cities, and officiated for the High Holidays two years in succession in Toledo, Ohio.

When Rabbi Matt first came to Minneapolis he stayed with Dr. and Mrs. George Gordon. Years later Dr. Gordon's son Theodore (who had become a rabbi himself) described the family environment in which Rabbi Matt found himself:

Dr. George Gordon

"My parents, Dr. George J. Gordon and Sophie Weinberg Gordon, were early and long-time members of Adath Jeshurun. My father came to the United States in 1890, to Philadelphia, to join his older brother. He peddled for a short time in Maryland and then decided that was not the future he was going to pursue. He came to Minneapolis because my mother's family was there and they were distantly related. He enrolled in high school in 1895-96. In 1896 he returned to Philadelphia and enrolled in Jefferson Medical College. He graduated in 1900, returned to Minneapolis, opened his practice and married in 1902. He settled down to do two things; one was to build up a medical practice, and the other was to build a Talmud Torah.

"We lived on the South Side, on Portland Avenue. My grandmother, Baila Weinberg, lived with us, and I used to walk with her to services to the Adath Jeshurun on Shabbat morning. I must have been no more than eight or nine years old. It would have been about 1917.

"I attended Talmud Torah across town with my sisters. [From the inception of the Minnepolis Talmud Torah, both boys and girls attended.] I started at the age of six. We went by streetcar and frequently got a ride home. My dad would very often drop into the Talmud Torah to look around and observe, and he would say, 'Wait for me and I'll drive you home.'

"Rabbi Matt came to Minneapolis in 1912, the year before he was ordained. He came here because the Adath

In the formal picture taken at the wedding dinner of Lena Friedman and Rabbi C. D. Matt at the bride's parents home, the following people were among those present: Meyer D. Mirviss (at extreme left), Menashe H. Harris, Leo Cohen, Dora Friedman Harris, Ellis Harris, Jennie Harris, Rabbi Deinard, Rabbi Simon, Rabbi Silber, Sophie Gordon, her husband Dr. George Gordon, Baile(Malkin) Weinberg, Mrs. A.I.Harris, Mrs. David Friedman (Lena Matt and Dora Friedman's mother), Sam Zalkind, his wife Molly Zalkind, Bernard "Barney" Harris and his wife Pearl.

Jeshurun was beginning to knock at the doors of modernity. It was felt that a rabbi from the JTS could lead the congregation out of a more traditional mold into the modern Conservative mold. He came to Minneapolis, and one of the first people that he met was my father.

"Rabbi Matt, a young, single man, asked my dad for some help in finding a place to live, and he did come to live with us. It took him one year to find a new place to live, and after that he established a home with his new bride, Lena Friedman. They were married in our home. I was five years old when he was married in 1913. I remember Rabbi Matt as a very warm, genial *haimish* kind of person. He used to sit me on his knee and tell me stories."

Theodore's sister, Stella Gordon Birnberg, recalled: "[Rabbi Matt] lived at my house for a while when I was a little girl. The memories that I had of him are pleasant. He had all sorts of pictures and educational cards that I can remember so clearly. He must have used them in his Sunday school classes and he would show them to us."

Rabbi Matt's new bride, Lena Friedman, was a girl from the neighborhood. Her family lived at 9th Street and 14th Avenue.

Jacob Mirviss described Rabbi Matt: "My brother, Harold, had his Bar Mitzvah at the Adath Jeshurun in September 1912, and mine was in December 1913. I still remember my *haftorah* taught to me by Rabbi C. D. Matt. He was a venerable, kindly scholar, with a good sense of humor, soft-spoken, but convincing. He wrote poetry.

"Rabbi Matt was hired in 1912. Father continued to conduct the services. Rabbi Matt delivered the sermons. At my Bar Mitzvah at the Adath Jeshurun, I read the *maftir* and I chanted the *brachot* and the *haftorah* and everybody said that I did well. There was a kiddush after, with home-baked things that Mother made, and also some things that we got from Bearmon's, the Jewish bakery on the South Side. Rabbi Matt was a very kindly man with a warm personality, a good sense of humour, and he use to play with us by giving us riddles.

"His sermons dealt largely with Jewish topics—history and Jewish personalities. He was a very close friend of the family. He and father use to carry on discussions all the time. Father came from a traditional background and Rabbi Matt came from the Conservative movement; and he, eventually or gradually, converted father to some of the new ideas of the Conservative movement. He Americanized father. He instituted the late Friday night services after the Shabbat started but there was also an early service for those who wanted to follow the traditional type of service.

"Our cousins, the Seltzes, lived on Chicago Avenue near Franklin, and we exchanged visits frequently. Living in such proximity to the synagogue, we were imbued with a strong identity with Judaism and a Jewish way of life. After my older brother and I had our Bar Mitzvah, we were awakened early every morning for the minyan. We learned the traditional melodies for the daily, Shabbat and holiday services as my father used to chant them, and they remain with us even now."

Saul Meyers recalled: "The first experience that I had at the Adath was when Rabbi C. David Matt was hired. My dad, Michael D. Myers, first cousin of Meyer D. Mirviss, was on the board. Dad's original name was Mirviss but it was changed.

"When I was 11 or 12, Mr. Mirviss's father use to ride in a horse and wagon. [Saul was born in 1909 so this would be around 1920.] He use to make the rounds, visiting his sister, his daughter, and my father and mother, because we were related. I was a nephew. I use to get into the wagon on Friday after school, ride down to the Adath and stay at the Mirviss' until Sunday night. Every Friday afternoon, Sammy Mirviss, myself, and a cousin of ours, Joe Seltz, used to

Herman Mirviss and Florence Glick

go to the synagogue with Herman Mirviss, and we would vacumn the carpets and dust every Friday.

"The Mirviss family lived on the second floor in the back of the sanctuary. We'd shovel coal into the furnace in the winter, haul out the ashes, and Sunday morning when they'd have the services, there'd be a pounding on the pipe. Mrs. Mirviss would holler down, 'How many?' and they'd holler 2 - 3- 4, whatever they were short for the minyan. We would have to bounce out of bed, get dressed and run downstaiars so it would make a minyan. I was already a Bar Mitzvah by then. This would happen many times. They had five right there. They had Harold, Jack, Sammy, Herman and me. All we needed were four other members. If they had women at that time, Mrs. Mirviss could have come down, Rose and Sophie, and we could have had a minyan all by ourselves!

"On Sunday afternoons, after Sunday school, we would take the bottoms out of the waste baskets, hang them up and we'd play basketball. We had a heck of a time.

"Friday night services were not like today, but they'd have 40 or 50. Saturday they'd have a nice crowd. On the High Holidays they

Children of the Ghetto, a theater production of the Menorah Society

were much more full. In the early days, Mr. Mirviss read the Torah. They didn't have Rabbi Matt yet. After they had Rabbi Matt, Mr. Mirviss still read the Torah. He would point out who received an aliyah, whoever had a yahrziet or something. They were one of the only synagogues where the women and men sat together. On Sukkot they had a little sukkah in the back and we used go back there and eat. Like all kids, we use to take the apples. Simchas Torah we used to tie all the *taleisim* together and when one man walked off, he'd pull everybody's *tallis* off."

Hy Mendow related: "Rabbi Matt came in 1912 and that synagogue became the center of activity for the young people of the Jewish community, particularly the university students. At that time the total number of Jewish students on the university campus was about 50, of whom eight were women. The Jewish plays were rehearsed at the Adath. There was the Menorah Society, which used to meet there occasionally, and they put on one play, *The Children of the Ghetto*, which was staged at a theater on 7th St. and Hennepin for money-raising purposes.

"The Adath was a meeting place for college students. I went to services there from the time I graduated college in 1915. I used to attend, and we gave musicals and stage plays. Sig Harris coached the theatricals. Irving and Leo Frisch, Jennie Harris, Dave Phillips and others were in the production of the *The Children of the Ghetto*. Rabbi Matt was very good with the young people.

"The Adath Jeshurun had a little rival synagogue a block away, B'nai Abraham/Sons of Abraham. Originally it was known as the Rumanish Shule. I lived in the neighborhood and attended both. My father attended the Orthodox and I attended Adath.

"It seems to me in my childhood recollections that a number of Romanian Jews broke off from the Adath Jeshurun...Rabbi Matt developed a method of having congregants deliver sermons or lectures on Friday nights. Friday services were slightly beyond the formality of the Orthdox services, and the services were partially in English for the first time. But you wore a *tallit* and a *yarmelke* or a hat because prior to that time for years in the Orthodox synagogue the chief rabbi, and also at the Adath, there was a Rabbi Silber who was a chief Orthodox rabbi who used to come in a tall silk hat to the services. The Reform Jews also wore a *tallit* in the early days on Portland and 10th Street, and wore silk hats. They could wear a *tallit* if they wanted to. The *tallit* and the hat went out much later there.

"Early on, everyone had a *melamed*, a tutor, who came to the house during the noon hour. He would take, say 20 minutes, and have three kids for 20 minutes each. I went on with that until—practically—I was in college. My *melamed* was a fellow name Kiefferstein. The Kieffers around town; that was their grandfather or great grandfather."

Most of the Reform and Orthodox sons of the early immigrants in Minneapolis had a Bar Mitzvah. Sons would be given private tutoring, often for no more than several months before the 13th birthday. There were some fathers that provided longer periods of study. The Bar Mitzvah boys were given set speeches to memorize, either in Hebrew or Yiddish, as English speeches would have been unintelligible

The Halpern Family circa 1917

to many of the congregants. Members of the family and friends were invited to the synagogue for the service. Following the service, a meal was served in the boy's home. Congratulatory addresses were given, and good wishes exchanged. The young man was given gifts by his family and friends and he was almost sure to receive a gold watch from his parents.

The parents of Esther Schanfield Rosenbloom had come from Rumania, and her father, Noah, was Joe Schanfeld's older brother. [Somehow the names were spelled differently.] Originally their family had also belonged to the Rumanishe Shule on 15th Avenue, but as Esther told the story: "Many of the Jewish people we knew belonged to this synagogue, the Rumanian Shul, so I would go there for holidays with my mother, but that was all. There was nothing special for us. But then Uncle Joe [Schanfeld] realized that we needed to have a synagogue where the children would be educated and participate. Uncle Joe and Dr. Gordon worked so hard. They got people to come, and they organized the Adath Jeshurun. It took a while. Rabbi Matt was very nice, and we so enjoyed coming and singing. On Friday nights Rabbi Matt led services.

"Sunday we didn't really have services. We just went to Sunday school. My aunt, Sarah Schanfield, taught at Temple Israel first. She was a teacher in the Minneapolis public schools and was very good. Rabbi Deinard asked her if she would teach a class there at Shaarai Tov/Temple Israel. She thought it was a good place to take me, so I went there, and then, of course, when we decided to have the Sunday school at Adath, we went there." Sarah Schanfield helped to organize the Adath Jeshurun Sunday school. That was probably around 1904.

Esther continued about the days when she was a little older: "I remember that we were invited to come. Rabbi Matt had arrived and he was deciding to have classes. We decided to organize and get all the Jewish girls and boys that we could to meet Friday nights with Rabbi Matt. He was wonderful for us. We use to have very interesting evenings on Friday nights and we always discussed things and sang. He taught us all kinds of Hebrew songs and had wonderful Friday nights for a number of years. It was just lovely.

"They also had a Hebrew School, and my brother Morrie went. They had certain teachers who would come and teach Hebrew. The Adath Jeshurun became right away a source of Jewish education for the community. On Sunday mornings we would discuss all the different parts of the Bible and that sort of thing. We had more fun because it was just for children, and it's different than a Friday night service that takes care of the whole congregation.

"There were probably about 30 or 40 of us. We came together and always sat in a certain row. There was a pianist, and we would sing with him and he would teach us a song. The rabbi was always right there. It was a lot of fun and we enjoyed it. We made a lot of nice Jewish friends. We lived at 9th Street and 15th Avenue and would walk the three blocks to the synagogue.

"My uncle Joe was a prince, always so thoughtful and helpful. Even on the High Holy Days, he would say, 'Esther, I am going. Would you like to go with me?' and we would go and sit downstairs in the Adath Jeshurun so that we could just read together. We had wonderful times at the holidays. They had only one service in those days. It was satisfying and we all met together.

"We used to have plays too. we had a Queen Esther story play every year on Purim and, of course, Esther had to be Queen Esther. My aunt saw to that. I always thought it was kind of unfair, but she would always say, 'Esther, you're the best, you have to do it!'"

Gazella Kantor, another early member of the Adath, moved to Minneapolis with her family around 1912. Her father had been born in Romania, but didn't want to serve in the Romanian army, and he also wanted his children to have good schooling. He worked in a bakery in New York, then brought his family to Pennsylvania where he worked in a pop factory, before finally moving to Minneapolis. Gazella had two brothers and one sister. She graduated from

South High School. She met her husband, Morris Kantor, in Minneapolis, and in 1916 Rabbi Matt married them.

"Rabbi Matt was very sweet," she recalled, "Quiet sort and full of fun. He always had time for the young people. He found time to do everything."

Louis Goldstein said, "The president of the synagogue used to give a speech in Yiddish. Rabbi Matt conducted the services and gave a sermon in English. Mr. Mirviss was the *baal kriah*. The *aliyot* (honors) were given to most of the older members of the congregation. Honors on the High Holidays were usually bid on for money. Women sat with the men at the Adath, whereas in the Rumanian Shul the women sat upstairs. Since many of the women could not read, one woman would read to them."

Rabbi Aronson recalled the early years: "There were very few Jews in Minneapolis that were regular dues paying members to a congregation. In fact the officers and the board were not too interested or too anxious to take in members. The income of the synagogue consisted primarily of selling tickets for the holidays and they auctioned off *aliyot* and whatever honors. In most cases they were just seat holders."

In those years the man that bid the most money was awarded the honor of holding, dressing or reading from the Torah. They would have an auction and yell out their bid. Many of the younger generation found this practice very distasteful and undignified.

In 1912, the *S.S. Titanic* sank on her maiden voyage. and former president Theodore Roosevelt formed the Progressive Republican Party, but on November 5, Democrat Woodrow Wilson won the U.S. Presidency. Sarah Bernhardt starred in the film *Queen Elizabeth* that year and five million Americans were visiting the cinema daily.

At Adath Jeshurun Congregation, a new era of Conservative Judaism was beginning under the direction of Rabbi Matt. He reorganized the religious school and Hebrew classes, and either led or influenced such organizations as a Bible class, the Herzl Literary Society, and a young women's group called the Deborah Society. The Ladies Auxiliary, which had done very supportive work in the past, now raised funds for the installation of a modern heating and plumbing system.

Joe Schanfeld later reminisced: "With the Deborah Society, which Rabbi Matt organized, and the excellent assistance by the Ladies Auxiliary, we forged ahead as the first Conservative congregation in the Northwest!"

In Schanfeld's yearly Yom Kippur address for 1914,

he underscored the need to continue supporting the Adath Jeshurun and the Associated Charities financially: "Most of you were greatly surprised when you came to the synagogue and found the building had been thoroughly remodeled into an ideally arranged and attractive synagogue. It was the donations you made toward the building fund on Yom Kippur in 1912 and 1913 that made it possible…"

Schanfeld went on to give detailed figures of the expenses, the new mortgage, and debts. He asked those that were not members to join the congregation, especially members of the younger generation.

Previous to Rabbi Matti's arrival, there had been annual "graduation exercises" at the end of each school year. This was noted as early as June of 1907. It was not until 1915 that anyone referred to the graduating class as a confirmation class of the Adath Jeshurun. In an interview with Dorothy Harris Weiner she said she believed that she was in that class in 1915. Other members of the class were: Evelyn Schanfeld, Vera Weisman Fischman, Marsha Harris Corwin, and Florence Shapiro Hersh. Florence and Dorothy recalled that they wore white dresses and sat on the stage for the ceremony. Each girl had to write an essay and then present it. At the end each one received a diploma. Some of the teachers they remembered were Belle Woolpy

Baila Weinberg and grandchildren

THE AMERICAN JEWISH WORLD

A Weekly Journal of Modern Jewish Life and Labors

In 1912, the same year that C. D. Matt arrived to become rabbi at Adath Jeshurun, a new Jewish weekly newspaper was launched in the Twin Cities, with Dr. S. N. Deinard, rabbi of the Jewish Reform temple, as editor, George Kaufman as printer, and Leonard H. Frisch as the publisher. *The Jewish Weekly* (as it was originally titled), was to serve as a forum for Jewish culture and tradition and to foster Jewish education. With the passage of time it broadened its purposes to include promotion of interest in Israel, unification of diverse elements within the community, encouragement of Jewish philanthropy, education, and aid to Jews that were in need abroad.

Dr. Deinard was quoted at the time as saying:

"The Associated Jewish Charities of the Twin Cities especially needs such a paper, to place its wants and plans before the Jewish residents of the community… There are also a great many miscellaneous Jewish organizations and the needs of all will be looked after in the columns of the new weekly."

Two years later the name of the journal was changed to *The American Jewish World*, because publisher Leo Frisch felt that *Jewish Weekly* was too similar to *Jewish Weakly*, and he figured the paper might have a national circulation one day: "Too many people spell weekly - weakly! I didn't like that idea - so *The American Jewish World* it became!"

Rabbi Deinard's view and the general theme of the *AJW* was the desire to create a unified, self-identified Jewish community. Deinard also called for a strong Hebrew education for Jewish youth: "A study of Hebrew must awaken in the child a consciousness of Jewish unity, a sympathetic brotherly feeling for all our fellow Jews, no matter what clime they may dwell or from what country they may hail." Deinard's newspaper reinforced the Americanization and English classes in which many of the Eastern European immigrants took part and the regular public school classes which their children attended.

When Rabbi Deinard died suddenly in 1921, Leo Frisch became the editor of the *AJW*, and he held that position for more than fifty years. Frisch said about Rabbi Matt, who became an associate editor soon after he arrived in Minneapolis: "…He was at the AJW office very often, at least once a week, to see how we were getting along. Either he brought his editorial in or else he wrote something while he was there. Every year he would write the article on what was new in Minneapolis and what had happened during the previous year. After he left in 1927, he continued to write editorials for a number of years from out of town."

Today Rabbi Matt's yearly summaries remain a valuable source of information concerning the early history of the local Jewish community.

Rauch, Esther Woolpy Himmelman, Sarah Schanfeld, Sylvia Schwartz, Manuel Sgutt, and Ralph Wilk.

The confirmation ceremony was a new concept for traditional and Conservative Judaism, but it had the effect of revitalizing the attendance on Shavuot, which had been decreasing in Orthodox, Conservative and Reform synagogues alike.

Rabbi Albert Gordon later remarked: "At first we used to regard the confirmation service, which was conducted by the Reform Temple on the first day of Shavuot, as something non-Jewish in form and content. We all connected it with the Christian confirmation services. But we found the service seemed to mean something to the children. They loved the pageantry. They learned something about their own people, its history, and its ideals; they gave public affirmation of their faith and what is more, because all this took place on Shavuot as part of the service, it brought their fathers and mothers and friends into the synagogue.

Sarah Berman on "Converting the Jew," Dr. George Gordon on "Palestine, the Diaspora and the Jewish Youth," and Dr. S. Deinard on "Intermarriage."

Among the topics of Rabbi Matt's sermons that year were: "Old Faith in New Surroundings," "When Marriage is a Failure," "Where Will the Blue Laws Lead Us?" "Who wants Immigrations Restricted?" and "What Have Jews Contributed to Art?"

At the synagogue there were daily services and on High Holidays and at Friday night services there were English sermons. The interior of the synagogue's auditorium had been completely renovated. M.B.Heiman and J.B.Ravitch helped Rabbi Matt conduct the High Holiday services.

And that year, the congregation mourned the death of Michael Jeffrey. He had lived in Minneapolis since 1887 and served the Adath Jeshurun in various capacities, including president and in the early years as a lay rabbi. In 1941, his grandson, Ira Weil Jeffrey, would be the first Minneapolis casualty of World War II at Pearl Harbor.

By this time the religious school had 120 pupils, six teachers, and 35 students in the Hebrew class that met daily. Assisting the rabbi with the Hebrew class was Harold Mirviss, son of M. D. Mirviss.

The holidays were celebrated with various activities and programs. On Tu B'Shevat, the children were given figs, dates and carob fruit that were eaten in the land of Israel. On Purim there was a program, and on Passover, lantern slides were shown, followed by old fashioned nut games. Prizes were also given, and the school picnic was again held at Minnehaha Falls, where hikes, sightseeing, games and ice cream cones furnished an afternoon of enjoyment.

Ruth Brockman Stillman (in an interview in 1982) recalled her religious school graduation confirmation in 1921, which was held on Shavuot: "I was confirmed in 1921 with Rabbi Matt. It was just a ceremony. The group got together and the rabbi blessed us. There were no plays or musicals or anything like that. We said prayers and we were blessed with our parents present. That was it—very short. I can close my eyes and recall that ceremony.

"My grandparents, Marvin and Rachel Kahn, were some of the earliest members of the original Adath, charter members in the 1880s. They came from Lithuania between 1878 and 1880. My parents, Laura and Abraham Brockman, were born in Romania. My great-grandchild is the

The Adath graduating class of 1922

fifth generation in this country and the fifth generation to be a member of the Adath Jeshurun."

1921–1922

Many of congregants of the Adath had been moving to the West Side of Minneapolis, and plans began to take shape to transfer the synagogue's activities to that neighborhood, and to begin the search for a suitable site on which to build. That year the synagogue also decided to use a uniform book, the Adler prayerbook, for the High Holidays.

On Yom Kippur, October 12, 1921, the Minneapolis Jewish Community was deeply shocked and grieved by the death of the esteemed Dr. Samuel Deinard. Thousands attended his funeral on October 16, and Rabbi Matt delivered the eulogy: " ...When the sun sets at eventide, its light is gone, because the night comes. But when the sun sets at mid-day, although it is obscured, does not its light linger on? And therein lies some small measure of consolation to us, ever in the tragedy that has, all too soon, ended so splendidly promising a career. We can feel that bodily he has ceased to exist, yet his spirit, his influence, his inspiration, still lives on..."

In the fall of 1921, the Adath Jeshurun had 160 pupils and had added two more classes, making eight. A Chevra Kadisha Society had also been formed by the congregation.

In his annual High Holiday message, Joseph Schanfeld spoke to the congregation about the importance of a mod-

Rabbi Matt (center of picture, behind casket) gave the eulogy at Rabbi Deinard's funeral, held at Shaari Tov on October 16, 1921.

ern Talmud Torah and a new synagogue. During his address he referred to Miss Grace Gordon (who had been in the first Minneapolis Talmud Torah Bet Hamidrash graduating class of 1919) as a model for what Jewish children in America should be.

"Grace Gordon's secular education as not been affected in the least by her Jewish training. She is a young lady, a student at the University of Minnesota. There are a very large number of Jewish students, young men and young women at the University, but how many of them possess the Jewish knowledge and the Jewish spirit that Miss Gordon has? She is the product of the Talmud Torah of North Minneapolis which is considered the best of its kind in the United States..."

Schanfeld went on to argue that, as more of the Adath's congregants moved to Minneapolis's West Side, sooner or later someone would start a Talmud Torah and synagogue there. "All they are waiting for is someone to lead them. Why not we? Why not now?"

Following Mr. Schanfeld's appeal, pledges of $35,000 were secured. The response was admirable. However, the economic conditions of the time made it inadvisable to collect the pledges, and for the time being the project remained just a hope, and a dream.

Later that year, the Adath Jeshurun opened a West Side branch of the Minneapolis Talmud Torah at Lagoon Hall over the Lagoon Theatre, at 2906 Hennepin Avenue. The instruction was uniform with that of the main Talmud Torah school at 8th Avenue North and Fremont. Initial enrollment was 34. A benefit was given for the new branch at the Shubert Theatre downtown and the proceeds were used to buy equipment for the school.

In February, Rabbi Matt attended the United Synagogue Convention and the Rabbinical Assembly, where the Women's League and the newly formed Young People's League also met. The meeting convinced him that the Union had not yet "found itself," though the steady growth in interest boded well for the forces of Conservative Judaism. "As the United Synagogue movement grows," he wrote, "assuming more and more its important position as the stabilizing force in American Jewry; it will no doubt prove one of the greatest monuments to the wisodm and foresight of its founder, the late Professor Solomon Schechter."

In May of 1922, Rabbi Matt made an appeal for the Jewish Theological Seminary, which was threatened with bankruptcy. Four of its graduates were serving in Minnesota, he pointed out, and he urged the Jews of the Northwest to help out.

The Adath Ladies Auxiliary held its 14th Annual Dance at the Curtis Court Ballroom and its first Shabbat Tea in the vestry rooms of the synagogue. The Shabbat Teas were an innovation by several of the other Women's Leagues of the United Synagogue movement. The purpose was to make the Sabbath more meaningful to Jewish women. At the first tea in Minneapolis, Rabbi Matt and Sarah Berman spoke on "Sabbath and the Jewish Mother."

The synagogue started to hold Friday night services at Lagoon Hall and the attendance was large.

On August 20, 1922 Joseph Schanfeld's niece, Esther Schanfield, was married to Eli Rosenbloom at the Adath Jeshurun. (Somehow, the two branches of the family spelled their names differently: Joseph had removed the 'i.') It was unusual to hold a wedding in the synagogue at that time, as most weddings were held in homes or halls, but Esther's parents had also been married in the synagogue's facilities. A hundred and fifty guests attended, and Esther's mother designed and made the canopy for the *chupah*. She then donated it to the synagogue for future weddings.

In 1922, the *American Jewish World* celebrated its 10th anniversary, and Rabbi Matt also celebrated 10 years as the rabbi at Adath Jeshurun. Two-hundred and fifty people attended a testimonial dinner in his honor at the Radisson Hotel, sponsored by members of the congregation.

During Rabbi Matt's first decade in Minneapolis, he

Esther (Schanfield) Rosenbloom on her wedding day, 1922

had spread his influence far beyond the synagogue, having served as president of the Minneapolis Lodge I.O. B'nai B'rith, the local Zionist organization, secretary of the Jewish Conference of Minneapolis, and on the Board of the Associated Jewish Charities.

He was frequently invited to deliver lectures on Jewish topics before non-Jewish organizations, and was a member of the Executive Committee of the United Synagogue of America and of the Rabbinical Association of the Jewish Theological Seminary. He contributed verse, reviews, and interviews to the *American Jewish Press* and was Associate Editor of the *American Jewish World*. By 1922, Rabbi Matt and his wife, Lena, had three sons: Joshua Leonard, Joseph Zalmon and Hershel Jonas. Twin girls would be born to them soon.

Dr. M. Lefkowitz, who had been a Reform rabbi in Duluth before moving to Minneapolis, has left an interesting description of Rabbi Matt: "Somewhat of a diffident disposition, he springs forth at the call of any worthy cause, Jewish or non-Jewish. Modest and unassuming in demeanor, his readiness to give of himself and his ability without stint has forced upon him the leadership in many public movements and always to the great good of movement. Lacking entirely in the qualities of pushing and self-advertising, his name has become a sort of household word. Woefully

deficient in knowledge of business and finance, he is yet one of the most popular 'marrying rabbis' I know, having launched more hopeful couples on the sea of matrimony accompanied invariably by his suave, soothing blessing, than any other colleague in the Northwest.

"Kindly and genteel by nature, he is yet a most firm and formidable opponent in debate, yielding not one iota when principle is involved and never descending to acrimony or recrimination, being saved there by his fine sense of humor. Simple and unaffected in manner, he meets all his fellows with the same winning smile, leaving upon each and all the impress of a good, helpful, consecrated man."

Dr. Lefkowitz went on to note that although the recently deceased Dr. Deinard had been as beloved by the Conservative Jews of the city as Rabbi Matt was by those of Reform leanings, Rabbi Matt had succeeded in countervening that powerful magnet, more than doubling the synagogue's membership in a single decade.

1922–1923

In September, 1922, the *American Jewish World* carried an article describing the Adath Jeshurun as "the most progressive and most active in all that pertains to the welfare of the younger generation and the desire to make Judaism palatable to them." Rabbi Matt had been instrumental in fostering clubs for adolescents and organizations for young men and women, including the Bible class, Deborah Society, Herzl Library Society and the Young People's Forum. These organizations spread the knowledge and the love of things Jewish among scores of young people.

Josie Mendow recalled in an interview in 1983 that when they moved to Minneapolis from Milwaukee in 1920, she and her husband, Hy, joined the Adath because, "We didn't want to belong to the Orthodox synagogue where Hy's father belonged. We were looking for a different social atmosphere. I got involved because my father always told us that we had to make a place for ourselves in the community where we lived and the only way to do that at that time was through a religious organization."

On September 15, 1923, Rabbi Albert G. Minda was installed at Temple Israel in Minneapolis. That fall, Hebrew classes were being held at Adath's West and South Side branches.

At High Holiday services, Rabbi Matt exchanged pulpits with Rabbi Heller from the newly formed Beth El Synagogue, the first Conservative synagogue on the North Side. Also that month Hebrew classes at the Adath Jeshurun

South were merged with the South Side branch of the Minneapolis Talmud Torah and held at the synagogue building on 12th Avenue.

The Ladies Auxiliary continued to function in full force, decorating and furnishing the vestry rooms and providing floral decooarations on Shavuot, and also providing substantial financial aid. They paid the cost in full for installing a complete heating and plumbing plant. They also took on a special function—paying off the mortgage on the synagogue. This feat was accomplished on September 1, 1923. The women provided a piano for the religious school, and gave treats to the children on each of the holidays. Palestinian fruits were given out at Tu B'Shevat.

Raleigh Gross Cable recalled Sunday school in the old synagogue: "My dad used to drop us off and go to the office. He then would forget to come and pick us up. That was on Sunday. When we were waiting, we would go to the Mirviss's apartment, and we'd play there. They were a wonderful family. Mr. Mirviss made you feel real welcome. There were always other kids, like the Selcers, who were always waiting for their father too, so we had someone to play with. We went to Talmud Torah too, because of my uncle, Dr. Gordon. He insisted!"

That fall, Dr. Alex Josewich spoke to the Young People's Forum on "Jewish Dietary Laws from a Medical Point of View." His family had been members of the Adath dating back to its early years on the South Side. His father, Joseph Josewich, had come over from Russia, and his mother, Anna, from Lithuania, during the 1880s.

The 1922-23 year ended with Adath Jeshurun negotiating for a site on the West Side. The need for a new synagogue was becoming more acutely felt, not only because the congregation had doubled in size, but also because many congregants now lived west of Nicollet Avenue and south of Lake Street. This was a newer section in the city. The site that was decided upon was on 34th Street and Dupont Avenue South. At that time the street wasn't paved.

The synagogue had also considered buying the plot of land overlooking Lake Calhoun where the Greek Orthodox church now sits, but the "price was right" on Dupont, perhaps because the land had poor drainage.

Hy Mendow later recalled that a few years earlier, three Minneapolis synagogues—Adath Jeshurun, Beth El, and Temple Israel—had been considering the possibility of consolidating. "We had organized a group to consolidate all three of them into one large cathedral-like structure, close to downtown. The Reform Rabbi Minda was agreeable, as was Rabbi Matt, but Rabbi Aronson scotched it. So each one built their own. I wrote the project up in the *American*

Jewish World so everyone would know, and Rabbi Aronson called me a *chutzpanik!*"

Joseph Schanfeld made several appeals that fall for contributions to fund both the building program and the Talmud Torah which had accrued a $20,000 deficit

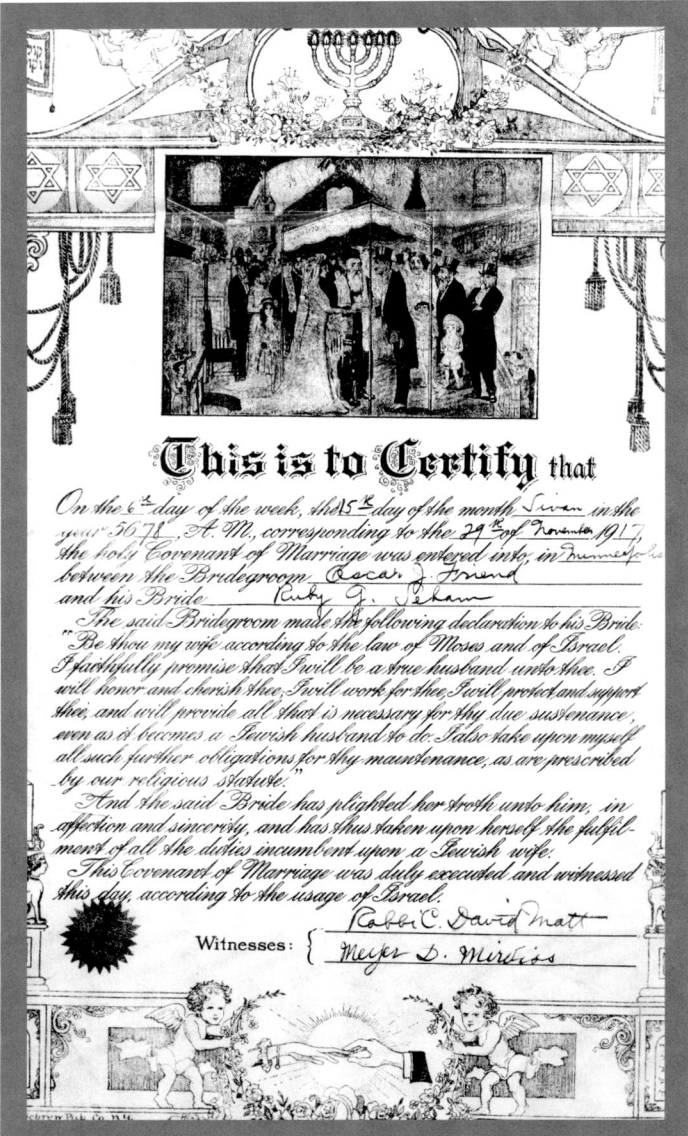

A typical marriage certificate of the era, signed by Rabbi Matt and M.D. Mirviss

during the previous year, though it still had ambitious plans to open a West Side branch and also a Jewish high school.

The tenth anniversary edition of the *American Jewish World* noted that Dr. Chaim Weitzman, leader of the World Zionist Organization, had visited Minneapolis to raise money for the Keren Hayesod/ United Jewish Appeal. The War Sufferers and Jewish War Relief were still in need, as were the Disabled American Veterans. Hy Mendow became the first Jew to be appointed a judge in Minneapolis, and Adath member Samuel Maslon received the Sears Prize at Harvard Law School.

Dr. M. Lefkowitz offered an appraisal in the *AJW* of the state of Minneapolis Jewry. He noted that they had been successful in supporting their own institutions, and well-organized in their philanthropic pursuits, but were not highly esteemed by local non-Jews. It pained him to report that not a single non-Jewish organization had welcomed Jews into its midst in Minneapolis. There were no Jewish teachers in the schools and no Jews on any city boards. In fact, in his view Jews stood far lower in Minneapolis than in any other community in the United States. Why?

Dr. Lefkowitz answered, somewhat lamely, that the Jews must first "understand themselves, and be well-versed in their background religion before they could interpret it to the non-Jewish community." In short, education was the key.

Many years later, in his book *Jews in Transition* (1949), Rabbi Albert I. Gordon asked the same question, but came up with a different answer.

"The World Fundamentalist Movement has its headquarters in Minneapolis and the Northwest Bible School, one of the major Fundamentalist schools, is located in the city. There is a large Lutheran population in Minneapolis, almost twice as large as the Lutheran population of St. Paul. On the other hand, St. Paul has a considerably larger Roman Catholic population and Roman Catholics play a greater role in the civic affairs of St. Paul than they do in Minneapolis."

Gordon went on to draw attention to the large Scandinavian population of Minneapolis, which had little contact with Jews in the Old World and tended to retain medieval notions of the Jew as the incarnation of the devil. He also pinpointed the many prominent New Englanders among the founding families of Minneapolis.

"These people are not to be regarded as anti-Semites in any sense. They are, rather, a self-contained and a self-sufficient class, unaware that the problem exists or, if aware, choosing rather to ignore it and go about their own affairs. Thus, those groups and persons who are anti-Semitic for reasons theological, political, economic or national are provided with the opportunity to carry on their anti-Semitic campaign, for the real leaders of the community appear not to be too concerned about the issue."

1923-1924

Representatives from the Council of Jewish Women, B'nai B'rith, and Keren Hayesod were beginning to venture out to small communities in Minnesota to establish Jewish activities. President Woodrow Wilson died and

Rabbi Minda, Temple Israel, delivered the prayer at the community Memorial Service. Young feisty Rabbi David Aronson was the new spiritual leader of Beth El Synagogue on the North Side. A graduate of the Jewish Theological Seminary, he spent short periods of time working in Salt Lake City and Duluth before coming to Beth El in Minneapolis in 1924. Three years later he married Bertha Friedman, a teacher and Adath Jeshurun graduate.

The Adath began holding Friday night services, religious school on Sundays, and Hebrew classes on Tuesdays and Thursdays, in the new Irwin Building at 1406 West Lake Street (near Hennepin Avenue) while the building on Dupont was under construction.

In his yearly review, Rabbi Matt made special mention of a radio program that was being broadcast under the auspices of the United Synagogue of America. The new medium was being used for instruction and entertainment on Jewish holidays.

A benefit for the Adath Talmud Torah and Religious School was held at the Shubert Theater in March. There was no graduating class of 1924.

1924-1925

There was considerable controversy that year as to where the High Holiday services would be held. Many who had been attending services at the Lake Street location requested that the Adath also hold High Holiday services there, but it was finally decided to hold them at the 9th Street building. The main auditorium had been redecorated and people were asked to make reservations for pews. There were free seats for the young folks and a special Young People's Service.

Mrs. Solomon Schechter, who had founded the National Women's League, died that fall. The Adath Jeshurun's women's group had been among the founding members. A memorial was held for her in Minneapolis in December.

The Young People's Forum's changed its name to the Young People's League. They had become associated with the national organization under the auspices of the United Synagogue of America. The forum sponsored a debate in which representatives from Beth El, Temple of Aaron, and Adath Jeshurun—the three local Conservative congregations—disputed whether Zionism was the only means of preserving the Jews.

On February 25, 1924, President Joe Schanfeld sent a letter to the Adath congregation informing them of a very important quarterly meeting that was to take place in the Irwin Building on Lake Street. In the course of the letter he lamented the discrepancy between what it cost to educate a child at one of the synagogue's two locations, and what the families of those who attended were actually paying.

...Either we must send the children away and doom them to grow up in ignorance of things Jewish or else teach them. If we send them away we would be penalizing the children and not the parents. Instead we have tried to teach the children...

We wish it were unnecessary to speak of money matters on these holy occasions, but so few of us enter the synagogue during the year other than these three holidays or attend a meeting of the congregation that this is the only opportune time we can enlighten you of our situation.

We had hoped during the last year to do something decisive in our building program but frankly, with our deficit staring us in the face, we had not the heart or the courage to proceed. The Adath has a reputation for generosity, perhaps that is why they consider us "the rich Shul."

That year the United States drastically reduced its immigration quotas: the mass migration from Eastern Europe was over. In Minneapolis, Rabbi Silber died and

M. D. Mirviss accepting a contribution for the synagogue

a young men's organization, AZA, the junior auxiliary of B'nai B'rith, was formed. The first president was Ben Bernstein.

The *American Jewish World* ran a series profiling various eminent men in the community, including several from Adath Jeshurun. An article about M. D. Mirviss described him as a "specialist in prying open the hearts of Jewish businessmen for various causes....Getting a donation gives him the sensation that 'a big killing' on the stock exchange gives to the stock speculator." The article went on to point out that Mirviss never begged. Rather, "He makes a person feel that it is a special privilege to be called upon to participate."

In the same issue Joseph Schanfeld, A. Morris Gross, Dr. George J. Gordon, and Dr. Moses Barron were also profiled.

1925-1926

Three Minneapolis synagogues—Beth El, Tifereth B'nai Jacob and Mikro Kodesh—completed new synagogue structures that year, and both Adath Jeshurun and Temple Israel had building programs in the works. Adath's plans were complete and the contract was ready to let out for bids.

The Deinard Memorial Library at the Talmud Torah was also dedicated that year. Its fine collection was bolstered by Dr. Deinard's and Rabbi Silber's outstanding bequests to the Talmud Torah. The Jewish Relief Fund became the United Jewish Appeal (UJA). Many distinguished speakers and educators came to Minneapolis, and also the premier Yiddish star of the time, Ben Ammi.

On October 30, 1925, at the Adath Congregational Dinner, President Schanfeld delivered an address thanking the congregants for their generous response to his previous appeals, and once again arguing the case for a new synagogue to be built on the west side of town.

...To my mind, a synagogue should be the center of Jewish influence, the source of inspiration, the place of assembly and a place for entertainment and diversion. We cannot do all that in the old building. Some day in the near future, we are going to build on the West Side. If we won't, some one else will. Why should it not be we of the Adath Jeshurun?

That evening the congregants made the momentous decision to go ahead with plans to build a new synagogue, to be completed for use by the High Holidays of 1927.

Josie Mendow, who was president of the Woman's League at the time, later recalled the situation: "I thought we needed [the new building] very much. I was sick and tired of meeting in the old hall. We had to have a kitchen. I felt that our outward symbols had to be as important as our inward symbols, and the only outward symbol of a religious organization was its meeting place.

"We used to have bazaars and raffle books. All the members had to take five or 10 raffle books, sell them and turn the money in. And I have a very vivid recollection of the food sales we had at the Radisson Hotel. There was a vacant store in the Radisson Hotel building and I talked to Mr. Krauss, the president of the hotel. I must have had an awful lot of *chutzpa* but I told him what we wanted. I said, 'Do you suppose we will interfere with your restaurant business if we serve food there?' He said, 'Not at all. What do you want?' So—we went in there and had the food sale which was very, very lucrative."

The architectural firm of Liebenberg & Kaplan was selected to draw the plans for the new synagogue building and to supervise its construction. One of their plans was accepted, and the Balkin Construction Company was given the contract.

Hy Mendow said, "One of the disagreements was that some of the members of the board wanted to build as cheaply as possible. My wife, Josie, put up a fight for Jack Liebenberg and for a grand building, which it became, one of the grand buildings of its time."

That fall Rabbi Matt's father fell ill and subsequently died. While the rabbi was out of the city, Dr. George Gordon, Dr. Moses Barron, and Samuel Maslon were on the pulpit. Theodore H. Gordon and Samuel Mirviss served as cantors and conducted services that year.

In December, 1925, it was announced in the *American Jewish World* that the old Adath synagogue at 12th Avenue South and 9th Street had been sold to the Council of Jewish Women, who planned to remodel it as the South Side Neighborhood House, for the recreational needs of Jews in that part of the city. On January 5, 1926, a Farewell Get-Together took place at the synagogue and the congregation bid good-bye to the edifice it had occupied for more than 20 years, with the satisfaction of knowing that the building would continue to be used for Jewish purposes.

The following day the daily services, minyan, and all of the synagogue's other activities were transferred to the West Side's temporary quarters. This shift gave even greater urgency to the fundraising activities that various groups within the congregation continued to sponsor.

In April the plans for the new synagogue were unveiled. A picture appeared in both the *Minneapolis Evening Paper* and the *American Jewish World*. Work was set to commence within the month.

The plans revealed that the edifice was to be built on four lots at 34th and Dupont Avenue South. The plans included a school and community center in addition to the synagogue structure. Twelve classrooms, a gym, a theater, an auditorium, a kitchen, a banquet room, locker and shower rooms, a library, a rabbi's study, a choir room, and women's and men's lounges were among the proposed spaces.

The exterior of the building was to be of pink marble stone with monolithic columns carried to two-and-one-half stories in Renaissance style—which was considered a departure in synagogue construction. The interior was to be carried out in Travertine stone finish, accentuated in Roman golds and soft grays. There would be no woodwork in the interior. The main sanctuary would hold a thousand, arranged in such a way that the bema would be visible from every seat in the auditorium.

1926-1927

The Adath Jeshurun congregation held their High Holy Days that year at Temple Israel's unused building at 10th Street and 5th Avenue South. By a happy inspiration, the services had been turned over to a group of young men. Samuel Mirviss and Theodore Gordon were the *chazanim* with Sam Gershowitz, Sam Grais, Harry Rosenblum and Mortimer Weinberg as their choir. Many felt that the services were the most impressive, beautiful services ever held in the city of Minneapolis, and 54 new members joined soon afterward—a number that nearly doubled within the next few months.

On Yom Kippur, Joseph Schanfeld once again spoke to his congregation, touching upon its temporary homelessness, its increasing attendance, the vitality of its Young People's League and Ladies Auxiliary, and the exciting prospect of a new building. As usual, his thoughts at that point went to the ever-present deficit that lingered like a ghost above the synagogue.

He went on to discuss relations between the synagogue and the Minneapolis Talmud Torah, which was about to assume the supervision of the Talmud Torah on the West Side. It was also proposed to establish a night school for boys and girls who were beyond Talmud Torah age or who had never had a chance to go to a Hebrew school. "For them the Talmud Torah is about to start an extension course, like a Jewish high school. This is so that at their most impressionable age, our Jewish youth may not be neglected to grow up in ignorance. We must do something for them and the Talmud Torah is about to make a very important effort."

Theodore Gordon recalled, "When I was 15, I joined the choir of the Young People's Synagogue at the Talmud Torah in 1923. The two chazanim then were Jacob and Harold Mirviss (sons of M.D. Mirviss) and Sammy Mirviss was in the choir. There were a few others who sang with us and we conducted the services on Rosh Hashanah and Yom Kippur at the Talmud Torah. It was a wonderful service and used to attract many adults who had their High Holiday service upstairs in the Talmud Torah's auditorium. We met downstairs all through the day on Yom Kippur. The adults would filter down and visit with us for awhile.

"When the Young People's Synagogue was dissolved because it was felt that it offered competition to the newly established Beth El congregation, we were a choir without a congregation. Adath Jeshurun, which was then really pushing across the threshold to become a modern Conservative congregation, invited us to conduct the High Holiday services for their congregation. Rabbi Matt was the rabbi. Jack and Harold Mirviss were not available, as they had gone off to their professions or schools so Sam Mirviss and I became the *chazanim*. We trained a choir and we sang.

"Once we knew that we were going to be conducting the Rosh Hashanah and Yom Kippur services, Sam and I camped on the trail of the *balabateem* at Adath Jeshurun. There was a Mr. Heiman and Mr. Shore with several others. We went to them and said that we needed to know a melody for this prayer—teach us.

"I really acquired my knowledge of *chazanut* almost entirely from those laymen in Adath Jeshurun who had been carrying the congregation until the time of Rabbi Matt's arrival. And of course, Mr. Mirviss taught us a great deal during that time. We never felt comfortable about his singing voice, but he had a mastery of the traditional melody.

"Sam and I learned a great deal, too, from cantorial records. I don't remember who made the approach to us but I am sure that it was a common consent, and Rabbi Matt was definitely part of that initiative. He and the lay people felt that we had something to contribute toward this wonderful process of moving Adath Jeshurun into modernity.

"The first year that we conducted the services was when the Adath met at the old Temple Israel building on 10th Street and 5th Avenue South in 1926. We were really young kids (18) but it was a very well received service.... We stood on the bema and the choir stood around us like in the traditional Orthodox synagogue. There was no musical accompaniment except for a pitch pipe. We conducted these services through the Holy Days of 1932."

The Annual Congregational Dinner was held at the Radisson Hotel that year, and the enthusiasm displayed by the congregation was so great that the building committee was instructed to let the contract out for bids.

Architect Jack Liebenberg

Jacob Josephus "Jack" Liebenberg had come to Minneapolis from Milwaukee, Wisconsin, to attend the first class of the University of Minnesota School of Architecture in 1912. He later recalled: "There were 18 or 19 more men, and out of that group, about 11 turned to dentistry instead of architecture, because the prospects were rather meager. There weren't many people that could afford an architect at that time. It was a luxury!"

In 1916 Liebenberg became the school's first graduate, and also became the first Jewish architect in Minnesota. He went on to receive an M.A. from Harvard University in 1917, and that same year he also won a gold medal and Diplome Par LeGouvernement Francais for his architectural designs.

During World War I he was an aviation instructor, and after the war he taught architecture at the University of Minnesota. In 1919, he founded Liebenberg & Kaplan with his brother-in-law, Seeman Kaplan. The firm was later called Kaplan, Glotter and Associates and much later, Liebenberg Associates, Architects.

In an interview he gave at the age of 89, Jack Liebenberg recalled: "When I was going to the university, I got acquainted with Rabbi Matt. He and Joe Schanfeld were very progressive. I used to go to the Adath Jeshurun Synagogue. I was involved with and helped to organize the Young People's League at the synagogue...At the university we organized a society called the Menorah Society, and it was the first chapter in the country. Jewish boys and girls would come to the meetings and from that group a bunch of activities and the religious group started in the Twin Cities.

"Jews were not allowed to join fraternities, and there were no Jewish fraternities. There were not many Jewish men on campus—you could count them on one hand. The Menorah Society played a very imporant part in tying the Jewish society together. Our Menorah Society was vigorous

THE PINK FAMILY JOINS THE ADATH

Dena Pink explained: "Dave and I broke away from the B'nai Abraham. We couldn't sit together there. Father would have Dave sit in front with him and I would sit in back with the ladies. That went on for a short while and then we decided to join Adath Jeshurun so we could sit together. That was after we got married in 1927." In the 1940's Dr. David Pink would be a president of the Adath; Dena would be president of the Women's League; and their two sons, Norman and "Buddy" would also each be president of the Synagogue.

and effective activity and later out of it came the Hillel House and many other things.

"At that time a Conservative Jewish group lived in South Minneapolis near Franklin. When I was a student, I boarded with the Wonderman family, Hy Mendow's uncle. I would attend services at Rabbi Matt's temple. Mr. Wonderman was a janitor at City Hall, a public job, but they were a very fine family. They were walking distance, so I could save streetcar fare and go over the bridge to the University. It was near the Seven Corners area, where the old Rumanishe Shul was. I used to walk to school. It was very convenient. I lived there until I graduated and went to Harvard.

"Being the only Jewish architect in Minneapolis at the time, the Beth El Synagogue got us involved in designing a synagogue for them in North Minneapolis. It was a small congregation, but they had changed from the Orthodox to the Conservative approach to Judaism, and we completed that building, more or less, in the medieval historical tradition of Jewish buildings, keeping with tradition in many things. Later on, the synagogue had trouble, couldn't pay their bills, and the architect, the builder, the suppliers, everybody compromised. Beth El was built in 1925. They already had financial problems. But I held my membership in the Beth El so that I had somebody to talk to—to get paid for the services that our firm had performed.

"...After the Beth El was built, it was only natural for Rabbi Matt to get us to build their new synagogue. When they finally did build it in 1927, it was automatic for me to become a member, after all I had designed and built the building!"

During the last week of December, it was announced that the Balkin Construction Company had been awarded the general contract for the new synagogue. The building

was to be completed by August, 1927, at a cost of about $182,000. It had been decided that the classic Renaissance architecture exterior would be built of variegated oolitic Bedford stone. By the first of the year, the first unit was nearing completion.

Jack Liebenberg recalled: "The Adath was the first synagogue to have a chapel. It was downstairs on the main floor. The building sits on pilings. It was actually built on a swamp. This was the first building in Minneapolis to be built on pilings. We dug down 50 to 75 feet. I think the land was about $2500 an acre. they owned the land across the street on Dupont but in order to pay off the mortgage they sold the land. Adath Jeshurun Synagogue was one of the first buildings in Minnesota to have plaster on the wall made of straw and gypsum.

"Liebenberg & Kaplan worked up the ideas and I did the sketches of the stained glass windows. The final design was done by a local man, Chester Leighton. He worked with Rabbi Matt and a committee. The money was raised for the windows after they were completed and installed. Individual families bought them 'In Memory' and 'In Honor' of family members. During the construction, additional frames were made to protect the windows on account of driving the piles."

Jack also said that the Adath had assigned seats with names on each pew. Some of the elders were always in the front and other people in the back. "You could pick your seat wherever you wanted behind the assigned seats. They were the only congregation that did it that way."

Jack continued: " I helped them finance their mortggage with a company that is today called the Farmers Safe Insurance Company in St. Louis, and they sold bonds in those early days to farmers all through the Missouri and Kansas area to finance the Adath Jeshurun. When the Depression came and they couldn't make payments, Adath finally mitigated their morgage commitments by paying half, or other.

"They couldn't pay the architect's fee as they had to pay the creditors. I got paid some but not what was in the contract. They made up for it a little bit. We had a good relationship there. It was no one's fault. It was the times."

Louis Shore recalled that on all the holidays in the early days, the men wore frock coats and top hats. Louis was married to Mr. Woolpy's daughter, Tess. Louis' father, Zelick Shore, was a lay cantor at the Adath and at other congregations but he didn't get paid.

Jack Liebenberg said about Mr. Woolpy: "He was a merchant. He was the kind of man that could attract attention because of his background and knowledge. He even went to the Unitarian church once in a while to listen to the sermon and would come back with information so that the rabbis gradually changed as the Conservative movement was young."

The original expansive plans to have an educational and social wing, with a gym, locker rooms and lounges for men and women were left out in the final plans.

The ground-breaking ceremony took place on October 16, 1926, with several hundred members and friends of the synagogue in attendance. The program included a reading by Theodore "Ted" Gordon; talks by Joe Schanfeld, J.H. Woolpy, Louis Rosenfield, Mrs. J. H. Gruenberg for the Women's League, Dr. George Gordon, and Rabbi C. David Matt. The benediction was pronounced by John Fligelman, the oldest member of the congregation. The privileges of digging the first shovelfuls of earth were auctioned off by Max Shallet prior to the event.

Towards the end of 1926, the Women's League held a White Elephant Sale to raise additonal funds. They continued their fundraising efforts with benefit teas, musicales, Mah Jong and Bridge parties, and sewing groups who made articles for the Food and Apron Sale.

Myer Heiman, pitcher for the Adath baseball team, circa 1917

The Asurens, the Adath's Athletic club, sponsored a Father and Son Banquet at the Gimel Daled Club in celebration of their winning the football championship in the Park Board League. The speakers were Sig Harris and Alex(Dutchy) Strauss. In January the Asurens basketball team were winners in the junior divison of the Municipal Basketball League and the Church League.

Between September and January, one hundred new members had joined the Adath Jeshurun, and on February 8 they were welcomed at the congregational dinner held at the Gimel Daled Club. At the close of the dinner, Joe Schanfeld announced that Rabbi Matt, who had served the synagogue since 1912, had tendered his resignation. He had recieved a call from Temple Beth David of Buffalo, New York, and after much soul-searching and deliberation, had decided to accept it.

At first the trustees unanimously refused to accept the resignation and made every effort to induce Rabbi Matt to reconsider, but the rabbi insisted that his resignation stand.

On March 1, a farewell dinner was given for Rabbi Matt at the Flame Room of the Radisson Hotel. Five hundred men and women—leaders in every walk of the city's communal and religious life and personal admirers of Rabbi Matt—gathered to honor him. Many speeches were given by the rabbis of the community and by the presidents of the various synagogue and communal organizations.

Rabbi Matt left for Buffalo the next day. He would return in June for his family and to attend the Bar Mitzvah of his nephew, Lawrence Harris. Special exercises were held on June 12 with Rabbi Matt confirming the graduating class who had been his students.

Once Rabbi Matt had departed, various congregants spoke from the pulpit, including Julius Fligelman, Dr. Alexander Josewich, Dr. Moses Barron, N. Mininberg, Hy Mendow, and Dr. Lefkowitz.

In spite of the rigorous winter, work on the new building was ahead of schedule, and on Sunday, April 10, 1927, the cornerstone of the Adath Jeshurun Synagogue was laid. Close to a thousand people witnessed the ceremony. Mr. and Mrs. L. J. Rosenfield, the Building Fund's largest contributors, placed the stone and were given a gold trowel. The next highest contributor, Max Graceman, received a silver trowel; Arthur Brin, the third, was given a bronze trowel. The fourth, Charles Selcer, was given the honor of placing the archives of the synagogue in the cornerstone. Rabbi David Aronson opened the ceremonies and John Fligelman, the oldest member of the congregation, delivered the principal address. Other speakers included Harry Brown, H. T. Bearman, Hy Mendow and J. H. Schanfeld. Small trowels were distributed to all that were present as souvenirs.

Looking back on Rabbi Matt's contributions to the synagogue, Rabbi Theodore H. "Ted" Gordon remarked: "Rabbi Matt played a special role in carrying the congregation from a traditional past to a more modern outlook and structure. He opened the door to modern Judaism in his organization of young people, bringing them into the synagogue. He changed the character of the Adath Jeshurun from what it had been in the old days when it was run by laymen, and the *chazan* and *baal kriah* were all members of the congregation. There was hardly any professional staffing of the congregation. He was the first modern rabbi. He led the congregation through that doorway. I have the feeling that the congregation he thought to create took root faster than he ever dreamed, and in a sense outran him.

"He was not a polished, pompous forager. He was deeply rooted in tradition and was a very warm, lovable person. He did not fit into the pattern of the kind of modern rabbi that ultimately the Adath Jeshurun had to acquire. Many of his congregation felt that he was unable to represent the Adath Jeshurun adequately in the non-Jewish community, in the larger community. I think that the congregation that he had created rapidly outgrew him, which was the reason that he left rather abruptly and went to Buffalo."

On a more personal level, Eddie Schwartz remarked: "He was such a mild-mannered, easy-going guy. To me he was a gentleman and a scholar. I liked him very much, and a kid of 13 can remember that very distinctly. Rabbi Matt was the rabbi who was there at my Bar Mitzvah in 1916. He was an upright sort of man with a small mustache. He was very pleasant, an easy man to get along with. You could talk to him; even as a kid you could talk to him. Rabbi Matt seemed to be a family type rabbi and a teacher."

Pauline Weise Cohen: "Rabbi Matt would show slides that were lantern shows. When the children didn't behave, he would put the slides on the ceiling to get our attention. I remember the Sunday school picnics at Minnehaha Park Pavillion. We would play games and put on plays by the falls."

The young Rabbi Matt

When Rabbi Matt died in 1951, his contributions to the wider community were also noted. For example, as secretary-treasurer of the Jewish Conference, Kehilllah, movement in Minneapolis, he contributed toward the state of mind which prepared the way for the organization of the Minneapolis Federation for Jewish Service in 1930. As member of the Charity Board, he helped in the organization of what is now the Jewish Family & Children's Service. As first secretary of the Jewish War Relief committee, which functioned during World War I, he prepared himself for a leading role in advocating the community's acceptance of the United Jewish Appeal. He represented this district at the early sessions of the American Jewish Congress.

He represented Minneapolis Jewry effectively at many civic meetings and committees. He was one of the organizers and vice president of the Goodwill Club in 1924, a meeting ground for clergy of different denominations, which paved the way for the later formation of the Minneapolis Round Table of the Conference of Christians and Jews.

The *American Jewish World* wrote:

"It is difficult at any time to carry the torch of truth in the crowded marketplace without the danger of singeing someone's hair, and Rabbi Matt wanted to carry the torch without hurting a hair on anybody's head. It was he, therefore, who was often hurt. But he took it with a smile. He loved his neighbors more than he loved himself.

"He was exceedingly humble in all his efforts. He would not spare himself, but he always endeavored to spare the sensibilities of others. He was well aware of such a delicate position in the life of a public man and he was sensitive of this conflict within himself- the urge to speak out and the doubt whether he is justified in causing pain or in upsetting anyone. He saw the pain and the hurt he might cause as immediate evils but his modesty and humility made him question the good he might accomplish thereby. He preferred to look for a more peaceful solution.

"He met the pressure of his impatient friends and the apparent urgency of the times with a smile, a story, or a witticism. Behind the smile, however, there was often a suppressed tear. The story was sometimes a cover for his aching heart, and the witticisim were an effort not to lose faith in the midst of the complexities of our civilization. 'This too, will pass,' his smile seemed to say. 'Don't take yourself and your difficulties too seriously' it suggested. If the rabbi was the first to laugh at his own stories, it was because he directed them against himself and his own problems even as he endeavored to calm and to encourage his friends.

"In an age of brass, his was the soft, still voice; in an age of strife, he was the great peacemaker; in a world of arrogant leaders and of inordinate ambitions, he served humbly and selflessly; in a world of speed and of emphasis on quick results, he was patient, never losing faith in human nature and in the ultimate triumph of the true and the good."

(Top) The new Adath building at 34th and Dupont Ave. S., ca 1930;
(Left) Rabbi Jesse Schwartz; (Above) The Women's Dramatic Club
presenting a play, *She Must Marry a Doctor*.

4

THE RABBI SCHWARTZ YEARS
(1927-1929)

With a new rabbi on the pulpit and Joseph Schanfeld at the helm of the board, the Adath congregation made full use of its new synagogue, filling its various spaces with ceremonies, socials events, meetings, dinners, and concerts. But as the years passed, one question resurfaced again and again—how were they going to continue paying for it?

At the end of June 1927, it was announced that Rabbi Jesse Schwartz of New York City would become the new spiritual leader at Adath Jeshurun. He would arrive in August and begin his association on September 1st. Rabbi Schwartz was known as a forceful pulpit orator. He had spoken in Minneapolis at Shavuot services and made a favorable impression on members of the congregation.

Jesse Schwartz was born in New York City in 1892. He received a B.S. degree from New York City College in 1912 and a law degree from Columbia University three years later. In 1918, he joined the army, and following the Armistice, he enrolled in Jewish Theological Seminary. He graduated in 1925, having been elected president of the student body during his senior year.

After graduation Rabbi Schwartz occupied a pulpit in Toronto for two years. By this time he had become well known for his Zionist activities. He had served with the Young Judea Organization and was Director of Adult Educational Activities of the Zionist Organization of America in 1920 and 1921. Interested in Jewish education, he also had been an instructor in the Extension Department of the Jewish Teachers' Institute of New York City.

During the summer of 1927, it was announced that Samuel Mirviss and Theodore Gordon would be the cantors for the High Holiday Services, accompanied by a choir of six young men that would be trained by Rabbi Schwartz upon his arrival in Minneapolis.

Beginning on August 15 of that year, morning and evening services were moved from the Lake Street quarters, which the congregation had been using for three years, to the first floor of the new synagogue. On Sunday, August 21, members of the congregation were given the opportunity to purchase memorial windows in the new synagogue. On August 24th Rabbi Schwartz finally arrived in Minneapolis and addressed the members at the annual meeting that same evening.

Howard Brin later recalled:

My own memories go back to 1927 when my grandmother, Tobie Fligelman, died and Rabbi Jesse Schwartz conducted the funeral in the present building. I was seven, and this was one of the first public events to take place in the new building.

On Sunday, September 11, an impressive program took place to dedicate the new Adath Jeshurun at 34th Street and Dupont Avenue South. President Joseph Schanfeld opened the ceremonies and Rabbi Schwartz gave the dedication address. Rabbis Albert G. Minda of Temple Israel, David Aronson of Beth El, and S. Levin of Shaarei Zedeck Synagogue, participated and lent emphasis to the fact that the new synagogue was an achievement for the entire Minneapolis Jewish community. Although Rabbi Matt was unable to attend, he sent his regrets, saying that it was impossible for him to leave Buffalo. The man who had helped to mold the congregation would not see the fruit of his labors.

Josephine Mendow, president of the Adath Jeshurun Women's League, delivered a greeting. (The Women's League had dropped their old name, the Ladies Auxiliary, and taken the new name that was becoming popular nationally.) Other features of the dedication program included remarks by Jerome H. Woolpy, a violin solo by Phyllis Bearman, a procession with Torah scrolls, and synagogue music by Theodore H. Gordon, Samuel Mirviss and the choir. The congregation sang "America," "Hatikvah" and "Yigdal." The Adath congregation's dream had become a reality!

The Women's League held a tea and reception at their first meeting of the season in honor of Mrs. Jesse Schwartz, wife of the new rabbi. At that same meeting Josie Mendow was re-elected president. Later that fall, the women helped with the Congregational Dinner—a testimonial for Mr. Woolpy, chairman of the Building Fund and a longtime member of the congregation. He had been chairman of the Religious School, the Ritual Committee, and been active in many other programs.

The Annual Bazaar took place on December 20-23. Businessmen's lunches were once again a big draw, and sales of fancy needlework, dolls, aprons, candy, novelties, baby clothes, stationery, nightgowns, food delicacies, and other articles were brisk.

Various organizations continued to raise money for the Building Fund by staging benefits. The Jeshurun's Athletic Club held its football banquet at the Radisson Hotel, marking the second championship for the team. Gold footballs were presented to 15 members and much credit was given to the coach, Harry Vermes.

Rabbi Schwartz lost little time in organizing new groups, including a study group for men and women ages 16 to 18, and a Men's Club, with Louis B. Schwartz as president. At one of their first meetings, a University of Minnesota professor spoke on "Anti-Semitism in Western Europe." A new name had appeared in Germany—Adolf Hitler. He had been making speeches during the past year, and Jews had been attacked by students at a summer resort.

Rabbi Schwartz was officially installed at the synagogue on Februrary 5, 1928. The topic of his address was "The Functions of the Rabbinate Today." Among the other subjects he addressed during the year were: "Building a Land Ourselves;" "Is a Universal Religion Possible?"; "A Self-Respecting Program for Better Relations Between Jew and Gentile;" "World Peace: How Shall We Achieve It?"; "Leisure: Is it a Threat or a Challenge?"; "Atheisim: Does It Really Exist?"; "Is Democracy a Failure?"; "What Can

the Bible Mean to Us Today?"; "The Tragedy of the 19th Century Jew;" "How Shall We Face Anti-Semitism?"; "The Meaning of Religious Experience;" "The Jewish Book and the People of the Book;" "The Return of the Jewish Intellectual;" and "Torah and Life."

Clearly, Rabbi Schwartz was introducing new ideas to Adath Jeshurun.

At the March 1 meeting of the trustees, Mr. Woolpy read the Building Committee report and once again emphasized the need to raise additional funds. By March 21, when the committee met again, the issue had become more pressing, because the Mississippi Valley Trust Company had submitted a communication with reference to $2,550 interest due. After discussing various options, the trustees decided to send bills to congregants and a more detailed letter to those owing substantial sums. Other plans to raise funds were also discussed, including a dinner at $10 a plate with a renowned speaker; movies at frequent intervals at $.50-$1 per ticket; the issuance of debenture bonds at $100 a piece; and the more aggressive sale of Memorial Tablets.

A new innovation at the synagogue that year was a public Seder. It was held the second night of Passover, April 5, and was open to both members and non-members. Sam Mirviss lead the singing.

A Women's league production of the 1920s

That spring the Junior League Dramatic Club sponsored a vaudeville show, with Esther Berg, Donald Graceman, Helen Mannes, Sylvia Orenstein, Horace Greenberg and Stanley Kronick in the leads. There was dancing in the vestry rooms following the show.

The United Palestine Appeal, along with the Minneapolis Hadassah Chapter, held their banquet at the synagogue in April. The funds were earmarked for the Jewish National Fund, Hebrew University, Palestine Foundation Fund, Keren Hayesod, Hadassah Medical Unit and the Mizrachi Organizations. The national quota for 1928 was $7,500,000, of which the Minneapolis quota was $40,000.

The school year ended on May 25th with the Sunday School's closing exercises, which included a tableaux based on the Book of Ruth. Students participating were Margery Ellison, Roslyn Engler, Bernice Goldstein, Lorraine Horitz, Firley Kronick, Harriet Rifkin, Geraldine Silver and La-Verne Shedlov, with coaching by Mrs. Louis Gross. Hy Mendow, chairman of the Sunday School Committee, distributed the prizes for Scholarship and Attendance given by the Women's League.

On the first anniversary of the opening of the new building, June 16-17, the Women's League organized a carnival at the synagogue, designed to resemble the carnival and market held tri-annually in Jerusalem in ancient times during the Pilgrimages to the Temple. A fish pond, fortune telling, a cafeteria supper, dancing, and a popularity contest for "Her Queenship," were all part of the festivities. The proceeds were used for the Sunday School and Educational Funds.

In July, the trustees discussed the matter of Rabbi Schwartz's contract renewal, and voted that he would be re-elected for two years, at a salary increase of $500 for the second year of the contract. Samuel Mirviss and Ted Gordon were re-hired for the High Holidays.

At the August meeting Joseph Schanfeld was once again elected by unanimous ballot as president, as were A. M. Gross, vice president; Dr. A. Josewich, recording secretary; M. H. Harris, treasurer; M. Dockman, financial secretary; and trustees: J. H. Woolpy, H. Goldberg, and D. Phillips.

In review of year 5668, Rabbi Matt (who no longer lived in Minneapolis but continued to write for the *American Jewish World*) wrote:

The year began with one important dedication and ended with another. The Adath Jeshurun gave to Conservative Judaism in the Northwest its newest, most beautiful and most pretentious edifice, equipped with facilities that have made it increasingly useful in all types of communal endeavor. On the eve of the New Year. Temple Israel had its dedication of its new beautiful and commodious Temple and school building at Twenty-fourth and Emerson Avenue So.

Another occurrence was the appointment of Dr. George J. Gordon as Superintendent of the Talmud Torah of Minneapolis ... His idealism and love of Jewish education were strong enough to induce him to relinquish the practice of his profession and dedicate himself henceforth entirely to the sacred

task of Jewish education which makes the status of the Minneapolis Talmud Torah and its director unique in American communities.

1928-1929

In the September 14th issue of the *AJW*, Rabbi Schwartz examined what he took to be the waning vigor of Jewish life in the aftermath of the Great War, when there would be less of a call for mass activity. He predicted that the outstanding Jewish movements of the day would be minority movements, and suggested that even the movement for the Jewish redemption of Palestine had never won the full support of the Jewish masses.

Nor did he consider this an altogether bad thing.

A calmer period will afford too an opportunity for a more careful analysis of the slogans emblazoned on the banners of the various wings of Jewry ...Orthodoxy, Conservatism, Reform—what do these terms mean today to the average American Jew? One gets the impression at times that the claim to Orthodoxy is based on the predilection of one's grandfather for unleavened bread on Passover, that Conservatism is to many a form of evasion, and Reform a symbol of successful social climbing.

Parts of Rabbi Schwartz's article no longer ring true (and who in the late 1920s could possibly have envisioned the Holocaust?) but much of it has the same validity today as when it was written.

In his Yom Kippur talk that year, Joseph Schanfeld felt it necessary once again to bring up the financial problems facing the congregation. He compared the situation at Adath unfavorably to that of Temple Israel, where, he noted, "as a result of remarkable teamwork among their members, they succeeded in securing for their building fund most liberal contributions from every one of their members...with the result that notwithstanding their building is a very costly structure, they are excellently financed and they were able to take possession of their edifice with practically very little, if any, deficit in their building fund."

And what was the situation at the Adath?

We too have erected a beautiful synagogue and community center which rebounds to the credit of the Jews of Minneapolis to which even future posterity will point with pride; but because of insufficient amount of donations up to the time the building was dedicated, we had a large deficit to carry over which has been and still is a serious handicap to us.

Schanfeld applauded the money-raising efforts of the Women's League, and also praised the facilities and programs at the Adath itself. What the synagogue lacked was a level of giving commensurate with the services it provided. Thus, new members needed to be recruited, and current members and seatholders who had not yet given to the building fund needed to open their purses.

During 1928-29, Samuel Mirviss and Theodore Gordon officiated as cantors, assisted by choir members Sam Gershovitz, Sidney Meadow, Edward Rosenberg, Leo Gross, and Sidney Scherling. In the interests of cultivating a greater degree of uniformity, Rabbi Schwartz requested that those who had the Adler Machzor and a prayer cap should bring them to services.

The Saturday evening following Yom Kippur, Rabbi and Mrs. Schwartz announced they would "be at home" from 8 to 11 p.m.

Among the topics Rabbi Schwartz spoke on that fall were: "The Meaning of Forgiveness;" "Gratitude and the Modern Man;" "Public Worship: Do We Need It?"; "The Challenge of the Conservative Synagogue in America;" "Where Science and Religion Meet;" and during the winter and spring: "What Others Think of Judaism;" "Judaism and Modernism;" "The Revolt of the Parents;" "Training the Jewish Child;" "Right and Wrong: Do They Still Exist?"; "How Non-Jews Misrepresent the Jew;" and "The Jews are Different: Shall They Remain So?"

The year was once again an active one for the Women's League at the Adath. They held luncheons, fall and spring rummage sales, a December food bazaar, a series of bridge and mah jong parties, the annual Congregational Dinner and Spring Carnival. The Women's Dramatic Club presented a play, *She Must Marry a Doctor*, at a get-together supper.

The Adath Junior Auxiliary held a debate between Kalman Goldenberg and Hershel Kaufman on the subject: "Resolved: That Jewish Palestine is Necessary for the Preservation of Judaism." In February there was a Goodwill dancing party, and in June, the third annual Vaudeville and Dance took place.

The basketball team continued to play, and the Beth El and Adath teams met in a benefit game.

Stanley Kronick recalled: "As a youth, I participated in some athletics which the synagogue sponsored. I played

D r. Sidney Scherling recalled his days in the choir:

I remember being at Adath Jeshurun approximately in 1926 or 1927. Sam Mirviss called me and said, "I heard that you like to sing. Would you like to join our choir?" That's when I first met Sam. I joined the choir. There were just four or five of us, Sam and Ted Gordon, who is now Rabbi Theodore Gordon, the son of Dr. George Gordon, Leo Gross, and Ed Rosenberg, who was the bass. At first there was only a male choir.

Sammy (Mirviss) was a very handsome fellow. He had a beautiful tenor voice. He used to be involved at the university too, mostly with his voice. He could read music very easily. I couldn't. We would practice and learn the songs by rote.

During Rabbi Gordon's first year, 1930-1931, Sidney led the services on Friday nights with the Adath Jeshurun Choir. "I conducted the services on Friday nights in the early '30s. That was part of my tuition for college, which I didn't collect very often because that was the Depression. Now and then I would go to Mr. Schanfeld, and he would give me a hard luck story and say $50 a month was too much for four services. I did not sing on Saturdays. I chanted the Friday Night Services. There weren't too many attending. Maybe 50 were there. If there was a Bar Mitzvah, maybe 100 would attend. The service was at 8:00 p.m. and the rabbi would give a sermon. He was an excellent speaker. I enjoyed him very much."

basketball and football and we had a baseball team. We were called the Asurens. Hy Mendow was our basketball coach and Harry Vermes, the football coach. The boys who played on the team were part of the Young People's Synagogue groups."

The Adath confirmation class of 1929. From left Florence Goustin, David Copeland, Bertha Novich, Russell Schwartz, Rabbi Jesse Schwartz, Peggy Gross, Sol Alcalay, Jerry Margulies, and Gertrude Zimmerman.

In March, two new groups emerged: a club to discuss present day Jewish topics and a Synagogue Boy Scout Troop, for ages 12 and 13, with Harry T. Bearman as scoutmaster.

On the second night of Passover, the Second Annual Congregational Seder was held. There were special children's holiday services, and on Saturday Religious School students led the 10:30 a.m. service.

At the May meeting, the ever-present problem of funding once again emerged and those in attendance voted unanimously to assess each member $50 or more, if possible.

The first Confirmation exercises in the new synagogue were held on Friday evening, June 14, 1929, the second night of Shavuot. The class included Sol Alcalay, David Copeland, Florence Goustin, Peggy Gross, Jerome Margulies, Bertha Novich, Faye Rigler, Russell Schwartz, Frances Seltz and Gertrude Zimmerman, all of whom gathered on the bema of the synagogue to have their picture taken. The theme of the confirmants' talks was "The Jewish Holidays." Certificates of Confirmation, prizes and Bibles were presented to the class.

The United Palestine Appeal's Campaign opened at a banquet held at Adath Jeshurun. Nahum Sokolow, associate of Chaim Weitzmann, was the principal speaker.

During the summer the Adath Holiday cantors, Samuel Mirviss and Theodore Gordon, assisted by Sidney Scherling and Edward Rosenberg, gave a program at the Lake Harriet Band Pavilion. It was an all-Jewish musical concert with the Lake Harriet Municipal Band, sponsored by the Council of Jewish Women. The young men sang "Kol Nidre" and other Jewish liturgical and folk songs. This was the first time that such a concert was held publicly in Minneapolis.

At an August meeting, Mr. Schanfeld, president of the board of trustees, advocated a complete change of officers. But on September 10th it was announced that Rabbi Schwartz had resigned. Though the immediate cause is uncertain, it would appear that both Rabbi Schwartz and members of the congregation approved of the idea. Rabbi Schwartz went back to Canada, where in 1933, he served with the Zionist Organization of Canada in Montreal.

Howard Brin later recalled:

Jesse Schwartz left Adath to go back to Canada to become the Executive Secretary of the Canadian Zionist Organization. He expressed great pleasure that he would be returning to the East for a more active Jewish life. He was the Adath's first Reconstructionist rabbi. The Reconstructionists were people who were influenced by Mordecai Kaplan and his teaching at the seminary. The feeling was that in order to be viable, Judaism had to adapt to society; that Judaism was not just a religion but a religious civilization, and we lived in two civilizations: the Jewish and the American. We had to come to some kind of accommodation with these two forces and factors.

Sidney Scherling described Rabbi Schwartz as "a demanding type of individual. He seemed to be a stern person. I don't know why he didn't stay long."

Sam Mirviss had not been impressed by the rabbi: "I cannot remember anything about Rabbi Jesse Schwartz except his inability to establish a good rapport on the pulpit in presenting services!"

But Rabbi Ted Gordon could see his merits:

Rabbi Schwartz brought more of what the congregation felt was needed after Rabbi Matt left. He was intellectually stimulating. He was a more polished speaker and was able to represent Adath Jeshurun in the way that this new congregation wanted to be represented. I had the feeling that he was essentially an Easterner. At heart he was never quite able to embrace the Midwest and I think that he left because he never really felt at home here.

He was a good speaker. I don't recall any special relationships that Sam Mirviss and I had with him. He had his department and we had the choir and conducted the service. Rabbi Schwartz was a more stern personality, a little harder to reach than Rabbi Matt, but he moved the congregation through the next phase of its growth into a modern Conservative congregation. He had experience with working with Young Judea and Zionist youth before he came here. His successors, building upon what Rabbis Matt and Schwartz had created, were able to make of Adath Jeshurun the congregation that it has become today."

At the September 10th meeting the trustees discussed who might be available to serve as a spiritual leader for the High Holidays. And, once again, there was a suggestion to raise dues—there was a big mortgage to take care of.

Leo Gross later recalled:

From the time the building was built, until a long time later, they couldn't make ends meet. The building was built in 1927 and two years later they ran into the Depression. It was extremely difficult. Frank Grouse, Helen Winer's father, very frequently paid the electric coal bills. Raising funds was a terrific effort and there was always a crisis when one or all of them had to guarantee electric, heating, and fuel bills. Jack Liebenberg was the architect and had the respect of everybody. I recall that Hy and Josie Men-

dow were very active.

The final crises came with the Depression and the building was foreclosed. At that time there were extensive negotiations to consolidate with the Temple which was also having problems. I was much too young to be involved, but I recall how seriously my father worked on that project. How the foreclosure was worked out, I don't know, but Dad worked like a Trojan to keep the place afloat. There were serious discussions about the merging. I can't recall who it was who objected or what group it was, if it was the Temple, the Adath or both.

1929-1930

After the resignation of Rabbi Schwartz the idea of electing a new slate of officers beacame less attractive, and Joseph Schanfeld stayed at the helm. It was felt that continuity of leadership was necessary until a new rabbi could be secured. Dr. George J. Gordon accepted the chairmanship of the Adath Jeshurun Sunday School Committee for the ensuing year, with Rae Berman as supervisor and a competent staff of teachers in tow.

For the High Holidays, and through Sukkot and Simchat Torah, Rabbi Peter Halpern of Brooklyn, New York (on the recommendation of the JTS) occupied the pulpit. On succeeding Friday nights, Louis B. Schwartz, Dr. Maurice Lefkowitz, Dr. George J. Gordon, and Jesse Calmenson from St. Paul spoke. Samuel Mirviss conducted the services, as usual.

In December, Rabbi Irwin M. Melamed from Germany lectured, and during Shabbat, Chanukah, and on Purim, Adath and Beth El held joint services at Beth El. Rabbi Aronson helped out the congregation and Sam Mirviss and his choir sang at Beth El one Shabbat. During January, Rabbi Henry Rosenthal, a recent graduate of the JTS, spoke. The rest of the winter, Sam Mirviss conducted the services with the support of the choir.

Although the rabbi was gone and the nation's economy was deteriorating day by day, various groups within the synagogue continued to organize activities and sponsor events. The Women's League in particular maintained a number of committees, including Ways and Means, Programs, Sunday School, Membership and Cooperation, Calling, House Committee, Hostesses, Sick Committee, University, Hospital, Publicity and Membership.

Evelyn Siegel, Sophie Singer, Ruth Stillman, and Dena Pink later described the activities of the Sick Committee in a joint interview:

The men would call on the men and the women on the women...The Sick Committee would know who was sick and they would call on them. They went to the homes. Who went to the hospital in those days? When you were sick, you stayed home. Dr. George Gordon delivered the babies, and Dr. Josewich was the treater-for-nothing. Sometimes Dr. Gordon would leave money under a needy patient's pillow instead of getting paid. We had dedicated people that lived for their synagogue.

In October the stock market, which had been teetering for months, finally tumbled. With no permanent rabbi in the pulpit and bills mounting at 3400 Dupont Avenue South, the energies of the Women's League were directed towards keeping an equilibrium. They held a Simchat Torah Get-Together and Buffet Supper; saw that the children got their treats at holidays; conducted fall and spring rummage sales; held card parties to raise more money; had their Annual Food Sale of homemade delicacies, and served lunches, tea and dinners.

At the January 22 Trustees Meeting, a committee of three was appointed to invite Dr. M. Lefkowitz to occupy the Adath pulpit temporarily. Also at the meeting M. K. Lifson was named chairman to solicit ads for the Shubert Benefit to be held on March 18. Temple Israel had issued an invitation to attend a public dinner on February 12 and the invitation was accepted.

That same month, the Congregational Dinner was held, and in February, congregants enjoyed an old fashioned Basket Social with dancing and prizes. There was a Purim Party in March; and to culminate the spring season, the Annual Carnival in May. It was called "A Carnival of Joy" commemorating the third anniversary of the opening of the new building. A capacity crowd chose Edythe Levine and Adeline Aberman as the Queens of the Carnival.

At the March 17 meeting, the trustees passed a resolution authorizing Meyer D. Mirviss, the Sexton and Assistant Rabbi of the Adath Jeshurun Congregation, to distribute wine for sacramental purposes to the members of the congregation, within the provisions of the Federal Prohibition Law.

And it was announced that pledges totaling $10,055.26 had been received that year from 131 members.

A committee of Herman Liss, Michael Dockman, and Mrs. Sophia Raymond was appointed to make the necessary arrangements for the Congregational Passover dinner to be held Sunday, April 13, in the vestry rooms of the synagogue. Dr. Lefkowitz and Samuel Mirviss conducted the Seder; and at the final Passover services that year, Theodore Gordon spoke. He was now a student at the JTS and was home for the holidays visiting his parents.

In the spring, Al Weinberg, Guita Bearman, Abraham Harris and Reuben Berman, university students active in debate

Harriet Hoffman, one of the Adath's first nursery school teachers, circa 1930

and oratory, gave a series of talks on Friday nights. On March 14 the A.Z.A. National Sabbath was observed with one of the national leaders speaking. Also that evening, Sidney Scherling, winner of the Northwest Regional Oratorical Contest, spoke on "Louis Marshall—A Hebrew Hero," and Harold Zadle on "The Psychology of the Jew." Sidney and Sam Ziff were the co-chairmen of the evening with A.Z.A. president Morris Besner and Irving Dachis helping. The Women's League hosted a social hour after the event.

On May 16, 1930, another young rabbi came to visit the Adath Jeshurun and occupy the pulpit temporarily—Rabbi Albert I. Gordon of Temple Israel in Washington Heights, New York City. His address that day was on "Why I am A Jew."

The final Adath Jeshurun Sunday School assembly for the season was held in June, and confirmation exercises were held at the synagogue on June 2 with Beth El's Rabbi, David Aronson, in charge.

5

THE RABBI ALBERT I. GORDON YEARS
1930 – 1946

IN THE SUMMER OF 1930, the world was in economic turmoil and the United States was entering into the worst depression in its history. The Adath Jeshurun congregation found itself with a new edifice and a large mortgage, but no rabbi and few funds with which to remain afloat. But on July 2, 1930, it was announced at the Trustees' meeting that Albert I. Gordon was to arrive shortly, accompanied by his wife, Dorothy, to assume the duties of rabbi. The arrival of the newly married couple brought a breath of fresh air to Adath, infusing new blood, inspiration, hope, and love into the congregation, which was now in its 46th year of existence.

Albert I. Gordon was born on May 11,1903, and raised in Cleveland, Ohio. He received his BA from NYU and was ordained at the JTS in 1928.

Rabbi Gordon was very active in communal affairs in New York City and was a member of the Executive Council of the United Synagogue of America. He served as chairman of the Committee on Eduction of Young People's League of the United Synagogue, on committees on Passover Relief in Washington Heights, the Committee on Cooperation, and the Allied Jewish Campaign.

Dorothy Davis Gordon was a Minneapolitan by birth, the daughter of Mary and Max Davis. Her father had been president of Knesseth Israel Synagogue in North Minneapolis. Dorothy, a graduate of North High School and the University of Minnesota, had won a scholarship to the New York Training School of Social Service and gone on to work with the Jewish Social Service in Chicago before marrying Rabbi Gordon in November of 1929.

"It was after our marriage," Dorothy later recalled, "when Rabbi Gordon was at Temple Israel, Washington Heights, and teaching Speech at NYU, that the seminary kept calling him to accept other positions. One was Kansas

City, another was Omaha and a third was Adath Jeshurun. When Joseph Schanfeld invited Albert to accept the position here, my father sent us a telegram and said: 'Don't you dare come. It's a dead congregation!' Whereupon my dear husband said, 'Well, I guess that's something for me to tackle.'"

The first issue of the Adath Jeshurun *Clarion* (October 15, 1930) carried the headline

WELCOME RABBI AND MRS. GORDON!

Josie Hechter remarked: "When Rabbi Albert Gordon was expected, my mother, Sophie Weingarten Raymond, was the only woman as part of the committee that met him at the train. ... We (my husband and I) were very fond of Rabbi Gordon. We dearly loved him. We knew Dorothy, as I had gone to school with her, and we were close."

And Leo Gross remembered: "When Rabbi Gordon came, things began to perk up again. He was a fine man, dynamic, and he could generate enthusiasm. He created a feeling within the synagogue and really got things going."

But things had already begun to percolate in anticipation of the new rabbi's arrival. The inaugural issue of the

Clarion also announced that a membership campaign was underway, with a goal of one hundred new members. President Joseph Schanfeld was heading the drive.

At the time, there were 157 children registered in the Sunday School, the largest number in the history of the school. The curriculum was being completely reorganized. A new feature that fall was the High School Department, to be composed of confirmants from the last two years. Beginner classes for Talmud Torah were starting. Saturday mornings Junior Sabbath Services were held at 10:30 a.m. All children and mothers were invited to attend.

1930-1931

The High Holidays were led by Theodore Gordon and Samuel Mirviss with the Adath choir participating. The Annual Congregational Election on September 30 saw Joe Schanfeld re-elected President; Dr. Harold Cooperman, Vice President; I.D. Schulman, Recording Secretary; and H.L.Altman, Financial Secretary. The Men's Club was reorganized. The Women's League had gained 54 new members, and study groups were set up to acquire greater knowledge of the Bible and Hebrew. A student government was also started. Each class was to have a representative and a school newspaper was going to be published. Jenny Gross was Women's League President and Josie Hechter was the Program Chair.

On Monday, October 27, 1930, at 8:00 p.m. Rabbi Albert I. Gordon was installed as Rabbi of the Adath Jeshurun. On the previous Saturday the *Minneapolis Tribune* (October 25, 1930) had described the synagogue building as one of the largest and most beautiful edifices in the country, while the *Minneapolis Journal* reported: "Christian as well as Jewish Ministers to Join in Adath Jeshurun Greeting." Rabbi Solomon Goldman of Chicago delivered the address. Dr. David Bryn-Jones, pastor of Trinity Baptist church, Rabbis Moses Romm, S. I. Levin and David Aronson brought greetings and Arthur Brin presided. The Women's League gave a reception with musical entertainment following the service.

At his installation Rabbi Gordon stated his aim to reacquaint the Jewish youth with the history and values of Judaism. "I seek not alone to preserve the Jewish heritage, but to make it function. Israel's past must be explained and reinterpreted in terms which modern men and women will understand." And Rabbi Gordon was, indeed, part of a new breed of American rabbi who considered Judaism to be a universal religion. One member of the congregation, Anna K. (Mrs. Louis) Schwartz, characterized him at the time as "a Herzl of the synagogue."

Dorothy Gordon later remarked that although her father had been exaggerating when he used the phrase "dead congregation," the Adath was in a very bad state in those days. "The synagogue had a brand new building but was financially distraught, absolutely without any funds. We came here for $5,000 a year. When we first came, dear Mr. Mirviss *was* 'The Synagogue!' He conducted the morning and the evening minyan."

Rabbi Gordon turned his attention immediately to developing a good school and having the Talmud Torah in the synagogue. He got the Men's Club, Sisterhood, the Young People's League, the Junior Congregation and the Shabbat Morning Service going again. He insisted that the newly-established Hebrew School be open to girls as well as boys. (As mentioned earlier, girls were also educated at the Adath and this was very important to Rabbi Gordon.)

Rabbi Gordon also worked hard to make the Adath part of the larger community, often sharing the pulpit with leading laymen in discussions about vital issues. Under his direction the Adath Jeshurun Lecture Series was introduced, and outstanding personalities were brought to speak to the community. He also frequently invited Jewish organizations to the pulpit, including Hadassah, Council of Jewish Women, AZA, and the Minneapolis Federation for Jewish Service. Each held a special Shabbat service during the year.

But Rabbi Gordon did not neglect his role as advisor, friend, counselor and guide to his congregants. The Gordons' home was always open, they were present at all synagogue functions, and they also shared in the congregants simchas, illnesses and bereavements.

Clearly, Rabbi Gordon had a great capacity for work, but he also inspired others to pitch in. He recognized that through idealistic work in the synagogue and community, people could channel their energies and become fulfilled. He also gave due attention to the social functions of the synagogue, fully aware that many came to the synagogue not only to pray but for social reasons.

"I joined the Adath in 1930," Sophia Singer later recalled, "when Rabbi Albert Gordon came. I immediately joined the choir. Evelyn Siegel was in the choir. In those days nobody got paid to sing. You did that because you loved it. It was an honor to belong to a choir and to be part of it. There was no money paid but some did get their dues free."

Evelyn Siegel remembered: "The first time they got women in the choir was in 1927. At first, the men used to stand around the bema: Sammy Mirviss, Sid Scherling and

Teddy Gordon. Then they got women: Sophie Singer, Phyllis Bearmon and me. In the beginning we all stood around the bema and sang until they got the organ up in the balcony. I sang from 1927 until 1971 - almost 45 years! Never missed a Friday night!"

In October, an article in the *Clarion* spelled out the need for funds to purchase books. It was announced in November that a Young People's League was to be organized for men and women of college age and older. Rabbi Gordon announced about the Junior Council Sabbath:

> *Too often, in the past, the Jewish young woman has been ignored by her elders. Jewish education and training was accorded to young men only. We have recently awakened to the fact that the future of Israel depends as much, if not more, upon our young women than it does upon our young men. Our Jewish institutions, religious, social and cultural, are maintained only through the zeal, enthusiasm and hard work put forth by our Jewish women.*

That November, Birthday Blessings were introduced as part of the Children's Service on Sabbath mornings, and each Saturday a different child gave a sermonette. Among those who gave such sermonettes in 1930-31 were: Bernice Segal, Laverne Shedlov, Harold Schein, Harriet Rivkin, Dorothy Bearman, Geraldine Silver, Sam Weiner, Edith Abrams, Monroe Crystal, June Schaffer, Firley Kronick, Marjorie Ellison, Donald Braman, Milton Minkin, Abbott Barron, Shirley Rigler, Alvin Isaacs, Grace Codden, Bernice Goldstein, Irving Gilinsky, Geraldine Pink, Marcella Gross, Edward Bramn, Earl Rosen, David Crystal, Joyce Cooperman, and Maxine Siegel.

At the 5th Annual Congregational Dinner held in the new building, Rabbi Herman Cohen, from Temple of Aaron in St. Paul, spoke. His address was on "Depressions and Their Prevention." Sidney Scherling directed a community sing following the talk.

On December 8, Adath held a debate with Beth El Synagogue. The subject was: "Do Present Tendencies in Jewish Life Assure the Survival of American Israel?" Representing the pro-argument for the Adath were Harry Gainsley, Viola Hoffman Hymes and Arnold Karlins. Beth El took the opposite position led by Harry Bikson, Guita Bearman Gordon and Max Shapiro. It was one of the highlights of the season, both socially and intellectually.

That year the Women's league began to host Sabbath Teas and Receptions following Friday evening services. Youth Services were also held.

Financial problems remained acute. In fact, throughout the early '30s, the trustees repeatedly discussed how to pay the bills; whether dues should be raised, and what the High Holiday seats should cost.

January, 1931, at the Men's Club Dinner, Dr. Tobias Birnberg, a St.Paul pediatrician, spoke on his recent tour of Europe and Russia. The 70th birthday of Henrietta Szold, founder of Hadassah, took place that month; and Albert Einstein, visiting the United States, said he would not return to Germany if the Hitlerites obtained control. Also that month the new Sunday School paper, *Ner Tamid*, surfaced, with a page in Hebrew written by pupils of the Hebrew school.

During February, the Men's Club Open Forum had Dr. David Siperstein, Dr. David Ellison, and Arnold Karlins leading a discussion on: "Can Liberal Judaism Satisfy the Needs of 20th Century Jews?" Questions that were dealt with were: "What is Jewish Liberalism, What Are the Needs of Our Generation, and Will Liberalism Result in Assimilation?" Rabbi Gordon felt it was necessary to win young people back to the synagogue and suggested that less dogmatism and emphasis on conformity would be required to achieve that end. He advocated, instead, making better use of the synagogue for airing ideas, debates, and forums.

That month a committee headed by Israel D. Fink began to plan the Jubilee. It was to consist of three days of fun and festivity with dancing, games, a Chevrolet car being given away, and a popularity contest (which Firley Kronick won). A Boy Scout Troop was organized for boys 12 and older. Harry Vermes and Ralph Bearman were chosen as scoutmaster and assistant.

In March there was a Purim Masquerade, with more than 115 children attending. Costume contest winners were Betty Swiler, Mendel Engler, Jean Shapiro and David Barron. Also in March, Rabbi Gordon was installed as the local district president of the Zionist Organization of

> ## "Moses went forth to his brethren and saw their suffering."
>
> Albert Gordon went out to the arena of life, believing that Jewish values were still relevant for the modern Jew and for world civilization. He felt that intelligent living was impossible without reference to the past, but that we must also acknowledge the changes that have taken place and apply the philosophy of the past to contemporary living.
>
> This commitment to "moral and ethical nationalism" drove Rabbi Gordon to shoulder responsibilities beyond the synagogue. He worked as a labor arbitrator and also alongside Hubert Humphrey [Mayor of Minneapolis at the time] on the Human Relations Council. He spoke out on timely issues, both on his own national radio program and through his pen, with books, newspaper articles, and a column in the AJW.
>
> These were the observations of Anna K. Schwartz. She was very close to Rabbi Gordon and planned to write a book about him. The closing remarks of her manuscript were: "May our rabbi's memory be for a blessing, for his unselfish dedication to survival, Judaism and the building of a better world...May his memory live on in the hearts and minds of all of us who had the privilege of working with him."

America. On Passover, the Memorial Library Fund for the Synagogue was inaugurated.

In May the First Annual Adath Jeshurun Spring Frolic Dance, sponsored by the YPL, was held with a five piece orchestra. The spelling of the synagogue was now officially "Adath Jeshurun" instead of "Adath Yeshurun."

In the spring issue of the *Clarion* Rabbi Gordon wrote: "Anti-Semitism exists here and abroad. Hitler is a menace to Jews everywhere. In the U.S. there are more delicate shadings...percentage clauses against Jewish students at universities...barring Jews from social and athletic clubs. Prejudice is at the bottom of it all...The problem will be solved when we learn how to overcome prejudice based on ignorance."

Among the topics of Rabbi Gordon's sermons during his first year in Minneapolis were: "Are Jews Clannish?" "Are 'We Moderns' Really Religious?" "Is Honesty the Best Policy?" "Has Youth a Place in the Synagogue?" "Converts to Judaism - How Shall We Receive Them?" and "Is There a Solution to the Problem of Anti-Semitism?"

On April 2, the second night of Passover, a Family Seder was held at the synagogue. The price per plate was $1.75 for adults and $.75 for children.

Reviewing the year, Rabbi Gordon described it as "sad and discouraging." The economic climate had not improved, and anti-Semitism was clearly on the rise. The situation in Germany was dire, and legislation was taking shape in the United States Congress to register aliens, an act clearly aimed at Jews. Jewish students in universities were facing obstacles, as were Jewish businessmen, and the outbreak of animosities between Jews and Arabs in Palestine was also discouraging.

What hope? Rabbi Gordon drew strength from a paraphrase of Theodore Herzl, "If you will it, it is no dream." He wrote. "We must first of all will to remain Jews...If in the face of difficulties we are determined to survive as a people, nothing—not even anti-Semitism in its worst manifestation, economic disorder or political maneuvers—can swerve us from the path we have chosen. It is this spirit Israel must have if it wishes to save itself."

Rabbi Matt, writing in the *AJW*, echoed these sentiments, describing the year as "a trying year for Minneapolis Jewry." Yet he also noted that "...Adath Jeshurun celebrated its 47th anniversary with a bazaar and Jubilee... To be able to continue when so much is distressing and discouraging is also an accomplishment."

1931-1932

The struggle to make both ends meet continued for both Adath and it congregants. As a means of raising funds, the Congregation sponsored a symphony concert with Sophie Breslau as the soloist, and Rabbi Matt noted that it was "difficult to separate the elements of profit-making and attractive, instructive entertainment." Mrs. Arthur (Fanny) Brin was elected National President of the Council of Jewish Women.

The congregations of Adath Jeshurun, Beth El and Temple Israel jointly sponsored a lecture series with nationally known speakers, Jewish and non-Jewish.

Gazella Kantor recalled: "We helped to the organize the first Lecture Series. The speakers we had were some of the most oustanding of that period. In order to pay the speakers we had program/ad books and I remember soliciting ads at pharmacies, furriers and numerous other businesses for $10 to $25. I opened my home for formal dinners for the speakers, officers and rabbi. At the synagogue dinners we women would do all the cooking ourselves."

Rabbi Matt observed at one point that although times were tough, "when we contrast our own position in this country with the plight of East and Central European Jewry ... we are by far better off than the rest of world Jewry."

Howard Brin later recalled: "The Depression clearly influenced life at the Adath. In those days Joe Schanfeld really held the organization together. Often the Trustees paid the bills for the Congregation. Rabbi Gordon had good forums, and the Adath was certainly one of the leading Jewish institutions in the community.

"Rabbis Gordon and Minda [from Temple Israel] were concerned that the Jewish community should not separate itself. They had Thanksgiving services with some of the churches to help combat the intense anti-Semitism in Minneapolis."

The Adath *Clarion* announced that the Sunday School had revised its curriculum and improved its teaching staff. The Talmud Torah beginners class for children seven years and older was meeting twice a week from 4 to 6 p.m. and the children also had to attend Sunday School. The Sunday School had 150 registered students.

Felix Moses, Sam Margulies, Kitty Ellison and Rabbi Gordon became the new editors of the *Clarion*. The library, with Marjorie Liss as volunteer librarian, put out a call for more books. With hundreds of men and women in urgent need of work, the congregation was asked, "Can you give a job?" They were also asked to pay their dues, come to services, and attend synagogue functions. And for those that could afford it, a new product appeared on the market—a fully electric refrigerator for home use!

In January Rabbi Gordon began his famous weekly radio talks on WCCO on Sundays. That first year the overall topic was: "Jewish Contributions to American Life." After the introductory broadcast Rabbi Gordon answered questions. He received no remuneration for his program, but did it as a public service to help combat anti-Semitism.

Among the topics he spoke on that spring were "The Puritans and the Jews," "Lincoln and His Jewish Friends," "Below the Mason-Dixon Line," "Maryland and Tolerance," and "Religious Liberty in America."

Menachem Heilicher of the Talmud Torah spoke at the Adath in December. The first Fathers and Sons Banquet sponsored by the Men's Club was held in January in the vestry rooms. On Tu B'Shevat there was a Hobby Show exhibit which consisted of interesting avocations of

the boys and girls such as old coins, maps, and doll dressing. The admission of 15 cents went to the Library Fund.

The biggest undertaking ever sponsored by any synagogue in the Twin Cities until that time took place on March 21, 1932, when the Minneapolis Symphony Orchestra under the direction of Eugene Ormandy performed with Sophie Breslau as its soloist.

It had become apparent that a large proportion of the children were unable to read Hebrew, and Hebrew reading was introduced into the Sunday School classes.

Both Hadassah and the United Synagogue of America celebrated their 20th anniversaries that spring. The first Hebrew broadcasting station was opened in Tel Aviv.

Rabbi Gordon gave the principal address at the Talmud Torah graduation. Adath Boy Scout Troop number 208 celebrated its first anniversary on April 15. Bob Camp was scout master and Harry Bearman, chairman of the troop committee.

Among Rabbi Gordon's sermon topics that year were: "Israel's Symphony," "Intellectuals and the Synagogue," "What's Happening to Religion in Russia?," "The Jewish Woman Takes a Hand (In honor of Hadassah Sabbath)," and a series on "Great Movements in Israel" devoted to Karaism, Messianism, the Pharisees, Hasidism, Hellenism, and Rationalism.

That April, Adath Jeshurun treasurer Dr. David Pink, and his wife, Dena, received Mazel Tov on the birth of a baby boy, Norman. (Fifty years later he would become an Adath Jeshurun president.)

In 1932 there were 17 boys and girls in the confirmation class.

In the June 3, 1932 *AJW* various headlines proclaimed: "Hitler Control in Germany Appears Certain," "Nazis Begin a Reign of Terror Against Jews," "Anti-Semitic Riots Close Universities," and "Professor Felix Frankfurter Named to the United States Supreme Court."

1932-1933

On September 19, at the Congregational Dinner meeting, Louis B. Schwartz took office as the newly elected Adath president. He said: "I assume the office of president at a critical period in the history of our congregation. If we are to pass through the present crisis successfully, it will require the earnest cooperation of every member and friend of the Adath Jeshurun. I ask your help in every possible way."

In his New Year's Greetings, Rabbi Gordon reiterated the problems facing the synagogue, but emphasized the

Vol. XXI   Minneapolis and Saint Paul—Nisan 4, 5693—Friday, March 31, 1933   N

Nazis Carry Out Anti-Jewish War Program
Shocked World Voices Protest To Hitler

Liberal America Denounces Anti-Semitic Activities In Germany

Minneapolis Meeting Deplores Nazi Outrages; Asks U. S. Aid

New York (W. N. S.)—A united Jewry backed by liberal America raised its mighty voice of protest against anti-Semitic war waged by Hitler.

From coast to coast, in almost every Jewish community, more than one million people gathered on the same day (March 27th) to denounce the Nazi Storm Troops and the Nazi leadership. A tremendous shout of indignation, —unimpaired by the statement of the American Secretary of State Hull that Germany's excesses against Jews are virtually ended in Germany,—was heard throughout the United States, demanding political and economic measures to safeguard the lives and property of German Jews.

In Albany, capital of the State of New York, Governor Lehman, addressing a protest meeting, in sober yet firm words said the situation in Germany. He said in part:

"I am convinced that what I say represents the views of the people of the State, regardless of creed or nativity. Christians and Jews, priests, clergymen, rabbis and laymen are joining with no animosity to the great German nation; with no intention to
(Continued on Page 3)

THE PROTEST RESOLUTION

WHEREAS, for a number of years a gospel of hatred and a campaign of extermination of the Jews has been preached by many of those who today exercise power in Germany,

WHEREAS, those doctrines of hate and persecution have during the last few weeks assumed a grave form, endangering the rights, safety, and very existence of the Jewish people in that country,

WHEREAS, many reports from reliable sources have reached this country from Germany of Jews being subjected to physical outrage, economic persecution and moral indignities,

WHEREAS, there has been no evidence of any serious effort on the part of the government to punish those guilty of attacking Jewish persons and property,

WHEREAS, many of the grave cases of persecution are not the actions of irresponsible individuals but are acts of an official nature; such as, the forcible closing of stores, the dismissal of physicians from municipal hospitals and First Aid stations, the closing of kindergartens and music schools, the exclusion of men and women from public employment, the elimination of judges, attorneys and notaries from the courts, the ruthless raiding of the homes; and the attacks upon the reputation of men prominent in the cultural and intellectual world; all of this for no other reason except that they happen to be Jewish;

THEREFORE, BE IT RESOLVED, that this mass meeting of American citizens held on this 27th day of March, 1933, at Temple Israel in Minneapolis, Minnesota, addressed by Floyd B. Olson, Governor of the State of Minnesota, Reverend H. P. Dewey, President of the Minneapolis Council of Churches; Reverend J. Austin Pardue, Rector of Gethsemane Episcopal Church; Father E. M. Peters, Chamlain of Newman Club, University of Minnesota, and at which messages of sympathy were received from the Most Reverend John Gregory Murray, Archbishop of St. Paul and Dr. Lotus D. Coffman, President of the University of Minnesota, hereby proclaims as false and malicious the doctrines that charge the Jew with responsibility for the political and economic difficulties of Germany. All attempts to make the Jew a national and political scapegoat are figments of a perverted imagination and are unworthy of the fine traditions of the German people.

BE IT FURTHER RESOLVED, that this meeting regards with horror and consternation reports of terrorism and violence in Germany, tending to crush the Jew economically, to suppress him culturally, and to wound his very soul out of which he has contributed in great abundance to whatever is best and finest in German life.

BE IT FURTHER RESOLVED, that this meeting appeals to the enlightened opinion and sense of fairness of the German people to check these destructive anti-Jewish actions, and

BE IT FURTHER RESOLVED, that the State Department be asked to use its good offices to convey to the German Government the grave concern felt by millions of American citizens regarding not only the physical mistreatment but also the official and institutional persecutions of the Jews in that country, a concern which cannot but affect the good-will between the German and American peoples.

BE IT RESOLVED FURTHER THAT copies of these resolutions be forwarded to the Secretary of State and to the Senators and Representatives of this state.

Boycott Against Jewish Activities To Start Saturday Morning

Declare Action Retaliation "Against Atrocity Propaganda Abroad"

Berlin (W. N. S.)—Stung by a world-wide protest, in which Jews and Christians expressed their horror of anti-Semitic excesses in Germany, the forces of the Nazi Government have been called into action to counteract the moral and economic rebuke which has isolated Germany in international public opinion. German Government officials issued statements in Berlin, tabled denials to England, America and elsewhere, and called upon representative Jewish organizations to issue similar statements denying pogroms.

With the Hitler government maintaining a "hands-off policy," the National Socialist party went ahead with its plans for a boycott against all Jewish business and professional activity starting Saturday morning. The Nazi party declared the boycott a in retaliation "against the atrocity propaganda abroad."

While the Nazi authorities maintained the boycott to be a defensive measure and that Jews now living in Germany were held responsible for these so-called "libels," the boycott announcement was seen as a victory of the left wing of the party, which had included a platform of reprisals against all Semitic activities in Germany for recent years. Actually, the Nazis...

PROTEST AGAINST HITLER'S PERSECUTION OF JEWS

Headline from March 1933. Note Rabbi Gordon, second from left.

opportunities that that lay ahead, including an expanded sponsorship for the Lecture Course that would give the congregation the opportunity to listen to some of America's outstanding thinkers.

At Louis Schwartz's installation dinner, former president Joseph Schanfeld, who had served for nearly a quarter of a century, was honored. Rabbi Gordon said of him: "Tirelessly, courageously, Joseph Schanfeld has served the Adath Jeshurun during its periods of stress and strain as well as in times of joy."

The second Adath Lecture Series had as guest lecturers: Rabbi Solomon Freehof; Dr. James Weldon Johnson, one of America's greatest African-American scholars at the time; Professor Morris R. Cohen, regarded as America's greatest living philosopher; Oswald Garr Villard, liberal and editor of the *The Nation*; Dr. Abram L. Sachar, historian and head of the Hillel Foundation at the University of Illinois; and Dr. Leo Honor, Dean of the College of Jewish Studies in Chicago.

Some members of the congregation had left the Synagogue to attend services at the Unitarian Church. Rabbi Gordon made every effort to bring them back, and even brought Unitarian ministers in to talk at Adath.

Among the congregation activities that year were the Women's League Rummage Sale; Annual Dinner Meeting in November featuring Sam Mirviss; a member of the

University Players portraying Spinoza in a radio drama; the Women's League monthly food sales; and Sunday night suppers and bridge get-togethers.

Lillian Krelitz Kaplan looked back fondly on those early rummage sales: "Mr. and Mrs. Mirviss were so sweet. They would give us their garage to keep our rummage in. We held it in the winter time, in November and December. I don't know why it was during the winter because that was the worst weather but people would buy for the holidays. I would go with the driver on Sundays and help him pack and load the truck. We'd drive in an old scrap truck down to 3rd Avenue and Marquette where we had the rummage sale. We would move in on Sunday morning and stay there until Wednesday or Thursday. We had to have detectives because many people tried to walk out with two coats."

At the Hadassah Sabbath, Anna K. Schwartz (Mrs. Louis) was the guest speaker. Members of the Women's League organized a public speaking class. A high school Junior League class was organized. The Council of Jewish Juniors sponsored a Chanukah essay contest for pupils from five Sunday schools and the Talmud Torah. Adath student Roslyn Engler won first prize.

At the end of November, a tragic auto accident shocked the city and congregation: it claimed the lives of Jennie Gross, former Women's League president, and her grand nephew, Robert Fink, age 4, son of Israel and Esther Fink.

By 1933 the United States' economy had spiraled down to a point near complete collapse. One-fourth of the working force was unemployed, banks had closed and hungry people hunted for scraps of food in trash heaps.

Franklin Delano Roosevelt had been elected the 32nd President of the United States, and millions of Americans feared what would happen next. In Roosevelt's inaugural address, he called for faith in America's future. "The only thing we have to fear is fear itself," he declared. His inauguration marked a turning point of sorts, and in time his efforts to revive the economy through government programs began to bear fruit.

The hit songs of 1933 were: "We're in the Money," and "Smoke Gets in Your Eyes." Katharine Hepburn and Charles Laughton were the best actress and actor of the year and the public listened to Will Rogers on the radio. Wheaties, "the Breakfast of Champions," was introduced and Jack Armstrong was the All American Boy. A new Ford cost $490 and gas was $.18 a gallon. At the Adath, the *Clarion* was reduced to one page to save money.

Rabbi Gordon's thoughts on 1933: "The New Year brings with it new hope and new courage to mankind...So long as the mind of man continues to function; so long as he does not lose faith in himself, there is a way out."

In February, a Girl Scout troop was organized with 13 members, age ten and older. Mrs.(John) Sarah Segall and Mrs. Strauss acted as scout leaders and LaVerne Shedlov and Geraldine Silver were the assistant leaders. Meyer D. Mirviss was elected first vice-president of the newly elected Talmud Torah Board of Directors. Menachem Heilicher, head of the Talmud Torah High School department, spoke at services in February, and in March the annual Sunday School Purim Masquerade was held with Deborah Miller and Ida Brochin arranging the program.

Maxine Goldie Smiley recalled: "I was scared to death of Rabbi Gordon as a child. Gladys Davis (Miller) was my fifth grade Sunday School teacher and she made costumes and we put on lots of plays, having costume and Purim parties. The classrooms were on both sides of the social hall downstairs. There were folding doors with dividers."

And the topics of Rabbi Gordon addresses that spring were: "The Legacy of Israel"; "The Church in Politics"; "I Believe in Spinoza's God"; "Why Do the Righteous Suffer?" and "In Praise of Fanatics."

Rabbi Gordon's Purim sermon was on "Germany Chooses Hitler." The *AJW* March 24 headline read: "Government Intervention Is Sought to Curb Nazi Excesses and Mass Meeting Here On Monday." More than 3,000 persons gathered at Temple Israel that week and a resolution was unanimously adopted protesting the anti-Semitic activities of the Hitler regime in Germany.

Also that month Rabbi Gordon became the chairman of the 4th Annual Minneapolis Federation for Jewish Service Campaign. A "Share Your Clothes" campaign began. Sixty thousand people were receiving relief in Minneapolis and were desperately in need of clothing. Congregants were urged to contribute whatever they could for the needy. The Jewish Free Employment Agency helped to provide labor, skill and unskilled.

Dorothy Gordon later recalled,

I was in the background for the first few years. Fortunately for me, Pearl Salsbury, director of the Minneapolis Jewish Family and Children's Service, had been my teacher at he University of Minnesota. It was during the Depression and she needed help. She called me in. I wasn't involved in the Sisterhood then, so I accepted the position.

It was during the third year, I believe, when Albert was getting no salary and I didn't have a warm coat.

My dear brother-in-law, Freddy Orenstein, was a furrier and he said to Albert, 'Listen, Dorothy needs a coat in this town. You've got to have a warmer coat for her. Let me bring you some of my samples.' Al thought about it and the next thing I knew one night he came home with a fur coat. It fit me perfectly and I said, 'All right, I'll wear it.' I wore it until Fred needed it to take as a sample out on the road. Then he came home with another fur coat, and took the first one back. So I wore that one until he needed it. During that cold Minneapolis winter, I wore three fur coats, and - what do you think happened? We got an anonymous letter saying; 'Here we are all suffering and the Rabbi's wife is wearing three different fur coats!'

I remember stopping over at my father's home, and I cried to him, because I couldn't cry to Albert and let him know that it hurt me deeply. My father felt badly and he said I should write a letter to the Clarion *and let people know, but I didn't. That next year I worked at a non-Jewish agency and so we were able to manage. Not only didn't they like my fur coats but they didn't like my working. I had our daughter, Judy, in 1934, and then I stopped working.*

And Dorothy Weiner recalled, "Albert Gordon went through the difficult times. Dorothy Gordon was working and she didn't come to the meetings at first and everyone complained. Then when she came, they complained that she would tell the rabbi everything that went on at the meeting."

Sophie Singer said, "I joined Adath in 1930 when Rabbi Gordon came and when they had nothing. They had wooden floors in the kitchen. When I came to Minneapolis from Chicago, I brought a girl with me so I didn't have to scrub floors in my own house, but I scrubbed those wooden floors in the synagogue. There were beautiful people: Jennie Gross, Mrs. Harris, Dorothy Gordon's mother, Mrs. Davis. All those older people took me in as a young sister and taught me what it was to belong to a synagogue that needed help.

"A. I .Gordon was a beautiful man and we were very close. We lived in Cleveland for a few years and became very close with his family. He had a beautiful background. He did everything with the children. He confirmed, married, and buried. He did everything. When we moved to Minneapolis we didn't know much about it, but we joined the Adath and it became our home. In those days everyone was poor and no one had a lot of money. Many times the rabbi did not get paid."

That spring, Rabbi Gordon announced that there would be no confirmation exercise due to his desire to increase the age level for the confirmants from the eighth to ninth grade, but for the first time, a high school graduation took place. During the year, 175 children had received Jewish training at the Adath. Also that spring, the rabbi spoke at the Talmud Torah graduation exercises. The summer's activities culminated with the Adath annual picnic at Antler's Park on Lyndale Avenue South.

Rabbi Matt's review of local Jewish life in Minneapolis for 5693 said: "Those who 'survived' until now may be reasonably sure that they have weathered the worst and that a new lease of life seems to be in store for them. There has been 'hard sailing' for the community, individually and collectively. Fortunately no single major activity had to be discontinued. Retrenchment and merging of effort resulted in greater efficiency and usefulness as well as in greater economy."

Among other notable events mentioned by Rabbi Matt were the projected organization of the Kosher meat industry in the city; a protest meeting following the victory of the Hitler regime; the 60th birthday of the Hebrew poet Bialik; Henry Bank became the first Jew to be elected to the City Council; Theodore Gordon graduated from the Hebrew Union College as a Rabbi; Joseph Gerstein won distinction in his studies at the Jewish Theological Seminary; Jennie Gross met a tragic death on the highway; Arthur Brin became the First Vice President of District 6 of the B'nai B'rith; I. S. Joseph was appointed by the mayor to the Public Welfare Board; and Fanny (Mrs. Arthur) Brin was one of 52 women designated by Eleanor Roosevelt for national welfare work, making her Adath's ranking Jewish fellow-citizen.

1933-1934

In August of 1933, Rabbi and Mrs. Matt returned to Minneapolis for a visit. A reception was held honoring them with music furnished by Marion Bernstein Bearman, violinist; Esther Woolpy, pianist; and Phyllis Beskin Bearman, vocalist.

During the summer of 1933, the Gordons paid a surprise trip to Palestine. After some coaxing on the part of Rabbi and Mrs. Herman Cohen from St. Paul's Temple of Aaron, who were just on their way to Palestine, Rabbi Gordon called Arthur Brin, who was on the board of the synagogue, and said, "Would it be possible for you to pay part of my year's salary so we can take a trip to Israel?' (As mentioned previously, Rabbi Gordon had not been paid that

year.) Arthur said, "I'll call a meeting of the board tomorrow noon and I'll let you know." The board decided to get a loan from the bank and pay $300 of the rabbi's salary.

Dorothy Gordon later described that exciting visit: "We went by boat leaving from New York and it took us four weeks to get there. We were there six weeks. We saw Tel Aviv, lived on many kibbutzim and I was ready to stay. We had no children then."

But friends advised them that they were needed back in the United States. And on their return Rabbi Gordon became the District President of the Zionist Organization of America.

"Our biggest distress," Dorothy later recalled, "was informing our local people adequately about the international picture. On our return through Europe, we were confronted with the refugees fleeing. There was so much conflict. The Fascists were rising and it was so emotionally distressing."

Rabbi Gordon engaged Nettie Elazar to conduct Talmud Torah classes at the synagogue. Her husband, Albert, a native of Palestine, taught at the St. Paul Talmud Torah and the two couples had spent time together in Eretz Yisrael that past summer.

In October the rabbi spoke from the pulpit of the many changes which he had noticed on his trip. A new volunteer choir was organized by Joseph Burnstein for Friday services and special occasions and Sidney Scherling chanted the services that year.

Golde Rapaport Borsten wrote:

My association with Adath synagogue was between 1930 to 1937. Albert I. Gordon was the rabbi. Three of us—Deborah Miller, Rivia Rosenberg and myself—all friends from North Minneapolis, were hired to teach Sunday School.

My classes were usually second or third grade. One of my pupils was Rodney Schanfeld Wallace, as rambunctious as he was adorable. He was the grandson of Joseph Schanfeld. My memory of the Sunday School was preparing assembly programs, cold Sunday mornings waiting for streetcars until my brother Hy took pity on us both and picked us up, and waiting for our $2 per Sunday, which was sometimes months in coming, and which we all depended on for the week's carfare to and from the university.

Borsten was unable to find a job after graduating, and Rabbi Gordon lined up a job for her compiling a Jewish cookbook for the Pillsbury Flour Company.

I translated their recipes for blintzes, knishes and other baked goods, which used a lot of flour. My dad helped with the Yiddish. Since we were unable to find a Yiddish typewriter in Minneapolis, my notes were sent to Chicago and the booklet was printed there. From that experience, he also recommended me to another flour company to read and translate contest entries on 'Why I Use Sarasota Flour.' The company advertised their contest in the Yiddish newspapers in Chicago and got about one hundred accounts of how the contestants came to America, the hardships and joys they encountered, and why, therefore, they used Sarasota Flour.

When that term of employment ended, Rabbi Gordon set Borsten to work cataloging books in the Adath's Sunday school library.

One day Mr. Mirviss came back from a visit to a rug company where he had shnorred *a small carpet for our library. A few weeks later, during Jewish Book Week in 1934, our library was dedicated. After that, I did get work and my association with Adath Jeshurun was no longer as an employee, but I was always welcome and did attend services, lectures and social affairs until 1937, when I left Minneapolis to work for the National Council of Jewish Women in New York.*

In later years, when I returned to Minneapolis for visits with my family, it was always a great pleasure to see how the synagogue had grown and its membership increased. I think now the teachers probably get paid on time too!

The '33-'34 Lecture Series was largely devoted to international themes, including John Haynes Homes speaking on "Russia and Our Western World;" Leland Stowe speaking on "France and Germany's New Militarism;" and Sherwood Eddy on "The World's Danger Zones."

Howard Brin remembered, "I had my Bar Mitzvah December 24, 1933. M .D. Mirviss would stand behind the Bar Mitzvah boy. He was always about a half a word ahead of what the boy was going to say. It was very difficult. On the day of my Bar Mitzvah, well, that was a great tragedy. We had a sleet storm that morning and it made it almost

Morris Kantar

impossible to drive to the synagogue. The streets were just a sheet of ice, so there weren't a lot of people. I remember my mother cooking gefilte fish for a week or more for the big event. Then only 32 people, except for the people that were within close walking distance of the synagogue, were able to get there. My uncle, Sol Fligelman, came from St. Paul and he said he had to drive up on the curbs and get in a patch to get up the hills. There weren't a lot of people at the service and after there was a kiddush with herring, gefilte fish, bread, lox and wine. As I recall, I don't think there was a big sit-down lunch. Ultimately the relatives got together when they were able to move around after the ice melted."

The big news nationally was that after 13 years, 10 months, and 19 days, Prohibition had finally come to an end.

On January 12-14, 1934, the Adath held its Fiftieth Anniversary Golden Jubilee Celebration. A special Friday night service was held with Rabbi David Goldstein as guest speaker, followed by a children's service in the synagogue on Sunday. That evening, a dinner dance was held at the Hotel Nicollet with a kosher dinner and a speech by Rabbi Max Kadushin, director of the University of Wisconsin Hillel Foundation. Morris Kantar was chairman of General Arrangements and Mame Breslow headed a committee of women for the sale of tickets. Guests received a souvenir booklet containing photos and a history of Adath Jeshurun.

More that four hundred people attended the celebration. Dr. Moses Barron presided over the evening's program, which included words of greeting from representatives of various branches of the congregation's activities. Mr. Schanfeld told of his experience before, during and after his years of service as president, and Phyllis Beskin Bearman gave a vocal recital accompanied by Dr. N.M.Levine on the piano.

The *AJW* reported: "The future of the Congregation in the sphere of its possible influence holds forth great promise, yet is fraught with difficult problems. The Depression, which may be just ending, has tried and tested all manner of organizations, and Synagogues are no exception. There are difficult days ahead for many a congregation. The future of the Adath Jeshurun must depend upon the need it serves and the specific work it does. If it supplies the spiritual requirements of its clientele, if it satisfies their Jewish needs it is bound to exist, and even to thrive. If it is but a duplication of other institutions, the mere sentimental attachment of its members will scarcely suffice to keep it alive."

Efforts to increase membership continued throughout the winter and by the end of March 40 new members had been secured. A new Junior League was organized for boys and girls of 15 years and over.

The *Minneapolis Star* of April 30, 1934, carried a story reporting that "Christians, Jews Here Stage Brotherhood Day - Aim is to Destroy All Religious and Racial Hatred." It was sponsored by the National Conference of Christians and Jews to promote the common good of the community and the nation.

At the May 23 Board Meeting it was moved and seconded and passed that Rabbi Gordon's salary be increased from $3,000 to $3,600, and that a note of $625 be given to Mr. Mirviss for past indebtedness.

Also that year, symposiums were held at Friday evening services for the first time. Among the topics were "How Can Goodwill Be Attained?" with speakers Albert Bank, principal of Lincoln Junior High School, Esther Rosenbloom, representing the mother's point of view, and Rabbi Gordon on the part churches and synagogues play.

Among the topics of Rabbi Gordon's sermons that year were: "Is Palestine the Answer?" "The NRA and Future of American Jewry;" "Is Universalism the Goal?" and "The Jewish Community of the Future."

At the Annual Meeting on June 6, the 1934-35 slate was elected. At the July 5 meeting Ben Segal broached a plan to refinance the mortgage.

In his appraisal of Minneapolis in the *AJW* that year, Rabbi Matt took note of the participation of the city's three English-speaking Rabbis—Aronson, Gordon and Minda—in the observance of Brotherhood Day at Westminister Presbyterian Church. He also drew attention to Rabbi Gordon's work as head of the Board of Arbitration in the laundry and cleaners industry and Arthur Brin's new position as President of District 6 of the B'nai B'rith. Joseph Gerstein was also ordained rabbi by the JTS that year.

These local successes notwithstanding, the *AJW* described the year as "The Hitler Year." More than half a million Jews were living in terror in Germany. Public opinion throughout the world continued to remain hostile to the Nazi regime and impassioned protests emanated from nearly every country in the world. The only hope was that a new regime would come into power in Germany.

1934-1935

Dr. Mordecai M. Kaplan prepared a special booklet of prayers and meditations for the New Year which was introduced at Rosh Hashanah services. Eugene Gottesman, of Youngstown, Ohio, was elected cantor. His responsibilities included leading the synagogue's 14-member choir and managing the musical program of the entire synagogue.

The lecture season that year featured Ludwig Lewisohn speaking on "Jew and Christian"; Roger Baldwin on "Civil Liberties Under the New Deal"; Professor Harry A. Overstreet on "Frontiers of a New Social Order"; and Norman Thomas on "Which Way, America?"

That year a number of symposiums were heard from the pulpit, which once again underscored Rabbi Gordon's commitment to exploring a variety of ideas and beliefs.

Early in his Minneapolis experience, Rabbi Gordon had become friendly with Rabbi Levine of the Orthodox synagogue and Rabbi Albert Minda of the Reform pulpit, and before long he was being asked to settle disputes among the Orthodox congregations. This led to his election to the Presidency of the Vaad Ha Kashrut, the most Orthodox group for settlement of disputes and the determining of standards of kashrut for the community.

Dorothy Gordon later recalled: "His association with Rabbi Albert G. Minda of Temple Israel, the Reform Temple of Minnneapolis, was always close. The two men served on many community agency committees together and showed mutual respect for the ideology and philosophy of the other. On Brotherhood Day or Thanksgiving, they held joint services for the community and always represented a united Jewish voice for the Christian community."

By this time there were more than two hundred pupils registered in the Sunday School and Talmud Torah. The Boy Scouts Sabbath was held in February and the Purim Carnival in March. Both a Mothers-Daughters and a Fathers-Sons dinner were held. The Boy Scouts celebrated their 4th Anniversary and an Adath Cub Scout Troop was formed with Sidney Harris as cubmaster.

The eighth Freshmen Banquet for Jewish University of Minnesota freshmen was held at AJ, sponsored by the Council of Jewish Women, B'nai B'rith, Temple Israel Sisterhood and the Women's Leagues of Adath and Beth El. More than 160 freshmen attended.

Bernice Cowl Gordon later recalled, "I remember when I was a freshman at the University of Minnesota. We had the welcoming dinner at the Adath Jeshurun. It was a wonderful occasion for all of us to get together and meet other Jewish students who were on campus. We were from all over the city. In those days not many students had cars so it was rather difficult to get back and forth."

The Young People's League was responsible for a wide and varied program. Hannah Lea Harris was president of the Young People's League. Activities included meetings, dances, drama group, Chanukah membership party, sleighride, and guest speaker Max Shapiro. A debate was held with Beth El on "The Desirability of Settling Jews in Biro Bidjan," the autonomous Jewish state, which had been recently established by the Russian government. The group presented several one-act plays and an original musical comedy, *Whoops, My Dear* with a cast of 35, held on May 28 and 29. It was a smashing success.

Earlier in the year, on January 12, the Adath in cooperation with the Repertory Theatre sponsored the Northwest premiere of the stage production, *The Jazz Singer*, at the Women's Club, with fifty people in the cast. It was a fundraising activity for the Synagogue with Dr. David Pink and Gazella Kantor as chairpersons.

Gazella Kantor said, "I remember we put on the play, *The Jazz Singer*. The lead was Sammy Mirviss. He was a wonderful young man and had a beautiful voice."

In fact, Sam Mirviss's own life paralleled that of the lead in the play. He had served as a cantor for more than seven years, and had been in the choir before that. In 1934, he turned to the stage, touring with a road company, and the next year he went to Hollywood for a screen test.

As Mirviss tells it: "When I was in Hollywood they said I looked like a Michael and I should take that as my first name. They asked what I would like my last name to be. I had always liked Loring Park in Minneapolis so I took the name Loring."

In the next few years Mirviss appeared under the name Michael Loring in several films, including *Postal Inspector*, *Yellowstone*, and *Flying Hostess*.

Lois Josewich recalled: "Through the years, my parents were regularly invited to attend the second Seder at the M. D. Mirviss home, being among the very few non-family guests present. Attending these Seder observances was always a treat, and particularly so when the Mirviss' handsome son, Sammy, still lived in Minneapolis. Sammy had a beautiful singing voice and delighted one and all with his fine singing at the Seder observances. Sammy's talent for singing was so exceptional that he went to Hollywood where he did some acting in films for a few years. One could say that he was the Minneapolis version of the famous entertainer, Al Jolson. As a matter of fact, I recall my father having mentioned that M. D.

Mirviss was a distant relative of Al Jolson."

That year at Adath, Rabbi David Aronson showed motion pictures he had taken on his recent trip to Russia. The registrar of the JTS, Professor Louis Finkelstein, was a guest speaker. The Women's League sponsored the movie, *This Is America*.

Graduation exercises took place June 9 for nine members of the Sunday School High School department. The young people had completed a three year course of study following their confirmation.

Sam Mirviss, Adath member and Hollywood actor

At the Annual Congregational Dinner, June, 1935, Morris Kantar was elected President; Dr. David Pink, Vice President; Harry Rubenstein, Recording Secretary; Fred Orenstein, Financial Secretary; and Dr. Louis H. Winer, Treasurer.

Reflecting on the previous year, Rabbi Gordon noted a break with the pessimistic spirit of the past, and the arrival of greater optimism and hopefulness, bringing with it "a host of activities which the community entered with unparalleled zest."

Golde Rapaport (Adath Sunday School teacher) became the president of the newly organized Minneapolis Jewish Youth Federation composed of representatives of all Jewish Youth organizations within the community.

Zionism and Zionist activity were more pronounced than in past years. The Friends of Hebrew University led by Dr. Moses Barron celebrated the 10th Anniversary of the founding of Hebrew University on Mount Scopus in Jerusalem.

Dr. David Pink recalled: "The Men's Club sponsored the lecture series and each member was asked to sell a certain number of lecture tickets. We did very well and we also had a program book. The rabbi decided on the speakers. Ludwig Lewisohn was one of our lecturers. We use to make $500 to $1,000 every year on the Lecture Series."

In February Rabbi Gordon was among those highlighted in a Minneapolis newspaper article entitled "Minneapolis Profiles in 1935." The article mentioned his radio talks on WCCO, which were in their fifth year, and the annual lecture series, which remained popular with both Jewish and non-Jewish audiences.

The writer went on to say: "Rabbi Gordon is a man of vitality and enthusiasm and has the ability of attacking a problem and staying with it to the finish. When he accepts a job, he asks only one thing - that he be allowed to do it in his own way without interference. His success as arbitrator for the Laundry and Dry Cleaning Industry in Minneapolis was an example of what he accomplished when his conditions were accepted. In 1934, when the industry was in the turmoil of labor-employer disagreements, Rabbi Gordon was named arbitrator heading a board of three employees and three employer representatives. Meeting semi-monthly, Rabbi Gordon's board has virtually eliminated the distrust that existed on the part of both employers and employees. Price wars, labor disputes, wage and hour difficulties gave away to a harmony and cooperation within the ranks of the entire industry."

The reporter noted the rabbi's hobbies as "taking motion pictures, baseball, reading light fiction for relaxation, a little golf and some bridge."

Rabbi Gordon was also appointed a member of the Advisory Board of the Public Works Administration, and received an appointment to serve as a member of the Council on Youth Administration.

Sammy Mirviss recalled: "I had an excellent relationship with Rabbi Albert Gordon, who was a most forceful personality. He had a strong impact on both the Jewish and general community in which he involved himself. Our professional relationship in presentation of services was good. Since my father was such an integral part of Adath's growth and existence, I welcomed Rabbi Gordon's warm relationship with M.D. Mirviss since there was quite a difference in age and backgrounds. [M. D. was a fine

Hebrew scholar, European, broken English; Rabbi Gordon was modern, American, fluent English, articulate] They respected each others strengths and skills and utilized these qualities in harmony to build Adath. Mrs. Gordon was a gracious lady."

Adath members Fanny Brin and Leah Barron were among 13 women chosen as the most influential women in America by the National Conference of Christians and Jews. All the city rabbis joined in the drive for clean films, and Minneapolis Jewry, at a protest meeting presided over by Dr. Maurice Lefkowitz, urged the United States to make a formal protest against Nazi excesses in Germany.

By 1935, there were 300 families at the Adath, a Cub Pack, Boy and Girl Scout troops, Young People's League, a Men's Club, Women's League, study groups and lecture courses. They were all part of the activities taking place at 3400 Dupont Avenue.

1935-1936

In his New Year message Rabbi Gordon praised the excellent leadership of Morris Kantar as president of the board of trustees. In an effort to improve the tone of services, he suggested that for the High Holidays men should leave their hats downstairs and wear yarmulkes, and that congregants resist the temptation to walk in and out during the service.

Howard Brin recalled: "Albert Gordon used to speak regularly on the subject of decorum. We should be more orderly, there should not be so much talking; and furthermore, the men were not to wear their felt fedoras in the synagogue. You were to change and put on a yarmulke. Ultimately everybody wore them. The other thing I remember as a kid was that the older men, who regularly sat near the front of the synagogue, always used to wear their *kittles* on Yom Kippur. They maintained that tradition for some time. I think it stopped sometime in the '30s."

Sophie Singer was pleased to recall that in the old days, families often sat together.

I remember we always had our seats designated to us. That was wonderful. A lot of people sat in the same seats on Friday nights. I remembered Mrs. Barron [Dr. Barron's mother]. She used to stand up and pray thoughout the whole service on Yom Kippur. The services lasted all day long from nine in the morning until sundown. There was a lot of running in and out on Rosh Hashanah and Yom Kippur.

In the earlier days they would auction off the

aliyahs. The shouting would go on and on. They called out how much money and whoever would give the biggest offer would be called to the pulpit. In those days $5 was a lot of money. According to Rabbi Gordon that was not how the Jews were supposed to operate. It's not what you have. It is what you do with dignity.

And Josie Hechter recalled," Rabbi Albert Gordon expected and received respect. Services were quiet. There was no chaos and he was a fine speaker."

That season, Joseph King, a Minneapolis Talmud Torah faculty member, served as cantor. Previously he had conducted services on the High Holidays for the Talmud Torah Alumni.

At the Women's League October meeting, "Betty Crocker" spoke, and a kitchen shower was planned to replenish the synagogue kitchen with much needed supplies.

Consecration of kindergarten and first grade children took place at Sukkot. All children were to bring fruits and flowers to decorate the pulpit and the sukkah.

Bernice Cowl Gordon said,

I attended the University of Minnesota and graduated with a degree in Education, Nursery School, Kindergarten and Primary. First I taught at Beth El Sunday School and then at the Adath with Rabbi Albert I. Gordon. I taught first grade when I was in college.

The Sunday School was excellent. We celebrated the holidays beautifully and the one I remember the most at Adath was Sukkot. It was a procession. Every child was asked to bring a basket of fruit or vegetables. It was like a pilgrimage in Israel. Each class marched with its teacher carrying a basket of fruit, bringing the harvest to the Temple for a gift. We did it in the sanctuary. We put our baskets on the bema and it was beautiful. We had a program with singing. ... Then the fruit and vegetables were given to some worthy organization.

The Rabbi introduced a change in the form of the regular Friday evening service. It began at 8:15 p.m. conducted by Rabbi Gordon, Mr. King and the choir. At the conclusion of the service, Rabbi Gordon spoke on important problems pertaining to present day beliefs under the general heading, "What Can We Believe?" Following his presentation, a discussion took place.

The 5th Annual Lecture Series was inaugurated by Wisconsin Governor Phil LaFollette November 5, 1935,

> "When it was time for a minyan, Mr. Mirviss would put up a white flag outside the synagogue on Dupont. That would show they needed a tenth man (for the minyan). One day a neighbor came along and saw the white flag and walked in and said, 'Good Morning.' He stayed there during the minyan and then they found out afterwards he wasn't Jewish. He heard that when they were in distress at the synagogue they would have a white flag. He didn't know what they meant by distress so he walked in to help them and stayed while they were praying."
>
> – *Lillian Krelitz Kaplan*

speaking on "Where Are We Going?" Other speakers that year included Emil Ludwig; North Dakota Senator Gerald P. Nye; two local scholars who debated the question "Is Civilization Doomed Under the Capitalistic System?"; and Dr. Angelica Balabanoff, an activist of international renown who spoke on "Mussolini and Hitler."

Madame Balabanoff had been a friend of Mussolini, and Dena Pink later recalled inviting Balabanoff to a dinner at her home. "I remember distinctly when Madam Balabanoff came to our house. I thought, *How are we going to take care of her*? She was a little woman and talked very little as she was afraid. Such a little character, you would not believe she was going to be the speaker. Her subject was on 'Conditions in Europe.' She was raised in a wealthy family in Russia and left there because she saw her brother whip a man. That turned her against him and the system. She did not think it was democratic enough. She never forgave her parents. They were very well-to-do and they didn't have to mistreat anyone, she felt. She was a Socialist and had just come from Italy. She was one of the few Jews to get a passport. She didn't like to be asked questions as she was afraid that she may be saying something which she shouldn't."

Another exciting guest speaker that December was Goldie Myerson (Golda Meir). She spoke from the Adath pulpit on "Palestine, As I Know It." At the time, she was described as one of the most important figures in modern Zionism.

Sue Rubel recalled: "The Lecture Series we had at the Adath was filled to overflowing with Jewish and non-Jewish audiences. Rabbi Albert Gordon wanted to elevate and expose his congregants to the great minds of the times... He brought great honor to us. He was a 'Man For All Seasons.'"

(Above) an announcement of Golda
Meir's visit. (Right) A Womens'
League costume party at Rabbi and
Dorothy Gordon's home

The 3rd Annual Chanukah luncheon of the Minne-apolis Conference of Jewish Women's Organizations, rep-resenting 14 women's groups, was held at the Curtis Ho-tel ballroom. A number of Adath women participated in a tableau.

Rabbi Gordon, seeking to counter the appeal of Christmas displays among Jewish children, advised mem-bers of the congregation to "....light Chanukah candles each night and tell the Chanukah story on the first night. Hanging stockings is not only a non-Jewish practice but definitely anti-Jewish. Chanukah is the season of gift giv-ing. Arrange a Chanukah party and distribute gifts to those present. The house ought to be decorated in some unusual way to make the children realize that the Jewish people too, have a festival which is both beautiful and meaningful."

The Men's Club and Women's League jointly spon-sored a Chanukah party and carnival. That fall the Wom-en's League program was dedicated to the ideal of peace. They presented a play by Rabbi Gordon himself entitled *Dreamers of Peace*.

In January Adult Jewish Education classes began to meet on Wednesday nights devoted to the contemporary Jewish world, a survey of Jewish history, and instruction in elementary Hebrew.

Bernice Gordon recalled, "On Purim, the children dressed up in costumes. There was always a play and of course, hamentashen. Parents came with their children to a separate service for the megillah reading in the synagogue."

The youth activities included a model seder, a Fathers and Sons Banquet celebrating the 5th Anniversary of the Boy Scout troop and the 1st Anniversary of the Cub Pack, plus the Spring Mothers and Daughters Dinner.

Beatrice Cohen (Mrs. Louis) Abrams said, "I remember Rabbi Gordon as being a most wonderful person.... He was responsible for helping us to open our store, the Abrams Delicatessen on Lake Street and Emerson Avenue South. We couldn't get a permit so he got the alderman to okay it and he would stand good for us."

On March 3, 1936, the dedication of the Jennie Gross Memorial Library took place, honoring the late Adath Women's League president. It had been the unanimous decision to dedicate the newly established synagogue li-brary in her memory for the many years she had devoted to Adath. The library chairman at that time was Kitty Ellison.

In the Jewish community, Talmud Torah celebrated its 25th Anniversary. For the Minneapolis Federation's 1936 Campaign, Dr. David Pink headed the Adath team, Arthur Brin was the Campaign Chairman, and Rabbi Gordon head-ed the Speakers' Bureau. The Minneapolis branch of Polish Jews of America was conducting a campaign for old and dis-carded clothing on behalf of the destitute Jews of Poland.

Sammy Mirviss signed a five-year contract in Hollywood with Universal Films, and a local newspaper reported:

Minneapolis' home-grown 'chazan' is coming back to the scene of his first successes—only this time he will be on the screen.

Samuel Mirviss - beg pardon, Michael Loring - who only last year conducted Rosh Hashanah and Yom Kippur services in a Twin City Synagogue, makes his film debut in Postal Inspector, *playing the part of 'Charlie Davis.' The picture will be shown in Minneapolis for the first time Sunday and Monday, September 6 and 7, at the Homewood Theatre, Plymouth and Newton Avenues North. Sam is the son of Mr. and Mrs. M.D.Mirviss, 3513 Bryant Avenue South.*

Everyone who has attended any sort of a Jewish social function in the Twin Cities in the last few years knows Sammy. His Yiddish songs have warmed the cockles of many a Jewish heart. His Jewish program several years ago over WTCN was one of the feature broadcasts of local radio entertainment.

Sam made a hit here when he portrayed the leading role several years ago in The Jazz Singer, Al Jolson's favorite piece. He appeared in numerous other productions both here and in the Northwest. Intending to study medicine, Sam gave up the medical profession for his first love, the theater. And now he's on the screen.

1936-1937

The Adath's new cantor, Solomon Winter, arrived in 1936. He was the first cantor to have studied at the Jewish Theological Seminary. A graduate of the City College of New York, he had also studied at the Julliard Foundation in New York City. He was from New Haven, Connecticut, where he had built a reputation as a singer of religious music. He and his wife had two children, Myra and David.

In the fall of 1936, Cantor Winter organized a new choir. At the Women's League first meeting of the season, he delivered a beautiful program of Hebrew songs. For the first time in the history of the Adath there is mention of an organ.

Although Rabbi Gordon felt that an organ would enhance the music at services, others were not so sure. Sophie Singer later recalled, "When they got the first organ, was there a split! The people that did not want an organ fought like you wouldn't believe. There were those

Cantor Solomon Winter

that wanted the organ but it could not be downstairs in the synagogue. So they put it in the balcony upstairs and that's where we sat. At first Evelyn Siegel played the organ."

Evelyn Siegel remembered: "The first organ we had was an old reed organ and they had it up in the balcony. We used to get our signals from the cantor down on the pulpit. They wouldn't allow it down there. I played the organ and I sang alto at the same time. Then later on we got Esther Rosenbloom to play the organ. Then I finally sang." Howard Brin recalled that "there was a lot of unhappiness about the organ and it sat for several years before they ever used it."

And Esther Rosenbloom recalled: "I went into the Adath when they needed an organist. I played on a push organ and had to pump it. It was one of those old ones. We used to sing up in the choir loft. The organ was up there. We didn't have a large choir and we didn't have any director at first. After a while the Cantor would direct. Later on we got a director."

On April 29, 1937, the Trustees decided that the organ would not be used during the High Holidays.

The Sixth Annual Adath Lecture Series once again brought in eminent speakers to discuss the Fascist threat, the future of democracy, the world Jewish scene, and other topics. But the outstanding event sponsored by the Adath that year was the lecture given by Eleanor Roosevelt on November 10 at the Minneapolis Auditorium. It was attended by more than 4,000 people. Gazella Kantar and Sarah Engler co-chaired the event.

Rabbi Gordon later observed that the event had the effect of elevating Adath Jeshurun in the eyes of the entire community. In was also a financial boon to the synagogue itself, and beyond that, he pointed out, "it demonstrated that we have a zealous group of workers who, if given some goal and some objective, strive fearlessly to attain it. With such enthusiasm, we need not fear for the future."

Gazella Kantar recalled: "My husband, Morris, was President of the Adath Jeshurun during this period, and I was co-chairman when we had Eleanor Roosevelt. She stayed at the Nicollet Hotel and was the grandest lady in the world!"

Throughtout this period the Adath remained in bad financial condition, and was in danger of losing its building.

Negotiation for refunding the mortgage had opened with the Mississippi Valley Trust Company, and the Adath leaders eventually succeeded in refinance the loan.

"The hardest period was when I first joined the synagogue," Sam Bender later recalled. " They couldn't pay the rabbi. They had all kinds of financial problems and almost lost the synagogue. ... Morris Kantar and Louis Schwartz and many other people worked hard and long to save it. But it was also the best of times when the Depression was on and everybody worked together."

Sam Bender with Cub Scout

Bender and his wife Ruth had recently been married, and they lived half a block from the synagogue.

I was active in the Boy Scouts [Bender later recalled] *and one night I walked into a scout meeting. I told them I wanted to join the synagogue, the Men's Club and the scout troop as a committeeman. So I joined and became Cub Master and then for ten years was the Scout Master.*

At that time we had about 50 boys and one of the finest scout troops in the city. We went on overnights on weekends and the boys would conduct services on Friday night. Most of the boys were members of Adath. We met every week. We did have a conflict with Talmud Torah as they held their classes in our building but we worked it out. That was in the '30s. Before we had the school building we had classes in

every nook and cranny of the place.

Rabbi Gordon was a terrific individual. Some people thought he was cold but he was the warmest fellow that I had run into in my lifetime. When I went into the service, he came to my house and said, 'If you ever need anything, I want you to call or write me. I don't care if it is money or what it is. If you ever have any problem, feel free to contact me.' ... It was a nice reassuring feeling to know I could call on my rabbi if I needed help.

Lillian Krelitz Kaplan shared her impressions of Rabbi Gordon:

I enjoyed working with Rabbi Gordon. He was a highly intelligent man and knew exactly what he was doing all the time. He taught us plenty by having wonderful programs on Passover with a seder for the Sunday School children and on the High Holidays we would all participate.

When my husband, Cecil Krelitz, and I joined in 1933, I brought in some younger friends. We started to have skits about what we were doing at the Adath in order to create an interest for new members. Sophie Burnstein would write them and Evelyn Siegel did the piano playing and all of our musical arrangements. We would direct each other. Sometimes I directed and sometimes Sophie directed. Shortly after I joined in the '30s I became program chairman for seven years.

The Sisterhood did most of the things there. The Men's Club was just getting started but we had Chanukah parties together. We would have home talent and get big crowds because everybody wanted to see their friends in the skits.

Norman Pink recalled: "My earliest experience would be going to the synagogue with my dad (Dr. David Pink) on Sunday mornings. He, George Stillman and Morris Kantar would try and sort out the problems of the congregation in the office which was behind the pulpit [in the building on Dupont.]

"At the time there was one secretary, Reva Ziff, at the synagogue. She was a one-woman executive secretary and bookkeeper. She ran the office and for the directors and officers she was their person. She would be there every Sunday. I would sit at an empty desk and doodle on paper. I wasn't old enough to go to Sunday School so I must have been around four. I remember Rabbi Gordon's study. It is now the Ida Fink room behind the pulpit and on the other

The kitchen crew for an Adath sleigh ride in January 1938. Doc Axelrod and Dan Shinder stand in back, with Pearl Finemean, Ann Bloomfield, Esther Mozofsky, Harriet Lasky and Reva Ziff (Rabbi Gordon's secretary) in the front row, left to right.

side where Cantor Kula had his office [where he used to have his office]was one of the two or three Talmud Torah classrooms."

Reva Ziff was secretary to Rabbi Gordon from 1930 to the fall of 1943. Here is the way she rememebered it:

When I graduated high school I was looking for a position where I would be able to observe Shabbat. Mr. Schanfeld was the Adath Jeshurun President. I went to see him and he hired me as the secretary to Rabbi Gordon and of the synagogue office. I was the only office employee at the time. I was there when Rabbi Gordon first came in 1930. Rabbi Gordon was very innovative, ambitious and industrious. He organized a great many activities. I served as his secretary and kept the records, books, wrote up minutes, sent out the bulletins and did everything that had to be done in the office.

Mr. Mirviss embodied just about every wonderful characteristic you could think of. First of all, he had a marvelous personality that people were attracted to and I think that everyone who came in contact with him, loved him. There's no doubt about it. Secondly, he had a marvelous cultural background. He had studied the Hebrew tradition. He could read the Haftorah. He was well trained. He led the daily minyan and trained the Bar Mitzvah boys. He was a marvelous mediator, an honest person. You knew that if he told you something, he meant what he was saying. Sometimes he

had a difficult mission to perform but he was always able to do it well.

He would go to people that nobody else could approach and get a response from them. He was welcomed where ever he went. A person may not want to see anyone else in the congregation but if Mr. Mirviss came, he was welcome. He was a very unique person.

He read the Torah, conducted the daily minyan and influenced a great many people to become closer to the synagogue. He was so learned. He did not just perform routine services such as organizing the minyons and looking after the synagogue but did whatever had to be done. I think that people regarded him not as someone who was doing menial tasks, but someone who was an authority they could respect and look up to.

Joseph Schanfeld was a prince with a heart of gold. He was helpful to people in any way that he could be and just a marvelous sweet person. He made you feel at ease. He was an authority in the community at large and a man that everybody respected, but in talking to him he was just always so sweet and understanding. You know you don't frequently find the head of an organization to be that type of a person. He was always willing to discuss things.

That fall Franklin Delano Roosevelt was elected to a second term as president. The Men's Club and Women's League held an Election Night Party to follow the returns.

After 30 years of service to the Adath, Mr. and Mrs. Mirviss were honored at a Testimonial Dinner in the synagogue vestry rooms on December 14. Joseph Schanfeld was toastmaster and Rabbi Matt returned from Philadelphia to be the guest speaker. It was one of the season's outstanding affairs.

On March 13 and 14, the Men's Club sponsored a minstrel show, and Cantor and Mrs. Winter hosted the members of the choir at their home. The Purim carnival was also a smashing success, as Sam Bender recalled: "It was a unique situation as it was before the synagogue was enlarged. We had it downstairs and it was jammed. We had different types of booths with products such as salami, spinning wheels and so on. We went out and scrounged as much as we could."

In April the Minneapolis Federation's annual campaign opened with "Federation Sabbath." Temple Israel and the Adath Jeshurun held a joint service. Rabbi Gordon said, "It is one of tthe largest campaigns to be conducted by any relief organization. It is American Jewry's campaign for sacrifice. It is up to us to give—not as charity but for the privilege of living on this side of the Atlantic...If not for us, they stand alone."

On July 12, 1937, the trustees proposed a settlement plan with the Mississippi Valley Trust Co. It involved raising $43,000 in eight annual installments of about $5,000 each without interest. The end result would be to relieve the synagogue of an obligation of $125,000.

The plan met with many obstacles and necessitated a trip to St. Louis and contacts to Rochester, N.Y. by Rabbi Gordon, the drafting of legal documents by L. B. Schwartz, a search of records by Maurice Engler, and last but not least, 209 individual subscriptions to the building fund.

1937-1938

In 1937 Ernest Hemingway's new novel *To Have and Have Not* appeared and Walt Disney produced his first full-length film, *Snow White*. There were bitter union conflicts. Hitler swallowed Austria and moved on to Czechoslovakia. The Munich Conference brought false promise of "Peace in our time." War threatened Europe.

In the September 3, 1937, issue of *AJW*, Rabbi Gordon spoke of the wave of anti-Semitism that was engulfing Europe. "The real Jew will not cringe. He will remain true to his trust and to his faith, and continue to challenge humankind until it has acquired an understanding of the meaning of civilization."

In his New Year's Greetings the rabbi acknowledged that "the sunshine is at last breaking through the clouds" with regard to the synagogue's financial woes, and expressed hope for the future.

The big news that fall at Adath was the founding of the Jewish Nursery School, for children aged three to five—the first of its kind to be held in any synagogue. Bernice Cowl and Harriet Engler, graduates of the University of Minnesota Child Welfare Department, were in charge of the program, under the direction of the Department of Child Welfare and Rabbi Gordon. In addition to the usual nursery school curriculum, the children were introduced to Jewish holidays, festivals, customs, stories, handicraft work, and ceremonies. The school had an outdoor playground adjoining the synagogue, and it also provided transportation for the children.

Bernice Cowl, the Adath's first nursery school teacher said: "The nursery school was Rabbi Gordon's brainchild. He was very progressive in his thinking and felt that it was very important that children come to the synagogue as preschoolers and get to feel at home with the blessings, customs, ceremonies, and celebrations of the holidays."

The children were ferried to and from school in taxis. "Isabel Berman did psychological testing of the children. Ann Orenstein was our advisor and I remember Mildred Stillman helping. The rabbi's secretary, Reva Ziff, would come down and help us get the children dressed for home."

Bernice recalled that although the school charged tuition, most of it was immediately spent on the transportation bill.

That year the Adath once again brought in eminent senators, authors, photographers, and other experts to share their perspectives on world affairs. In the final lecture, held on March 2, Dr. Abram L. Sachar, director of the Hillel Foundation, spoke on "What Next in Europe?" (A few years later Dr. Sachar became the first president of Brandeis University.)

In October, threats of foreclosure resurfaced. Many who had been involved in building the synagogue had since departed, and money was hard to come by. The synagogue's offer to rent the building was rejected by the trust. Dr. David Pink later recalled:

The Mississippi Valley Trust held the mortgage. They were really serious about foreclosing. They wouldn't consider renting. The cost of keeping it up would be more than we could pay them. We offered them $5,000 a year and then finally went a little bit higher.

(Above) Bernice Cowl, the Adath's first nursery school director, with (front row from left) Judy Gordon, Arnold Blumberg, Norton Stillman, Joanne Sheldov, Barbara Winer, Tommy Kassmir; (back row) Sue Zipperman, Bernice Cowl, and Albert Kapstrom.

(Left) Joan Siegel, an unidentified boy, and Barbara Winer, at the Adath nursery school, 1937.

We finally paid it up by 1942. Money wasn't easy to come by and we went out on a drive. Mr. Mirviss, Morris Kantar and I went to members who had resigned from the synagogue within the year prior. It wasn't very easy to get money then like it is today. Now you go ask for $2,000 or $3,000 but when we got $300 we thought we were lucky. We kept plugging away.

One day Leo Frisch walked into the office. He said, 'O.K. I'll write you out a check for $300.' I said, 'Leo, that's very generous of you. You don't make that much!' 'Well,' says he, 'it's my synagogue too!' Fortunately we had Mr. Mirviss and no one ever turned him down.

New plans for the Women's League were the inaugurating of "Oneg Shabbats," presenting reviews, having Hebrew Study Classes, a class for mothers on "Bringing Up the Jewish Child," a Kitchen Fund Shower, and establishing a "Happy Day Fund" for contributions.

In November, the Men's Club held a discussion on bitter labor problems that were then sweeping the country; in December they staged the 2nd Annual Minstrel Show. In January, along with Beth El and Temple of Aaron, they hosted a symposium on "What Can the Jew Contribute to the Betterment of the Social Order?" with Max Shapiro, I. D. Fink, and Jesse Calmenson speaking. A Purim Carnival was held for three days in March and the year ended with

the Fathers and Sons Dinner in April.

Ruth Stillman said: "We had a carnival on Purim. I worked like a dog and George (my husband) went around getting all the merchandise. We use to have congregational dinners and not have one solitary person get paid and we served oodles, maybe three hundred. We made and served everything and didn't have caterers. We did it ourselves and had fun doing it. We use to do our Friday cooking at home, hurry and get our own done, and then go down to the synagogue and do all the baking for Shabbat for the next day. Then we'd go home and serve our own Shabbat dinners. We made all the dinners at the synagogue. We cleaned chickens, washed dishes, and afterwards scrubbed the wooden floors. It was our synagogue. It was our second home. When the rabbi was ill, everything went on."

That year a Junior Choral group was started. Rabbi Gordon compiled a special booklet on Chanukah. AZA was holding their meetings in the synagogue. A youth group was organized for those fifteen and older, with Phyliss Goldie as president. YPL continued to flourish, and planned to sponsor a production of Rabbi Gordon's play, *So Let Them Foreclose.*

Rabbi Gordon was invited to address the Jewish Theological Seminary in New York, and that week, Jacob Mirviss spoke from the pulpit.

Nine students graduated from the 2nd High School class: Harriette Chauss, Sylvia Harris, Herbert Kantar, Robert Kerner, Louise Medalie, Edwin Neff, Leah Schulman,

Talmud Torah class, 1939. Front row, left to right: Sheldon Kieffer, Pearl Silver, Cantor Solomon Winter, Rita Bernstein, Myron Rubenstein; back row, left to right: Jack Bernstein, Normand Diamond, Elliot Spring, Sherman Hechter (fifth student unidentified).

Ruth Schwartz and Delphia Silver.

Rabbi Gordon spoke often that year on the tribulations facing Europeans living in the shadow of war. Among his other topics were: "Shall It Be Evolution or Revolution?" "The Jewish Attitude Toward Intermarriage;" "War and Human Nature;" "Light, the Symbol of Understanding;" "When the Messiah Will Come;" "Jews On A Diet;" and "What Is Sacred About Human Personality?"

The situation in Europe was very bad and the call was "Send Warships For Refugees." The residents of *Eretz Israel* remarked on the continuing uncertainty:

"One remembers the sense of utter helplessness experienced by the 'Yishuv' in the face of the disasters which have befallen the Jews of various European countries and of Austria in particular. In Eretz Israel we have had to look on passively at their agonies while knowing that we could give them effective help if only our hands were not tied. Our grievance against restrictions on immigration (which has now been almost completely throttled) is one

of long standing; but never before have we been so outraged as when seeing the gates of Eretz Israel barred by cool political calculations against multitudes for whom it is a last hope, the ultimate refuge...That Eretz Israel should be closed to the Jewish masses in this hour of bitterest persecution is not among the least of the enormities committed in this era of brutality and denial of elementary human rights..."

They went on to describe the settlements of middle-class German Jews that had recently been established on National Fund land, which they described as "irrefutable proof of the constructive assistance that could so readily have been made available for Austrian refugees as well were not the gates of Eretz Israel hermetically sealed."

A lead article in the August 1938 *Minneapolis Journal* was titled, "Hate Crusades." It dealt with an anti-Semitic group, the Silver Shirts. Rabbi Gordon responded with an impassioned letter to the editor about the group.

1938-1939

In Rabbi Gordon's fall message, he once again underscored the growing barbarity in Europe and its threat to the well-being of the Jews. In October a mass meeting was held in St.Paul to discuss Great Britain's reported plan to stop Jewish immigration to Palestine. Fourteen hundred people signed a petition and sent it to President Roosevelt, asking him to issue a public statement on the matter, and making a plea for united action on the part of the United States to express opposition to the proposed nullification of the Balfour Declaration.

During the High Holidays many of the German-Jewish refugees, who were then residents of Minneapolis, attended the services at Adath as guests of the congregation; and, Rabbi Gordon secured the release of all WPA workers for the holidays so they could attend synagogue services.

On October 23 the first Midwest Regional Conference of Women's Leagues of the United Synagogue of America opened its sessions at the Adath.

Among the luminaries brought in for the Eighth Annual Lecture Series were the novelist Stefan Zweig, Dr. Jerome Davis, and Dr. Abram L.Sachar.

The nursery school and Sunday school continued to thrive. Jerome Fischbein recalled: " My wife, Bernice, was a Sunday School teacher when Albert Gordon was there. He married us and we were close to him. At first I thought he was cold but he really wasn't. After you got to know him on a one-to-one basis, he was warm. He was very strong from the pulpit and the decorum was good."

In 1938, Rabbi Gordon's radio program was back on Sundays at 11:45 a.m. Among the rabbi's sermon titles that year were: "Can Youth Build a New World?," "Why Remain Jews?," "The Weapons of Israel," and "What Ickes Learned From Hitler."

Employers and employees in the fur and bakery industries asked Rabbi Gordon to continue arbitrating their disputes. The first payment for the bonded indebtedness against the synagogue was finally paid off.

A city-wide Chanukah program was held at the Lyceum Theater on Sunday, December 25, with children of the Adath, Talmud Torah, Beth El, Temple Israel, the Hebrew Free School and the Emanuel Cohen Center participating. The Adath Religious School raised money for the American Jewish Joint Distribution Committee for their relief work in connection with German refugees. The children made the contributions instead of spending the money for personal Chanukah gifts. The Junior Supper group for young people between the ages of 15 to 18 met and Lillian Gross was the club leader.

Lillian (Mrs. Leo) Gross said: "We were married in 1935. It was taken for granted that I would be involved with the Adath. We kept house for Leo's father because his mother was gone. We lived at the house which was two blocks from the synagogue."

Leo Gross added:

Adath was very convenient for us…We were regular attendees on Friday night and after services, a whole group, including the Gracemans, Englers and others, would come for a 'glassel tea.' We would sit around our round dining room table and talk and tell stories. After we were married we began to have a more mature relationship with the synagogue.

Adath had an influence on Lil and me. We grew to like and respect Al Gordon and felt a loss when he moved to New York. From a personal standpoint, Adath has always been a part of my life. I see Rabbi Al Gordon as a wonderful leader, a strong personality and a dedicated Jew. He did much for our Synagogue at a time when strong leadership was necessary.

Lil and I were active in Study Groups, the Men's Club and the Women's League. For many years I was a member of the Board and an officer. We had a wonderful group of young people and we worked very hard putting on carnivals with raffles and all sorts of fundraising activites. We put on plays, shows and any kind of activity that we thought would raise funds. At the same time, there was a great comraderie with people like Lou Cohen, George Stillman, Ben Grossman, Dave Spivak, Archie Miller, Sam Bender and many, many others.

And we had an Adath orchestra. Max Levinson was the conductor and Sam Segal was the pianist. I played clarinet. We played at the Talmud Torah Graduation, at Hastings and would give concerts around.

There is no doubt in my mind that the Adath and the Talmud Torah, together, had a much greater effect on me than either institution alone could have had. One without the other would have left a serious void. That is one reason I am so grateful for Adath providing facilities for the Talmud Torah for the many years it did.

That year, with the Grosses as advisors, the YPL had attorney Amos Deinard as a guest speaker, held a sleigh ride and raised $250 on their wonderful musical production *Heading South*. They participated in the National YPL

Convention in Atlantic City and were guests of the YPL of Judson Memorial Church.

A scene from the play *Headin' South*. Bernice Cowl Gordon, the Adath's first nursery school teacher, is 2nd from right.

A highlight of the year was the Festival of Nations program held in St.Paul. Groups representing various nations and races living in the Twin Cities participated.

The Temple Israel/Adath Jeshurun Annual Federation Sabbath was held at the Adath in April. Alexander Easterman, the noted English newspaper correspondent, spoke.

The Jewish Theological Seminary was in its fifty-second year and Adath members contributed to help keep its doors open. During its existence the seminary had sent out 327 rabbis to lead congregations and 680 teachers in almost all the states of the union and several foreign countries. Its first graduate, Joseph H. Hertz, was then Chief Rabbi of the British Empire.

The year 5699 ended with 62 new members and their wives being welcomed at the Congregational Dinner, Confirmation Exercises and the Annual Picnic with Sam Bender as chairman.

On May 17, 1939, the infamous British White Paper on Palestine was issued.

1939-1940

The year 1939 was critical for world Jewry. On September 1, Adolf Hitler's blitzkrieg invasion of Poland stirred Great Britain and France to retaliate and World War II began. Hitler's ally, Soviet Dictator Joseph Stalin, seized eastern Poland and attacked Finland. The forces of Franco had won the Spanish Civil War earlier in the year, and the long shadow of dictatorship was spreading across Europe.

In the United States, a World's Fair was taking place in New York. And it was a vintage year in Hollywood with the unforgettable *Gone With The Wind*, *The Wizard of Oz*, and Gretta Garbo in *Ninotchka*.

In Minneapolis, Rabbi Albert and Dorothy Gordon marked their tenth year at the Adath. The Rabbi stated in the opening *Clarion*: "We remain uncertain as to whether we shall have peace or war. The thought that civilized men and women stand upon the brink of war is indeed horrible to men and women who have, for these many centuries, yearned for the blessings of peace. The Germany of Hitler, which was founded upon the principal of force and power, seems as unready today to plunge the world into war as do the democracies....Not only Jews suffer today. The whole world is wracked with pain and anguish. What the morrow will bring no one knows...Let us pray for peace."

The interior of the synagogue was decorated through the effort of the Women's League that fall. *Clarion* editor Elliot Hoffman reported, "The soft tones of the choir, the pleasing voice of Cantor Winter, the new interior of the synagogue with its subdued lighting effects, the attentiveness of the congregation all served to imprint on our minds the spiritual beauty of the High Holy Days."

Anna K. Schwartz was elected president of the Midwest branch of the Women's League that year. Eighty-five delegates representing 13 communities in seven states attended the conference in Omaha. Among the resolutions adopted was the endorsing of a campaign to build a Jewish center in Rochester, Minnesota, for patients visiting the Mayo Clinic.

Rabbi Gordon was often ill that fall, and a number of outstanding speakers were secured to speak at Friday Evening Services, including Dr. George J. Gordon, Dr. Moses Barron and Rev. F. Zietlow. Cantor Winter presented "An Evening of Jewish Music" on the Council Sabbath with Viola Hymes, Fanny Brin, Bea Grossman and Dorothy Rosen participating.

Looking back on Rabbi Gordon's tenure, Albert Louis Cohen recalled:

I had the good fortune of being actively involved at the Adath while Albert Gordon was our leader. Possibly I was prejudiced by the fact that his wife, Dorothy, a Minneapolis girl, was a long time childhood friend. Albert and I had numerous medical complications, so we commiserated with each other for many years.

He was a stern taskmaster with a heart as big as a pumpkin. He was a fine gentleman and a dear man. Many times he was not well. In my opinion, he was one of our leading rabbis. He brought decorum to the synagogue, orderliness and a business-like sense. He was more active in our civic affairs in Minneapolis than any other rabbi in the Twin Cities before or since…He brought identity and recognition to the Adath Jeshurun.

The YPL was again busy with their numerous activities. A Brotherhood Sabbath was held, and the rabbi continued his talks in the community. The Mothers' and Daughters' Dinner had an unusually fine program with a play entitled "The Eternal People," with original music by Esther Rosenbloom, special dance numbers coached by Sue Rubel, and choral music led by Cantor Winter. The script was written by Rabbi Gordon. The play was presented again at the Congregational Dinner on May 27 so all would have the opportunity to see the excellent production.

Esther Rosenbloom: "When the present Adath was built, I took part in organizing plays with texts arranged by Rabbi Albert I. Gordon and musicals written by me. Rabbi Gordon was a gracious, highly educated person who read a great deal and loved Jewish things. He was a real scholar and we became very good friends."

Sue Rubel, in an Adath production

Sue (Mrs. Barney) Rubel recalled: "Esther Rosenbloom wrote the music and I did the choreography with Biblical themes. The first time we danced on the bema we had to have permission. Mr. Mirviss said, 'Of course, she can dance before the Ark, because Miriam in the Bible danced before the Lord.' So once the Ark was covered, it was accepted."

Ruth (Mrs. James) Davis: "In 1939, I married into the Davis family who were very involved with every aspect of Judaism. My mother-in-law, Mary Davis, was very observant. Rabbi Albert I. Gordon was her son-in-law. I became exposed to a close and large family with a very rich Jewish background so I started doing more reading and became involved in Jewish activities.

"My sister-in-law, Dorothy Gordon, was extremely active not only as a rebbetzin but involved in the community. She had a background in social work. In those days I think all rabbis' and ministers' wives were married to the synagogue. They took their responsibilities seriously. Dorothy was always on call and felt very needed especially during the Depression. Things were difficult for everyone, not only the rabbi and his wife, but for everyone."

Bea Abrams said: "Rabbi knew if you had attended Friday night services. One Friday I wasn't feeling well and it was snowing. I couldn't trudge from my house to the synagogue. He stopped in the store and inquired why I wasn't at services. It wasn't only me he watched out for, it was everybody."

At a Commemoration Dinner, April 9, 1940, more than three hundred enthusiastic and appreciative persons hailed Rabbi Albert and Dorothy Gordon for their ten years of service to Adath. Those participating in the evening's program included Arthur H. Brin, the Program Chairman; Rabbi Albert G. Minda of Temple Israel; Rev. Morris Robinson, Rabbi David Aronson, and others.

1940-1941

Attempting to sustain a hopeful note in the fall of 1940, Rabbi Gordon wrote: "When Napoleon swept through Europe, men everywhere believed that civilization was doomed. Yet, in these and in a hundred more instances culled from the pages of history, it should be clear to us that the human spirit had actually achieved victory over the forces of darkness."

In September of 1940, Rabbi Abraham I. Millgram, an author and educator from Philadephia, became the first full time director of the B'nai B'rith Hillel Foundation at the University of Minnesota. He spoke to the Women's League that fall. Those who attended an Election Night Party that

November 5 learned that FDR had been elected the President for an unprecedented third term.

In his "Thoughts on Thanksgiving," Rabbi Gordon underscored the significance of the fact that millions of American citizens had gone to the polls and voted for the men of their choice, unchallenged by Gestapo agents or secret police. He lauded a system in which children could develop a sense of self-respect and dignity, families could worship as they chose and live by a code of justice based upon the idea of equality.

Bandmaster Glenn Miller was at a peak of popularity, and the Adath Men's Club, Women's League and YPL presented the musical, *So Let Them Foreclose*, on December 7, 8, and 9. It was billed as a scintillating musical comedy and a substantial profit was made on the production.

Evelyn Siegel recalled that there were sometimes rehearsals every night of the week—and she played for all of them. "We had dancing, singing, costumes, skits and plays. It was beautiful. Sophie Burnstein was a beautiful writer and we had a choreographer. In those days none of the young girls worked like they do now. You could get any-

body to come and do anything. One of the productions that the women did was *Sailors Beware*. We were all dressed in sailors' costumes."

In the rabbi's column, Rabbi Gordon answered the question "What Does the Rabbi Do?" describing the time he spent preparing sermons and the personal counselling service he rendered day in and day out to congregants with personal, marital, or financial problems.

"Further," he added, "There are those who simply need a friend, one in whom they can confide. The rabbi listens to these persons, advises them and tries to be of assistance whenever possible."

That winter the Adath Boy Scout troop camped at Camp Tonkawa during a blizzard, and received the highest award given to any troop that season for its decorum and general efficiency.

Norman Pink: "I was in Boy Scout Troop 108 and Sam Bender was our leader. One of the reasons the Adath formed the troop was that if you went to Talmud Torah, you couldn't belong to Boy Scouts, because troop meetings were after school. So they had our troop meet in the eve-

Meeting of the Young People's League music appreciation activity at Lucille Seltzer's home, April 25, 1940

A Gross family seder, 1941

nings or on days that we did not have Talmud Torah."

Under the leadership of Ruth Davis, a Girl Scout Troop was organized for girls 11-14 years of age.

"The girls that belonged to the troop were mostly members of the Adath but some were from the neighborhood. We would tie in our activities with the holidays and usually had an annual BoyScout/Girl Scout Sabbath."

Rabbi Gordon exhorted his congregants to give to the Minneapolis Federation to help save "thousands, nay millions, of children, fathers and mothers all through Europe who are faced with starvation." Louis M. Cohen and Dr. H.A. Diamond and Mmes. Ann Orenstein and Marion Figen were chairmen of the Adath Federation team.

Starting in 1941, all boys who were to celebrate their Bar Mitzvah publicly at the Adath would be expected to attend the Talmud Torah for a minimum of two years. And at the end of the year, the Liss family donated motion picture equipment to the synagogue.

1941-1942

The summer of 1941 was one of baseball's greatest, with Joe DiMaggio hitting in 56 straight games, and Ted Williams batting .406. The workers at the Ford Motor Company went out on strike for the first time. On November 2 there was a city-wide Balfour Day celebration to commemorate the day in 1917 when British foreign secretary Arthur James Balfour expressed "sympathy with Jewish Zionist aspirations."

The Women's League opened a gift shop that year, which included books, holiday ceremonial objects, menorahs, kiddush cups, and many other items.

Two days later Japan attacked Pearl Harbor, bringing the United States into World War II.

Rabbi Gordon exhorted the congregation to help the cause. The Red Cross was already meeting at the Adath as part of National Defense, and sewing, surgical dressing and first aid classes were set up. The Boy Scouts collected waste paper and magazines. The rabbi stressed the importance and significance of celebrating the holiday, TuB'shevat, the New Year of the Trees. The custom of the schoolchildren in Palestine was to utilize the day for planting thousands of trees; but, for those living in the Diaspora it was a time "to help to purchase land in Palestine to help our stricken brethren throughout the world so that they may find in that land a haven of refuge."

On March 20, 1942, a posthumous award was made in memory of Ensign Ira Weil Jeffrey, the first Minneapolis casualty at Pearl Harbor. His grandfather, Michael Jeffrey, had been one of the Adath's early presidents and a lay rabbi of the congregation in the 1880s, and his father, David Jeffrey, was the first boy to be a Bar Mitzvah of the synagogue.

Rabbi Gordon asked for the names of sons, brothers and other immediate members in families who were in government training or were in active service to be inscribed in the Congregational Roll of Honor. The YPL paid tribute to its departing President, Louis Rovner, who would soon be entering the Armed Forces. Two of the popular songs being sung across the nation were: "The White Cliffs of Dover" and "We Did It Before and We Can Do It Again," sung by Dinah Shore and Eddie Cantor.

The Men's Club sponsored a Golden Glove boxing night, and for the first time the Annual Father/Son Dinner had daughters present.

The Synagogue Council of America, representing the Orthodox, Conservative and Reform Rabbinical and Congregational Organizations of America, declared a Shavuot Affirmation. Calling the holiday the birthday of Judaism it said: "Approaching Shavuot, the Festival of Weeks, which Jewish tradition commemorates as the birthday of the Ten Commandments, the Charter of Judaism, we reaffirm these ancient truths, and rededicate ourselves to them as timeless imperatives. Keenly aware of their cogency at the present juncture in human affairs, we register our firm conviction that the principles of Sinai can achieve salvation for human society."

The Summer of '42 saw the Annual Congregational Picnic and the Men's Club sponsoring a baseball game under the chairmanship of George Stillman. Bess Frisch became president of the Northwest Region of Hadassah; Josiah Brill was named head of the USO; Nahum Schulman became the new rabbi of Mikro Kodesh; and Louis Cohen and Ellis Peilen headed the Adath Federation team.

1942-1943

Rabbi Gordon's New Year Greeting read: "Today, we are active participants in the great conflict. Well over 140 of the sons, husbands and brothers of our members are today in the armed services of our country."

The 12th Annual Lecture Series once again brought experts to the Adath Jeshurun, including M. Thomas Tchou, Secretary to Chiang Kaishek, and Admiral Yates Stirling, Jr., former commandant, Pearl Harbor and Chief of Staff of the U.S. Fleet.

Anna K. Schwartz, who for many years had been associated with the activities of the Women's League, became the new principal of the Religious School.

In October, the Adath Women sponsored a Basket Social with dancing, a program, an old time fiddler, and square dances. Each woman's admission was a decorated basket with lunch for two.

Helen (Mrs. Louis) Winer: "We were married by Rabbi Gordon at the Nicollet Hotel in 1933. When my daughter, Barbara, was born, I became interested in her religious education. Rabbi Gordon knew that I was a graduate of the Talmud Torah and he asked me if I would be willing to teach the Confirmation Class at the Adath Jeshurun. I said, 'I certainly would.' When Barbara was in the first grade of Religious School, she would go to her class and I would teach the Confirmation class every Sunday morning.

"During the war most of our activities had to do with helping to win the war. We got permission to grow vegetables in the the lot behind us and we and our neighbors raised all kinds of vegetables."

On Sunday, December 20, 1942, more than 300 men and women attended the Congregational Dinner in honor of the retirement of the synagogue mortgage. The thrill of the evening was when Meyer D. Mirviss and Rabbi Gordon were accorded the honor of burning the mortgage.

Louis Cohen recalled: "I have been a member of Adath since 1928. I was married there by Rabbi Schwartz to Tess Smiler, daughter of Bertha and Gerald Smiler who had always lived on the South Side. My family all lived on the North Side. After some years of inactive membership, I found myself becoming involved and making friends at the Adath…The Adath not only became our congregation and a house of prayer but it became a club. There was camaraderie.

"Financial problems were great in those days. We had trouble raising funds for the projects that we were desirous of undertaking. We did burn the mortgage."

That year three new practices were instituted at Friday evening services: Blessing the men who were about to enter the Armed Forces, reading the names of those whose yahrzeit dates occured during the following week, and preparing the boys who were to be Bar Mitzvah'd. They would chant the kiddush at the Friday evening service preceding their Bar Mitzvah.

Rabbi Gordon was appointed to the National War Labor Board. And he continued to share letters he had received from his constituents in the Armed Forces with the congregation. But as of 1942, the Young People's League was discontinued because many of the people who had made up that group were in the armed forces.

On February 5, 1943 a very exciting "first" took place at the Adath Jeshurun. Sybil Wolk, a member of the graduating class of the Talmud Torah and also a student in the Religious School, was honored with the first Bat Mitzvah in Minneapolis and one of the first in the country. Her parents, Mr. and Mrs. Isadore Wolk, extended an invitation to the congregation to be their guests at a social hour following the service. (The Bat Mitzvah had come about as part of the movement to accord equal rights to women, including the right to religious education.)

Sybil Wolk Marblestone:

My parents were Isadore and Janet Hersh Wolk. My father was from Russia and my mother's parents came from Romania and they belonged to the orthodox Romanian shul. Our family lived at 3343 Emerson Avenue South just across from the synagogue. I started Hebrew School when I was nine. I was the only girl in my Hebrew class at the Adath Jeshurun. My teacher was "Mar" Kahz. Some of the boys that were in my class were Norton Furman, Seymour Hartzberg and Bobbie Sokol. There were about 15 in the class. Mr. Kahz was a vegetarian and at that time we thought it was strange; but, I felt he was a good teacher and he inspired me. I loved Hebrew and still do.

Every Saturday I attended services and I remember Rabbi Gordon as strict and stern but very loving. I was mesmerized by him. As far as I can remember one of the reasons that I had a Bas Mitzvah was because my brother, Marvin Ronald, died. He had a brain tumor. We were born three years apart to the day, July 29; he in 1932 and I, in 1929. My parents were very active in the synagogue. Mr. Kahz encouraged me to have the Bas Mitzvah and because of my brother's death, my parents thought it would be a good idea.

I was very excited and felt very good about it. I read some Hebrew and the rabbi blessed me. I was not allowed to hold the Torah even though they did take it out.

At the time there were five other girls who were attending or had graduated from Talmud Torah who had expressed interest in being Bat Mitzvah in the synagogue. And on April 16 the second Bat Mitzvah, Loisclaire Friedman, daughter of Mr. and Mrs. Emanuel Friedman, took place at the Adath.

As Norman Pink remembers it:

Cantor Winter and Mr. Kahz conducted the Talmud Torah Hebrew classes. Cantor Winter was there

for my Bar Mitzvah. He was a very handsome man and had a beautiful voice. He led the services, sang, and at one time edited the Clarion. *We had Talmud Torah on Thursday after school and Friday morning was the cut off day for the* Clarion. *While we were reading out of the Chumash he would be editing the* Clarion. *If he told us to read page 47, sometimes we would just turn and read any page or skip lines. I remember he would always catch us. He wasn't looking at the book. He didn't seem to be paying any attention to us but he knew we were fooling him and he would tell us to go back to the right page.*

Mr. Kahz had the large classroom which was behind the balcony. He had the rowdier and larger class at one time. He use to chase his pupils around the balcony to get them to come back to his class. He was a very stern man and had to be in order to handle us. The decorum of the students in the '40s was no different than it is today, except the facilities weren't as good. There was another situation. World War II was going on and a lot of fathers and brothers were at war. There were many single parent families. I think this had an effect on us. The atmosphere was different.

At the May 27 Congregational Dinner meeting, Morris Kantar, who had served for eight years as president, relinquished the office and was succeeded by Dr. David Pink. During Morris Kantar's term in office, the membership of the synagogue had more than doubled, and the mortgage debt was retired. The *Clarion* reported: "Mr. Kantar's friendly, wholesome Jewish spirit has won for him and his dear ones a host of friends and admirers. We extend to him our sincere thanks for all that he has done and will continue to do as a member of the board on behalf of the synagogue."

1943-1944

In September 1943, Rabbi Gordon said, "The year that has passed has been hectic and trying for most of us." He was referring to the war effort.

For Sukkot the Women's League celebrated by having a Musical Tea with a special program which Esther Rosenbloom prepared and participated in with Sue Leonard, Evelyn Siegel, Ruth Libman, and Cantor Solomon Winter. The synagogue was selling War Bonds and stamps weekly plus operating a booth for that purpose at the Nicollet and Radisson Hotels.

Ruth Davis recalled that "during World War II, our Scout Troop had a huge Victory Garden on 36th and Irving opposite the Greek Orthodox Church. Through Al Gordon the land was made available to us. We went to the canneries and even did our own canning."

On November 2, 1943, Hubert H. Humphrey spoke to the Women's League on "Under Cover," a review of the daring expose of Fascism in America.

Ruth Stillman: "Hubert Humphrey was Mayor of Minneapolis and was speaking that day. We even had our little kids involved. Tommy was five years old, [her son, now Dr. Thomas Stillman] and in kindergarten. We took him out of school to come to the luncheon to sing the opening prayer."

Will Rogers, Jr., California Congressman and son of America's greatest humorist of that time, opened the 13th Annual Lecture Series speaking on "From Washington to London, Algiers, Rome and Back Again." Later in the series General Victor A. Yakhontoff, authority on Russia and the Far East, spoke on "Is Cooperation with the U.S.S.R. Possible?" (At the time, Russia was our ally.)

At the end of 1943, Chairman George Stillman announced that the Adath had opened its School Building Fund Drive. The funds would be used to erect a building to house the Religious School and Talmud Torah classes and provide other badly needed facilities for the congregation. Negotiations had recently been completed for the purchase of a building site next to the synagogue with funds raised by the Men's Club.

As of January 9, 1944, Sophie Haveson, supervisor of music in the Minneapolis public schools, was appointed principal of the Adath Religious School.

Norman Pink said: "My dad brought the first professional educator to the Adath's staff. She was Sophie Haveson, one of the heads of the Music Department for the Minneapolis schools. She came in as principal of the religious school at a time when leadership was needed. Rabbi Albert Gordon was sick and the lay leaders just didn't have the time to handle the school properly. Sophie Haveson came and not only did she run the religious school but she also did the music program for the congregation."

In February, the Women's League held a cooking school, and Ruth Stillman, Dena Pink, Edith Grouse and Anna Daskovsky demonstrated how to stretch dough for strudel and baigalach, and how to make kreplach and taiglach.

"I learned to make all kinds of dishes in those days from my friends at the Adath," Helen Grouse Winer later recalled, "And even today I make those dishes. I learned to make strudle from my Romanian friends. They were wonderful cooks."

The Women's League asked women in the congregation to provide 3,000 cookies for servicemen: the cookie jars at the various canteens had to be kept full. The League also assisted the Office of Civilian Defense with the project of sending Christmas gifts to servicemen without families.

WAC Pvt. Tillie Goldberg was one of many who wrote expressing their thanks: "It is indeed gratifying to men and women in the service to know that the 'folks' at home are thinking of them. The girls at the barracks think it is wonderful that we have such considerate organizations. They also appreciate the goodies I receive."

Rabbi Abraham Millgram and son

During 1944 Rabbi Gordon was often ill, and Rabbi Abraham Millgram frequently offered his services.

I arrived in Minneapolis in September, 1940, to assume my duties as director of the newly established Hillel Foundation at the University of Minnesota and found an apartment in South Minneapolis near the Adath Jeshurun synagogue. The congregation offered the family free honorary membership but we refused the offer and insisted on becoming regular dues-paying members.

In the mid-winter of 1943-44, Rabbi Albert Gordon called me and said that he was going to the hospital for surgery and that this would necessitate his absence of six weeks. I assured him that I would take care of all his rabbinic duties for as long as my services would be required.... Before the six weeks were up, the family and congregation were informed by the physicians that Rabbi Gordon's condition was critical and that there was nothing that they could do except to advise the family and the congregation to pray. And so we did and many of us lined up at the hospital to donate blood for the necessary transfusions.

A congregational committee came to my home and asked me to continue to serve as acting rabbi for the rest of the congregational year. I informed the committee of my promise to Rabbi Gordon and that I intended to substitute for Rabbi Gordon until he fully recovered. As to the compensation, I considered myself a volunteer.

Rabbi Gordon recovered from his illness and resumed his duties in the fall of the year.

On March 3, 1944, the Minneapolis Jewish community held a mass meeting, during which they adopted a resolution asking President Roosevelt to urge Congress to act on behalf of a Jewish Commonwealth in Palestine; and the ZOA began a campaign for a thousand new members of the Minneapolis district.

The National Women's League endorsed the work of the Jewish Council for Russian War Relief, a new project to ship sorely needed supplies, clothing, and household kits to designated areas in the Soviet Union in which there were heavy concentrations of Jewish people. The Soviet government had approved the undertaking.

Penicillin reached the civilian market in 1944, and a starlet named Elizabeth Taylor made her debut in the film *National Velvet*. The hit songs of 1944 were "Long Ago and Far Away," "Mairzy Doats," "I'll Walk Alone," and I'll Be Seeing You." On June 6, the Western Allies invaded Nazi-occupied France from the beaches at Normandy. General Dwight D. Eisenhower was the Allied Commander and General George S. Patton commanded the armored divisions. That July, in Minneapolis, Dr. Moses Barron told the Jewish Federation that it was time to think of building a Jewish hospital.

In Poland, the war took on a terrible new dimension as the Allies arrived at Maidanek, the first of many Nazi extermination camps to be liberated.

"The worst of times was when we became aware of what was really happening in Europe," Ruth Davis recalled. "The horror of it was beyond human conception... We knew things were happening and our family sent many things over with the Army and Navy surplus. We knew of the needs but not the particulars until the camps were opened up."

1944-1945

Rabbi Gordon returned temporarily to the Adath pulpit for the High Holidays. In the September *Clarion* he expressed gratitude for the friendship and concern extended to him during his illness. And David Spivak, the Men's Club President, wrote, " For the first time in a decade, Jews the world over can look to the coming New Year with a ray of hope in their hearts. "

But that fall, on the advice of his doctors, Rabbi Gordon turned over most of his duties to an array of other rabbis.

The Board of Trustees approved a plan to require three years at Talmud Torah for boys who planned to be Bar Mitzvah.

When we were studying for our Bar Mitzvah [Norm Pink recalled] Mr. Mirviss would teach us our Maftir and Cantor Winter would teach us the Saturday morning service. We went to services from the time we were 10 or 11 years old. We had Children's Services and learned there. By the time we were 13 we could conduct the services. On the High Holidays we had Children's Services that were in the afternoon at about 2:00 p.m. Several of us, Burt Abramson, Burt Cohen, Eddie Kieffer and myself, conducted them but it was less than the young people are doing today. The liturgical part was the same as today. What was really significantly different was that we learned the Torah by rote. We weren't taught the notes of the Torah. We didn't read out of the Torah and we literally memorized our Haftorah.

In those early years, Mr. Mirviss taught the Torah readings. You studied down in the old chapel which became the storeroom behind the kitchen. He stood there and you read and he sang, and you sang and he read. You just memorized. We didn't do anything in comparison with what the young people do today as far as reading Torah. Our Torah portion was shortened and we didn't read the whole Haftorah.

I remember Rabbi Albert Gordon as a very stoic,

stern and somber individual. He had been quite ill but he was a very dynamic person. Services under him were very formal. There were assigned seats on the High Holdiays. You didn't have to look for your parents or for seats, and I still remember the people that sat around us. My dad was usually on the pulpit when he was president. I don't recall sitting with my dad very often. He was either on the pulpit or ushering so we always had an extra seat and plenty of room in our row.

The young people did not sit in the services as they do today. We would go to services and then we would hang around outside... It was really a time of socializing. There was no participation on our part in the main service.

Another thing I remember is that I had never heard maftir read on Yom Kippur by anyone else other than Jay Phillips, the leading philanthropist in our congregation and one of the leading ones in the city. Every year he was selected to read the Maftir.

Ellis Peilen recalled that "Mr. Mirviss was the one that convinced Jay Phillips to have the maftir on Yom Kippur and he trained him and worked with him... Jay has had the same aliyah since the days of Mr. Mirviss."

Norman Pink remembers Mr. Mirviss blowing the shofar. "It's nothing like we have today with Mel Sigel and Mel Orenstein and some of the other pros. There were times we barely heard the shofar blown. As he got older Mr. Mirviss just couldn't get up enough wind to blow the shofar. When he did get out a clear note, there was a lot of excitement in the congregation.

"There was a tradition on the High Holidays that the mothers use to have gardenia corsages. They would come to services with their flowers and the synagogue reeked of gardenias. On Mother's Day they had a service and every mother was given a rose.

"I remember Sukkot because that holiday was especially beautiful. During the war, we used to have a sukkah in the synagogue where the chupah would be on the bema. Ruth Stillman, Mrs. Libman and my mother would collect leaves in the vacant lots around our house and the lakes. We would cut down branches and bring them to the synagogue and decorate the sukkah. Then we would bring baskets that were decorated very beautifully and filled with food and fruit. The different classes would march up to the pulpit and deposit their baskets. It was a beautiful sight. The food was later donated to needy organizations and families."

I. D. Fink undertook the responsibility of raising the funds needed to continue with the School Building Campaign. The Men's Club fall meeting held a symposium on the subject, "Does Minneapolis Need a Jewish Hospital?"

Dorothy Gordon recalled: "Albert had been ill and had surgery at the University Hospital. One day the president of the hospital came into our room and said, 'You know, you Jewish people haven't done anything for our community.'

"Al said, 'Oh, is that so?' and he said, 'Yes. You have your Federation and you have your own funds, but we need a new hospital here. We need another hospital.'

"Well, that was enough for Al. He came out of the hospital and thought about it a great deal. Then he called Jay Phillips and said, 'Jay, this is the story I heard in my hospital room. Can you do something about it? You're the fellow to do it, and it has to be a hospital with a Jewish name.' So they had a meeting with Amos Deinard, Sam Maslon, Al and Jay. And that's the way that I recall that it was organized."

The other reason that Mount Sinai Hospital was backed so strongly by the Jewish physicians and community was that it was very difficult for Jewish doctors to get on the staff of many of the hospitals. Once Mount Sinai opened its doors, that problem disappeared.

On November 7, 1944, Franklin Delano Roosevelt became the first president to be elected to a fourth term, and another election-night party was held at the synagogue. The 14th Annual Lecture Series brought Louis Fischer, Marquis Childs, and Waldo Frank to town.

On Sunday, December 17, the synagogue observed its 60th anniversary with a dinner in the vestry rooms. Framed photographs of the four presidents who served the synagogue from 1911 until that time were presented to the congregation. They were: Joseph Schanfeld, 1911-1932; Louis B. Schwartz, 1932-1935; Morris Kantar, 1935-1943, and Dr. David Pink, the incumbent. A photograph of Rabbi Gordon was also presented.

It was announced that Adath had a membership of 355 families and also served an equal number not directly affiliated as members. There were nearly 300 pupils enrolled in its religious school and the Adath branch of the Talmud Torah had 106 pupils.

February saw two of the young lights in the Conservative Rabbinate speak at the Adath. Director of the Midwest Region of the JTS, Rabbi Stanley Rabinowitz spoke on the 16th, "To Be Or Not To Be;" and on February 23rd, Chaplain Morris Gordon of the Army Air Field at Sioux Falls, South Dakota, spoke on his experiences as a chaplain in Burma.

In March, Rabbi Albert Gordon returned to the pulpit.

Rabbi Albert Gordon, his wife, Dorothy, and family at the Adath's 60th anniversary dinner

But with V.E. Day (Victory in Europe) and spring around the corner in 1945, a sad announcement was made in the *AJW* and the *Clarion*: Two young members of the congregation, Myron Silver and Willy Billig, had been killed in action. The *Clarion* described Willy Billig as "the neighborhood refugee boy" and he had made an impression on the community. He was raising money to bring his father, mother and sister over to this country. But that was not to be.

Rabbi Gordon memorialized the passing of Willy Billig, and everybody in the congregation stood up to say Kaddish. Rabbi Gordon said, " His family had been destroyed by the Nazis. Not one of Willie's family is left to say Kaddish for him. I am sure that neither I nor the many friends whom he won by his friendly manner and gracious smile will soon forget him. "

In June of 1945 it was announced that Cantor Solomon Winter was leaving the Adath to accept a new post as cantor of the Germantown Jewish Center in Philadelphia. He had served the Adath for nine years and had also been a member of the Minneapolis Talmud Torah faculty, teaching at the Adath branch.

On April 12, 1945, Franklin Delano Roosevelt died of a cerebral hemorrhage and Harry Truman became the 33rd President of the United States. On May 8, the forces of Germany surrendered. The Allies had defeated Nazi Germany.

Three months later, the United States dropped two atomic bombs which destroyed Hiroshima and Nagasaki, forcing Japan to surrender. Albert Einstein, the Jew who had left Nazi Germany, was the mind behind the atomic formula and Dr. J. Robert Oppenheimer, physicist from the University of California, had set up the key establishment at Los Alamos, New Mexico.

World War II had come to an end.

1945-1946

In 1945 Americans were singing the hit songs, "Sentimental Journey," "It's Been a Long, Long Time," "Till the End of Time," and "It Might as Well Be Spring!"

But in the *AJW*, the Jewish year of 5705 was called: "DEATH OF NAZISM" and reported that not only Jews, but all of mankind, was turning a new page in history.

The synagogue had always been a refuge during dark days; but, in the war years from 1941 to 1945, Adath was a beehive of activity. It was no longer just a house of worship but served as a center for Red Cross activities, War Bond drives, Civilian Defense, first aid, and emergency functions that arose.

With the lifting of the clouds of the devastation of war, the first post-war congregational year began with a tremendous increase of activity.

The Amsels were welcomed into the Adath family. The 15th Annual Lecture Series was announced, and the Women's League's opening luncheon featured Mayor Hubert Humphrey. A new innovation of discussions was begun after Friday Evening Services, with Maurice Grossman presiding and Max Levinsohn, Herbert Joshua, and Louis B. Schwartz speaking on a variety of issues.

On November 26, 1945, Mr. and Mrs. Meyer D. Mirviss were given a reception honoring them on their 50th wedding anniversary. More than 1,000 people attended the party, which was sponsored by the synagogue, and it seemed as if all Minneapolis Jewry had turned out, along with a substantial part of St. Paul's, to greet the most beloved Jewish couple in the Northwest.

The couple was given a trip to Eretz Israel by their many friends in the congregation.

Council Camp was about to become a reality with plans being made for the construction of a permanent, much needed vacation camp for children in the area. People were also making pledges to the proposed Dr. George J. Gordon Memorial Talmud Torah Building. Adath and Beth El were concerned with their building funds for the new religious school addition and community house. The

A NEW ERA AT THE ADATH

On June 29, 1945, Morris Amsel of Cleveland was guest cantor for the first time, during memorial services for Pfc. Sanford Berkwitz and Pfc. Harold Benjamin who had died during the war. On August 1 he began his duties as the cantor of the Adath, and a new era began that would last for 30 years. The couple would soon become a beloved part of the synagogue family.

Cantor Amsel had an excellent musical background. Born in Czechoslovakia, for the previous 12 years he had been the cantor of Oheb Zedek congregation in Cleveland, Ohio. He and his wife, Sabine, arrived in Minneapolis with two daughters, Myrna and Joy, and two more daughters, Toby and Michelle were born.

"I knew it was a nice congregation," Amsel later recalled, "and I was willing because I figured it is a Conservative congregation and I will have an opportunity for a better living and musically it will be better too."

Sabine Amsel remembered: "From the very beginning, Rabbi Gordon was looking for a cantor to introduce congregational singing. My husband was well known in Cleveland as he had introduced singing to his congregation. They were the 'singingest' congregation in the city. That's what interested Albert Gordon."

Cantor Amsel added: "On the High Holidays I use to take off about five to ten minutes and teach the Congregation a Chasidic song. It was a highlight. When I first came, attendance at Friday evening services was very small, not over 40 to 50 people. I'll never forget how Albert Gordon told me, 'Morris, we had a cantor for nine years and he did the same Kiddush and service for the nine years. I hope when you become the cantor you can vary it and have some changes.' So I promised him and the first year I was going to have four services for the season and I did it. When I started to do the sixth and seventh he said, 'Morris, stop!' I made a bet with him, if you ever repeat a Kiddush that I sing in the congregation, I will give the congregation a year's service for nothing. I really liked it when he said, 'Stop, stop, enough!'"

Sabine Amsel: "He was so personally involved with the congregation that when Sisterhood would order something for the Gift Shop, he would examine it to see if it was exactly what they had ordered…Everything bothered him if it wasn't right. He was completely dedicated to the Adath. He was very reserved on the pulpit and in the

Cantor Morris Amsel

synagogue but at home, he was completely different and was a lot of fun. He would unwind and relax."

Rabbi David Younger: "My relationship with Cantor Amsel goes back to Cleveland, Ohio before I was Bar Mitzvah and Sabine lived across the street from our home. She was in her early twenties, and was was a very, very beautiful woman. People would walk down the street in the summertime and they would always turn back to see the beautiful young girl they saw sitting on the porch.

"Cantor Amsel, at that time was the cantor at the old synagogue in Cleveland. He came to my Bar Mitzvah. Our families were very friendly. We became even closer in Minneapolis than we had been in Cleveland. Instead of being across the street we lived upstairs from the Amsels in a duplex on Dupont and 36th. Many times we had breakfasts and lunches together when we were living in the duplex.

Ruth Davis: "I remember the first time Cantor Amsel came to Minneapolis because we had occasion to meet him at Dorothy and Al's house. A very warm, wonderful man, not at all a tempermental singer but a real cantor in every sense of the word. We felt that he was very warm, sincere and traditional with a true feeling for Judaism."

Anniversary celebrations were frequently held at the synagogue. The August 9 *AJW* carried a description of the Golden Wedding Anniversary of Daisy Gruenberg and Mayer Schwartz held at the Adath. They had been pioneer members of the congregation and had been married, August 11, 1896. Mayer had a little print shop downtown on 4th and Washington North where he set the type for the invitations, and Daisy read proof and addressed the envelopes.

The article continued:

"Thirty-one years ago Mayer was paralyzed on one side and with total loss of speech. After three months in Rochester, flat on his back and three months in bed at home, he was advised by Dr. Charles Mayo to get up and go to work.

"This time Daisy had to be the front. She met the customers and when she asked the questions about the details of the work, Mayer had to write out the answers. The Gruenbergs and the Schwartzes were the pioneer Jewish families of those days. It was a little lonesome for the 'greeners' that came in to settle in these parts. There was shul business and lodge business and there was the dancing class. That dancing was a very important feature of this early Jewish community life in Minneapolis. Come evenings, Mayer would take off his printer's apron, wash up and put on his fancy tie, snatch a bite to eat and trip it to the dancing school a block away. He loved to cheer up the young people and bring them together. Eddie figures, he overdid it, [Eddie Schwartz, the son of Mayer and Daisy] But Daisy and Mayer buckled down and worked it out together without any help from anybody."

Gimel Daled Club had a new name, the Standard Club, and it was being done over; plus, the Oak Ridge Country Club was in the process of a new building program. Rabbi Abraham E. Millgram left Minneapolis and accepted the post as head of the Department of Education of the United Synagogue of America in New York City.

New Bar Mitzvah requirements for Adath students were added (in addition to attending Talmud Torah for three years or the equivalent). They were to attend:

1)   Shabbat morning services regularly.

2)   A special class on Sunday mornings conducted by the cantor, for at least a year prior to their Bar Mitzvah so they would become familiar with the liturgy and know how to chant the service.

3)   Religious School to get to know the rabbi and the philosophy of Judaism which was taught at the Adath.

In February the rabbi reported that the Minneapolis Federation had set a goal of $1,000,000 to be raised by the Minneapolis Jewish community for overseas relief and rehabilitation work in Palestine. There was an urgent need to help the surviving Jews of Europe not only to keep their bodies alive but to give them the opportunity to re-establish themselves in Eretz Yisrael. In view of the gigantic undertaking, all community organizations were asked to refrain from engaging in any campaigns for the raising of capital funds.

This meant that Adath would be unable to carry out their plans to raise the necessary funds for the planned new school building which was so urgently needed. There would have to be a temporary lull in the Adath's campaign efforts in the interest of world Jewry.

Rabbi Gordon was chairman of the Minnesota State Drive for Overseas Needs. The reports of the people that had liberated the concentration camps were horrifying. It was now American Jewry's duty and task to save those who had survived.

Cantor Amsel was bringing a new type of participation to the congregation. "An Evening of Jewish Song" was held on Friday nights in November and February, and Sabine Amsel had immediately become an important part of the congregation.

The Conservative Congregations Women's Groups held their annual joint Seminary Tea at Adath in February which was also Jewish Music Month. The program was arranged by Betty Berkman. Cantor Amsel and Esther Rosenbloom presented liturgical music. Esther had written an article about the need to awaken Jewish potential in the folk art forms. There was no Jewish dance group for adults in Minneapolis, nor was there a group devoted to Jewish poetry or fiction, a Jewish theater or a lay singing group. She said it was time to plan a project to meet the challenge of developing the Jewish arts in Minneapolis.

Jay Phillips, president of the Minneapolis Jewish Hospital Association, was named "Man of the Year" by the Jewish War Veterans for his leadership in the raising of $1,800,000 for the construction of Mt. Sinai Hospital, which would serve patients of all races and creeds. He was cited as the outstanding Jewish citizen of Minneapolis for 1945 at a dinner on April 30 at the Nicollet Hotel. In prior years the award had been given to Arthur Brin, Joseph Schanfeld, Dr. George Gordon and I.S. Joseph, all of whom had been members of the Adath synagogue. He was called in the *AJW* "the Aladdin with the magic lamp—the lamp of *tzedekah*."

In June, the 1946-47 officers of the congregation were announced at the 62nd Annual Meeting. George Stillman was the new president; Arthur Figen, vice president; Maurice Grossman, recording secretary; Irving Naiditch, financial secretary; and Herman Neff, treasurer. New board members were: Ellis Peilen, Arnold Karlins and Harold Gottlieb.

Adath Jeshurun Sunday school teacher and Minneapolis businessman, Herbert Joshua, flew to Palestine to visit his parents and sisters in Tel Aviv. It was 36 hours to Cairo on the maiden flight of the TWA airliner, "The Sphinx." A group of diplomats and other Jewish people chartered a plane to Lydda airport. In one more hour and seven minutes they were in Eretz Yisrael.

In August, after 16 years of service as the rabbi of Adath Jeshurun Congregation, Rabbi Albert I. Gordon resigned to accept the position of Executive Director of the United Synagogue of America, with headquarters in New York City. He was to assume his new duties by November 1.

During Rabbi Gordon's years of service, the Adath grew from 85 families to 410. From 1934 to 1945 he was a labor arbitrator for 23 different industries. Among his other distinguished roles, he served as president of the Minneapolis Federation for Jewish Service, president of the Minneapolis Zionist District, president of the Minneapolis Kashruth Council, and a vice president of B'nai B'rith Lodge No.217. He had been an active member of the Minneapolis Round Table of the National Conference of Christians and Jews and served as a member of the boards of the Minneapolis Talmud Torah, Jewish Family Service Society, and numerous other organizations including the newly organized Mount Sinai Hospital.

He also served as a member of the Advisory Council of the Minneapolis Federal Housing Project and the National Youth Administration. He was a contributing editor to the *AJW* and had written articles for various publications including *Jewish Social Studies* and *The Reconstructionist*.

During his years of service to Adath, the congregation's debts were paid off and a constructive program was planned and carried out. He had started the famous Adath Lecture Series in 1931.

When Rabbi Gordon assumed his duties as United Synagogue of America Executive Director, he was to be in charge of all phases of the congregational life of Conservative congregations throughout the country. Upon leaving he told his congregants: "It is only because the post to which I am going offers such a tremendous challenge and so great an opportunity for constructive and creative work on behalf of all of the Conservative congregations of the United States and Canada that I felt obliged to accept this new responsibility. I would say 'l'hitraot,' I shall see you all again, many times in the years to come."

1945-1946

During the first year of peace, a Jewish research institute released a grim report disclosing that 60% of the total Jewish population in Europe had been murdered by the Axis, not including the military casualties among the Jews. A large number of those Jews who *had* survived were homeless, and many had little desire to return to the cities where they had recently escaped extermination. The majority wanted to go to Palestine.

But the Holy Land was in turmoil. In Palestine, curfews were imposed upon the *Yishuv* and there was brutal deportation of survivors of Nazism's concentration camps from Palestine to British detention camps in Cyprus. British troops had been ordered to use all devices in their hunt for "illegal" immigrants and "illegal" weapons while the navy patrolled the Mediterranean to run down wretched vessels carrying undernourished and sick survivors of concentration camps.

In October, 1946, there was a reprint in the *Minneapolis Star* of the Carey McWilliams article published in *Common Ground*, in which Minneapolis was called the capital of anti-Semitism in America. It brought from Rabbi David Aronson an editorial challenge to the general community: "Now that you've been publicly told of the situation, what are you going to do about correcting it?"

That same October, Jay Phillips became chairman of the committee to secure a new rabbi for the Adath. A farewell reception was held at the synagogue to honor Rabbi and Mrs. Gordon on October 29.

Following the reception, Rabbi Gordon sent the following letter to George Stillman, president of the congregation: "Dorothy and I were deeply moved by the fine outpouring of sentiment at the reception of last night. We are of course deeply grateful to you and to the congregation, both for the gift as well as for the effort taken to make the affair so beautiful."

October 25, 1946, Rabbi Albert I. Gordon delivered his final sermon as rabbi of the Adath in Minneapolis, but on November 29 he returned for a visit with his family and spoke once again from the Adath pulpit. On that occasion he said:"I want you to know that in my travels I found that Cantor Amsel is doing things with the Adath that it will take the rest of the country another ten years to catch up to.'"

On November 8, representatives of the Jewish community met with experts to help plan a community self-survey under the auspices of Mayor Hubert H. Humphrey's Council on Human Relations.

During December Rabbi Joseph Gerstein, Harold J. Goldenberg and Rabbi Moshe Goldblum were guest speakers. First Lieutenant Moshe Goldblum, Army chaplain, and the grandson of Adath founder Kive Goldblum, delivered a dramatic and inspiring post-Chanukah sermon and then spoke informally on the Talmud Torah fundraising campaign. He said, "I would not be standing before you tonight if it were not for the Minneapolis Talmud Torah. Everything I am today I owe to our Talmud Torah. It is the finest school of its kind in America. Its graduates are among the finest Jews, rabbis and teachers in America."

(Top) Rabbi Gordon leads an adult discussion group,
featured in *Look* Magazine; (Above) Rabbi Gordon in
uniform; (Right), Rabbi Gordon and Cantor Amsel at
Leland Fleischer's Bar Mitzvah

6
THE RABBI MORRIS GORDON YEARS
(1947 – 1952)

Rabbi Morris Gordon arrived at the Adath as a World War II hero, just when the returning G.I.s were getting married and the Baby Boom began. He influenced many programs, including the newly formed Married Couple's League, and introduced the Hebrew language to the nursery school. When Israel became a state, his enthusiasm was contagious. The membership more than doubled during his stay, and he helped accelerate the drive for the synagogue educational addition. Also among his accomplishments was a national first: the High Holiday Double Service, for which the congregation received a Solomon Schechter Award.

Radar was being used in airplanes, Princess Elizabeth married Prince Phillip, and designer Christian Dior's "New Look" sent hemlines plunging. The dog, Lassie, had a radio show, Alec Guiness starred in *Richard II*, and Albert Schweitzer was at his hospital in Africa.

A number of guest speakers occupied the pulpit at Adath Jeshurun during the early months of 1947, including Rabbi Gerstein, the well-known author and lecturer Oscar Leonard, and from Minneapolis, Reverend Carl Zietlow and Dr. Kalman Friedman, rabbi of Tifereth B'nai Jacob. But the first sermon of 1947 was given on January 3 by Rabbi Morris Gordon, from Temple Anshe Emeth in Youngstown, Ohio. And on March 13, President George Stillman made the announcement that Rabbi Morris Gordon (no relation to Adath's previous rabbi, Albert Gordon) would arrive in late spring to become the rabbi at Adath Jeshurun.

Born in the Bronx, Morris Gordon grew up in Albany, New York, in a home where only Hebrew was spoken. His father, Isaac, was the principal of Hebrew Education in Albany, and insisted on the use of Hebrew in the family home.

The family later moved to New York City and Morris continued up the academic ladder as an honors graduate at City College of New York and the Teachers Institute of Yeshiva University, where he was the youngest graduate in his class. In college he played varsity basketball for Yeshiva and City College, and earned varsity letters in basketball, tennis, and baseball at both CCNY and Columbia University, where he received his Master's Degree. Ordained as Rabbi with Distinction from the Jewish Theological Seminary in 1940, he also received awards for Hebrew literature, public speaking and *chazanut* (cantorial music).

Rabbi Gordon's first pulpit was at a millinery center in the garment district in downtown New York where he converted a small kaddish temple over a candy store to a modern three-story, air-conditioned, well-attended synagogue. His early efforts led to the establishment of a number of successful synagogues in New York's commercial district. After a year at Temple Zion in the Bronx, he went to Temple Anshe Emeth in Ohio.

The following year he joined the United States Air Force as a chaplain and served in the African and South Asian theaters of war. He was the first chaplain to go up the Burma Road under sniper attack. He ministered to the needs of Catholics, Protestants, and Jews along that dangerous route, and later received the Bronze Star and three decorations for service beyond the call of duty. He was the only chaplain to receive the Chinese Medal of Honor, awarded personally by Madame Chiang Kai-Shek in

Morris Gordon (left) and two buddies in Burma.

Peking for his service with the Flying Tigers under General Chennault.

Following World War II he returned to his pulpit in Youngstown, where he also was appointed State Chaplain of the Reserved Officers Association.

Prior to his speaking engagement at the Adath in January of 1947, Rabbi Gordon had spoken to the congregation in 1945 while still in the service. When he recieved the call to become rabbi at the Adath, he was reluctant to accept at first. "I had just returned from overseas and to the Youngstown congregation," he later recalled. "My mind wasn't set to go elsewhere. But, the *shidduch* with the Adath had a providential push because we all liked each other very much. A few months later I accepted the call."

The first issue of the the religious school newspaper, *Sunday Morning Post*, appeared on January 19, 1947. In one early issue Judy Silverman described the project C.A.R.E. effort on the part of the Girl Scout troop to raise money to send food overseas to a Jewish family. The girls also sent "friendship bags" to Girl Scouts in Holland.

On Tu B' Shevat, Jewish Arbor Day, the Sunday school classes planted a hundred trees in honor of Florence Kunian, the Minneapolis Hadassah President. The goal that year was to buy 100 trees honoring Dr. Moses and Leah Barron. I.S. Joseph, president of the Minneapolis Federation for Jewish Service, had announced in January that a Jewish National Fund Forest in Palestine had been named for the Barrons.

On January 29, Dr. Theodore Bramdel, professor of educational philosophy at the University of Minnesota, spoke on "The Atomic Age—Education's Final Chance." In February the Women's League's held a Food Bazaar and donated the proceeds to a fund for improving the synagogue's kitchen facilities. At the Talmud Torah dinner, James Gross, Harvey Abrams and Sandra Lieberman of the Adath branch said their pieces well, although Sandra had to be reassured by her mother, Mrs. Harold [Adelle] Lieberman, who told her, "These people are all your friends, honey."

A new radio program sponsored by the Jewish Theological Seminary, *The Eternal Light*, began airing on Sunday mornings. And on March 27 Rabbi David Aronson was the guest speaker at Adath high school graduation exercises. The graduates that year were Howard Karon, Edward Kieffer, Edith Bloch, Ruth Rosen, Burton Cohen, and Charles Frisch.

An article on Adath Jeshurun appeared in the *American Jewish World* on March 14, reviewing the 35 years since the inception of the weekly paper. It noted that the Adath planned to expand its facilities, but found it difficult to gather a daily minyan. "It is even difficult to gather a minyan for Saturday morning," the article went on. "Thirty-five years ago a minyan was a matter of course. That difference, in itself, tells a story of the evolution of the Jewish community. Jewish divorce, once a rarity, now occasionally bobs up. Intermarriage, likewise once a rarity, is not quite so rare now." In short, the Jewish community had become integrated into the American way of life.

At Passover, the religious school featured a model seder and for the first time, the Adath Women's League honored mothers at an annual mother-daughter dinner.

By May 16, Rabbi Morris Gordon had arrived and he took part in confirmation exercises on the following Sunday. In its June 6 issue the *American Jewish World* welcomed Rabbi Gordon and his wife, going on to state:

"Adath Jeshurun is among the larger congregations in the country. Located in the center of a large and growing Jewish population, its rabbi will have ample opportunity for his services. But a rabbi in Minneapolis must serve more than his congregation. The Jewish communal organizations are well advanced, and rabbis serve on practically all committees where they can make a distinct contribution. There are many civic areas where the leadership of rabbis is called for. We are confident that Rabbi Gordon's background, his native ability, his experiences as rabbi in Youngstown and as chaplain in the U.S. Army, have well qualified him for these tasks."

Not long afterward, Rabbi Morris and his wife, Francis, attended their first congregation dinner (the Adath's 63rd) and heard speeches by George Stillman, president,

Archie Miller, Men's Club president, and Marion Figen, Women's League president.

At the annual meeting the Board of Trustees presented a written statement of the congregation's finances for the first time, and announced that it had been operating on a budget for some years. The 1946-47 budget was $32,382, or $71.17 for each of the 455 members.

That June the Men's Club sponsored its Third Annual Fish and Fun Trip at the new Lakeside Inn on Lake Mille Lacs. It cost $5 for sleeping quarters and extras with the food ala carte.

George Stillman

At the Board of Trustees meeting in July the trustees considered a plan to eliminate reserved seats at High Holy Days services. It was decided, instead, to hold an auxiliary service. A letter was sent to congregants announcing that due to the growing size of the congregation, it would not be possible to seat everyone in the main auditorium. However, a "very beautiful High Holy Day Service" would be led by Samuel Mirviss in the vestry rooms. Sammy had returned from World War II, where he had commanded a fighting craft in the Pacific. Prior to entering the service his tenor voice had brought him screen and radio fame. Rabbi M. Gordon would deliver the sermons. The new services were intended for the younger married group and teenage members. It was announced that Sheldon Gensler would read the Torah and lead the English readings and Dr. Reuben Berman would blow the shofar.

Rabbi Albert I. Gordon returned to Minneapolis that summer for a vacation. In an interview he gave to Janet F. Kroll for the *AJW*, he said:

"There is something about Minneapolis...it's unique... even though St. Paul does have the edge on us in having the oldest congregation in the Upper Midwest (Mount Zion Temple)."

Rabbi Gordon had been working on a book about Minneapolis Jewry, *Jews in Transition*, for his doctorate, and during his visit he took the opportunity to make inquiries and update some of the information he had collected during his tenure at Adath Jeshurun.

"My book is not so much the story of the Jewish community in Minneapolis," Gordon told Kroll, "as the story

of certain changes over a number of decades. I am convinced now, as I was before, that Minneapolis is a unique community, particularly in a sense of cohesiveness. It's not splintered like some of the others that I have visited. There is a very healthy relationship between the rabbis and community, between the various rabbis to each other, and between the rabbis and non-Jewish clergy. It's not flashy like Los Angeles, nor does it have the pace of New York, but I like it."

That same summer Rabbi Schwartz, who had served at Adath from 1927 to 1929, traveled to Zurich to represent the Zionist Organization of Canada at a meeting of the Actions Committee of the World Zionist Organization.

1947-1948

In the fall of 1947, the United Jewish Appeal launched the greatest philanthropic drive in American history, and a special session of the United Nations was held about Palestine. A Supplies for Overseas Survivors (SOS) drive was staged in Minneapolis to gather supplies to ease the suffering of 250,000 Jews in Europe's displaced persons camps, and to aid the million and more survivors seeking to rebuild their shattered lives in Europe.

That same fall, Rabbi Morris Gordon instituted the first Hebrew High School class on Sunday mornings. Among the guest speakers were I. S. Joseph and Guita Gordon.

The first Zionist camp in the Northwest, Herzl Camp, which had opened the previous year, purchased a new site on Devil's Lake near Webster, Wisconsin. Rabbi Gordon, who had visited the camp during the summer as a guest of its director, Rabbi Walter Plaut, spoke at the dedication dinner.

The new organ was dedicated on October 10 at a special service led by Cantor Morris Amsel and the choir, with Esther Rosenbloom at the organ. Esther's childhood friend, Mrs. Leon (Pearl) Knight, had donated the money for the organ, in memory of her mother, Amelia Kleckner, and she returned to Minneapolis from Youngstown, Ohio, for the ceremony.

Cantor Morris Amsel recalled that both Albert and Morris Gordon had been instrumental in getting a better organ. "Before then we had a little tiny box. Esther Rosenbloom wrote the music for the cantatas and I used to conduct them."

"In the beginning the choir stood around Morris on the pulpit," Cantor Amsel's wife Sabine recalled, "until Ruth Libman said one time, 'You know, we should really change that. It looks bad with their backs to us. Isn't

Ruth Davis and Girl Scouts at the presentation of a Swiss flag by the Minneapolis Consul

there some way we could get the choir upstairs? You would need a choir director.'" At that time the choir consisted of Evelyn Siegel, Maxine Siegel, Joseph Burnstein, Phyllis Bearmon, Charlotte Miller, Arnold Weisman, and Jerome Lane.

The 1947-48 lecture series was devoted, for the first time, to Jewish artists, rather than to outstanding thinkers and lecturers.

The Adath congregation now included nearly 500 members. The educational program included a religious school, kindergarten through high school age with 310 children enrolled, and Talmud Torah classes with 85 enrolled. For those who did not attend Talmud Torah, special Hebrew classes were conducted Tuesdays, Saturdays and Sundays, with an emphasis on Jewish history, customs, and ceremonies. Due to increased enrollment and lack of classroom facilities at Adath, classes were held Sunday mornings at Calhoun School.

Prior to World War II, the Adath had prided itself on having one of the outstanding youth organizations in the Twin Cities, and it now began to reorganize its programs. The Boy Scout Troop 108 was revitalized and a new Cub Scout pack was started. The congregation continued to sponsor a Girl Scout troop, a social Junior Supper Group for teenagers, and the Young People's League, which had been reorganized the previous year. The league, which was composed of singles and married couples ages 18-35, held a series of programs and activities to make it easier for the many young people who had recently returned from military service to meet new people, see old friends, and keep up with the happenings of the community.

Joseph Gitlin, chairman of the youth activities committee, appointed S. Louis Shore as advisor to the Young People's League. Sheldon Gensler was director of youth activities. Harold Rifkin was YPL president. Plans for a Hebrew pre-kindergarten were being discussed, and the Young People's League's first project was to outfit and guide a day nursery for 3-to-5 year olds. Their first social event, a Fall Frolic, featured dinner, dancing and entertainment.

The Artists' Series opening was a joint recital by soprano Margerite Kozenn and pianist Julius Chajes, in a repertoire of traditional Chassidic, Yiddish and modern Palestinian selections. The other artists that year were: November 30, Irving Davidson, the "Jewish Ripley;" January 4, 1948, Sidor Belarsky, world renowned opera singer, "A New Repertoire from Palestine;" and February 1, Rabbi James G. Heller, music critic and lecturer, "What is Jewish Music?"

Rabbi Gordon was the principal speaker at the opening session of the Women's League Midwest Convention held that November in Kansas City.

On November 7, funeral services were held at the Adath for pioneer Adath member and Minneapolis civic and business leader, Arthur Brin. At Sabbath services that evening, the Armistice Day Service sermon was "Memorial Tribute," for the servicemen who had given their lives for their country. All veterans had been invited to attend, and the Jewish War Veterans Ladies Auxiliary catered the reception.

In November, an article by Meyer Levin appeared in the *American Jewish World* about conveying Jewish families on the underground route to Palestine. He said it was like slipping through enemy lines in wartime. The outstanding motion picture of 1947, voted by the New York Film Critics Circle, was *Gentleman's Agreement* with Gregory Peck, in which for the first time aspects of anti-Semitism in America were dealt with in a film.

At its November meeting, the Board of Trustees took up the issue of building a new religious school building to accommodate the synagogue's expanding educational programs. It was hoped that construction could begin the following year.

During the 1940s, Dorothy Weiner was religious school chairman and Women's League representative. She recalled: "My responsibilities included the registration of students, office work, seeing decorations were made for the various holidays and that they were observed, having the sukkah put up, and seeing to the teachers' salaries. Members did not have to pay for their children to attend religious school but non-members had to pay $25. There were some families who could not afford to send their children, but I saw to it that they could attend. During Rabbi Morris Gordon's time the child that wrote the best essay got the floral offering at confirmation and the second best got the final prayer. I felt Rabbi Gordon was gutsy."

The year 1948 was one of great promise, according to the editors of the *American Jewish World*, who expressed the hope that in the coming months a new Jewish state would be formally established in Palestine, and the United States would enact legislation allowing many of Europe's Jews to resettle here. They also looked forward to the successful completion of the $250,000,000 campaign of the United Jewish Appeal and the start of construction of the new Mount Sinai Hospital in Minneapolis.

That spring Rabbi Gordon attended a Leader Training Fellowship (LTF) convention in Chicago. Charles Frisch, who also attended, later recalled: "The purpose of the conference was to get us and other young people interested so we would start groups in our cities. LTF was to provide future leadership for the Jewish community."

According to Norman Pink, "LTF started as a select group. Rabbi Morris Gordon, in conjunction with Rabbi Cohen and Rabbi Aronson, selected young people that were interested in Judaism. We would meet one Thursday a month at a different congregation in study groups and for discussion. Then we had dinner and the *birkat* and after we would meet until 8:00. Every Saturday afternoon Rabbi Aronson would invite the same group for a luncheon or a snack and discussion group."

Through such meetings, as well as conferences and summer workshops, members of LTF began to develop a deeper love for Judaism and took a more active role in organizing dancing groups and junior congregations.

There were plenty of youth-oriented activities at Adath Jeshurun—AZA, Scout Sabbath, Young Judea Benefit Dance, Bar Mitzvah Brotherhood, children attending Shalosh Se'udoth with a Havdalah service on Saturday afternoons, Senior High Discussion Group, and Basketball Leagues (which played in schools and churches). Rabbi Gordon played basketball with one of the groups at Southwest High School each week.

Adath's basketball team: (Front, left to right) Stanley Schweitzer, Marshall Miller, Marv Sternberg , Bruce Levine, Allan Goldberg; (standing, left to right) Amos Rosenbloom (coach), Stanley Goldberg, Mert Cherny, Neil Naftalin, Bill Lifson.

"What I liked about Rabbi M. Gordon," Saul Meyers remarked, "were the programs that he brought in. We had some very exciting ones and he was excellent. Morris Gordon got the kids involved. AZA used to meet in homes. We felt the kids should meet in the synagogues and temples where they could learn a little bit of religion. Rabbi Aronson agreed and then we got Temple to give us one night. When we came to the Adath, Morris Gordon said, 'You can have every night except Friday and you can have as many groups as you want.' That guy was all for the kids."

Rabbi Morris Gordon: "The Saturday evening service was not being well attended, so I decided to have a Havdalah program. The evening service with Havdalah had a very magical touch to it...I went to the teachers and said, 'I'm going to invite your class Saturday night, November 10, to the synagogue. The topic for this year is 'the Sabbath.' I want your youngsters to learn something extra-curricular about the Sabbath—a poem, a song, a dance.' Then I went to the USY and said, 'We want you to supply us leaders for one hour of just pure fun. I want USY to be part of it.' Then

I went to to the Men's Club and asked them to supply the money and to the Women's League and asked them to serve a hot dinner. Nothing was too good for our youngsters.

"The Havdalah program was just for Adath but kids from all over the city started to come. After the University of Minnesota football game you'd find cars coming to the Adath and we would have 250 to 300 people every Saturday night."

An Adath Jeshurun Forest was planted in Palestine with the purchase of 200 trees by the children of the congregation. Adath branch Talmud Torah teacher, Haim Bernstein from Palestine, drew a hugh tree which had 200 blossoms representing the children's contributions in memory of Rabbi Morris Gordon's father, who had died at the end of 1947.

At the Talmud Torah's first consecration service in February, Cantor Morris Amsel sang a memorable duet, "V'Shomru," with his daughter Myrna, aged 11. Rabbi Gordon later confessed, "One of the things that pulled me into the heart of this congregation was to hear that lovely little voice of Myrna from up there (in the choir loft), harmonizing with her father on the pulpit. It was a tingling, ringing, singing spiritual sensation."

Norman Pink was also impressed with Amsel's voice: "It was fun to be in the congregation when Cantor Amsel and Morris Gordon were on the pulpit. The voice that Cantor Amsel brought the congregation was unbelievable. People would put down their prayer books and they would be mesmerized by his singing. He knew that, too, and could 'milk' a note to its fullest. He was a real showman."

Rabbi Morris Gordon was formally installed as Adath Jeshurun's spiritual leader on March 5. An impressive array of dignitaries attended the dinner the next day, including Minnesota Governor Luther W. Youngdahl, Minneapolis Mayor Hubert H. Humphrey, Reuben K. Youngdahl, Pastor of Mount Olivet Lutheran Church, Rev. James H. Moynihan, Pastor of Church of the Incarnation, and Amos S. Deinard, representing the Jewish community. Rabbi David Aronson, vice president of the Rabbinical Assembly of America, gave the installation address.

Few details have survived regarding the first Midwest Jewish Youth Conference, though this group later evolved into the first USY (United Synagogue Youth) group in the nation. The youth groups of Adath, Beth El and Tifereth B'nai Jacob synagogues, Minneapolis, and Temple of Aaron, St. Paul, organized the conference, and invited representatives from chapters in Duluth, Tulsa, Omaha, Kansas City, Sioux Falls, and Lincoln to attend.

Shirley (Mrs. Kassel) Abelson later emphasized that the Midwest branch of Women's League playedd an important role in the formation of USY. "Through Lee (Mrs. Maurice) Gordon who was president of the Midwest branch at the time, and the other officers, they passed a resolution that everyone in the Midwest branch would pay $.25 per capita to be used for USY. This was the way the branch youth commission was funded…It's fine to start an organization but in order to have any kind of a branch organization one must have the funding."

Rabbi Kassel Abelson recalled that he had just arrived in town when the first conference was taking place. He noted that the different synagogue youth groups were called Youth Canteens at the time and had no formal structure or organization. "When we came [to Minneapolis] Shirley and I talked at length with Rabbi and Bertha [Aronson]. They had dreamed of starting a youth movement but had no idea how to do it, how to proceed. Shirley and I began to work with our own youth. We quickly saw that youth had to have a sense of being part of a larger group. You couldn't organize in one synagogue alone, so we set about organizing the other Conservative congregations. But since kids went with each other and were friends with each other, just the Conservative congregations would not serve at that point. We also spoke to our colleagues in the Orthodox and Reform congregations, and they, too, agreed that there was a need for a youth movement. Hence movements got started virtually simultaneously in all congregations in Minneapolis and in St. Paul."

That year, Fanny Burnstein read her sister-in-law Sophie Burnstein's script, "A Woman's Place In the Synagogue." It started out: "Since time immemorial the Jewish woman has been charged with the responsibility for the perpetuation of Judaism. You may ask, 'How can mere woman fulfill this role, when within the traditional faith of Israel she is not formally counted in the congregation?'"

The program emphasized the woman's role in molding the family into the Jewish pattern, but concluded that women must first attain self-fulfillment as enlightened, observant Jews.

According to Lil Krelitz Kaplan, it was during Rabbi Morris Gordon's tenure that women started becoming more active in the religious life of the synagogue. "At first the elders of the congregation didn't like it, but like everything else, they became accustomed to it. When it included a member of their family, they were happy. That's how it

The Jewish refugee ship "Pan-York," carrying new citizens to the recently established State of Israel, docks at Haifa. The ship sailed from southern Europe to Israel, via Cyprus, landing in Haifa on, July 9, 1948. (National Archives)

grew and I think it was a wonderful idea. Why should we be in the background?"

The prizes on offer at the Men's Club Bingo party that spring reflected a new-found post-war prosperity after years of scarcity. They included a Philco Deepfreeze, Launderall Automatic Washer, Martin Outboard Motor, Glad-Iron Automatic Ironer, Stewart Warner FM-AM Radio Phono, and Cory Coffee Makers, Toasters and Presto Cookers.

On May 14, 1948, the State of Israel was proclaimed by the Palestine Jewish authorities, one day before Great Britain relinquished control. The previous year the United Kingdom had acknowledged its inability to implement the mandate it had endorsed in 1920 acknowledging its responsibility to implement the Balfour Declaration. In response to this abdication of responsibility, the United Nations General Assembly had established a special committee to inquire into the question, and the committee, in turn, had recommended the establishment, in Palestine, of both a Jewish and an Arab state. The State of Israel was proclaimed and recognized in the United Nations but the Arab armies invaded Israel instead of developing their own state.

In Minneapolis a solemn two-day observance signaled the birth of the new Jewish state. The Rabbinical Associa-

tion called upon the Jewish people of Minnesota to assemble in their synagogues on the Sabbath, May 14 and 15, and to congregate at Adath Jeshurun on that Sunday "...to express our encouragement and support in words of prayer and praise for that determined band of fighting dreamers which has dared to raise its ensign of faith in a moment of fear; its banner of God in days of godlessness; its call to freedom in the midst of force."

The rabbis called upon the American Congress to recognize the independence of the new state. The program for the "City-Wide Celebration for the Rebirth of the Jewish People" consisted of the audience singing "America"; opening remarks by Leo Gross; Hadassah greetings by Mrs. I. C. Marks; an address by Ezekiel Leiken, "New Paths for Zion"; the singing of Israeli songs; a movie, *House in the Desert*; and a rededication service led by Rabbi Morris Gordon and Cantor Morris Amsel.

Rabbi Gordon later recalled, "We had a tremendous celebration for a whole week. There was music, songs, Israeli dances and an Eternal Light Program for Israel and hundreds of youngsters. It was a very exciting weekend. We filled the synagogue and then moved outside and went dancing in the streets. That's how we celebrated the creation of the State of Israel!

"We had some plans for it but it was almost a spontaneous eruption of young people coming from all over to celebrate with us...there was a certain sense of pride, a sense of dignity, of wanting to know more about Israel. I feel that the whole concept of the Israeli state suddenly made them feel that they were not a classless people in the state of humanity. The land of the Bible and the land to which the prophets returned. It was a tremendously climactic experience."

An article in *Time* magazine offered this perspective: "After 2,000 years of exile, the Jews had regained their homeland. The birth of Israel arose from the ancient aspiration, the hope of an ingathering after the long centuries of the Diaspora...After the terrible revelations of the Nazi Holocaust, the impulse was to create, to will a Jewish state into being in the desert."

The author went on to note that many European Jews arrived in Palestine "as if they had come to colonize the moon." It's early history had been one of strife, as the visions of Israelis and Palestinians collided. But recent events had been exciting and revolutionary.

"Unhindered now by the British, the refugee ship, Andria, brought 360 immigrants into Haifa. Other ships brought war supplies to Tel Aviv. The new government announced its adherence to the principles of the United Nations Charter. At 21 minutes past midnight, Palestine time, President Harry Truman announced: 'The U.S. Government recognizes the provisional government as the de facto authority of the new State of Israel.'"

Not all observers were so eager to recognize the new state. Israel's neighbors in Transjordan, Egypt, Syria and Lebanon wasted little time before sending troops across the border to sieze and occupy villages, while Egyptian planes began to strafe Tel Aviv.

That spring the Adath SOS Committee reported remarkable success in shipping more than 2,000 tons of medical and dental supplies to the displaced persons camps in Europe. And in June the Minneapolis Talmud Torah opened a new branch in St. Louis Park after having been temporarily housed at Lenox School.

In mid-June Golda (Meir) Meyerson spoke in the Twin Cities at mass meetings held by the United Jewish Appeal. She was the only woman cabinet member of the new state.

In the June 25 issue of the *American Jewish World*, Adath Talmud Torah teacher Sol Kahz told the story of the origin of the Haganah, the Israeli army. His story went back to 1914 when, at the age of 15, he was a student at the Teachers' Hebrew Seminary in Jerusalem. When the war broke out he joined the Jewish Legionnaires fighting to free their homeland from the rule of the Turks. He was assigned to the Mule Corps, which meant that he loaded the mules with petrol, cans of water, ammunition and other supplies. This first Judean battalion later became the nucleus of the Haganah.

At the 64th Annual Congregation Meeting, Louis M. Cohen was elected president. Prior to holding this position, Cohen had served on numerous committees, and had chaired the dues committee for many years. "We were always short of money," he recalled, "and there were always people who weren't paying enough for their dues. It was a nasty job. We made numerous enemies but we were very firm because we knew we needed the money and the people could afford to pay. This experience got me to know the congregation better and to appreciate the complex and numerous problems."

That summer Camp Adath, a day camp sponsored by the synagogue, opened. Campers received daily swimming instruction at Lake Calhoun's main beach, went on picnics, visited farms, made handicraft items, and engaged in other camp activities. City buses were used to provide transportation. More than 100 children attended. Lenny Neiman was camp director with the help of Mickey Nathenson, Louise Lasker, Marv Kahner, Merle Ann Epstein, and Sissy Beugen.

Merle Ann (Epstein) Kremen recalled: "All of us had been counselors at Council Camp the summer before. Lenny Neiman was a real organizer and I enjoyed being a counselor under him. He had such rapport with the children and teenagers. I taught dramatics."

At the Annual Adath Synagogue Picnic on Sunday, July 11, synagogue members bid farewell to Arthur and Marian Figen and their family, who were moving to California.

1948-1949

The religious school continued to hold classes at Calhoun School due to a shortage of space in the synagogue. Fanny Brin chaired an essay contest on the United Nations for Sunday School children, and the Adath Hebrew preschool opened in October. The idea for this school had come orignally from the Young People's League (YPL), but a congregational committee had been directing policy and supplying the backing. The YPL Nursery School Board, with Rabbi Gordon, now began to supervise the school's activities, map the educational program, grant scholarships and originate ideas for raising funds to supplement tuition payments by pupils' parents. The Adath Jeshurun Nursery School was the first of its kind in the Upper Midwest to emphasize teaching Hebrew. Dr. Louis Sher was elected chairman of the nursery school board.

According to Rabbi Gordon, the rationale behind teaching children Hebrew so early was to "evoke a pleasant emotional response in the child to his entire heritage, so that years later, he can establish a happy relationship to the Hebrew words and prayers he hears in the synagogue." Hiam Bernstein and his sister, Shoshana Wolf, both from Palestine, were the nursery school instructors. They would speak in Hebrew and English to the children so the children would become bilingual without knowing it. The school was open to South Minneapolis and St. Louis Park children, 3 to 5 years old, and operated from 9:00 to noon, Mondays through Fridays.

The Young People's League sponsored a dance at the Calhoun Beach Club to raise funds for the school. Irving Brand, who chaired the dance preparations, later recalled,

"We had a tremendous turnout. The Young People's League was very active with monthly meetings and study groups." At the time, Brand was teaching in the religious school.

The Twin Cities Youth Congregation held a basket social in October at Adath, with the girls bringing decorated basket lunches that the boys bid for. Jeans were the common mode of dress.

The purpose of this organization, as stated in a brochure of the time, was to "create a wholesome Jewish personality—spiritually, culturally and socially," through fellowship, friendship, and fun, and to nurture connections between young American Jews and Jews in Europe and Israel. The organization sponsored dances, Sukkot barn dances, Chanukah latke parties and sleigh rides, Purim parties, matzoh balls, Lag B'omer picnics, wiener roasts, and basketball and baseball games.

That fall the Minnesota Rabbinical Association made the historic ruling that limited Jewish weddings to homes and synagogues. The ceremony would no longer be allowed in hotels or public places.

In the November, 1948, United States elections, Harry S. Truman was elected president. Bell Telephone Laboratories demonstrated a small, simple device called a "transistor." A novel about World War II, *The Naked and the Dead* by Norman Mailer came out, and in Israel the young American conductor, Leonard Bernstein, gave a special concert during the battle for Jerusalem.

On November 19, 1948, Minneapolis Mayor Hubert H. Humphrey, United States Senator-Elect of Minnesota, received a copy of Israel's Declaration of Independence from Rabbis David Aronson and Morris Gordon, in recognition of his efforts on behalf of the new Jewish state.

Rabbi Gordon contributed an essay on the theme "Why a Jewish Artist Series?" to the 96-page program book printed for the "Cultural Arts in Jewish Life" series. It read, in part:

"...Our fathers knew the value of giving aesthetic expression to emotional experience. They emphasized the *hiddur mitzvah*, the embellishment of the customs and ceremonials. They beautified the bema. They delicately wrought the silver decorations of the sacred scrolls. They artistically wove the *parohet* and the tapestry to adorn the Holy Ark. They graced their homes with exquisite Sabbath lamps, kiddush cups, golden *mezuzahs*, and silvery spired havdalah ornaments. Tall, stately books of the Talmud and Midrash lined the *mizrach* wall. We do not know of any great Jewish artists in the Middle Ages, yet, the beauty of Jewish art gave an aesthetic touch to every home and synagogue.

"Today we have outstanding Jewish artists but no Jewish art....Why is it that at the very time when the cultural horizons of the Jew are broadest, when there is a deeper interest in art than in most generations of the Jews who preceded us; that at this very time in our history there is a dearth of Jewish art?..."

The answer he gave was that Jews no longer take much of an interest in specifically Jewish art forms. The purpose of the Artist Series at Adath Jeshurun was to revive that Jewish aesthetic as a means of insuring the future of Jewish artistic expression.

The program book was dedicated to M. D. Mirviss, "whose serene, sweet and spiritual personality, graced 41 years of endless endeavors on behalf of our synagogue and our community...He has been an integral part of the Adath Jeshurun since 1907 when he was not only the sexton, but rabbi, cantor and even janitor."

In December the Jewish National Fund Dinner also honored Mr. Mirviss, the beloved "Mr. Adath Jeshurun," with a grove of trees in Israel. $1,500 was contributed for 75 trees purchased by the religious school children. Mrs. Mirviss thanked the crowd on behalf of her husband who was convalescing at his home from a lengthy illness. She said in Yiddish that in her opinion, "The Jewish people should plant trees in Israel, not in sorrow, but only for *simchas*."

That evening Rabbi Morris Gordon credited Mr. Mirviss with fostering a rare spirit of comeraderie on the pulpit between rabbi, cantor, and sexton, which spilled over into a feeling of harmony within the congregation itself. "His kindliness, compassion, gentle stroking, his touches, and real *yiddishkeit* were a wonder to behold."

On the evening of December 3, 1948, the congregation welcomed Adath Jeshurun's first executive director, Abraham Kastenbaum, and his wife, Naomi. Rabbi Gordon spoke on "Behind the Synagogue." A reception for the Kastenbaums followed the service.

Abe "Dutch" Kastenbaum would become not only the first executive director at the Adath, but also the director of youth activities. There were no exact working hours for the job. It depended on the type of work that was needed. The salary was $5,000 for the year. Kastenbaum was in charge of secretarial and janitorial help, building maintenance, and the synagogue calendar, which entailed scheduling events and seeing that the requisite rooms were made ready for them. He was also in charge of contacting new members, following up on negligent dues, and seeing to synagogue publicity in the local newspapers, the *American Jewish World*, and the *Clarion*.

As youth director, Kastenbaum was in charge of all youth organizations in the synagogue, including athletic programs, social programs and entertainment, and youth-oriented discussion and study groups. His miscellaneous duties would include helping to carry through the various synagogue projects, such as Shalosh Seudot, Stay-at-Home camp, and the Bar/Bat Mitzvah Minyannaires.

The Minyannaires was a new group established to acquaint the young people with the meaning of Bar and Bat Mitzvah ceremonies. It was intended for boys and girls who were at least 12½ years old.

Previous to coming to Adath, "Dutch" was associated with leading Jewish communal agencies in the field of Jewish social service and camping. He had a master's degree from New York University. During World War II he had served with the Information and Education Division of the European Theater of Operation.

Many remembered "Dutch" and Naomi Kastenbaum as exciting people. They remembered Dutch with his big pipe and the two of them as father and mother figures.

Beginners and Advanced Hebrew Classes were formed at the Adath as the Adult Institute in November. Rabbi Gordon delivered a memorial tribute to 13 Minneapolis servicemen killed in World War II, and a bronze memorial plaque bearing the names of the Adath war dead was presented by Charles Silver to the synagogue. He had lost his son. The inscription read: "In Memory of the Sons of Adath Jeshurun Synagogue who gave their lives for our beloved country during World War II - 1941-1945: Harold M. Benjamin, Sanford Berkwitz, William Billig, Alvin Brody, Harry Chersonsky, Nat Eiser, Albert Feigelson, Morley Horwitz, Julius Margulas, David Sherman, Myron Silver,

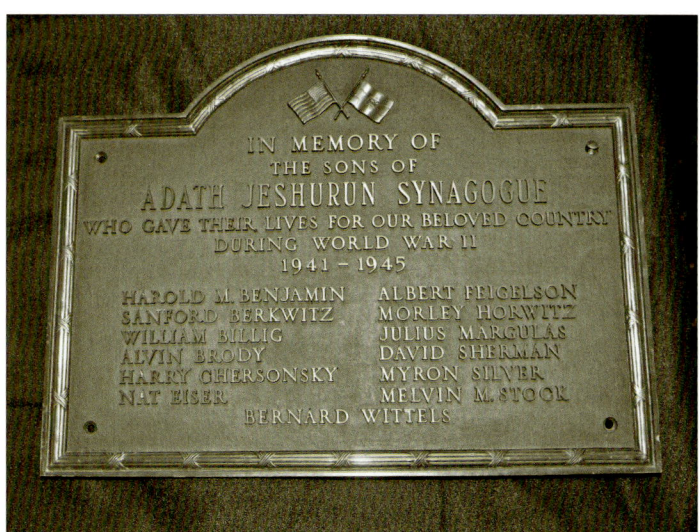

Melvin M. Stock, and Bernard Wittels." A total of 296 men and women from Adath served in the armed forces during World War II.

UNITED SYNAGOGUE YOUTH

Alongside LTF, a new national youth group for Conservative high school youth was in the process of emerging. At the Adath, it was still called the Junior Young People's League, and the four St. Paul and Minneapolis Conservative synagogues called it the Twin City Youth Congregations (TCYC), but at the first Midwest Conference held in Omaha, Nebraska, the name United Synagogue Youth (USY) emerged. As described earlier, this group started in the Twin Cities in 1948 with a conference at Temple of Aaron. At the convention in Omaha it began to take on a larger dimension.

Five delegates—Carolyn Blicker Abramson, Adele Weisman, Norman Pink, Jerry Weil and Stanley Shapiro—represented Adath Jeshurun at the convention in Omaha, the stated purpose of which was to organize the Midwest as part of the National Junior YPL movement. They attended workshops, listened to lectures, and participated in various ceremonies and social outings. Committees were set up, officers were elected, dues were established, and the organization passed a set of resolutions in an effort to define its purpose.

It was noted later in an informational bulletin for YPL leaders that more than 220 teenagers had attended the conference in Omaha. The Twin Cities had the largest delegation—five from St. Paul and 30 from Minneapolis. Melvin B. Sinykin of St. Paul was elected president.

He later recalled, "We went down to Omaha on the train in a private car… They wanted to have a president from the Twin Cities. The night before the voting, a group came and asked me to run for president as they thought I might have a chance to win. I was 17, the same age as the seniors in high school, but I didn't know how much time I would have to spend on the group as I had just started at the university. They persuaded me to run. I did and became the first president of USY. I remember I was given a beautiful olive wood gavel that had been made in Israel."

On December 17, a reception tea was held to honor Rabbi Albert I. Gordon, who had recently received his doctorate degree—the first School of Anthropology Ph.D. to be awarded at the University of Minnesota. His doctoral thesis, "The Jews of Minneapolis—A Study in Acculturation," later became the book *Jews in Transition*.

At the time he was still executive director of the United Synagogue of America.

The year 1948 ended with a joint Chanukah service with Temple Israel on December 31. It was the fourth successive year that joint services had been held on the eve of the secular New Year. The families of Mrs. Sarah Schwartz and Sidney Goldish won first and second prizes for the Chanukah decoration contest.

Sabine Amsel later recalled that Morris Gordon had started the Chanukah decorating contest to offset the heavy Christmas influence. "He started the home decorations contest and it went through the whole city. Lou and Tess Cohen really went all out. There was a committee that would go around and judge the homes and the winners won prizes."

Sabine also noted Rabbi Gordon's efforts to reverse the widespread anti-Semitic feelings that prevented Jews from joining AAA and other clubs in Minneapolis, which was known at the time as "the city of anti-Semitism."

By all accounts Rabbi Gordon was a likeable and persuasive individual. Said Dena Pink, "Morris's sermons were very interesting. He kept your attention. He would roll his eyes up to heaven and was very impressive. His wife, Francis, was a lovely person."

In December the Second Annual Leaders Training Fellowship (LTF) Midwest Conference took place at the beautiful estate of the North suburban synagogue, Beth El, in Highland Park, Illinois.

The Polaroid camera, which could take and print a finished picture in one minute, was unveiled. Milton Berle was the top performer in the new American TV industry, and *Death of a Salesman* opened on Broadway. The book, *1984*, by George Orwell was released, giving a depressing vision of what the world might become. But that same year the outstanding new musical, *Oklahoma*, opened, and jazz trumpeter Louis Armstrong showed there was still plenty to sing about.

In January, Herbert Joshua's eighth grade class put out the first issue of the religious school paper, although a name had not yet been decided upon. Milton Bix and David Brown were the co-editors. At Friday evening services on January 28, a memorial plaque was dedicated in memory of Arthur Brin, former board member and leader in the Jewish and civic communities.

On February 13, the religious school celebrated Tu B' Shevat with songs, plays, and dancing; and a grove of trees was purchased in Israel in honor of Mr. Mirviss's 70th birthday, which coincided with the date of the holiday, February 14, 1949.

Rabbi Gordon's course in the University of Life series at Hennepin Methodist Church was eminently successful, with some 60 non-Jewish students attending.

At the Adult Institute Sabbath in March, the question at hand was whether there should be a unified Jewish community in Minneapolis, so that a single contribution would support a variety of synagogues, community centers, children's and aged homes. Max Levinsohn and Percy Ross took the affirmative, and Sidney Cohen and Newton Atlas upheld the negative position. Ross took a tip from Rabbi Gordon and contacted Rabbi Max Vorspan, of Pasadena's B'nai Israel Congregation, where such a unification had been successfully established.

In April the opening session of LTF was held at the Adath. A combined training program had been undertaken by the three Conservative Twin Cities synagogues: Beth El, Adath Jeshurun and Temple of Aaron. Some of the early Adath members were Mendel Abrams, Karin Becker, Philip Bloom, Margory Cohen, Daniel Frisch, Roslyn Fryer, Sue Garber, Lonnie Garvis, Jimmy Greene, Phyllis Halpern, Eddie Lazar, Stephen Lieberman, Thomas Litman, Myrna Noodleman, Paul and Norman Pink, Albert Kapstrom, Donald Schwartz, Stan Shapiro, Jo Anne Shedlov, Norton Stillman, Ned Waldman and Adelle Weisman.

The first Thursday in every month was selected as the meeting day for the combined Minneapolis and St. Paul meeting, while the local chapters met about twice a month with their respective rabbis. The meetings typically consisted of discussion, a *maariv* service, dinner, and then singing and Israeli dancing.

Members of the group were also expcted to become involved in community activities on their own initiative, and each of the Conservative synagogue in the Twin Cities set aside one Friday night and Saturday morning service at which their LTF representatives would participate.

What the progenitors of this movement hoped to accomplish—to foster Jewish leadership in those young people for when they became adults—definitely came about. Throughout the 1960s, '70s and 80s, leadership positions in Minneapolis and St.Paul synagogues were taken by men and women who had been LTF participants. And Rabbi Gordon deserves an added measure of praise for the enthusiasm he brought to the Jewish community and its institutions through this program by his energetic and positive personality. Many young congregants had never before met a rabbi that they could relate to and have fun with.

The Bat Mitzvah on April 8 of Arlene Burnstein, daughter of Jack and Fanny Burnstein, was Rabbi Gordon's first at the Adath.

On April 26 an FBI agent spoke at the Men's Club meeting, and George Mikan of the Minneapolis Lakers presented awards to the Adath basketball champions.

The 22nd Annual National Convention of YPL of the United Synagogue was held in Atlantic City on April 1-3. Senator Hubert H. Humphrey was one of the speakers. More than 750 youth leaders from all parts of the United States and Canada reevaluated the role of Jewish youth in America in the light of developments in Israel and through out the world.

On May 21, 8th and 9th graders had a hayride as a *m'lavah malkah* party at Eaton's Ranch. Gertie Abrams was commended for the wonderful way she handled and managed the catering. Other synagogue events that month included a lecture by University of Minnesota professor Wayne Anderson on the subject "Adjustments in Early Marriage," followed by a discussion on "Is Sex Education Necessary?"

The 65th Congregational Dinner was held on May 25. An original skit, "The Parade of the Years," by Sophie Burnstein, the synagogue's "author exceptionale," traced the history of the Adath. Jack Burnstein and Arnold Cohen were narrators. The skit highlighted the great strides the synagogue had taken in recent years, but also noted that it was experiencing growing pains due to the rapid pace of expansion in many areas. "We are too big for our breeches," the skit concluded.

1949-1950

A new practice was instituted at Adath Jeshurun that September, when Paul Herman became the first Bar Mitzvah to chant the Torah portion without the use of vowels or help of a book. He also recited the haftorah and conducted the service. A kiddush followed the service.

A new group had also been formed, the Young People's Club for singles 17 and up. Advisors were Murray and Ruth Abry and Harry and Marilyn Karasov.

On the year's agenda for USY was the regional convention in Kansas City, a camp session, finding a meeting and activities room, and equipping it for work.

In the summer of 1949, the first LTF Summer Institute had been held at Camp Ramah-Wisconsin. Rabbi Bernard Mandelbaum had been appointed LTF National Faculty Chairman.

The LTF Midwest Convention, Kinnus, took place at the South Side Hebrew Congregation in Chicago from December 30 through January 1. Mendel Abrams and Donald Schwartz were the Adath delegates. Upon their return, Mendel reported:

"...I was thoroughly amazed at the ease with which all of these boys and girls conversed in Hebrew. In fact, only Hebrew was spoken during the whole reunion. I always prided myself on knowing how to speak a little Hebrew—after the first few minutes there I realized how descriptive the adjective 'little' really is. I honestly knew just a little, however, Donald was more fortunate in that he attended Camp Ramah last summer. After spending the afternoon at this reunion I realized the wonderful job Ramah is doing.

"At 11:30 Rabbi Hillel Silverman, the field director of LTF, and also director of Camp Ramah, gave the opening address. He particularly stressed the fact that LTF members must spend at least six hours a week in Hebrew study..."

At the business meeting, the city of Minneapolis won overwhelming approval to host the next convention.

In the October *Clarion*, Rabbi Gordon announced that a double service was to be added for Kol Nidre, so that parents and children could be together at those services. "Today there are so few occasions when an entire family partakes of a religious experience that we must do all we can to recapture this source-spring of faith. It is with this end in mind that we establish a double service on Kol Nidre night, the night when religious ties are most sensitive; when Jewish hearts are most Jewish."

That issue of the *Clarion* also announce a new fund drive for the Talmud Torah, which desperately needed a new building, with Leo Gross as campaign chairman. The 1949-1950 Artist Series was also unveiled. It included Richard Tucker, tenor with the Metropolitan Opera and former cantor; Ruth Kobart, singing actress (and niece of I. D. Fink); the humorist Baruch Lumet; and comedian Molly Picon.

The 19th Annual Lecture Series program booklet was dedicated to Joe Schanfeld, who had served as the president of Adath Jeshurun Congregation for 20 years. It described his "Horatio Alger" career, and his many contributions to the community.

"...even to this day he is frequently confronted by older men who remind him that he gave them their first job when they came to Minneapolis from the old country. Starting in humble beginnings, he has carved a niche for himself in this community and is a millionaire if measured in the love, honor, and respect bestowed upon him by the entire community, both Jewish and Christian alike..."

The Schanfield Family: (back row) Rodney Wallace, Marcella, Jane Levin, Julie Ratner. (front row) Gladys, Joseph and Pauline Schanfield, Susan Ratner, Vera Ratner

That fall a long-awaited publication, *United Synagogue Youth—A Guide For the Organization and Programming of Teen-Age Groups in the Synagogue* finally made its appearance. And the Women's League of the United Synagogue of America held its Seventh Midwest Regional Conference in Omaha. Participating from Minneapolis were Mrs. Maurice Gordon, Dorothy Gitlin, Shirley Abelson, Lillian Krelitz, Helen Ziff, and Bertha Aronson. Rabbi Albert I. Gordon gave an address on his newly published book, *Jews in Transition* and Rabbi David Aronson also spoke.

In an atmosphere of almost overwhelming hospitality, the Midwest Region of the United Synagogue Youth held an outstanding 2nd Annual Convention, November 25-27 at Temple K.I.B.S. in Kansas City. Adath sent as delegates Norman Pink, Jim Greene, Daniel Frisch, Edwin Agranoff, Adelle Weisman, Naomi Sezer, Roslyn Fryer and Arlene Green. Mel Sinykin, the Midwest Regional USY President, was to have presided at the convention but due to illness was unable to attend.

Delegates from the entire area participated in a highly diversified program of workshops on programs, membership, dances and songs, LTF and religious activities.

To counteract the general pattern of indifference to Judaism portrayed by many college youth, and the distinctly anti-religious bias of many philosophy, humanities and political science professors, a group of university students formed a College Leadership Training Fellowship. The group met with rabbis from the various synagogues to discuss the significance of their heritage.

A plea went out in 1951 to every male member of the congregation to give one week a year to save the morning minyan. And members of the congregation began a new practice of arranging for a consecration service upon moving into a new house. The candlelight service lent inspirational beauty to the tedious task of moving. Young couples were also coming on Sabbath mornings to name their sons and daughters. This ceremony took place in front of the Ark. The rabbi pronounced the child's name in Hebrew and English and offered the blessings of the sages upon it.

The Youth Activities Department held a contest to name its newspaper, and Sam Abrams won with the entry *Nu?* which means, roughly, "Well?" or "What about it?"

On March 3, Reverend Dr. Howard Conn from Plymouth Congregation Church spoke as part of Brotherhood Month. Rabbi Gordon had spoken at Reverend Conn's church on February 19.

On March 28, at the annual donor party, the Women's League presented *Frivolities of 1950* with script and parodies by Sophie Burnstein and Frieda Margulas.

On April 28, a dedication, service and reception took place honoring Mr. and Mrs. M.D. Mirviss, for whom the newly remodeled chapel was being named.

An entry in the Minneapolis Federation Chronicle said that an army of 1,000 volunteers, in a city-wide mobilization, had been launched to raise $1,300,000. Abba Eban, Israel's representative to the United Nations, was guest speaker at Federation's Advance Gifts Division.

Rabbi M. Gordon had been chosen to chair the Federation campaign, and he also spoke at the event. "It is a privilege to head the movement which not only serves us in Minneapolis but reaches out to embrace our people in Israel and our refugees around the world. God has saved our brethren from death at the hands of a brutal pharaoh. God has helped us bring them from the bestial bondage of Europe to the beaches of Israel. In God's name let us bring them their final freedom now. Let us make them free to live, to love, to laugh; to release the genius in their souls so that they may take their rightful place in the cultural symphony of mankind."

Other Adath members serving with Rabbi Gordon were L.S. Grossman, Jay Phillips, I. D. Fink, Dr. Moses Barron, Jules Ebin, Sig Harris, Samuel Maslon, Leo Gross, Thomas Levitt and Joseph Linoff.

The Adath chapter of USY-TCYC worked up 12 vaudeville acts for the annual talent show of the Twin Cities group held on April 23.

The editor of the Midwest USY regional newsletter offered a portrait of Rabbi Abelson and his wife Shirley, who were at the forefront in helping to organize USY: "Rabbi Abelson has been assistant rabbi at Beth El in Minneapolis for two years. Chances are many of you have met him either at Camp Ramah, where he was head of the LTF last year; at Young Judea Camp the year before; or perhaps at USY Camp last summer.

"His favorite pastime is reading, and his ambitions are to be in the rabbinate and to go to Israel. The rabbi, who came from Brooklyn, feels there is a great future for today's youth and has much faith in them.

"The other half of this invincible team, known to all as Shirley, is a St.Paul gal. As a graduate of Teachers' Institute and Columbia, she's a full-fledged teacher and makes use of her training by teaching Sunday School, an adult class in Hebrew, and a group of LTF members who plan to be teachers. She's a sensational cook...ask any of the kids; a wonderful wife...says the rabbi, and he should know; is a swell sport and likes to be with the young people."

On May 13 and 14, the Adath service groups staged the Second Annual Adath Variety Show. It was written by Shirley Rivkin, directed by Harold Rivkin, and produced by Max J. Levinsohn, who also conducted the Adath Orchestra.

Rabbi Gordon (right) with Abba Eban at a Minneapolis Federation dinner in 1951.

The 66th Congregational Dinner took place on May 16 at the synagogue. Joseph Schanfeld was the evening's honored guest. He was presented a testimonial with a hand engraved scroll encased in a custom-made leather frame folder as a token of appreciation.

During the summer Adath Day Camp sessions, children between the ages of 5 and 10 were given the opportunity to swim daily at Lake Calhoun, go on field trips to the Museum of Natural History and Radio Station KUOM at the University of Minnesota; or tour the Ford automobile plant, the *Star and Tribune* newpaper plant, Como Park, and the Northland Milk Company. Some took a train ride to St. Paul.

Campers from Minneapolis, St.Paul, Kansas City, Chicago, Omaha, Des Moines, Superior and Milwaukee met in Aitkin, Minnesota, on August 22-29 for the United Synagogue Youth Midwest Regional Conference.

Two campers wrote a synopsis of their week in a camp newsletter, *Kolenu*: "What an experience!—riding 140 miles into the wilderness of Minnesota with 35 other enthusiastic and unsuspecting campers. The trip by bus from Minneapolis was uneventful, save for the joyous singing and laughter of those aboard. I knew then that week at Council Camp would be one I'd long remember.

"It was a short time until Rabbi Aronson was standing

before a roaring fireplace roaring. That is to say, he was giving us a formal welcome and introduction to the week's course of study, the prayer book. Then we adjourned to our chosen workshop, either programming, journalism, or singing and dancing. Before retiring, we met on the porch to elect our camp officers. The politics were interesting, as politics go—but, in spite of them, Norman Pink was elected president and Carl Puritz secretary."

The report went on to describe various outdoor activities and also a series of classes, lectures, and debates on Jewish themes. It described a beautiful havdalah service on the lakeshore, "a most impressive scene with the boys' trio singing and eight girls, dressed as angels, presenting the Sabbath story by interpretive dance."

For two years the question of unassigned seating for the High Holidays had been a subject for discussion at the executive committee meetings. In the spring of 1950 executive director Kastenbaum conducted a survey of 25 synagogues similar to the Adath in city population and membership size. As a result of the survey, the committee decided to eliminate assigned seating, in the interests of utilizing seats more fully and insuring that the congregants come early and remain throughout the service. A system of ushering would be set up to minimize problems.

In June, President S. H. Libman sent a letter to all of the members of the Adath announcing the decision as tactfully as possible.

"Democracy is rooted in the Bible. Equality stems from prophetic idealism...In order to serve all of our members, in order to use to the utmost advantage all our facilities in the most democratic manner possible, the Board of Trustees proposes the following plan for use during the coming Holy Days..."

The letter went on to announce the abolition of reserved seating and the addition of an auxilary service in the Mirviss Chapel.

"...Only so, can we claim to be a true *bet tefilah*—a house of prayer and worship—for all."

But the proposed plan did not go into effect that fall. After receiving a number of letters complaining about the change, President Libman sent another letter to the members in July, announcing that some sections of the congregation were not yet ready to accept the change. The implementation of the new system was therefore delayed until a general meeting of the membership could be held following the High Holy Days.

Rabbi Gordon returned from the Summer Institute of the Jewish Theological Seminary in July, full of thoughts inspired by the theories of Mordecai Kaplan, who had spoken there. Professor Kaplan had advanced his well-known thesis of "Unity in Diversity" by which Orthodox, Conservative, Reform and Reconstructionist Jews could be brought together to enhance the likelihood that Judaism would survive in the United States. The question was, could these various branches work together while maintaining their distinctive ideologies? Rabbi Gordon had also been inspired by discussions of how the relationship between Israeli Jews and those of the Diaspora would evolve over time.

1950-1951

In September, 1950 "Dutch" Kastenbaum tendered his resignation as executive director and youth activities leader, in order to further his studies at the university. The September *Clarion*, with Rose Zimmerman as the new editor, welcomed Louis Haber as the new educational and youth activities director. He would also assume the position of principal of the religious school. He had formerly been educational director of a congregation in Denver.

Ella Weiss Braverman, from Vancouver, B.C., was hired as the new choir director. She had been a music specialist on the Vancouver High School staff and was a graduate of the University of British Columbia, an Associate of Trinity College of Music, London, a graduate of the Vancouver Talmud Torah, and had extensive experience with Jewish liturgical music.

Rabbi Gershon Rosenstock, from the Jewish Theological Seminary, was engaged to conduct the services in the Mirviss Chapel for the High Holy Days. He trained a junior choir to participate in the chapel service. On Erev Rosh Hashanah, Rabbi Rosenstock delivered the sermon in the main synagogue to give the entire congregation an opportunity to hear him speak.

With the easing of the American immigration laws, survivors of the concentration camps were arriving from European displaced persons camps and other parts of the world. In Washington D.C., the top leadership of U.S. Jewry convened October 27-29 to plan a program of aid to Israel.

For Sukkot, the Women's League and Men's Club sponsored their annual festival. Entertainment included square dancing, songs, monologues and community singing. A food sale was held with the proceeds going toward the maintenance of the religious school.

The Adath Men's Club booked Jan Peerce, leading tenor of the Metropolitan Opera, for a one night engagement in October at the Minneapolis Auditorium.

At the opening late Sabbath service, October 27, new members of the congregation were welcomed and an Oneg Shabbat followed in their honor. On November 3, guest speaker Dr. Stephen Kayser, curator of the Jewish Museum, New York City, gave an address on Jewish art.

With the High Holy Days behind them, the issue of reserved seating was once again brought up for review. The new executive director, Louis Haber, sent a letter to all members announcing a forthcoming meeting which all members of the Adath were encouraged to attend.

NATIONAL WOMEN'S LEAGUE CONFERENCE

Minneapolis hosted the National Women's League of the United Synagogue of America Biennial Convention for the first time on November 12-16, 1950. The group had been started in 1917 by Mathilda Schechter, wife of Solomon Schechter. The aims of the League remained the same as originally formulated by Schechter: "To foster the observance of traditional Judaism among our women; to spread Jewish ideals; to strengthen Jewish sentiment in the home; to further Jewish education of our women and children, and to awaken Jewish women to their responsibility as members of their communities and as Americans."

The Radisson Hotel was chosen as convention headquarters, and more than 800 delegates attended, representing more that 100,000 Jewish women affiliated with the Conservative movement in the United States and Canada. The theme of the convention was *Lilmod, Le-lamed, La-asot*" or " To learn, to teach, to do," though there was much discussion during the event about the problems that Jewish women faced due to a world of changing values.

In his address, Rabbi David Aronson noted that in the past, "the opportunities for women to study Torah were very limited. Since scholarship and familiarity with the principles and practices of Torah played a major role in determining a person's postion in the synagogue, the position occupied by women was consequently minor and inferior."

The purpose of the convention, he went on, was to "return our people to the wells of living water, to Torah in its historic, threefold implication, to study, to teach, to do." He noted that in modern America, it was the men who had no time for study, and had largely lost the art. Women, on the other hand, had been emancipated. They now had the time to study, to read, to attend discussion groups, whereas the "poor men who have no intellectual opportunities during the week find a Friday night service painful." In conclusion, he recommended that it was a bad idea to separate the sexes when inculcating Jewish values.

Dr. Louis Finkelstein, president of the Jewish Theological Seminary, spoke at the Monday night banquet. In his message he said: "I remember the earliest beginnings of the Women's League from the time of its founder, Mathilda Schechter, the wife of that great scholar and great man, Solomon Schechter. What a small organization it was in the days of Mrs. Schechter and how few grounds we then had for envisaging this mighty organization!"

Dr. Finkelstein talked that evening of the great sages and rabbis who thought of life as a school. But, he added, "what we need today again is not a group of rabbis together, not a group of scholars alone who can lead us—but men and women of the 'Great Synagogue.' The emancipated women of our time must participate equally with men in the formulation of policies and the clarification of problems in preparing a curriculum of education for our children, in implementing the programs of great institutions, so that they will not be ends in themselves, but merely the means toward the greater service of God. The 'Great Synagogue,' must be brought into being, not only because it is necessary for the survival of our people and our faith, but also because it is an instrument for a far greater service. The world today needs men and women of character."

At the Torah Fund Luncheon on November 14, Minnesota Senator Hubert H. Humphrey was praised for championing the FEPC Plan in the National Democratic platform. "...every blow that we strike against bigotry and discrimination, against selfishness and greed," he said, "is a blow in behalf of human freedom. "

The afternoon's program continued with Rabbi Kassel Abelson introducing Morris Sherman, a Minneapolis high school student and member of Beth El LTF, who spoke on the subject: "What is our youth doing today?" Then the Adath's own Adele Weisman described the efforts of the United Synagogue Youth to involve young people in various aspects of Jewish culture and service.

MOUNT SINAI HOSPITAL

In the third week of November, 1950, the new Mount Sinai Hospital of Minneapolis was dedicated. Jay Phillips, president of the Mount Sinai Hospital Association and one of the founders, made a pre-dedication week statement in the *AJW* in which he described the dedication as "one of the milestones in the life of Upper Midwest Jewry."

"It marks," he continued, "the beginning of an era which will see new developments in race, relations, in hospital care for all, without regard to race or creed, and in the research which the hospital will always stand ready to contribute for the benefit of all humanity." On the Friday evening services of November 24, a tribute was paid to the members of the Mount Sinai board of directors and to the many friends who had served selflessly on its behalf.

The YPL *Schrier* announced that the nursery school would break even financially that year. After only six weeks of school, the children had learned 150 Hebrew words and 12 Hebrew songs.

Chanukah celebrations included the annual Women's League and Men's Club Chanukah party for the entire Adath family with a skit called, "Malka Bakes Latkes." The evening included lighting the candles, Myrna Amsel and her Choral Octet, the 1950 debut of the Adath Symphony Orchestra conducted by Max Levinsohn, the Hillel Dancers, Community Singing, and a Chanukah quiz contest.

The 20th Annual Chanukah luncheon sponsored by the Minneapolis Conference of Jewish Women's Organizations was held December 7 with an original skit, "Our Women of Valor," by Sophie Burnstein. On December 15, the new executive and educational youth director, Louis Haber, and his wife, Louise, were officially welcomed at a reception following Friday services. The organist was Robert Johnson.

In the *Clarion*, Rabbi Gordon described the United Synagogue Convention he had recently attended: "For the first time in the history of the United Synagogue, awards were given out to those congregations who have shown the greatest progress in the past two years. We received honorable mention and a beautiful Solomon Schechter Award was given to our president, Samuel Libman. The *Shalosh Seudot* project, which was one of the reasons why we gained national recognition, is about to begin again at Adath. When you, our parents, receive a cordial invitation from the rabbi to be his guests at the Sabbath dinner, we would like you to make sure to attend with your children. This is one of the highlights of our congregational year."

Funeral services were held on December 16 for Mayer Schwartz. He had been one of the Adath's early members. He had come to Minneapolis in 1887 and had worked as a printer doing most of the Adath's printing over the years. He convinced his partner, a non-Jew, that it would be wise to invest $100, then a considerable business risk, to purchase Hebrew type in Chicago for shipment to Minneapolis. It wasn't long before his partner retired and from that day until the day of his death, Mayer retained his interest in Hebrew printing to help build up the Jewish community. For half a century, Mr. Schwartz carried on his work despite a paralytic stroke. His courage won him many friends in addition to those attracted by his community service and fine character.

Talmud Torah students who pursued their Hebrew education were given recognition by taking part in the Kiddush ceremony at services on Friday evenings. Harriet Goldstein and Michael Burnstein were the first two pupils honored on December 22, followed by Iric Nathanson and Robin Berman on December 29.

The year ended with a college youth night on December 29. Baruch Bloom spoke on "A Critique of American Jewish College Youth" and Robert Latz replied with "Meeting the Challenge." Also participating in the services were Eddie Kieffer, Ruth Rosen, David Himmelman and Edith Block. A discussion followed at the Oneg Shabbat.

At the first Shabbat of 1951 on January 5, plans were revealed for a series of Canteen Socials to be held at regular intervals during the coming months. They were to be called Saucy(s) which was an anagram for United Synagogue Young Adult Canteen. (USYAC)

Rabbi Morris Gordon was chairman of the Jewish National Fund dinner on January 7, and Dr. Moses Barron headed the committee arranging for participation of civic leaders. Minnesota Governor Luther Youndahl and Minneapolis Mayor Eric Hoyer greeted U.S.Congressman Franklin D. Roosevelt II at the Golden Jubilee marking 50 years of service to Israel by the JNF. Adelle Lieberman arranged for the kosher dinner held at the Radisson Hotel.

In February, Evelyn Silverman became the new editor of the *Clarion*. In the February issue Rabbi Gordon wrote about the 50th anniversary of the Rabbinical Assembly of America.

That same issue reported that a new Bar Mitzvah requirement had been unanimously endorsed by members of the Minnesota Rabbinical Association, namely, that children be required to attend Sabbath services in a synagogue for at least two years prior to such ceremony.

In mid-February Minneapolis hosted the Israel Philharmonic Orchestra. It was comprised of nearly 100 members that hailed originally from 13 different countries. The musicians had been unwanted, rejected strangers in the lands they had come from, but now they were proud citizens of Israel. An audience of 3,500 from the Twin Cities and the Upper Midwest celebrated the occasion.

March 2 was Mordecai M. Kaplan Sabbath, and the

sermon topic was: "What is Reconstructionism?" in honor of Dr. Kaplan's 70th birthday and his bold and dynamic new approach to Judaism.

RECONSTRUCTIONISM

Rabbi Gordon reported on the first meeting of the Reconstructionist Rabbinical Fellowship Conference in a February 1951 issue of the *Clarion*. He noted that for two generations, American Jews had been preoccupied with the problems of European Jewry and of Zionism, while neglecting their own religious and cultural growth. As a result, American synagogues had become devoid of spirituality, and the laity was now "more interested in administrative affairs than in religious and ethical problems."

Mordecai M. Kaplan, who spoke at Adath on "What Makes the Jewish Religion Jewish?"

The Reconstructionist rabbis were dedicating themselves to the task of rebuilding American Jewish life on firm spiritual foundations, and committing themselves to two vital propositions:

(a) the centrality of Jewish spiritual values.

(b) the belief that what holds Jews together is more important than what divides them.

To further such values, Rabbi Gordon recommended a number of initiatives in religion, ethics, and the field of personal guidance, "so that Judaism will remain true to its historic character as a way of life." These projects would draw fully upon the energies and insights of laymen and women. He recommended the wider use of Hebrew to foster cultural unity, and he also recommended setting up experimental societies and synagogues to further explore the possibilities for genuine Jewish community.

"In issuing this statement," he concluded, "we announce the establishment of the Reconstructionist Rabbinical Fellowship. We express our determination, as charter members of the Fellowhip, to work together, in cooperation and in a spirit of devotion, for the spiritual welfare of our people. Individually we retain and shall continue to retain our loyalty to our respective rabbinical associations, but we see no reason why such loyalty should preclude our cooperation in all matters affecting our sphere of activity. We shall welcome into the Fellowship any of our colleagues who share our beliefs and purposes. We assure our fellow American Jews that we have no intention of creating a new and competing denomination. Our whole purpose is to focus attention, amidst dis-

tracting circumstances, upon the real and crucial business at hand, namely, the uniting of Jews on the broadest possible base for the advancement of their spiritual welfare."

The Reconstructionsts also agreed that women could be counted in a minyan and called to the reading of the Torah in the synagogue—a radical departure from tradition in the eyes of some.

The youth groups of Sigma Ep, Tri-T, Bialik Chapter of AZA and the XV Club were hosted by USY and LTF for a gathering in May. The evening was a unique experience in the history of Twin City youth organizations for two reasons: first, the meeting was sponsored by the groups themselves; and second, the young people decided that they wanted not only sociability, but also inspirational appeal, and decided to hold four seminars.

The Women's League commemorated Jewish Music Month in February with a tribute to Evelyn Siegel, pianist and vocalist, for her 22 years of service to the League and the Congregation.

Also in April the first Mothers and Sons banquet was held with a Mother and Son Charleston Contest. Sara Garvis and her son, Allen, won first prize, and Lillian Gross and son, James, were runners-up. Min Himmelman ran the kitchen while the irrepressible Gertie Abrams, who practically lived in the synagogue, took it easy for once and also took the prize for having the most sons dining with her—Mendel, Harvey, Erwin and Sheldon.

At that time Lillian Krelitz Kaplan was president of the Sisterhood: "When I became president we used to give

THE ORIGINS OF UNITED SYNAGOGUE YOUTH

Rabbi Morris Gordon: "It was three years before we wrote to the Jewish Theological Seminary. Then we decided it was too good to keep just in the Twin Cities. I went to New York with 60 boys and girls and there we founded USY as a national movement. They thought I'd be lucky if I had 75 in attendance. At that time they didn't see kids after their Bar Mitzvah. They couldn't see 16 to 18 year olds coming to meet us. We went to the main auditorium at Columbia University. Despite what all of them said, we had over 2,000 young people filling the main hall and kids standing in the aisle. USY took off and then spread all over the country. It had started in our basement in Adath Jeshurun with Rabbis Aronson and Abelson and their Beth El group taking the most active part in its beginning."

Ellis Peilen: "Morris Gordon had a great deal of influence on the youth of our congregation. My daughter, Elizabeth was absolutely overwhelmed by Morris Gordon and instead of having pictures of movie stars on her dresser, she had pictures of Morris Gordon. She got very involved and went to Shalosh Seudot every Saturday afternoon until she went away to college. She sang with all the older people and loved it."

the Sisterhood presidents a pair of silver candlelabras. Every Friday night we would have to borrow one of the past president's silver candlelabras. I decided to have a Silver Tea. Betty Berkman Codden was our decorations chairman at the time. She and I went down to Sears and Roebuck and we bought a bird bath and covered it up with silver. We had silver invitations sent out and had a musical afternoon. Those that came to the Silver Tea dropped their donation into the beautiful bird bowl. The people were so generous and so thrilled that from that afternoon we bought a pair of silver candlelabras, a silver tea set, a sugar tongs and a tray. Thereafter the Sisterhood Board and I decided that we would ask people to donate a piece of silver to the Women's League whenever they had a simcha. That is how they acquired all the silver that you see used for various occasions."

The final religious school assembly was held June 3. Awards were presented to Mendel Abrams and Roslyn Fry-

er, whose names were inscribed on the gold cup in company with the names of previous award winners Thomas Litman, Adele Weisman, Jimmie Greene and Norman Pink.

Abba Eban, Israeli Representative to the United Nations, presented a major address to Minneapolis Jewry in June at Adath Jeshurun.

A memorial forest was planted by the JNF in Israel and would be known as the "Forest of Six Million" in commemoration of the six million Jews who were killed in the Holocaust. The goal of the synagogue was for one tree to be purchased for every member of the Adath family.

At the Men's Club annual summer outing, Rabbi Gordon was initiated into the art of fishing.

The Korean war had widened, the McCarthy witch hunts continued, and the Rosenberg atomic spy case made headlines. Danny Kaye played a straight dramatic role on the radio entitled, *Bricks Without Straw*, and Henry Fonda was the lead in *Mister Roberts* at the St.Paul Auditorium.

1951-1952

For the first Israel Bond Drive in Minneapolis, festivals were held on both the North and South Sides.

The big news for Adath for High Holidays was that a double service had been arranged to enable families to sit together at services. A more traditional service was scheduled for 7 and a less traditional service at 11:30 with an hour called "Prelude to Prayer" in between. Rabbi Gordon engaged Dr. Shalom Spiegel, professor and lecturer at the Jewish Theological Seminary, to speak during that interlude in an effort to reacquaint congregants with the deeper meaning of the prayers associated with Rosh Hashanah and Yom Kippur.

Rabbi Gordon felt that the increasing size of the congregation necessitated such a change. Several rabbis at the theological seminary counselled against the move, arguing that the High Holidays were sacrosanct, and some Adath board members feared that congregants would resign in protest, but Dr. Kaplan said, "If you combine it with study, it will be a breakthrough on the American scene."

"By the third year of the double service," Rabbi Gordon later observed, "I had as many as 300 students from the University of Minnesota write to me and say they heard about our services. They wanted to come and study and pray with us for the High Holidays...When we started there weren't any double services, youth movements or havdalah services like we were having in the entire country. The first double service in the Conservative congregations

Adath congregant Amos Rosenbloom in Korea

in the whole United States was started at the Adath. We always tried to do something a little different each year. I dedicated myself to that."

The Adath received an eviction notice that fall from the Minneapolis School Boards stating that public schools could not be used for religious purposes. The synagogue received a one-year extension to use Calhoun School, but it was clear that something needed to be done. A brochure showing a proposed addition to the synagogue was sent out to the congregants. It was titled: "Their Future Is In Your Hands" and ended with "Open the Door to Your Child's Future!"

Sam Libman noted in the brochure that the religious school had grown from 100 to 400 pupils, and went on to outline a plan for a new building with 16 classrooms to be built at a cost of between $300,000 and $350,000. By the end of October, $150,000 had been pledged. In January one of the Adath's newer members, Sim Heller, became executive director of the building drive.

The USY Midwest Regional Convention was held in Minneapolis that year on Thanksgiving weekend. The theme was "The Art of Jewish Living" and Twin City membership of all Conservative synagogues cooperated. More than 400 representatives from the Midwest attended an inspiring series of workshops, seminars, panels and dinners. There was singing and Israeli dancing.

Beginning on Friday, November 30, Rabbi Gordon presented a series of three sermons on professor Mordecai Kaplan's provocative views, with a discussion following each service. The following March, the Men's Club was honored to present Dr. Mordecai Kaplan himself as guest lecturer. Dr. Kaplan spoke on: "What Makes the Jewish Religion Jewish."

The newly organized nationwide USY held its first convention December 25-27 at Columbia University in New York. The delegates ate at the Jewish Theological Seminary and were housed at various nearby hotels. More than 500 delegates attended the convention in all, representing 65 different communities in 14 states and Canada. The Adath was represented by Alvin Gendein and Jim Greene. Paul Freedman, Connecticut, was elected the first national president and Arthur Oleisky, Minneapolis, was elected first vice president.

In February members of the Adath celebrated Tu B'Shevat. This festital had taken on new meaning in recent years, as Rabbi Gordon explained in the *Clarion*: "The trees of Israel, neglected during the centuries when the Jews were absent from their beloved country, are being replanted by Jewish pioneers. Already forests, symbols of life, beautify the countryside. The Forest of Six Million, an international project begun last year, which will commemorate the six million Jews who were done to death by Hitler, will be the focal point for the Jewish Arbor Day, international observance this year. The trees donated by members of Adath will be planted in the Deinard Forest, a part of the Forest of Martyrs."

The demand for Hadassah hospital supplies continued to grow. Thousands of immigrants were streaming into Israel and needed new garments. Volunteers were being sought to form a sewing group at Adath to help with Israel's needs.

No fewer than 15 separate youth activities continued under the auspices of the Synagogue Youth Program. New LTF members chosen from the congregation were Sandra Besner, Rhea Gass, Carol Ann Gross, Paula Phillips, Sheila Markus, Eugene Herman, Billy Silverman, Elaine Stern, Beverly Stillman and Richard Zelle.

In April of 1952, Rabbi Gordon surprised everyone at Adath by announcing that he planned to resign as rabbi due to ill health brought on by Minnesota's harsh climate.

He had planned to step down in June but was pursuaded by the board to stay until after the High Holy Days.

Rabbi Gordon planned to devote six months to study and writing, pay a visit to Israel, and then perhaps seek out a rabbinical position in a more clement region.

In the May issue of the *Clarion,* Rabbi Gordon quoted Rabbi Reuben Slonim of Beth Hamidrash Hagodol Synagogue in Toronto: "At a meeting of the board of governors the other day, when applications for membership were being considered, one of the newer members of the board asked, 'Will these families we are admitting into the congregation attend Sabbath services?' The question elicited laughter from some, but it startled most of us. The force of its pertinence struck home."

Gordon went on to suggest that perhaps few join a congregation primarily to participate in religious worship. "He has a host of reasons for joining—because his friends are here; because he wants a readily available place for his daughter's wedding; because his son is approaching Bar Mitzvah age; because he wants seats for the High Holidays—but attendance at regular services are furthest from his purpose."

The problem, he said, is that the major part of the synagogue's budget is spent on facilities for worship. "We choose a rabbi for the excellence of his sermons which we do not listen to. We conduct a Hebrew school in order to train children to feel at home in a religious exercise which they are not expected seriously to practice. Prayer is the *raison d'etre* to synagogue existence; all other activities may be duplicated in one way or another in the rest of the community. Yet the voice of prayer is almost inaudible."

To counter this unhappy trend, Rabbi Gordon proposed that congregations establish a trial membership. "A man will sign his application and write his check, but he is not to be regarded as a member until he proves that he is willing to change his habits to include worship, so that his very life becomes synagogue-oriented..."

In May, the *American Jewish World* carried an article announcing the establishment of a Cantors Institute at the Jewish Theologial Seminary of America. Upon the completion of a six-year program, gradutes of the Institute would receive a Bachelor of Sacred Music degree, qualifying them to occupy posts as cantors and directors of music in synagogues throughout the country.

In conjunction with the biennial United Synagogue Convention held in Boston, May 14-18, Adath was designated the outstanding Conservative congregation in the United States. The 1952 Solomon Schechter Award symbolizing the honor was presented to Rabbi Gordon for outstanding achievement in "Congregational Programming." The committee which made the selection cited Adath's steady congregational growth, its pioneering work in such youth activities as *Shalosh Seudot* programs, and the establishment of the first combination "learning and prayer" High Holiday services. The presentation was made as the highlight of the national convention which marked the 50th anniversary of the arrival in America of Solomon Schechter, the first president of the Jewish Theological Seminary of America.

The 68th Congregational Dinner was held June 3 and honored Cantor Morris Amsel for his service to Adath and the community. Cantor Amsel was cited for presenting two complete consecutive services with choir on Rosh Hashanah and Yom Kippur. Dr. Ephraim B. Cohen was master of ceremonies, Ruth Stillman was general chairman with Rose Zimmerman, co-chair and decorations by Betty Berkman. Betty had been recognized by the Minneapolis newspapers for her unusual talent in the field of decorations, which she generously contributed to community organizations for their fund-raising projects.

Ellis Peilen: "Cantor Amsel made Adath a singing congregation. Amsel would teach the choir and teach the members of the congregation to sing various tunes so there was response in Hebrew and not just in English amongst all the congregants."

Harry Goldberg and Joseph and Sophie Burnstein also received recognition for their contributions to congregational activites. The congregation said farewell to the Burnsteins who were moving to California. Joe had been associated with the musical growth of Adath since his boyhood when he sang with Sam Mirviss and Ted Gordon. He had sung with the choir from its inception. Sophie had been a bulwark of intellectual strength and stimulation behind the scenes. She wrote the testimonials to Joseph Schanfeld and Dr. Moses Barron, did most of the publicity for the important functions of the congregation and wrote the script for "Parade of the Years" that was presented at the 65th Anniversary Dinner. She was also a charter member of the Midwest Regional Board of Women's League.

Rabbi C. David Matt died in December, 1951, in Philadelphia. He had served the Adath from 1912 to 1927. Rabbi Gordon was chosen from among many hundred clergymen in the area to serve as chairman at a Minneapolis Auditorium rally welcoming Korean War heroes home. Rabbi

Gordon had also recently been elected president of the Minnesota Rabbinical Association. Joseph Schanfeld was honored at a testimonial dinner by the Jewish Home for the Aged of the Northwest, which he had served as president for more than 20 years.

And nationally, the McCarran Immigration Law, condemned by President Truman as being "racist," was passed despite the opposition of liberal and Jewish organizations.

1952-1953

For the second consecutive year, Dr. Shalom Spiegel lectured on the High Holidays on the basic meaning of prayers in the *machzor*.

After the High Holidays the fall festivals began. The Yom Kippur Dance was held again at the Calhoun Beach Club. The Bar and Bat Mitzvah Brotherhood opened the 1952-53 season with prayer sessions and breakfast. Rabbi Gordon made his last appearance at a LTF meeting at Beth El Synagogue, where his lecture was received with great enthusiasm by the young people.

In the *AJW* for September 19, 1952, Rabbi Morris Gordon speculated that congregants often find the services boring because they have "lost the throbbing reality of being in God's presence..." A month later, in his final contribution to the *Clarion,* he wrote, "We will never forget our heartwarming relationship with our Adath Jeshurun family. We know that no matter where the hand of Providence will guide us, one of the brightest stars in our destiny will be Adath Jeshurun Synagogue whose light will shine in our hearts forever."

In the *AJW*, October 24, 1952, Lewis Ginsburg interviewed Rabbi Gordon. The rabbi reminisced: "I came to this little island of peace, called Minneapolis, following three years of constant, on-the-move Army life in combat areas dominated by death. Perhaps that Army-engendered mobility accounts for my active participation in every communal endeavor during the first two years of my Minneapolis stay. During the last three years, however, I have concentrated on my congregational activities and personal ministrations to my congregational family. I have learned, as youthful rabbis must learn, that only through working with small groups, only by helping to inspire individuals, do we prove most effective in enhancing our Jewish heritage."

Rabbi Gordon went on to praise the harmonious cooperation he found among community leaders on the Federation board and in the Minnesota Rabbinical Association, and the excellence of the local Talmud Torah. What trou-

bled him the most about the local scene was that too many Jewish organizations lacked a genuinely Jewish character.

"There are some very worthwhile civic organizations which can elicit our leadership potential and with which we should affiliate as citizens of Minneapolis. These naturally make no Jewish demands of us. However, every organization which brings only Jews together should endeavor to help make Judaism meaningful and significant to its members."

On November 1, the Junior Congregation turned out *en masse* to bid farewell to Rabbi Gordon. Many a tearful eye was in evidence at the prospect of the rabbi's leaving. The Women's League had a tribute to the rabbi and his wife Francis a few days later, with Rabbi Gunther Plaut as guest speaker.

On Sunday, November 2, the synagogue held a fairwell reception for the Gordons. That day Women's League President Lillian Krelitz spoke for many when she referred to "Rabbi Gordon's outstanding ability, his warm and vibrant personality, his steadfast integrity and leadership."

And Paul Herman highlighted the rabbi's remarkable contributions to the youth programs at Adath: "During the years Rabbi Gordon was with our congregation, our youth made great strides forward. Five and one-half years ago, when he came to us, Adath young people were not organized at all. The Junior Congregation was non-existent. Our youngsters had no way of partaking in a service which was geared to their level. We had no United Synagogue Youth and Leaders Training Fellowship groups before he came. "

Herman went on the praise the rabbi's contributions to athletic programs. "Between halves of basketball games he would often be found out on the floor shooting baskets with our players. He was a good shot, too."

Annalee Lilienfeld said: "If the Adath membership were asked what qualifications they wanted in a rabbi, I think some would say humility and kindness; some would ask for a brilliant scholar, profound thinker and a fine orator; some would call for an excellent teacher, well versed in Talmud and tradition; others again might think it necessary to choose an administrator of great merit and tact who could combine all the activites of a great congregation into a smooth running machine. Some would call for a young man of vitality, who would attract youth and make the synagogue the focal point for their activites; others might think the most important attribute of a rabbi to be an understanding heart, a charitable soul and a fine character.

"There are few persons indeed who are endowed with a combination of all these attributes. Such a one would truly believe that 'what is true for him in his own private heart would be true for all men.' Such a man is Morris Gordon! And we are losing this man."

Thirty years later, in the early 1980s, the following people remembered Rabbi Morris Gordon:

Margie Cohen Zats: "He did it his way, he was his own man and he had the courage to stand up for his innovations and at the time, progressive thinking. He was very charismatic. His wife was lovely and very sweet."

Sam Bender: "He was a fantastic individual with kids and they idolized him. There were a few fellows who wound up at the Seminary because of him. If the Men's Club wanted to have a show, we would ask Rabbi Gordon for advice. He was the best salesman in the world and he gave good sermons."

Evelyn Siegel: "Rabbi Morris Gordon used to stand up on the bema and dance to 'Ein Keloheynu.' "

Gertie Abrams: "Rabbi Morris Gordon was warm, outgoing and beautiful. He was friendly to everyone and had a wonderful smile. My family and I knew him and his family very well. He gave wonderful sermons and had a marvelous sense of humor. He loved music but didn't sing too well. One time he sang along too loudly and Cantor Amsel stopped singing and said to the whole Congregation, 'Morris, you preach sermons and I'll sing.'"

Cantor Morris Amsel: "Rabbi Morris Gordon was a jolly rabbi. He made a lot of friends, the youth especially. He was the rabbi that loved children, loved to play ball with them, and loved to sing…He was concerned about the schools and wanted the children to stay out on the Jewish holidays. I remember he called in all the principals and some of the teachers and had them to a Friday night service and an Oneg Shabbat. He explained to them why the Reform children only stayed out one day and the Conservative children stayed out two days. He agreed that when a child came to services he would give each one a written ex-cuse that they could take back to school. He really pushed it and it was accepted."

From an interview with Rabbi Morris Gordon, September 26, 1983: "Among the highlights of my services in the rabbinate was the Jewish community of Minneapolis. If there was anything you really wanted to do that was educational for youth or spiritual; if you really wanted to do it, you could find the kind of people and the support you needed in order to accomplish your dream. That is not true in many places. There was always good lay leadership within the congregation. There were always people to fall back on. You could find within Adath Jeshurun those people needed for any project. As long as you developed and conceived of a project, you could find the people. They were diversified enough of quality and content to meet your needs."

He was the postwar World War II hero rabbi and was at the helm when the returning G.I.s were getting married and the Baby Boom began. He influenced the newly formed Married Couple's League, an outgrowth of the Young People's League. The emphasis of the Hebrew language in the nursery school was his innovation, and greater participation of youth in services.

When Israel became a state, his enthusiasm spilled over to his congregants. His leadership in the Federation and the general community was commendable.

The membership more than doubled during his stay, and he helped accelerate the drive for the synagogue educational addition. When he left Adath Jeshurun, his legacy included much greater religious participation, a more educated congregation, and a national first: the High Holiday Double Service for which the congregation received a Solomon Schechter Award.

Many of the youth he influenced in the late '40s and early '50s became leaders of the Jewish community and several became rabbis. And many still have very fond memories of him, as do their parents.

(Top left) Rabbi Stanley Rabinowitz; (top right) teacher Bonnie Seltz lights Shabbat candles with the children at
Adath nursery school circa 1953; (Above) The Adath Jeshurun Synagogue on Dupont with its new addition.

7
THE RABBI RABINOWITZ YEARS
(1953-1960)

Rabbi Stanley Rabinowitz arrived at the Adath with outstanding oratorical skills, but he also had a backgound in business, and it was during his years that a major addition to the synagogue was planned and built. A new group of leaders was coming of age, including several who had been groomed in the Leader Training Fellowship. Bat Mitzvah procedures were changed to more closely resemble the Bar Mitzvah, and an Adath Board of Education was established to coordinate recreational and educational activities at the Religious School, Youth Activities, and Nursery School.

Although the synagogue no longer had a rabbi, it was determined to forge ahead with the construction of a new school and youth center. To that end, $200,000 had already been raised and an additional $200,000 was anticipated. The proposed new addition would have a library, administrative offices, and a large foyer. The classroom section would have sixteen classrooms on two stories, and the gymnasium section would also serve as an assembly room and a stage. A hobby shop, a rumpus room, toilet facilities, and locker rooms for both boys and girls were also part of the plan.

Maurice L. Grossman, who was president of the congregation at the time, later recalled: "There wasn't a day when I didn't go to visit the building because we had to be sure that it was properly built on pilings. The soil was not very good. You will note there are no cracks in our synagogue nor in the educational building. It was built on good pilings.

"We had a lot of difficulty in raising money. In those days if we raised somebody's dues $10, there were a lot of complaints.

"The synagogue owned a couple of lots adjacent to the synagogue but it didn't own all of the space on Dupont where the educational building and the parking lot is. There were several lots owned by Louis Rose who also owned the two apartment buildings on the corner of 35th

and Dupont. I helped negotiate the acquisition of a couple of those lots from Mr. Rose. My recollection is that we paid in the neighborhood of $12,000 for them."

At the time there was discussion as to whether the synagogue should build or move to a new site. Grossman said: "At that time, most of the Jewish people were not living in St. Louis Park. They were in the neighborhood of 50th and Irving. They thought possibly the move would be that way. The real tragedy of the situation was that right across the street from the Adath, there was a whole block that belonged to the State of Minnesota and was forfeited for taxes. That whole block could have been bought for almost nothing and paid out over a period. But none of us had enough brains to think about it.

"Secondly, we thought the land was very poor, and…in those days you weren't supposed to consider parking places because of not riding on the Sabbath."

At the Women's League National Convention in Philadelphia, the delegates unanimously adopted resolutions aimed at increasing Sabbath observances in the Jewish home. And 21 delegates from the Adath attended the USY Midwest Regional Convention in Omaha.

Among the rabbis and speakers who occupied the Adath pulpit that year were Rabbi Ari Hyams of the Jewish Community Center in Teaneck, New Jersey; Rabbi Max

Linda Grossman was honored with the first Saturday morning Bat Mitzvah at Adath Jeshurun.

Kadushin, Director of Hebrew High schools in Greater New York; and Rabbi Joshua Stampfer of Tifereth Israel Synagogue in Lincoln. On March 20 Rabbi Albert I. Gordon returned to speak.

The synagogue that year hosted a Married Couples League Lecture Series on comparative religion. On December 22, at the Annual Chanukah Luncheon, a tableaux written by Mrs. Albert G. Minda was performed. It was narrated by Merle Ann Kremen, with singing by Myrna Amsel, Phyllis Bearman and Mrs. J. Teener, and Evelyn Siegel at the organ. And in January, in observance of Jewish Music Month and Brotherhood Month, the Women's League mounted a concert production of Judah Halevy's opera, *La Juive* (The Jewess).

In March, Rabbi David Goldstein, spiritual leader of Philadelphia's Har Zion congregation, came home to Minneapolis and addressed his old friends and classmates at the annual Talmud Torah Alumni Purim banquet. He said, "Minneapolis Jewry doesn't realize it, but this Talmud Torah is absolutely unique. You must treasure it, and sustain it constantly."

Although these and other organizations within the Adath continued to sponsor programs and events, it was difficult sustaining the synagogue's ceremonial functions without a rabbi.

"It was a hard period when I was president," Morrie Grossman recalled. "There were weddings that had to be performed, funerals that had to be arranged for. I couldn't have done it if it weren't for Lou Haber, who was executive director. Cantor Amsel pitched in and did what he had to do... That was a tough year because we had to get substitutes. One Friday night I would have Rabbi Raskas from St. Paul come over and speak. Rabbi Milgrom would come and then the seminary would send someone."

Marge Grossman added: "We had rabbis that came directly from the seminary. They came to our house for dinner on Friday night. Then, in rain, sleet and snow, the rabbi and Morrie would walk to the synagogue. Our lives rotated around the Jewish community and the synagogue. We were all involved when he was president. I was vice president of membership in the Sisterhood. Everyone went to Talmud Torah. We did everything as a family at the synagogue. That was how it was.

"Leo Gross had a sukkah built and it was beautiful. They made quite a practice of inviting a good many of their friends and members of the synagogue to the sukkah. On Chanukah we had a contest and everybody decorated their houses, particularly if they had children. We had committees that went around to inspect the various decorations. Confirmation was also a big thing in those years. I remember the receptions with the formal dresses on the girls. It was at night which they don't do anymore."

In April, Temple of Aaron hosted a Minnesota United Synagogue Youth convention. Sally Leafman (who later became the Adath president) was in charge of the cultural activities, and Sam Kaplan, president of the Temple of Aaron USY, extended greetings.

The first jointly sponsored Minneapolis celebration of Israel Independence Day was held at the Adath in May. The theme of the celebration was: "Partners in Democracy—The U.S. and Israel." More than 20 organizations participated.

Dr. Jonas E. Salk was in the news that year due to his work developing vaccines for polio and influenza; and America's first medical college under Jewish auspices, at Yeshiva University, was named the Albert Einstein College of Medicine.

The Rabinowitz family

A NEW RABBI IS INTRODUCED

In May of 1953, board president Maurice L. Grossman announced that Rabbi Stanley Rabinowitz had been appointed as new spiritual leader of Adath Jeshurun. Rabbi Rabinowitz was a native of Des Moines, Iowa, where his parents lived. His grandparents, the late Mr. and Mrs. Herman Rabinowitz, had been Minneapolis residents before moving to California. He and his wife Anita had three children, Nathaniel Herz, Sharon Deborah, and Judith Leah. Anita was the daughter of Nathan and Sarah Jane Lifson of Mansfield, Ohio, and granddaughter of Nathan and Mathilda Waisbren, of Minneapolis. Mr. Waisbren had been the first president of the Talmud Torah of Minneapolis, which he had helped to establish.

Rabbi Rabinowitz had graduated from the State University of Iowa and had a master's degree in sociology from Yale University. Following his ordination at the Jewish Theological Seminary in 1943, he had served the seminary as field director in New York City and later as head of its midwestern office in Chicago. He became acting executive director of the United Synagogue of America, an office he held until accepting the call in 1946 to B'nai Jacob Synagogue in New Haven, Connecticut. A former president of Aleph Zadik Aleph (AZA), Junior B'nai B'rith affiliate, a chairman of the New Haven community relations committee, he had been active in many other communal and rabbinical organizations.

The Adath congregants met their new rabbi at the Congregational Dinner on June 3, and later that summer the Rabinowitz family settled in at 3520 Humboldt Avenue South.

Maurice Grossman, who was president of the synagogue at the time, was responsible for bringing Rabbi Rabinowitz to Minneapolis. He later recalled: "I got a telephone call one day from Sam Libman, my immediate predecessor as president, saying that there was a young rabbi in New Haven by the name of Stanley Rabinowitz. His wife's grandmother had died and the funeral was going to be in Minneapolis. He said, 'I understand he is a wonderful young man. You ought to contact him and go to the funeral and meet him.'

"Well, Sam Libman and I did go. I had never seen or heard of Rabbi Rabinowitz before but I fell in love with him. From the very moment that I saw and heard him, I was determined that he was going to be the rabbi at the Adath Jeshurun. I made life miserable for him. He was perfectly content to stay in New Haven although it was a smaller congregation and was located in the downtown area, with no possible chance for growth.

"His father-in-law owned a company that made electric coffee pots and appliances. He wanted Rabbi Rabinowitz to give up the rabbinate and go into his business because he was a smart young man and he could use him. ...Stanley was torn between the desire to do those things and his desire to be a rabbi. His grandfather was a very noted and revered rabbi in Des Moines who had been a tremendous influence over Stanley as a young man.

"Stanley was very active in AZA as a young boy and became the national AZA president. He was a wonderful speaker, a very handsome fellow, a wonderful guy and a very humble man. I thought he was the kind of guy that the Adath could really take care of and needed. The synagogue was not divided from a business point of view so that it could operate efficiently, and Stanley's background in business made a big difference.

"With Stanley, there was a sort of a love relationship—a personal friendship. I remember he was going to live in our present cantor's house and the house was pretty well run down in those days. I had the kitchen remodeled and did everything that was necessary including the plumbing. I even went and vacuumed the carpeting prior to his moving in there."

Rabbi Rabinowitz was already familiar with the region, having been born in Duluth and reared in Iowa. His wife, Anita, was a Minneapolis native and the couple had visited Beth El many times because her grandparents worshipped there. (His grandfather, Chaim Rabinowitz was a *shochet*.)

"The thought of working in Minneapolis professionally had never occurred to me," he admitted, "but once the opportunity presented itself, the prospect became very exciting. It was like recapturing a portion of one's youth. It was heartwarming. We fitted easily into the social and friendship pattern. We made many close friends in Minneapolis. I didn't find it necessary to protect my rabbinic dignity. Ours was a congregation that had always respected the rabbinate and learning, so the adjustment was an easy one."

Mendel Abrams, son of Gertie and Sam Abrams, was honored at Hillel for planning and conducting the Friday services during the year for University of Minnesota Jewish students. Rabbi Louis Milgrom, Hillel director, dubbed him, "The Erev Rov." That summer Mendel left for New York to attend the first summer session at the JTS.

In June Judge Irving Brand won a "smashing" victory in the Minneapolis general city election as a Municipal Court Judge. An editorial in the *American Jewish World* expressed the hope that Brand's victory, the largest majority of any victorious candidate, might help to dispell the city's reputation as the anti-Semitic capital of America.

A NEW SCHOOL

The final plans for construction of the school addition were approved in June. (Leibenberg and Kaplan were the general architects, with Lang and Raugland, associated architects, and Ralph Boom and Co., mechanical engineers.) Bids were formally opened on July 17 and contracts awarded July 28 to Naugle-Leck, Inc. for the general construction; Harris Bros. Plumbing Company for the plumbing and electrical work; and T.D. Gustafson Co. for the heating and ventilating. The total contract price was $249,500. The contractors promised to have the two-story building ready in 240 working days—10 months from the starting date.

Ellis Peilen later recalled one of the fundraising events held at Morris Grossman's house: "It was a cold wintry night and Morrie and I waited with bated breath for somebody to show up for the meeting. Finally the doorbell rang and in walked a person who introduced himself as Sim Heller. Neither of us had met Sim, as he had just moved to Minneapolis from Grand Rapids. We were kind of embarrassed to have a fund-raising affair for one person, but no one else showed up. We had such a pleasant visit with Sim and he gave us a big pledge so our evening was a success. From then on he became a candidate for the presidency. He did succeed me as president for four years which was a record, not since the days of Joe Schanfeld."

The formal ground-breaking ceremony took place at the building site on 34th and Dupont on August 4. Janet Kroll later described the event: " The atmosphere is a bit damp and muggy, but not so the spirits of the Adath Jeshurun building committee and the 200 congregants who came to witness the ground-breaking ceremonies. We can hear the rumbling of the approaching construction trucks with their cranes and bulldozers. A truck bearing lumber for the temporary building offices where Sukkot services used to be held, waits for the signal to unload."

Kroll went on to describe various friends greeting one another, including Rabbi Gordon's wife Dorothy "blond, elegant, alert, looking very Bostonian," who had returned from her new home in Massachusetts for the event, and Mrs. M. D. Mirviss "in her diminutive, bird-like dignity" trying hard to keep back the tears. Her husband was at that time too ill to attend the ceremony.

There was a momentary hush when Maurice L. Grossman, synagogue president, stepped forward with a sturdy, old shovel. Then came the voice of Cantor Morris Amsel ringing out in joyous solemnity: 'Mah Tovu Ohelecho Yaacov—How goodly are thy Tents, O Jacob!' The traditional ceremony had begun. Cameras began clicking and Adath Jeshurun history was being recorded. Another landmark was about to be created.

Ellis Peilen breaks ground for the Adath's new school wing.

Joseph Schanfeld dug up the first shovel of dirt, followed by old-timer Fred Zimmerman and the members of the building committee.

The arrival of Rabbi Rabinowitz and the ground-breaking of the new school were highlights of the year for the Adath, but it was an *annus mirabilis* for the broader Jewish community as well. Two of the city's leading Orthodox congregations, Kenesseth Israel and Tifereth B'nai Jacob, merged; the B'nai B'rith Hillel Foundation held a drive to construct a new building on the University of Minnesota campus; the Beth Israel-Chesed Shel Emes congregation built and dedicated a Bet Hamidrash; and a stream of visitors from Israel brought inspiring reports of steady progress in the development of the Jewish state.

A large Israel Bond drive had gotten underway, and Yehudi Menuhin, celebrated violinist, played a concert to a packed house at the Lyceum Theater. The Minnesota Jewish Council sponsored the first annual Institute on Community Relations. For the third successive year, the Institute for Adult Jewish Studies opened its season at the Gordon Memorial Talmud Torah building, with an expanded curriculum and enrollment. The first annual Chanukah Conference of Twin Cities Synagogue Youth Organizations took place in December. U.S. Senator Hubert H.

Humphrey spoke at the Jewish National Fund dinner and actor George Jessel addressed the kick-off dinner in April for the Minneapolis Federation for Jewish Service.

B'nai Abraham Congregation, an Orthodox group, (the former Rumanishe Shule) considered a move to St.Louis Park, and a change to the Conservative branch of Judaism to meet the growing needs of more than a thousand Jewish residents living there. Discussions were also taking place about building a Jewish Community Center in the same suburb. For the third year the Midwest section of United Synagogue held a retreat in August at Deer Park Lodge, Minocqua, Wisconsin.

1953-1954

For Rosh Hashanah, 5714, the Adath engaged Maurice Samuel, distinguished author, translator and lecturer, to deliver the Prelude and the Postlude to Prayer. Mr. Samuel had devoted more than 30 years to the transmission and interpretation of Jewish values to the English-speaking world. He told the Adath congregants that the survival of American Jewry would depend on the success of new survival techniques to match the pace and complexity of modern life—for example, the Jewish campus movement; the rise of the Jewish community center; and adult retreats.

The topics for Rabbi Rabinowitz's High Holiday sermons that first year were: "Balancing Our Books," "The Still Small Voice of Conscience," "Our Unfinished World" and "The Best Years of Our Life." Bella Braverman was choir director that year.

In September a group of a hundred young men were chosen by *Time* magazine as representative of Minneapolis' future leadership. Included from the Adath roster were Irving R. Brand, 34, municipal judge and Adath vice president; Howard Brin, 33, general manager of Brin Glass Co., district president of the Zionist Organization of America, and Adath secretary; and Rabbi Stanley Rabinowitz, 36, the newly appointed spiritual leader.

Women's League activities that season included a discussion of disciplinary problems in the home accompanied by the film, *The Angry Boy*; and the presentation of an Eternal Light script, *A Little Lower Than the Angels*, by University of Minnesota Radio Guild Players.

The Men's Club served a dinner in October with Bob Katz in the role of chief cook, and also put on a one-act play, *If Men Played Cards as Women Do*, by George S. Kaufman.

Sam Bender later recalled Rabbi Rabinowitz and his impact on the Men's Club:

Women had begun to serve on the Adath's board of directors by 1954, when this photo was taken. (Front row, from left) Ellis Peilen, Maurice Grossman, Rabbi Stanley Rabinowitz, Sheldon Gensler, Sam Libman; in the back you may pick out Cantor Morris Amsel, George Stillman, Gertie Abrams, Rose Filmer, Ruth Davis, Dr. David Pink, Lou Cohen, Jerry Fischbein, Irving Paradise, Art Fisen, Murray Abry, Sam Bender, and Barney Rubel.

We had a very successful Men's Club, about 350 members. I recall Stanley Rabinowitz very well because we became very good friends and he told it like it was... He asked me if I would take over as president of the Men's Club. I remember his exact words. I asked him about the religious part of the club. He said, 'You just get the Men's Club going, I'll take care of the religious part.' And he did!

The Adath held a panel discussion in December on the subject "Can There Be Peace For Israel?" with experts in geography, social science, and international finance from the University of Minnesota weighing in on the subject, and Rabbi Rabinowitz sharing his views on the United States government's role in Israel's foreign relations.

In September, the Adath Talmud Torah branch reached an enrollment of 200 for the first time. Meshulam Riklis was in charge at the time, with teachers Judith Riklis, Devorah Evers and Dalia Segal.

Linda Grossman Schibel shared her impressions of the school in those days: "I recall my Hebrew School teacher, Meshulam Riklis. His family came to the synagogue around the time of my Bat Mitzvah. There was also Haim Bernstein. He had fought in the Israeli War of Independence in 1948 and had lost a hand. The Riklis family were also Israelis. He and his wife, Judith, taught Hebrew School...I remember him and his good humor. He made it as fun as it could have been."

Elsie Perlmutter became the principal of the new Religious School on November 1, during its last year of classes at Calhoun School.

In December the board announced new Bat Mitzvah procedures. They would take place at the Sabbath Morning Services instead of the Sabbath Eve Service, in order to more closely resemble the Bar Mitzvah ceremony. Adath was becoming an egalitarian congregation!

The first Saturday Bat Mitzvah was Linda Grossman, the daughter of President Maurice and Marge Grossman. The ceremony took place April 10, 1954, during the Adath's 70th Anniversary year.

Linda Grossman Schibel: "It was the first time in the history of our congregation that there was a Bat Mitzvah on a Saturday morning. A very big deal was made out of it because a woman, a girl, actually held the Torah and participated in a Saturday morning service…As kids we regularly did participate in services and at Friday night services especially, but this was Saturday morning services."

The USY Midwest Annual Convention was held Thanksgiving weekend in Kansas City. Peter Edelman was elected regional recording secretary.

Mike Heiman was in charge of the Adath Basketball League. They played at the Temple Israel gym, Bethlehem Church, and at Southwest High School.

In December an article in the *Clarion* addressed the decline in appropriate dress among people, both young and old, attending services on the Sabbath.

"Ladies are expected to maintain the same regard for the proprieties of dress as they do for any other formal occasion. Hats are always appropriate for ladies in the synagogue. Young ladies who have reached the age of Bat Mitzvah are also expected to wear hats. It is permissible for them to utilize skull caps, if they do not customarily wear a hat. Young men should wear ties. The synagogue is not the place for open collars or sweaters, shirtsleeves or leather jackets…Attire should always be consistent with the sanctity of the synagogue at all times."

Proper procedure at a Bar Mitzvah was also spelled out. Bringing infants or young children to the ceremony was frowned upon, as were idle greetings and neighborly chatter that might disrupt the prayers. "A Bar Mitzvah is not a show, it is a religious service. You are not a spectator, you are a participant."

On January 24, 1954, the cornerstone for the new annex was laid, with a brass time-capsule containing permanent records of Adath Jeshurun Congregation's history sealed inside it.

Rabbi Stanley Rabinowitz and Talmud Torah director Lawrence Kaiser addressed the crowd, after which Morris Grossman called members of the congregation to come forth and place their items into the time capsule. Among those contributing were Harry Solomon, Max L. Levin, Sam Pink, Cecil Krelitz, Sam Bender, Mrs. H. Zimmerman, Murray Abry, Erwin Abrams, Elizabeth Peilen, and Daniel Lieberman.

Rabbi Rabinowitz applies cement to the cornerstone of the new annex.

The box was then set in position for sealing, and the trowel was passed from hand to hand as the elder statemen of the synagogue applied cement to the cornerstone.

The building itself was to be completed in April and dedicated on May 1, if all went according to plan, although it would not be put into use until Rosh Hashanah the following September, allowing time for it to be properly furnished and decorated.

During his first year at the Adath, Rabbi Rabinowitz distributed a detailed questionnaire to congegants to ascertian how they felt about the synagogue's programs. Gertie Abrams was chairman of the project, aided by President Maurice Grossman, Taube Masler, Marge Grossman, Lil Krelitz and Rose Zimmerman.

Upon the recommendation of the Women's League, Men's Club, Married Couple's League and Youth Committee, the Board of Directors voted to establish an Adath Board of Education. The objective was to coordinate recreational and educational activities at the Religious School, Youth Activities, and Nursery School. The board would consist of five members designated by the synagogue president (one of whom would be designated as chairman of the board) and four each from the Women's League, Men's Club, and Married Couples League. The Board of Education had begun its work when the congregation dedicated its new school building at a special Friday night service and open house April 30, 1954.

A celebration was held the first weekend after Passover, April 30-May 2, to celebrate not only the school annex dedication, but also the installation of Rabbi Rabinowitz, and the Adath's 70th Anniversary. Rabbi Morris Gordon spoke at the dedication ceremony for the building on Friday, and a touching note was injected into the Sabbath morning service when an old Torah rescued from pogrom-ridden Russia, the family possession of the Benjamin Wain of Chisholm, was installed in the Adath Ark.

The festivities included a ball at the Calhoun Beach Club and an installation banquet honoring Rabbi Rabinowitz, with Rabbi Albert I. Gordon delivering the address. An editorial in the *American Jewish World* noted that 70 years represented a mere sliver of time in the context of Jewish history, although in the context of *American* Jewish history, such a congregation "appears to have attained a venerable age."

"With the dedication of its new building," the article continued, "Adath Jeshurun will be properly equipped to perform the three-fold functions of the synagogue in history—a house of prayer, a house of study, and a house of assembly. In the pioneering stages of American Jewry, the old synagogues generally failed to meet these inter-related needs, with the result that so many of our Jewish activities became secularized and both the community and the personality of the individual Jew lost its vital integrated character. With its new facilities, Adath Jeshurun will be in a better position to make a distinct and creative contribution toward the integration and intensification of Jewish life."

It rained heavily during the weekend, and even snowed, but that didn't hold anyone back.

That summer Evelyn Silverman, editor of the *Clarion*, announced that for the first time, the publication would appear weekly from Rosh Hashanah through Shavuot. Bonnie Seltz was designated principal-teacher of the Adath Nursery School. She had been director and teacher for four years and also taught in the Religious school, city public schools and Emanuel Cohen Center.

Elsie K. Perlmutter, acting principal of the Adath Religious school, would become director of educational and youth activities. She had been a teacher in the Minneapolis public high school system and had been associated with Adath for 15 years in various capacities. A comprehensive program of adult education was being planned under her supervision, and also a complete recreational program including a youth canteen.

Also that summer the Talmud Torah board agreed, on an experimental basis, to a new plan submitted by Rabbi Rabinowitz for the Adath branch. The plan called for a revised and extended Hebrew education program for beginners. Sunday School classes would be eliminated for children who had reached eight years and were entering Talmud Torah (third grade in public school). The children would study Hebrew three days a week for 1¾ hours. One of the three days would be Sunday. Children in the next grade would also be urged to participate in the plan as a substitute for Sunday School. Rabbi Rabinowitz was convinced that this would be far more effective than a one-day-a-week system.

Other educational changes were also in the works at the Adath, due to the phenomenal growth in class enrollment that accompanied the Baby Boom. Classes would now be held on both Saturday and Sunday, though on Saturday the spirit of Shabbat would continue to be observed.

At about that time Rabbi Rabinowitz took it upon himself to revise the synagogue's funeral practices. He wrote to Morris Grossman on July 8, 1954, arguing that the synagogue ought to be available to all congregants for funeral services: "There is no question that in the past a funeral from the synagogue was reserved for an *adam choshuv* or an 'important, a learned, a saintly, and scholarly person'...today I fear that very few people could qualify under the limitations of the traditional definition. Moreover, who is to pass judgment on whether one is saintly, important, or honorable enough to merit a funeral at the synagogue?"

Rabbi Rabinowitz pointed out that in an age in which many Jews "do not think enough of their religion to affiliate themselves with the synagogue, but expect the synagogue staff to serve them at their pleasure," those who *do* become members should *ipso facto* merit a funeral in the synagogue. He went on to express his distaste for expensive ornamental caskets and vast banks of flowers, and set down guidelines that would return the attention of the bereaved to the grieving process.

Also during that year, Mount Sinai Hospital completed a $100,000 research laboratory, named in honor of president Jay Phillips; Temple Israel celebrated its 75th Anniversary; and B'nai Abram Synagogue, heeding the phenomenal rate of growth of the Minneapolis suburbs, took steps to move from 13th Avenue and 9th Street South to St. Louis Park and laid plans for constructing a synagogue at Ottawa Avenue and Highway 7.

On May 17, the Supreme Court ruled against racial segregation in public schools in the case of Oliver Brown vs. the Board of Education of Topeka, Kansas.

The movie of the year was *On the Waterfront* and the male lead, Marlon Brando, was voted, "Best Actor." Popular TV shows were *The Jackie Gleason Show* and *You Bet Your Life*. People were singing, "Fly Me to the Moon" and "Three Coins in the Fountain."

1954-1955

Formal Sabbath evening services began October 29 with a reception for members who had made pilgrimages to Israel during the past year. At the Oneg Shabbat following the service, Leo and Bess Frisch, Jennie Levitt, and Dr. William Medalie discussed "Israel Under Crisis," with Rabbi Rabinowitz as moderator.

Programs for children were many and varied that year. Cub Scout and Brownie troops were organized. The Board of Education endorsed a program with the Emanuel Cohen Center to establish a citywide Youth Canteen for young men and women ages 17-19, a concept Rabbi Rabinowitz had been working on with the Minnesota Rabbinical Association.

For adults there were Wednesday night classes sponsored by the Talmud Torah's Adult Institute of Jewish Studies, and a new Creative Arts program with Leon Sorkin, a well-known Minneapolis artist, teaching art classes; and Evelyn Raymond, former head of the Walker Art Center sculpture department, teaching sculpture classes. Adults and teenagers could also learn to rhumba, mambo and samba in dance classes taught by David LaVay.

In March the Arts Committee, composed of Marion Meyers, Shirley Rivkin, Ruth Heller, Sylvia Baker and Sylvia Levinsohn, with Theresa Berman as chair, opened the synagogue's art gallery with a series of events that included a display of ritual objects and an exhibit where members could purchase original works of art for their own collections or for the synagogue.

The 1954-55 year was a particularly busy one for Women's League. They published a cookbook and began a new fundraising project for the Religious School. Inspired by the Talmudic maxim that "the Torah is a tree of life to all who nurture it, and its supporters will find their lives enriched," Women's League members asked donors to purchase gold or silver leaves on a "Tree of Life" in the synagogue's assembly room, which would be individually inscribed with the donors' names. The family of Bertha Smiler dedicated the inscription on the tree trunk in her memory, "Who plants a tree benefits another generation," and the frame around the tree was dedicated in memory of Betty Halpern by the Dechter family.

Another successful fundraiser was the Phone-a-rama at the synagogue, where people could buy food, plants, and other things.

On the more serious side, Rabbi Rabinowitz was making an effort to encourage his congregants to observe a traditional Sabbath, spelling out the relevant practices in detail and giving each member of the family a set of responsibilities to make the Sabbath a more spiritual family experience.

Men were encouraged to leave work earlier on Fridays, to send or bring flowers for the Sabbath table, to dress for services before dinner. The wife would have spent the day cleaning the house, cooking Shabbat dinner and preparing meals for Saturday. The children were supposed to clean and decorate their rooms for the Sabbath, then dress "properly" for dinner and greet their parents with "Shabbat Shalom" or "Good Shabbos."

At dinner, father would bless the children and recite the kiddush. Mother would light the candles and welcome guests, if any. After dinner the father, having "steered clear of table-talk about business," would lead the *z'mirot* (songs for the Sabbath), recite the *Birkat Hamazon* (grace after the meal) and tell a Sabbath story to the children. Then it was time for the entire family to attend services, bringing friends if possible.

Saturday was to be a day to take time out to read a Jewish book or magazine. Mother would avoid all shopping and arrange an Oneg Shabbat party for the children, who were advised not to do schoolwork, write, draw, or paint.

In 1954-55, Rabbi David Younger came to Adath as principal of the Talmud Torah South Branch housed in the new education wing. He taught Bar Mitzvah lessons on Sunday and Talmud Torah classes Monday through Thursday, supervised the daily minyan service and the Junior Congregation's Saturday services, and took Rabbi Rabinowitz's place on the pulpit when needed. It turned out to be a demanding assignment, because the rabbi was much in demand as a guest speaker and also traveled extensively to participate in seminary functions.

Rabbi Younger stayed at Adath for 15 years. In 1969, when Talmud Torah moved its north and south branches to its new building in St. Louis Park, he left Adath to become Talmud Torah's Associate Director and Administrator of the High School and Bet Midrash.

During 1954-55 American Jewry celebrated the 300th anniversary of Jewish settlement in North America. The largest event in the Upper Midwest was a statewide rally on October 17, 1954, at Northrop Auditorium on

Rabbi David Younger, his wife Sara and son Bruce. Rabbi Younger served as principal of the South Branch of Talmud Torah at Adath.

tion "in one of the most exciting chapters in Jewish history," recommending that parents of all future Bar and Bat Mitzvahs give their children Israeli bonds as a "means of dramatizing the bond with Israel that a Bar or Bat Mitzvah service symbolizes."

It was also a year of mourning for Adath Jeshurun with the death of two of the most beloved and devoted members of the congregation. Joseph H. Schanfeld, 78, died in March, and on July 2, Meyer David Mirviss died at the age of 79. The synagogue chapel had been dedicated to M. D. Mirviss several years earlier. Now, in tribute to Joseph Schanfeld, the social hall of the synagogue was renamed Schanfeld Hall.

In September, 1955 the Adath inaugurated its own Wednesday evening Institute of Adult Jewish Studies, chaired by Morris Besner. This generated a degree of controversy, because the Talmud Torah was already sponsoring adult classes on the same night. Rabbi Rabinowitz pointed out no Adath members had enrolled in Talmud Torah classes the previous year because they had to go to north Minneapolis to register, and he went on to observe, with approval, that Temple Israel was also setting up their own Jewish Studies Institute. "Make it easier for all Jews to study, is my motto," he said.

Pearl Pearlman continued as Director of the Gan Hayeled Nursery School, with Janet Aelony, Dolly Rosenblum, Rita Neimark and Anne Dachis as teachers. Adath's was reputed to be one of the best nursery schools in town.

Pearlman later recalled that the student body was quite diverse. "We had Jewish and non-Jewish children, a Greek Orthodox boy, a black child whose family traced its history back to the Queen of Sheba, a Chinese boy. and many other interesting children. Gan Hayeled means Garden of Children, and it was literally a garden. They were beautiful."

The diversity of students notwithstanding, the curriculum at Gan Hayeled remained focused on Jewish themes. The school formed affiliations with other educational associations, and also with the Hennepin County General Hospital School of Pediatric Nursing. Pearlman enjoyed working with the nurses, many of whom were from small towns and had never met a Jew. "It was my job to take them on their last Friday into the sanctuary and open the Ark and tell them about the things in the synagogue."

During 1956 Rabbi Rabinowitz's sermons increasingly focused on Israel. In February he spoke on the Dead Sea Scrolls and joined with Cantor Amsel in a musical narrative, "The Judgment of Reb Yozifel," adapted from a story by Sholom Aleichem. In March he turned to "Politics and

the University of Minnesota campus, when 4,000 people gathered to hear Dr. Abram L. Sachar, Brandeis University's founding president, speak. As a tercentenary gift, 66 Minnesota Jewish organizations donated a large sum of money to the Minnesota Historical Society for purchase of Judaica.

The tercentennial year was also marked by creation of the Minnesota Fair Employment Practices Commission, after ten years of quiet lobbying. Governor Orville Freeman had supported legislation passed by the State Legislature in 1955, and he established the commission to administer the new law. The FEPC began by working with the local chapter of the B'nai B'rith Anti-Defamation League to put an end to anti-Jewish policy at northern Minnesota resorts.

At the Bar Mitzvah of Lyle Berman, his parents, Nathan and Theresa, presented him with an Israel bond and Rabbi Rabinowitz congratulated the young man on his participa-

Oil... Crude and Refined," the first of several additional sermons on the Middle East. Rose Zimmerman recalls that "the standing joke on Friday nights was 'Rabbi Rabinowitz is going to dig oil.' We didn't realize that he was warning us how oil was going to shape the Middle East and how it would affect us as Jews."

The focus on Israel continued at the annual Congregational Dinner, during which a painting by William Saltzman depicting the evolution of the State of Israel was dedicated in memory of M. D. Mirviss.

During the year the synagogue had received a number of other works of art as gifts, among them a mezuzah by Israeli artist Yehuda Walport which was hung at the Dupont entrance to the Education Building. It was a duplicate of the mezuzah on the entrance to the Weizman Institute in Rehovoth, Israel. Other Adath families picked up on the gesture, and soon mezuzot were hanging at the doors of all 16 classrooms in the new building.

1956-1957

Jerry Belenker had joined the Adath Jeshurun staff in 1955 as executive director, putting him in charge of the synagogue's burgeoning load of office and administrative work. In 1956 he resigned and Aaron Silman took over. During the transition, Harold Bernstein served as interim executive director, and then became youth activities director. Anna K. Schwartz, who had taught in the Minneapolis public schools as well as at Adath, became principal of the Religious School.

During the High Holiday services, Arthur Ballet, an Adath member and professor in the University of Minnesota drama department, gave a stirring reading from John Hersey's *The Wall*, the story of the Warsaw Ghetto. Local Israel Bond chairman and Adath member Howard Brin wrote a "thank you" to Rabbi Rabinowitz for his sermons about Israel, and also for the generous contibutions given by the Adath membership in response.

On December 7 the rabbi's sermon focused on the prospects for Conservative and Reform Judaism in the State of Israel.

Synagogue activities in 1956-57 included a masquerade ball in the tradition of Tel Aviv's riotous Purim "*Adloyada*" celebration, and a program for Jewish Music Month featuring Cantor Amsel chanting ancient ritual and Chassidic melodies, and Samuel Flor and his quartet of Minneapolis Symphony Orchestra musicians playing Eastern European folk music.

That spring David Jeffery established a Rabbi's Discretionary Fund. It would be used to publish the rabbi's sermons and purchase ritual materials which the rabbi might require but the congregation had not budgeted for.

As of September 1, 1957, Adath joined with the Minnesota Rabbinical Association to set new standards for Bar and Bat Mitzvahs. Every candidate would be required to have a minimum of one year's training at Talmud Torah, with the requirement extending to two years in 1958, three in 1959, and four years by 1960. Candidates and their parents would also have to attend Shabbat services for a minimum of two years prior to the time of their ceremony.

It was also understood that the candidate could be required to continue studying after the Bar or Bat Mitzvah, if specified by his or her synagogue. Exceptions could be made due to place of residence or other valid reasons, but boys and girls in this category would be required to pass a special examination administered by the rabbi at their synagogue.

In September, the Minneapolis Federation published a Survey of Jewish Education in Minneapolis by Louis L. Ruffman. The survey showed that a total of 3,034 children were receiving some education, although 56 percent attended only one day a week. Talmud Torah had shown a 63 percent increase in enrollment over the previous six years while the Adath Sunday School Elementary Department enrollment had declined 25 percent. This decline, of course, was the result of a 30 percent increase in Talmud Torah high school enrollment among Adath youth. At the time girls made up 40 percent of the total.

The study also showed that the basic problem facing Jewish communities was not the number of children who attended school, but the number of years they *stayed*. Yet the Adath's figure of 18 percent who continued on into the High School Talmud Torah after their Bar or Bat Mitzvahs was considerably higher than in other communities.

In regard to Adath's proposal that classes meet only three days a week, Ruffman felt it would tend to water down the curriculum. His suggestion was to maintain the four-day schedule at the Adath branch of the Talmud Torah, which was a blow to Rabbi Rabinowitz and his proposal that children spend two days at Talmud Torah and one day at Sunday School.

Friday night services were very well attended, and on Saturday mornings some 35 regulars were joined by 100 to 300 so-called "floaters"—guests of the Bar or Bat Mitzvah family. But attendance at the daily minyan remained weak, and that year both the daily minyan and the summer services were moved into the Mirviss Chapel.

Rabbi Rabinowitz's housing needs became a concern during the 1956-57 year. A committee headed by I. D. Fink was set up to investigate whether the synagogue could

Adath congregant I. D. Fink

provide a larger home for the rabbi and his growing family. Rabbi Albert Gordon had originally owned the home at 3520 Humboldt Avenue South, but when he left in 1946 the synagogue purchased it. Rabbi Morris Gordon had occupied the house from 1947 to 1952, paying $150 a month rent to cover the mortgage payments, and the Rabinowitzes had lived there since arriving in Minneapolis.

The synagogue proceeded to purchase a lot on Park Lane, on the east side of Cedar Lake, but later decided to buy a home from the estate of James Rappaport at 3916 West 28th Street, in St. Louis Park, for $50,000. The lot on Cedar Lake was sold.

The synagogue also purchased the duplex on 35th and Dupont Avenue where Cantor Amsel and Rabbi Younger were living. When the Rabinowitzes moved to St. Louis Park, Cantor Amsel moved into the house at 3520 Humboldt and Harold Bernstein moved into the duplex, which was later sold to the Youngers.

The 1956-57 congregational year ended with the annual meeting on June 13. President Ellis Peilen reported that 74 families had joined the synagogue that year, increasing membership to 830 families. The board voted a general revision of the dues structure to bring each member's dues to a level in keeping with his income.

1957-1958

That fall, joint Selichot Services at Beth El Synagogue underscored the ideological unity between Minneapolis's two major Conservative synagogues. Members of the recently organized B'nai Abraham Synagogue in St. Louis Park were also invited to participate.

The Women's League elected Lillian Gross president, a responsibility she referred to as "a full-time job." Rabbi Rabinowitz's wife, Anita, also took an active part in synagogue activities, sponsoring formation of a Women's League Book Review group that continues to meet.

In November, Ruth Stillman and Raleigh Cable chaired a Food Fair featuring cheese bagelach, blintzes, chopped liver and home-made preserves, as well as cakes and cookies. In February the Auxiliaries of Grace Presbyterian, St. John's Episcopal and Trinity Baptist Churches were guests of Adath Women's League for a program featuring "Favorite Hymns and Prayers of All Faiths."

In March, when Social Action chair Betty Rappaport planned a luncheon meeting with University of Minnesota Professor E. W. Ziebarth speaking on "Struggle for Survival: 1958," discussion session participants were Paulette Fink, Ruth Peilen, Betty Rappaport and Anita Rabinowitz. In April, they celebrated Israel's 10th anniversary with a program that included Habonim dancers and a movie depicting life in the Negev.

The Adult Studies Institute that year featured ten lectures on "Creative Personalities in Jewish Life" by Talmud Torah teacher Menachem Heilicher. For Men's Club, nationally-known celebrities who came to speak included Jewish humorists and television personalities Emil Cohen and George Jessel and stage and screen star Joseph Schildkraut. Members attending the Spring Dance and fundraiser had their choice of Grand Prizes—a trip to Israel for two, or a 1958 Chevrolet or Plymouth.

Twin Cities Conservative synagogues staged their second annual dinner in January, 1958 as a fundraiser for the Jewish Theological Seminary. The tenth anniversary of USY was also celebrated with a dinner honoring USY's founder, Rabbi David Aronson of Beth El. USY had grown from its beginnings in Minneapolis ten years earlier to 18,500 members in 340 congregations throughout the United States.

Two of Adath Jeshurun's most active members at the time were Ruth and Howard Brin. In October of 1957 they gave a "Dialogue Travelogue" Friday night sermon. In December, Ruth wrote a responsive reading for a homecoming service for university students.

Back in 1953, Rabbi Rabinowitz had begun to add new prayers and responsive readings to the service. "This was before so-called 'creative services' became popular," Brin recalled. "I began to write readings that were mimeographed as part of the Order of Worship for Friday nights. Rabbi Rabinowitz often mentioned his sermon subjects to me so the material could coordinate with his preaching."

Now Brin was being called upon again to write interpretations for the weekly Torah reading, because Rabbi Rabinowitz felt that many congregants couldn't follow the Hebrew and needed a short English version. "I began to work on this in about 1957," Brin recalled. "I had studied Bible in college and had taught Bible to Adult Jewish Study groups. Rabbi Rabinowitz supplemented this with suggestions for reading and with personal instruction so that I could understand the rabbinic and Talmudic interpretations."

Ruth's husband, Howard Brin, added that much of Ruth's writings for the weekly prayer reading came from midrashic material, though it also reflected her ideas about "contemporary implications—the Holocaust, civil rights, that kind of thing."

Rabbi Rabinowitz's 1958 semons included "Why Did God Create Cancer?," "Jewish Music in Hi-Fi," and "An Institute of Shame," which offered comments on an Institute on Middle East Affairs held the previous week under the auspices of St. Catherine, Macalester, Hamline and St. Thomas Colleges, in cooperation with the American Friends of the Middle East and the Foreign Policy Association.

At the 74th Annual Dinner that year, 350 congregants gathered to honor Adath's "first Bar Mitzvah boy," 80-year-old David Jeffrey, as a "humanitarian and citizen extraordinary." Jeffrey, who had celebrated his Bar Mitzvah at Adath on March 15, 1891, in the loft of a rented building in the old Gateway District of Minneapolis, near Washington and Nicollet Avenues, said "thank you" with an Endowment Fund for the study of Hebrew, which would cover scholarships for students and educational materials. Herman Neff and Harry Solomon were cited for many years of service to Adath, and Men's Club President David Gordon showed off the trophy Adath had received from the National Federation of Jewish Men's Clubs for "best all-around activities program for the year."

Judge Irving R. Brand, chairman of the Special Committee on Long Range Planning, was also on the program. He described how his committee had mapped out a program to keep pace with developing congregational needs for the next 12 to 15 years, including a $75,000 fund drive for building improvements. Martin Weinberger presented a check for $500 to the synagogue as the opening contribution to the campaign.

Another significant event in 1958 was the presentation of Samuel Bugatch's cantata, "Israel, A Dream Realized," adapted by Cantor Amsel, Ruth Brin, Rabbi Rabinowitz and Esther Rosenbloom.

In January Rabbi Rabinowitz was invited to New York to participate in an advanced seminar in international affairs sponsored by the Church Peace Union. In February he appeared on local television's "Religious Town Hall" discussing problems in the Middle East.

Earlier that day he had delivered a powerful sermon at First Universalist Church, identifying religion as the cause of much of "the bloodshed and strife which have made man his brother's murderer rather than his keeper."

"Wouldn't it be easier to achieve one world," he asked, "if man could achieve one religion, one mode of worship, one belief?"

But Rabbi Raboniwitz went on to reject this notion, arguing that "just because people have the same God doesn't mean they have the same history or tradition. To attempt to have one religion is to separate the ideals of a religion from the people that created those ideals... Religions can live together only if they can say, 'My religion is as good for me as your religion is good for you.'"

That summer, while the rabbi was in New York, eight young members of the synagogue delivered ten-minute sermonettes at well-attended Friday evening services. The speakers were Steve Bard, Harry Goldfarb, Zenith Kremen, Max Levinson, Daniel Frisch, Jerome Fischbein, Frederick Bob and Betty Rappaport.

1958-1959

Many special events were planned for the Adath's 75th anniversary year. In October Aaron L. Harris, 75, the oldest living active member of the congregation, was honored at a testimonial dinner. Harris had come to America from Lithuania in 1904, and in 1913 founded the Harris Brothers Plumbing Co. He had served on the Adath's board of directors for 18 years, 12 of them in the difficult post of house and building committee chairman.

At the dinner, the hardships and highlights of Harris's life were recalled alongside those marking the growth of Adath Jeshurun.

In November Sidney Goldish offered a survey of books of Jewish interest published during the previous year, followed by an exhibit of fine books from the synagogue's library and a preview tour of an upcoming exhibit by Israeli and local artists.

In December, Adath USY received the Outstanding Achievement Award at the 8th National USY Convention. The following year the first scholarships were awarded for the USY Israel Pilgrimage, an eight-week visit to Israel, in addition to Camp Ramah, Council Camp and Herzl Camp scholarships that were customarily awarded each year to 20 deserving Adath youngsters.

January, 1959, was kickoff month for the 75th Anniversary Improvement Fund. The money would be used to beautify the synagogue building. On March 6 Rabbi Albert I. Gordon returned as guest speaker at the 75th Anniversary Service and the annual dinner sponsored by Twin Cities Conservative congregations to raise funds

Leo and Lillian Gross, Ellis Peilin, Rabbi Rabinowitz and his wife Anita, Sam Bender (with mustache) and friends

for JTS. Shabbat services that weekend also featured the Adath's first B'nai Mitzvah for the Auerbach twins, Merrily and Ronald, children of Ben and Beatrice Auerbach, who had been married by Rabbi Gordon. Anniversary weekend festivities concluded Sunday morning with a speech by Dr. Simon Greenberg, vice chancellor of JTS.

In February of 1959 some 400 guests came to Adath for an interfaith luncheon sponsored by Women's League. Guests viewed a display of Judaica and listened to an original cantata, "Unfinished Journey," with libretto by Ruth Brin and music by Esther Rosenbloom.

In March Women's League celebrated Founders' Day, honoring five Adath women who had been "charter members" when the National Women's League was organized in 1918—Freda Abramovitz, Ida Selcer, Fanny Zimmerman, Lena Graceman and Mayme Shulman.

The women also held their first annual Awards Luncheon to honor "morning bowlers" Ruth Stillman, Mitzi Reiser, Juanita Farkas and Audrey Caplan. Men's Club brought in nightclub comic Jack Wakefield to celebrate Cantor Morris Amsel's "Bar Mitzvah"—his 13th year at Adath Jeshurun—and continued its 1950s innovation, Mother's Day Dinners. The men did the work under supervision of Sam Bender, a "take-charge" hobby cook who planned the menu and bought the groceries. "We served over 500 people on Mother's Day," Bender said. "That was a lot of cooking, and I was 'cooked' by the time it was through!"

For Married Couples League the year was one of service to the Gan Hayeled, installing coat lockers in the nursery school and buying additional playground equipment. They also sponsored monthly "socials" to integrate younger married couples and new members into Adath's activities.

The year 1958 was also Minnesota's Centennial Year of statehood. A Minnesota Centennial religious music concert at Northrop Auditorium featured traditional music of the four major religions.

As 1958 drew to a close, Adath was honored by the Jewish Book Council of America for its Jenny Gross Memorial Library. Minnie Zack, who had served as synagogue librarian for 20 years, was leaving town and William Silverman became the new full-time librarian. At Rabbi Rabinowitz's suggestion, a mourner's case was set aside for books that could be brought to a house of mourning for use during the week of Shiva.

The 75th Anniversary Year's final event was a Service of Tribute to those who had been associated with the synagogue for 25 years or more. The service took place during the annual meeting on June 7, 1959, and that day the first annual Shem Tov Award for service to the congregation was presented to Sam Abrams in recognition for his many years of Sabbath morning ushering and chairing many major committees, including the very successful Adult Education Program. (The Shem Tov award has become the most distinguished award for volunteer service given out by the Adath congregation.)

1959-1960

After many years of discussion and debate, in 1959 the practice of assigning seats for the High Holidays was finally brought to an end. For many members, giving up their seats meant real trauma, but for others it was a welcome change—and there were no more empty seats during services on the High Holy Days.

The previous year there had been no lecture on Rosh Hashanah, because the congregation was experimenting with the non-reserved seating plan, but now that the plan was in place, Rabbi Louis Milgrom was invited to speak for the High Holy Day prelude and postlude lectures on both Rosh Hashanah and Yom Kippur.

In the fall of 1959 Shelley Segal joined Adath as director of the afternoon nursery school, and Sander Latts was hired as activities director. Latts was a graduate of North High School and Bet Hamidrash and had been an early member of Beth El USY, LTF and AZA. He had a bachelor's degree in psychology from the University of Minnesota and was working on his doctorate in marriage and family relations.

One of the programs that Latts planned to co-chair with Rabbi Rabinowitz was a seminar for prospective brides and grooms. He also served as program chairman for the first Leadership Institute for Youth Advisors, held that November at Beth El. Some 50 club advisors participated in the workshops on synagogue club programming for boys and girls from grades 6-12. Representatives of the major synagogues and agencies in Minneapolis approved establishment of a Jewish Youth Council, with Adath member Murray Abry as chair of the adult advisory board.

Two distinguished members of the congregation won national honors that fall. Fanny Fligelman Brin was honored by the Jewish National Fund on her 75th birthday, October 20, 1959. She had been named one of the 10 out-

standing women in America and had been a consultant at the San Francisco conference where the United Nations was organized, representing the National Council of Jewish Women, which she had served as national president from 1932-38. The other honoree was Dr. Moses Barron, who was featured in a national medical publication as the doctor who had inspired Dr. Frederick Banting to use an extract that led to Banting's

Adath member Fanny Brin was honored by the JNF on her 75th birthday.

discovery of insulin as a treatment for diabetes. Dr. Barron had also celebrated his 75th birthday that year.

In December, architect Percival Goodman released a study commissioned by the Adath suggesting that its building was wholly inadequate for program needs, and that not much could be accomplished by adding to it or remodeling. President Sim Heller appointed Morris Besner, Dave Trach and Sam Segal to investigate possible locations for a new synagogue building.

On January 27, 1960, a letter was sent to the membership to inform them of the likely growth of the congregation. It described various alternatives that had been considered, among them plans to renovate the sanctuary, remodel the social hall, install an elevator, enlarge and improve the kitchen, build a new chapel and install air conditioning at an estimated total cost of about $175,000. Alternatives, according to the letter, were to build a new synagogue in the existing parking area and then raze the existing edifice, or to build a new synagogue at another, larger site.

In the months that followed, it became evident that the improvements outlined in the letter would cost considerably more than originally estimated. Total cost estimates were now $400,000 for the improvements already outlined, plus $100,000 for adding a third floor to the religious school building.

The board approved future construction of a new building, and directed the president to appoint a committee to begin the search for a suitable site for a new structure. The letter to the congregation pointed out that it would take at least five or six years before construction could begin. Actually, it would be more than 30 years!

Adath programming that fall included a series of three lectures on the subject of status, based on the then-popular book *The Status Seekers*, and Rabbi Albert Gordon's recently published study of the community's continuing flight to St. Louis Park, Golden Valley and other western suburbs, *Jews In Suburbia.*

In January the focus was on the Book of Job. On January 8, services consisted of a presentation of Archibald MacLeish's *J.B.*, with Arthur (Hecker) Rosenfield, a member of the Adath choir and president of Theatre in the Round Players, a community theater, in the role of J.B. Other cast members included Bud Goldstein, Muriel Levin Schuman, and Rabbi Rabinowitz, with Don Stoltz of the Old Log Theatre as director.

April brought a familiar topic back to the bema as Rabbi Rabinowitz spoke on the Middle East and its mixture of "water, oil and great power politics... in the light of the Passover story." Speaking on the prospects for peace, he compared the Red Sea, source of Egypt's undoing, with the waters of the Suez Canal, "which may yet be Egypt's undoing in the future, and the pathway to Israel's liberation in the present."

The successful summer Sabbath Eve sermon schedule of the year before was repeated with the theme "Words To Live By," with sermons by members Judge Irving Brand, Harry Goldfarb, Dr. Zenith Kremen, Max Levinson, Daniel Frisch, Jerome Fischbein, Frederick Bob and Betty Rappaport.

The 1959-60 year was also a busy one for organization members. The Women's League opened the season with "Accent on the Holidays - Your Table of Content," a musical presentation narrated by Cibi Neff with vocal solos by Claire Shore, musical accompaniment by Evelyn Siegel, original decorations by Shirley Rivkin, and commentary by Rabbi Rabinowitz. In a more serious vein, Federation President I. D. Fink, JCRC executive director Sam Scheiner, and Howard Brin participated in a panel discussion on anti-Semitism with Rabbi Rabinowitz moderating.

A January dinner meeting listened to Saadia Gelb, who had made aliyah to Israel in 1945. The Men's Club's Youth Leadership Award went to USY treasurer Gary Myers for his proficiency in Hebrew studies and leadership potential and active involvement at Adath.

USY member Howard Bard won the scholarship to attend the USY Israel Pilgrimage and spent six weeks that summer working on a kibbutz. The Adath basketball team went undefeated for the season and won the championship in the Minneapolis Church Athletic Association, with Mike Heiman coaching a team that included Tom Sklar, Bob Silverman, Harris Ravine, Myron Lazar, Paul Wernick, Sheldon Abrams, Bruce Peilen, David Broude and Herbert Levin. At the other end of the age spectrum, the Adath Social Club for retired members of the South Side Jewish community started meeting Tuesdays with a program of afternoon lectures, films, book reviews, socials, musical events, and monthly trips.

ADATH CONGREGANT
Carolyn Abramson

Adath has played a pivotal role in my life, at least the last 68 years, which were the most important ones of my life. I met Burton when I was 10 years old and moved to 3952 Ewing Ave So. He lived at 3804 Ewing, and the Adath is where we grew up together in our youth and for all of our married years.

I began my Sunday School years at the Adath. I remember our classes were rooms set up around the social hall. When Talmud Torah decided to have a class at the Adath, we met in the room upstairs, next to the balcony. The only bathrooms were two flights down. You can imagine it took up a lot of time when you asked to be "excused" from class!

There were three girls in the class along with maybe 10 boys. There was a group of us who didn't live near the synagogue, so we were picked up by taxi. When we started a chapter of Young Judea, we met in a room in the basement, next to the boiler room and another room where the janitor lived. I began my "teaching" career when I started teaching Sunday School at the Adath.

When Rabbi Aronson began a USY chapter in 1946, we had "mixers" events and when Adath was the host the food committee, all girls, of course, found themselves in the kitchen getting the snacks ready. When my own children got involved in USY, I was back in the kitchen, preparing dinners for their events.

If you wanted to talk with someone quietly, in a "private" place, you went into the small chapel which was next to the back door. You could say I knew every space of that building, including the office which was behind the choir loft!

All of my significant life events took place at the Adath. The Adath congregation was my "extended family." With each rabbi I had a different relationship, beginning with Rabbi Albert Gordon, who, when I was a child, was like the "voice of God."

For newly married couples, there was the "Married Couples' League." I'm not sure what all we did, but the pot luck dinners were great! I remember one meeting when Marty was a baby and I left him sleeping in the car, parked in someone's driveway!"

A Men's Club membership drive boating party on the *Tonka Belle*.

On May 14, 1960 two of Rabbi and Anita Rabinowitz's children, Nathaniel and Sharon, were called to the Torah as B'nai Mitzvah. The Rabbi wrote in the *Clarion* that because it was so difficult to be "both rabbi and father at the same moment," he would invite his uncle, Rabbi Max Schenk of Shaarey Zedek Synagogue in Brooklyn, New York, to become the rabbi of Adath Jeshurun for that Sabbath. "I shall be content to wear the tallis of a congregant," Rabbi Rabinowitz wrote, "and share the joy of the front pew with my wife and our family."

The following month, as the congregational year was coming to a close, Rabbi Rabinowitz announced that he had received a call from Adas Israel Synagogue in Washington, D.C. and would be leaving Minneapolis in June. He had occupied the pulpit there as guest rabbi during the last two days of Passover, and had told the Adath Board that he was considering an offer from Adas Israel. At the next Board meeting he made it official.

The congregation paid tribute to the Rabinowitzes at the 76th Annual Dinner June 16 at the Pick-Nicollet Hotel. Men's Club president Sidney Rich presented the Club's Bell-ringer Award to Rabbi Rabinowitz. The Shem Tov Award went to Herman Neff and a silver Yemenite Torah Pointer went to Howard Brin for the success of the Adath Jeshurun High Holy Day Israel Bonds appeal. But most of all, the focus was on the rabbi.

Emcee Fred Rappaport toasted the rabbi as "a truly great spiritual leader whose contributions have left an indelible mark on our Jewish and non-Jewish community." He also applauded the rabbi for living up to the *Time* magazine and Minneapolis Chamber of Commerce prophecy that he would be "one of Minnesota's 100 newsmakers of tomorrow," and lauded him for speaking out during the precarious, fearful times of the Sinai campaign, for his presidency of the Minnesota Rabbinical Association, and for his many other community activities. Rappaport also listed a string of accomplishments including the new school building and growth in membership to more than 3,000 individuals, representing 900 families.

In a farewell interview with the *American Jewish World*, Rabbi Rabinowitz said that "Washington is a capital city, but capital can mean many things. Minneapolis is a capital city in terms of Jewish activity, Jewish education, and Jewish life. Other communities have much more to learn from us than we have to learn from them. The cold climate here is more than compensated for by warm people."

Later he would write that "Jewish life was intense in Minneapolis... (and) it was easier to be a rabbi... The synagogue was more important to people... (and) the children found their social life in the synagogue.

"I recall the Adath Jeshurun congregation as one of the outstanding congregations in the U.S. in its commitment to positive Jewish values, its respect for education, for Hebrew, its response to liturgical creativity and its support of Israel. Adath pioneered the double services on the High Holy Days, a great experiment, one which helped other congregations resolve their attendance problems. I didn't like them, but it was necessary. We were innovative in Minneapolis. What we did with drama on the pulpit... *J.B.* and *Death of a Salesman*... The nursery school was an innovative effort... The idea of having a responsive reading based upon the weekly Torah reading was really original with Adath Jeshurun...

"One of the greatest problems of the rabbinate is that to be a successful rabbi, you have to admit to failure. We are all 'failures', because we can never satisfy all the expectations others have of us, much less the expectations we have of ourselves... So early on, the rabbi learns to feel that he is going to fail anyway, so he might as well give priority to the area which provides him with the greatest satisfaction and in which he is the most effective.

"In my case, I have given priority to the pulpit. A rabbi may be the greatest counselor and psychologist, a healer of the sick, a counselor of the bereaved, but... the pulpit is where the rabbi is measured... The r abbi wants to be a prophet. If he does his priestly functions reasonably well, he will have a chance to be the prophet. If he fails in the priestly functions, he'll never have a chance to deliver the prophetic message.

"It was Jacob who worked for seven years and then had to work seven more years for the woman he loved. Well, you will be the Rachel of my life, rather than the Leah."

Cantor Amsel, Rabbi Lipnick and congregants on Sukkot, 1964;
The 1964 Women's League Bowlers; Lillian Gross serving tea at Oneg

8

THE RABBI LIPNICK YEARS
(1960 – 1965)

Rabbi Jerome Lipnick arrived at the Adath with the desire to help its members become the best human beings they could be. He placed great emphasis on participation in services, study, and observing *mitzvot*. A man of keen intellect, his vision extended to issues of global dimension during that turbulent time.

The big news event of the Jewish year 5720 was the capture of Nazi Adolf Eichman by Israeli agents in Argentina. The Israeli Philharmonic made its first American tour and played at Northrop Auditorium as part of the University Artists Course series, and the first televised presidential debates took place between John F. Kennedy and Richard Nixon.

It was a time of mobility, and in Minneapolis many North Side and Adath families continued to move to the rapidly growing western suburbs of St. Louis Park and Golden Valley. The Talmud Torah, Emanuel Cohen Center and a number of synagogues remained on the North Side, and the South Side branch of Talmud Torah continued at Adath with Rabbi David Younger as principal.

Minneapolis was named an All-American City in 1964 with Major League baseball and football teams and a new airport terminal. The Minneapolis Symphony (which later became the Minnesota Orchestra) had a new conductor, Stanislaw Skrowaczewski, and the Tyrone Guthrie Theater was built adjacent to the Walker Art Center.

It was a time of triumph and tragedy, of economic growth and superhighways spanning the country; the beginning of the ZIP mailing system and the Peace Corps. The Civil Rights movement rocked the South, with Martin Luther King as its leader, and Fidel Castro led a social revolution in Cuba. The Cold War between the Soviet Union and the United States was at its height and more than a few families built bomb shelters in their back yards. Stereo sound and color TV came on the market, the Beatles appeared on *The Ed Sullivan Show*, John Glenn orbited the earth, and the world was shocked by the assassination of

President Kennedy in 1963. By 1965, Congress had passed the Civil Rights Act and civil disobedience over the escalating Vietnam War was on the rise.

At the Adath Jeshurun, the congregation was grappling with the departure of Rabbi Rabinowitz, who had been a charismatic orator and also an efficient adminstrator. A special board meeting was called on June 7, 1960 to interview Rabbi Jerome Lipnick, who was being considered as a replacement. The rabbi was questioned extensively about the daily minyan, pastoral duties, civic participation, pulpit presentation, attendance at social functions, the youth program and other areas of rabbinic participation. It was suggested that a committee member attend a service conducted by Rabbi Lipnick, and that additional candidates be interviewed. However, encouraged by the recommendation of Adath President Sim Heller, and the JTS placement office, the board unanimously endorsed Rabbi Lipnick to serve as the Adath's new spiritual leader. The family would use the rabbi's residence at 3915 West 28th Street in St. Louis Park.

Sim Heller, the recently elected president, was a retired businessman, soft-spoken but firm, who spent many hours on congregational administration. He had been a school principal in Grand Rapids, Minnesota, before his business success.

In Rabbi Rabinowitz's final talk to the congregation at the 76th Annual Meeting, June 16, 1960, he referred to Rabbi Lipnick as an excellent choice, "who is a deeply devoted and wonderful individual whom the congregation shall certainly appreciate." He said they should "welcome Rabbi Lipnick and offer their assistance in attaining a common purpose for the membership of the Adath Jeshurun Synagogue."

The period between rabbis was a rocky one. As Lillian Gross recalled, "Between Rabbis Rabinowitz and Lipnick was a period when we were afraid of losing the cohesiveness of the congregation. The Men's Club and Sisterhood combined to have a number of very successful Sunday night dinners to help keep unity."

Adath Jeshurun's new rabbi was born on February 4, 1918, in Baltimore, Maryland, to Augusta Kanowsky, from Kishinev, Russia, and Thomas Lipnick, from Lithuania. Rabbi Lipnick's parents had immigrated to Baltimore in the first decade of the twentieth century. Jerome "Jerry" Lipnick had a younger brother, Bernard, Rabbi Emeritus of the B'nai Amoona Synagogue in St. Louis. Jerry and Bernard were strongly influenced and inspired by their teacher, Dr. Louis Kaplan, dean of the Baltimore Hebrew College which they both attended.

Rabbi Lipnick had earned degrees from Baltimore City College, Johns Hopkins University, Baltimore Hebrew College & Teachers Training School, and the Jewish Theological Seminary of America, where he was ordained in 1945. Following a couple of temporary assignments, Rabbi Lipnick served as rabbi of Congregation Beth El, in Utica, New York, from 1946 to 1960.

Rabbi Lipnick met his future wife, Joan Leff, in 1947 through a former classmate, Dr. Jack J. Cohen. Joan was born in 1926 to Sally Zamzok and Dr. Jacob H. Leff and grew up in New York City. Her mother was an accomplished music teacher, pianist, and accompanist. Dr. Leff was a 1914 graduate of the New York University Dental School.

After graduation from Barnard College in 1946, Joan worked as a research assistant to Dr. Louis Finkelstein, JTS Chancellor. The Lipnicks were married on December 21, 1947 and had three children, Miriam Joyce, Robert Charles, and Jonathan.

When Rabbi and Joan Lipnick moved to Minneapolis in 1960 there were 22,000 Jews living in the city. The Adath Jeshurun had 921 families with a very active congregation of well over 3,000.

On Friday, September 2, Rabbi Lipnick assumed his rabbinical duties. Dr. Markel Karlen was guest speaker at services, and an Oneg Shabbat was held to welcome the Lipnicks. That fall various board members sponsored parlor meetings to get acquainted with the new rabbi.

When Rabbi Lipnick was asked in an interview for the *American Jewish World*, "Why did you pick Minne-

apolis?" He replied, "I have been surrounded by Minneapolitans all my life!" His best friends at the JTS had been his roommate, Rabbi Moshe Goldblum (grandson of Adath founder Kive Goldblum), Rabbi Kassel Abelson, and Rabbi Moses Sachs, a close friend since their Baltimore boyhood days at Talmud Torah and Hebrew College. He had been the best man at Rabbi Sachs' wedding to Francis Schwied of St. Paul and Rabbi David Aronson was one of his favorite instructors.

He was also acquainted with Rabbis Theodore Gordon, Norman Shapiro, Melvin Kieffer, and Max Vorspan; and Melford Spiro, anthropologist and author of *Children of the Kibbutz*. Stanley Rabinowitz, his predecessor in the Adath pulpit, had been president of the student body when Lipnick served on the executive committee in 1945. He also knew former Adath Rabbis Albert Gordon and Morris Gordon.

At his first Rosh Hashanah service in 1960, Rabbi Lipnick spoke to the congregation about Israel: "Our observances of Rosh Hashanah this past decade have been a paradoxical blend of fear for the safety of Israel and profound pride in its ability to withstand assaults from its surrounding foes while moving dramatically forward in the fields of creative life."

But his early efforts were also directed toward deepening the congregation's commitment to Jewish observance and values. Al Meirovitz said: "He tried to bring more tradition back into the congregation."

He felt the purpose of the synagogue was to help members become positive Jews and the best human beings they could be. This would involve assuming

Al Meirovitz

obligations including participation in services, study, and observing *mitzvot*.

Dr. Marvin Bacaner said, "I admired Rabbi Lipnick. He was a real scholar and I always found his views interesting and well grounded. He knew a lot. He was a fine man, a good pastoral rabbi and he never missed seeing the sick or bereaved. He was a teacher, a role model, a good person and very spiritual."

As a means of putting his ideas into effect, Rabbi Lipnick gave a series of monthly talks and workshops

From left, Rabbi Lipnick, a guest speaker, Morrie Grossman and Sam Bender

on Jewish customs and rituals at the Men's Club Sunday breakfast meetings. During his first year he also served as moderator for ten lectures on "Integrity and Compromise in Daily Life" at the Adath Adult Institute, where prominent members of the community discussed the ethical dimension of their professional lives. Among those who participated were *Minneapolis Star & Tribune* journalist Sidney Goldish; former Minneapolis mayor and political science professor Dr. Arthur Naftalin; Howard Appleman, manager of the Nuclear Warheads Division of Minneapolis Honeywell; and University of Minnesota Medical School Assistant Dean, Dr. William Fleeson.

On the weekend of January 13-15, 1961, Rabbi Lipnick was formally installed as the rabbi of Adath Jeshurun. At Friday evening services past presidents of the synagogue, Women's League, Men's Club and MCL were recognized.

In the *Clarion* that month, Rabbi Lipnick described the other events of the weekend, and on a more personal note, he also described an experience he had while interpreting Psalm 50 to a Lutheran church class. As he read the lines, "From the rising of the sun unto the going down thereof, out of Zion the perfection of beauty," he looked up and saw the sunset through a huge window. "The very subject of the psalmist's wonderment was being enacted outside while our noses were buried in a book. I interrupted my reading and invited everyone to look up at the glorious sight...Study is never a substitute for the thing itself, nor is a weekend of dedication," said the rabbi.

According to Ruth Brin, Rabbi Lipnick often drew inspiration from the remark of the French thinker Charles Peguy: "Religion begins in mysticism and ends in politics."

"That was Rabbi Jerome Lipnick," Brin said, "often going from inspiring psalms to a beautiful sunset to the demand for action, 'from mysticism to politics,' a journey he often made."

In Utica, Rabbi Lipnick had helped found a Citizens' Association that worked against corruption in city government, and for his efforts was the first person to be made an Honorary Life Citizen of the city. Rabbi Lipnick admired the political climate in Minneapolis and soon became involved in interfaith activities. He continued the tradition of holding jointly sponsored Thanksgiving services with neighboring churches Grace Presbyterian, St. Paul's Episcopal, Trinity Lutheran, and Temple Israel.

There was no assistant rabbi, but Rabbi David Younger helped out when needed. Rabbi Lipnick also assisted with each of the constituent organizations, conducted study groups, weddings and funerals, worked with program committees and attended board meetings. He was also a wise counselor and caring friend to those who approached him individually.

Through his *Clarion* column, "From Where I Stand," Rabbi Lipnick shared his thoughts on a variety of issues, including the role of the rabbi in Jewish life and the difficulties of getting to know the members of a large congregation individually—especially those who seldom come to the synagogue. He wrote about baseball, a sport he loved, and he tried to impart to prospective newlyweds the importance of having a good sense of humor. He wrote about how urgent it was that people know something of their roots, who their grandparents were, and where they came from. And he wrote about the privilege and responsibility of voting in a democracy.

Rabbi Lipnick had been deeply affected by the annihilation of European Jewry during World War II and by the inaction of much of the population during those dark years. During his seminary days, he and friends Moshe Sachs and Noah Golinken had proposed an action program. Now, 20 years later, his concern about the Civil Rights movement led him to participate in two voter-registration drives in Mississippi, and to go to Martin Luther King's "March on Washington" in August, 1963.

He was accompanied on this mission by Rabbi Moshe Sachs, Max Fallek, and William "Bill" Budd, director of the Minneapolis JCC, along with 54 others from Minnesota. They went as individuals rather than as representatives of the institutions with which they were associated.

Bill Budd gave his interpretation: "Those of us who flew to Washington as the Minnesota contingent to the 'March on Washington' grew up in an atmosphere of belief in human dignity and freedom for all people regardless of race, color, creed, or nationality. Many of us who went into the helping professions were deeply committed to the betterment of our society for all people.

"As leaders in our respective organizations, we were well aware of the fact that fighting hatred and bigotry wherever it appeared was also good for the Jews. We often went it alone. Many of the rank and file of our organizations were afraid to get involved. 'Don't rock the boat' was the attitude and many did not appreciate our involvement and did not want to be identified with these movements. We participated as individual citizens.

"I recall how committed Rabbi Lipnick was to these causes that were more global than administering to the needs of a congregation. It was also more rewarding and fulfilling to be involved with a group that needed our help and were appreciative. This was the first grass roots movement in the U.S. that attracted hundreds of thousands of people. There was an excitment for us to be involved."

At the urging of Rabbi Lipnick, the congregation started a social action committee in 1963 with Howard Brin as chairman. Some of the Adath congregants were very proud that Rabbi Lipnick participated in Civil Rights demonstrations, but there were others who felt that he should be minding his flock at home.

Harold Chucker said, "I think a lot of us were quite proud of him at that time because we wanted our leaders to be involved. This was a traumatic time for most Americans. Some of us who were liberally inclined wanted to help and also have our leaders do everything they could for the Civil Rights movement. We were delighted to see that Rabbi Lipnick joined in and was our representative there.

"I don't think that most of the congregation felt that way. Some thought his job was at home and not traipsing off somewhere. Some of us wanted him to be involved not only in Civil Rights but in nuclear disarmament and other major issues. He was very idealistic."

NEW IDEAS

Beginning in 1961, Rabbi Lipnick introduced a new three-week series as an orientation for new members. It was designed to provide insight into the synagogue and its activities, the Conservative movement and its meaning, and Jewish life in the home and synagogue.

The next year a "book of the year project" was started so that every congregant could participate in a book discussion. The first book suggested was *The Gentleman and the Jew* by Maurice Samuel, followed the next year by a new Torah translation; and in 1964, *Basic Judaism* by Milton Steinberg. The rabbi hoped that the various constituent groups within the congregation would incorporate the project into their own programs.

Another innovation in Adath programming was the Kallah Scholar-in-Residence program, through which scholars came to lecture for a full weekend. The first speaker invited was Rabbi Lipnick's former teacher, Dr. Louis L. Kaplan, Dean of the Baltimore Hebrew College. In the ensuing years, the congregation heard JTS Chancellor Gerson Cohen, and Dr. Mordecai Kaplan, founder of Reconstructionism and one of Judaism's great educators and writers.

André Trocmé, pastor of the Church of St. Gervais in Geneva, Switzerland, also spoke from the Adath pulpit. He became much better known after the publication of Phillip Hallie's book, *Lest Innocent Blood Be Shed*. The book detailed how the Trocmé family and their neighbors in the French village of Le Chambon Sur Lignon rescued more than 5,000 Jews during the German occupation of France in World War II. Among those rescued were Francelyne Oppert Lurie and Nadine Oppert Bicher, children of Paulette Oppert Fink, a heroine of the French Resistance and active in saving Jewish children through Youth Aliyah to Israel. Their father and her husband, Yves Oppert, a hero of the French Resistance, was killed by the Nazis two weeks before the Allies liberated Paris.

"Miss Dolly" Rosenbloom (left) and Cecil Kiperstein with an Adath Consecration class in in 1960

Paulette became an international speaker and fundraiser for the United Jewish Appeal and served as national campaign chair of the Women's Division during this period. She married Adath member, Israel "Iz" D. Fink, in 1954 and moved with her daughters to Minneapolis. Iz became a UJA activist and president of the Minneapolis Federation for Jewish Service. Both Paulette and Iz spoke from the Adath pulpit.

During those years the Adath had many leaders who also worked in the broader Jewish community. Leo and Lillian Gross were honored at the Israel Bonds dinner in 1961 with Israel's Ambassador to the U.S., Avraham Harman, as guest speaker. Leo had been Minneapolis' first Israel Bond Chairman; was Minneapolis Federation campaign chair in 1943; Jewish National Fund and Adath vice president; and Talmud Torah president. Lil was a chairperson for Israel Bonds and Women's Divison of Federation; president of Adath Jeshurun Sisterhood and vice president of National Women's League.

Also prominent among Adath community leaders were Jay Phillips, philanthropist and founder of Mount Sinai Hospital, elected in 1961 as the first president of the Minneapolis Chamber of Commerce; Dr. Moses Barron, ac-

tive in Zionist causes and honored by the JTS; Howard Brin, first president of Israel Bonds for Minnesota and the Minneapolis Jewish Community Center; Ellis Peilen, active in Federation and B'nai B'rith; Martin Ucko, president of B'nai B'rith Ira Weil Jeffery Lodge; Ruth Davis, president of the Women's Division of Federation, active nationally and locally in the Girl Scouts of America; Fritzi Hodroff, Israel Bonds chair; Pearl Pearlman, president of the Minnesota Pre-School Education Association; Fred Rappaport, 1961 Federation campaign chairman; and Mendel Abrams, ordained as a rabbi at the JTS.

In September, 1961, Fanny Fligelman Brin (Mrs. Arthur) died. She had been one of the outstanding Jewish women of her day. Her parents, John and Antionette Fligelman, were among the earliest members of the Adath Jeshurun. Fanny graduated Phi Beta Kappa from the University of Minnesota in 1906. She taught at West High School and was the first woman appointed to the Minnesota State Teachers' College Board.

She was one of the state's first suffragists; national president of the National Council of Jewish Women, 1932-38; named one of the 10 outstanding women in the U.S.; chair of the Minneapolis Women's United Nations

Committee; director of the Minneapolis branch of the American Association of University Women, and was also active in numerous other organizations.

An editorial in the *AJW* noted, "The passing of Mrs. Arthur Brin marks the end of an era of pioneering...She was reared in a home where the values of American democracy were fully appreciated and adopted without giving up the basic values and spiritual traditions which the immigrants brought with them. She was one of the first children of Jewish immigrants to become an English teacher in an American school, and to volunteer to teach in a religious school for Jewish immigrant children on the North Side."

In 1962, outstanding scholar and former Adath president Louis Schwartz died, as did former Adath Rabbi Jesse Schwartz.

Rabbi Lipnick had an egalitarian view of women's roles in the synagogue. He encouraged them to say Kaddish, to be counted in the minyan, to receive *aliyot*, and to be in leadership positions. In a column he wrote in 1965 he discussed Betty Friedan's book, *The Feminine Mystique*, saying that he "looked to the day that a woman would be elected president of a congregation and of the United States..." and felt that "Israeli women were an irreplaceable force in Jewish and human history."

Joan Lipnick was not only his helpmate as a *rebbitzen* but was a vibrant, involved participant in many phases of congregational and Jewish communal activities. She initiated, wrote, and participated in many programs for the Sisterhood and on occasion from the pulpit.

Al Meirovitz recalled: "Joan was charming, lovable, personable, a most outstanding lady—deeply involved with every facet of the congregation. She loved people and was everybody's friend...a truly great lady."

The Lipnicks were gracious hosts, and often invited synagogue groups to meet in their home.

It was during Lipnick's tenure that the Adath published congregant Ruth Brin's book, *Interpretations for the Weekly Torah Readings*. The book was begun with the help of Rabbi Rabinowitz and written over a seven-year period. It was completed with Rabbi Lipnick's assistance and became a congregational project. Published by Harry Lerner's company, Lerner Publications, illustrated and designed by Sharon Lerner, and printed by Leo Kibort, all Adath members. The poems in it have been reprinted in anthologies and prayerbooks of various Jewish movements.

This book and an earlier one by Brin, *A Time to Search*, were among the first to be published on prayers written for services, and, were among the first by a woman to find wide acceptance. During the 1970s, the Conservative movement would continue down this road toward greater equality for women and more lay participation in services.

Congregant and author Ruth Brin

A talented new local theatre group produced successful amateur plays and musicals that year. In May 1961 they put on *The Matchmaker* at the Prudential Theatre with Charles Brin, who had just returned from acting on Broadway, in the role of the director. Hannah Donsker and Sidney Rich led the talented cast.

The following year, 1962, Cibby Neff and Shirley Rifkin wrote *No, No, Noah*. Special kudos went to Bill Aberman who did a hilarious job with Yiddish as the philology professor, and to Leo Gross as a Talmud Torah teacher.

The Women's League had expanded by this time to more than 600 members and published a monthly newsletter, *The Adath Jeshurun Women's News*. In 1962 the women voted to change their name from the Women's League to the Sisterhood.

The Sisterhood traditionally hosted Oneg Shabbats on most Fridays, but beginning in 1961 congregants were encouraged to sponsor an Oneg Shabbat following services to honor happy occasions such as Bar or Bat Mitzvah, wedding aniversaries, birthdays and new babies. This soon became a tradition at the Adath.

In February of 1962, the Adath held an "Interfaith Tea" to help their Protestant neighbors understand the Jewish religion.

In 1962, Ruth Dechter was Sisterhood president and at their opening fall meeting they had a panel of authors including Bill Hoffman, Ruth Brin and Ruth Schulman, speak on "So You Want to Write a Book."

During those years the Sisterhood held institutes with other Conservative Sisterhoods on Sukkot and one on "The Jewish Woman and the Feminine Mystique." There were adult education programs including braille, social action, and Judaism in the home; religious school and holiday observances; helping feed and house foreign students; mental health group visits to Hastings Hospital; gift shop;

Torah Fund; Leagrams; Atida Fund; and Freedom Lunch for youth groups on Passover.

The Sisterhood furnished the synagogue with 100 cushioned chairs, 22 round tables, silver serving dishes and trays, wine glasses, and meat and milk services for 300 people. And they set up new committees—a "foster parent" and a "visiting" group to visit the chronically ill and shut-ins at home—at the request of the rabbi.

The Sisterhood and Men's Club gave gifts of membership in the Jewish Publication Society toor Bar Mitzvahs, candlesticks for Bat Mitzvahs, and prayer books for confirmands.

The Men's Club continued to take care of the ushering, sponsor dinners and lectures, and the very successful Sunday morning breakfasts. Some of the speakers included Drs. Velvl Green, Hyman Berman, and Daniel Elazar, Mayor Authur Naftalin, State Representative Robert Latz, Rabbi Louis Milgrom, local author William Hoffman, and Minneapolis JCC director, Bill Budd. During the transition year of 1963-64, Alan Abrams arranged the breakfast discussion series with members leading the discussion on subjects chosen by Rabbi Lipnick.

Sidney Rich later remarked that "the rabbi's off-the-cuff observations delivered at each discussion were positively brilliant, and unveiled a depth of knowledge, humor and penetrating thought which has, sadly, been missed by those who did not attend these breakfast discussions."

The Married Couple's League served as a meeting place for new couples, but it also acted as a bridge between the newly married and the wider Adath congregation.

Irving Nudell said, "This group had a very interesting function. A number of people were members for several years before they joined the congregation. The MCL was a recruiting device for the congregation. Much of the leadership of the congregation came out of it, a lot of committee chaipersons, officers, etc."

At the core of the MCL was a study group that met on nights another than when MCL met. It was the forerunner of all the study groups in the congregation and is still functioning. Rabbi Lipnick was the leader. Some of the original members were Jules and Dora Zaidenweber; Ruben, June, Esther and Marty Miller; Esther and Morrie Katz; Fred and Shirley Bob; Marilyn and Harry Karasov; and the Spitzes (who moved to Chicaco).

By 1965 there was large reduction in the number of children entering the Religious School. Some of this was due to the rule requiring Bar and Bat Mitzvah students to attend Talmud Torah.

In September, 1961, an Oneg Shabbat was held honoring Myrna Amsel who was leaving to take a job in New Jersey. Myrna, the oldest of Cantor and Sabine Amsel's four daughters, had directed the junior choir at the age of 14; had been a soloist and director of the Adath choir; directed confirmation cantatas, taught post-confirmation classes, and had sung and played the guitar at many Jewish weddings. No one who heard the duets she sang with with her father would ever forget them.

She had enriched the religious and cultural life of the synagogue through the warmth of her music, her service as teacher and leader of young people and her dedication to the congregation. Myrna with her parents gave much to the congregation during their years of participation. They were deeply loved.

Cantor and Sabine had been a link of stability at the Adath during periods of transition in rabbinical leadership. Sabine gave of herself completely. She edited the *Clarion*, she edited the *Women's League News*, she wrote skits, helped presidents write their speeches and helped in every way she could.

The Amsels were honored at an Oneg Shabbat for 16 years of service in June, 1961, before they left for their first trip to Israel. With their daughters, Myrna, Toby, Joy and Michelle, they had put on an outstanding evening program, "A Night With the Amsels," with English, Yiddish, Chasidic, Israeli, religious and folk music. Myrna narrated and played the guitar with Joy playing an Israeli drum.

Al Meirovitz became the synagogue's new executive director in 1961. He recalled, "The biggest change during Lipnick's leadership was with what we now call the Saturday Morning Program (SMP). This was patterned after a program that was started at B'nai Abraham and was looked down upon by the other congregations. It was a program run by the kids, for the kids.

"We always considered ourselves a very professional synagogue. The teachers all had to have teaching degrees or had to be college students, qualified to teach. B'nai Abraham showed us that a 15-year-old could teach a 12-year-old, a 16-year-old-could teach a 13-year-old, etc. Consequently, we learned that it was possible and this evolved into SMP. We had to start with nothing because we didn't have Torah readers. We started teaching Torah reading, cantorial skills and Israeli dancing and the real way to celebrate Jewish customs, traditions and holidays.

"Over the years SMP became the strongest religious educational experience that the kids could have. They learned how to read, write and spell in Hebrew at the

The Amsel family doing a Torah Fund luncheon concert for the sisterhoods of Adath Jeshurun and B'nai Abraham. From left to right: Joy, Myrna, Toby, Cantor Morris, his wife Sabine, and Michelle

Talmud Torah and that tied into SMP."

Howard Brin said, "Rabbi Lipnick encouraged younger members of the congregation in Torah reading classes. When our daughter, Debbie, had her Bat Mitzvah in 1963, our two sons, Aaron and David, each read from the Torah. It went so well that he asked them to read Torah for the 1963 High Holidays. I believe it was the first time and it created quite a stir. The question was raised whether young people could be a *Baal Kriah* for the congregation. This clearly was one one of the things Jerry was interested in doing. He gave it the impetus.

"Morris Amsel then started a Torah reading class open to all, but in the beginning it was the young people that took to it more than the older members."

In 1961, a special Shabbat was held to honor Eve Karon, who had taught in the religious schools for 20 years. The entire religious school staff was honored that day. The next year, Eve continued to instruct the four-to-seven year olds at a story hour on Shabbat mornings.

In 1961, Sol Serber was appointed youth director. A Talmud Torah graduate, he had been active in synagogue work for many years working as cantor and youth director at Tifereth B'nai Jacob, Kenesseth Israel, and Mikro Kodesh. He taught at Torah Academy and worked with Golden Age groups for the Minneapolis JCC.

Sol Serber was instrumental in revitalizing USY, preparing a blueprint for the Youth Congregation, Children's

Sabbath Hour, and forming a *Baal Kriah* group for boys ten years and older to learn to read Torah. Mr. Strimling led the Torah Reading Group.

Mike Yablonski directed the musical portion of the Junior Congregation Service and a Junior Congregation Choir comprised of 16 boys and girls received special choral training. Rabbi Younger offered explanations and background material for the understanding of the prayers, interpreted the synagogue rituals, and explained the highlights of the weekly portion.

A weekly Kiddush was served in room 101 at the conclusion of the service.

Between 1961 and 1963 the Adath and B'nai Abraham conducted an experimental Joint Youth Program combining the use of all physical facilities of the two congregations. An office was maintained at the Adath, expenses were jointly shared, and six members were appointed from each synagogue along with a chairman. Sol Serber was hired by the Joint Commision as the director to serve both congregations under the direct supervision of Rabbis Lipnick and Sachs. He organized bowling and roller skating parties, a social dance class, photography, chorus, Oneg Shabbats at the Lipnicks' home, and a conclave at Lyman Lodge with food prepared and served by Adath mothers. "Firsts" included a Brotherhood Banquet and a Freedom Luncheon held the first day of Pesach for the Junior Congregation, USY, and the religious school.

Approximately 125 children attended on Sabbath

mornings from Simchat Torah to the end of the religious school year. The basic aims were to offer the children a valid religious experience through public worship at their own level, to give them a better Jewish education by means of a pleasurable, rewarding activity, and to educate them for future participation and leadership in the religious life of the adult Jewish community.

In 1960, a Habonim program was added to the existing Adath Jeshurun youth program for a one-year trial. The group presented musicals in Hebrew, including *Oklahoma* and *The Wizard of Oz*. A year later the question of sponsoring Habonim was heatedly debated but a majority voted to continue their sponsorship at the synagogue.

DECISIONS

At the 77th Annual Meeting, June 4, 1961, Sheldon Gensler, chairman of the Site Committee, reported that potential sites in Minneapolis and the southwest area had been examined but no suitable property had been located for a new synagogue. He recommended that the synagogue remain in the present area contingent upon success in acquiring more property in the adjacent area.

A resolution was passed to give a free membership for the first year of marriage to all children of congregants.

The Adath By-Laws had not been updated since 1949. In 1962 a comprehensive revision was completed. One very important clause dealt with membership. Three types were established: family, individual, and honorary, which the board could confer. There had previously been memberships only for men (which included their families) and widows.

A completely new kitchen and an air conditioning system for the social hall were also installed that year. Arnold Karlins, on behalf of the Schanfeld family, formally dedicated the newly decorated and remodeled social hall in memory of Joseph Schanfeld, whose unparalleled contributions to the life of Adath Jeshurun and the welfare of the people of Minneapolis extended from 1905 to 1952.

Rabbi Lipnick had recently drawn up a set of Kashrut rules along with other Twin City Conservative rabbis. They were posted in the newly remodeled kitchen. For the first time, the kitchen was prepared for Passover. Luncheons for both the Junior Congregation and the Bar and Bat Mitzvah observances were held during the Passover holiday. The *Shalosh Sudoth* service on Saturday evening was expanded and participation increased.

ADATH CONGREGANT
Joni Kibort Sussman

"When I was a little girl sitting at a havdalah evening service at the old Dupont building with my dad, Leo Kibort, a survivor of Dachau Concentration camp, he remarked to me that here we were, just the two of us, but that some day he imagined rows of Kiborts all sitting together in "shul," and that would be his victory over the Nazis. I thought of this many years later on a Rosh Hashanah morning as we all sat together, my parents, my brother and sister, my Uncle Ben and Aunt Reva, their three kids, and all of our spouses and children. Where we had once been two people sitting on a bench, we were indeed now almost three full pews of Kiborts, just as my father had wished."

Leo Kibort, after his liberation from Dachau

The Kibort family in the early 1960s: Hinda and Leo, Joni and Chuck

In 1962 several Minneapolis Conservative congregations, including the Adath, jointly sponsored the Akiba School for Adult Jewish Studies. One of the best attended courses was on the "American Jewish Community" presented by visiting Professor of Sociology, Dr. Daniel Elazar, former Minnesotan who had made Aliyah to Israel.

David Goldenberg succeeded Leo Gross as president of the Minneapolis Talmud Torah.

Rae Abelson retired after 15 years of devoted service. She was honored at an Oneg Shabbat as "not simply a secretary in the office, but a friend always eager to help, even if it extended her day's work into the evening hours. At one time she was in sole charge of the synagogue office, with its complex duties. She saw the congregation grow from 400 to 900 families. Many young adults can thank her for interesting them in working for the synagogue and showing the way for them to build a life of positive Judaism with all its rich rewards."

Sam Abrams was commended in 1962 for his tremendous efforts on behalf of the daily minyan. He, more than any other person, had made them possible from the standpoint of assessing attendence, books, and other important details. The ordination of Rabbi Mendel L. Abrams from the Jewish Theological Seminary was celebrated at Adath services in July.

On March 23, 1962, the Adath celebrated a Hadassah Golden Anniversary Shabbat. Forrest H. Selvig, assistant director of the Minneapolis Institute of Arts, discussed the Marc Chagall stained glass windows that had recently been placed at Hadassah Hebrew University Medical Center in Israel after having been exhibited at the Louvre in Paris, and at the Museum of Modern Art in New York. Rabbi Lipnick and Mr. Selvig presented a slide lecture on the life and work of Marc Chagall and the symbolism of the windows.

A historic goatskin Torah scroll prepared by an early seventeenth-century scribe and encased in a nineteenth-century silver Torah case from Alexandria, Egypt. Donated by Leo and Lillian Gross in honor of their five children's B'nai Mitzvah on their son Jonathan's Bar Mitzvah in 1963.

It was an exciting time when Sidney Goldish was elected Adath president in June 1962. He had a master's degree in journalism, and had served in the U.S. Marine Corps in World War II. He was a writer and lecturer of note, *Minneapolis Star & Tribune* director of research, and the orignator of the Minnesota Poll. During his presidency, he began an ambitious program looking ahead to the synagogue's 80th year.

Envisioning a series of forums to be held in Schanfeld Hall, Sidney felt they should be devoted to some of the major issues of the times "as they bear upon our lives as Americans and as Conservative Jews," including the race crisis in America and in Minneapolis, Israel and the Arab world, medical and hospital care for the aged, the decline in moral values, and the prayer-in-the-schools controversy.

Sidney got his good friend and press colleague, Harold Chucker, to join the Adath and to become the *Clarion* editor. The two men felt it was absolutely necessary to have a weekly newsletter for better communication with the congregation. Chucker noted, "Sid was a very articulate person. He knew exactly what he wanted to say, both verbally and in writing and that made him a very effective leader. Everyone admired him."

At his first meeting, July 5, 1962, the new president offered an appraisal of where the synagogue stood, and concluded that it was in good shape financially, and had no major capital outlays looming for the first time in recent memory. "We should be considering now how to strengthen, develop and expand the programs of Adath..."

In 1963, on the occasion of his 80th birthday, Aaron Harris was described by William Hoffman as "a man who gave not only his dollar, but also his physical energies to our beloved Adath, a good man and a devoted Jew."

Until 1963, an Israel Bond appeal had been made at High Holiday services. On September, 25,1962, an Israel Bond dinner was held for the first time at the Adath with Maurice Samuel as guest speaker and Howard Brin as chairman. It was extremely successful and the practice was continued in subsequent years.

On June 9, 1963, Sidney Goldish was re-elected president. But he died suddenly at the age of 52 in late December, just one month after he had given an eulogy for President Kennedy from the Adath pulpit. His untimely death came as a shock to the entire community.

Rabbi Lipnick wrote, "His was a rare talent and a unique offering to our synagogue and to our people. Sidney had a total commitment. May his memory spur us to greater and purer effort."

Vice President Sheldon Gensler gave the message to the congregation: "It is a very difficult and painful task to present a message this year in the place of our beloved and most able president, Sidney Goldish, whose untimely death left a terrible and deep gap in our synagogue life and leadership. At the annual meeting last hear, Sid outlined an ambitions program for our congregation, having in mind that we were entering our 80th year of congregational history.

"Some parts of Sid's program were completed, others partially, and still others remain yet as goals and dreams...We should resolve, as a fitting tribute to Sid's memory and to his dedication to both the synagogue and the Conservative movement, to carry out his uncompleted goals." The remodeled bema area (completed in 1968) was named the Sidney Goldish Memorial.

The 80th Anniversary Ball was held at the Pick-Nicollet Hotel in downtown Minneapolis on June 7, 1964. Tickets were $15 per couple. Dr. Arnold Cohen chaired the programming. A vote of thanks was extended to the three vice presidents, Sheldon Gensler, Irving Paradise and Arnold Cohen, for their services following the recent loss of President Goldish. David Gordon became the new president in July of 1964.

In February 1964, a very successful Festival of Arts and Music was held with Adath artists and musicians participating. Later that winter the Sisterhood created a Hospitality Committee, chaired by Barbara Mark, to extend a welcome to new members. And another new program was also launched to help the Adath family get better acquainted. One night a month was designated as Congregation Night with a varied program of activities. Murray Abry, Lil Kaplan, Jerome and Bernice Fischbein were chairpersons.

The Sisterhood was also involved in sponsoring the first "Israel Economy Pilgrimage," scheduled to take place from September 30 to October 20, 1964, in conjunction with the observance of Israel's 16th anniversary.

Etheldoris Grais recalled, "I was education vice president and the idea of the tour began in 1962 when my husband, Arnold, and I took our son, James, to Israel for his Bar Mitzvah. We went on the National Council of Jewish Women Bar Mitzvah Tour which encouraged families to take their children to Israel. I thought it would be a great idea for the Adath to have a tour. I asked Pam Brin to help me and we organized it with the Travel One Agency."

Education Vice President Etheldoris Grais organized one of Adath's first trips to Israel.

Grais planned a program in April to acquaint members with the idea, drawing on the experiences of Adath members who had already been to Israel, including Howard Brin, Lil Gross, Ruth Davis, and Jean Grossman.

Adath members who made the trip were Lydia Millman, Mr. and Mrs. Ben Berkowitz, Pam Brin, Fred and Ann Orenstein, Jean Grossman, Leo Gross, Harry and Shirley Solomon, Harold Lieberman, Rose Klein, Gordon Savran, Laurie Fruen, Florence Bolter, Jany Myers and Lois Blaustone. They were honored the following spring at the congregation's celebration of Israel's 17th Anniversary.

Rabbi Lipnick tendered his resignation in the spring of 1965, and a search for a new rabbi was immediately started. The man who was eventually chosen, Rabbi Arnold M. Goodman, later offered this commentary on his predecessor: "The congregation wanted to hire a good pastoral rabbi. Rabbi Lipnick turned out to be a very good pastoral rabbi. But as Ruth Brin said, 'Anyone that followed Stanley Rabinowitz in the pulpit would have a very difficult time, for he would always be compared to Stanley who was such an outstanding orator.'

"This is what happened. The Adath Jeshurun wanted the dedication of Albert I. Gordon, the exhuberance of Morris Gordon, the speaking ability of Stanley Rabinowitz, and the idealism and pastoral qualities of Jerome Lipnick. No one person could fill all those expectations.

"Jerome Lipnick was an uncommon man. He was a teacher, a writer, an idealist—compassionate and concerned with humanity."

(Top) Rabbi Goodman at an Adath picnic circa 1980;
(Above left) Rabbi Goodman and Cantor Amsel at a
Tashlich ceremony on Lake Calhoun:
(Right) Rabbi Goodman.

9

THE RABBI GOODMAN YEARS
(1966 – 1982)

More traditional than his predecessors, Rabbi Arnold M. Goodman introduced many new programs to the Adath Jeshurun. The Shabbat Morning Program (SMP) became an integral part of the congregation, and a new generation became the most Judaicly educated in the Adath Jeshurun's history. All of the High Holidays were observed creatively, and on Yom HaShoah and Yom Ha'atzmaut special programs were held. The Kallah Center opened in Minnetonka to nurture a fuller exposure to Jewish living, and the nursery school, Gan Shelanu, added extended daycare and kindergarten enrichment programs. Rabbi Goodman led tours to Israel, and in 1976 he spearheaded the organizing of the Adath Jeshurun congregational burial society, the Chevra Kavod Hamet.

Rabbi Arnold M. Goodman became the new spiritual leader of the Adath Jeshurun Congregation early in 1966. The rabbi, his wife, Rae, and their children, Ariel, Daniel, and Shira, took up temporary residence near the synagogue at 3454 Fremont Avenue South, and he assumed the pulpit on January 21. Rabbi Moses B. Sachs of B'nai Abraham Synagogue welcomed Rabbi Goodman to the community with the following words, "Rabbi Goodman and I were colleagues serving the Greater Chicago Jewish community. During those years I developed a deep appreciation for his ability, his devotion to Jewish education and his commitment to the progressive enrichment of Jewish life. The Minneapolis Jewish community has many achievements, and many problems. We shall need his wisdom, his ability and his strength to continue doing our part as rabbis and congregants in building a Jewish community worthy of our tradition."

The new rabbi had graduated from the Jewish Theological Seminary in 1952, and served as an army chaplain for two years before becoming rabbi at Congregation Rodfei Sholom-Ohr Chodosh in Chicago. He served that community for a decade, and during that time he also earned

degrees in educational administration and law from nearby universities. In Chicago, Rabbi Goodman had risen to positions of leadership in a number of Jewish and legal organizations, and had published articles in the *Jewish Spectator*, *The Reconstructionist*, and other publications.

In one of his early addresses, Rabbi Goodman compared his relationship with the Adath community to that of the seedlings planted in Israel during Tu B'Shevat. "I have every confidence," he said, "that this young seedling will take root in the soil of Minneapolis and grow into a mighty tree which will nourish us spiritually. May we at this time, through our mutual efforts, make Judaism more vital, our synagogue—Adath Jeshurun—more effective, and our Torah a Tree of Life for us, for Israel, and for all mankind."

Among those who helped welcome the Goodman family and set up "instant housekeeping" were Esther Katz, Raleigh Brand, Edith Schept, Shirley Bob, and Carolyn Abramson.

Rabbi Goodman's sermons that year touched on such subjects as the Vietnam War, which was then escalating; an intriguing examination of Jethro, Moses' non-Jewish father-in-law; the relationship between environmental pollution and spiritual pollution; and how we benefit from our friends…and also our enemies.

Rae Goodman joined into synagogue activities, organizing a Pre-Passover Seder for March 29. The congregation, rabbi, cantor, Sisterhood, Men's Club, MCL, board of education, and religious school parents committee sponsored the evening. The goal was to teach or re-teach all fathers how to conduct a seder and all mothers how to prepare not only Passover food, but a Passover mood. Congregants were asked to bring their own Passover ritual items to use. Rabbi Goodman himself prepared a detailed guidebook with instruction, prayers, readings and songs in Hebrew with English translations for future reference.

Rabbi Goodman was in his office afternoons and Sunday mornings for those who wished to appoint him as their agent to "sell" their *chametz*. [The basis of this custom is the Biblical injunction "In all your dwelling places there shall be no *chametz*." Since it is impossible to remove all *chametz* utensils from our houses, Jewish law provides for a conditional sale of all *chametz* to a non-Jew; this sale being effective Passover week. The rabbi thus executes his agency by entering into an "agreement" with a non-Jew who for eight days has title to our *chametz*.]

On Library Shabbat Rabbi Goodman extolled the Adath library and commended the library committee who maintained it. "At Adath Jeshurun we have a fine library; it is an excellent collection of Judaica, which is well administered and properly displayed. Yet not enough of our members have acquainted themselves with this significant facility in our midst."

At the annual dinner meeting in early June1967, Rabbi Goodman was officially installed as Adath's spiritual leader. That summer the rabbi inaugurated a series of four classes at his home, focused on the relevance of Jewish tradition in contemporary Jewish life. It was open to all college students and recent high school graduates. The program was a success and that fall a committee was formed under the chairmanship of Murray Abry to explore other ways in which the needs of Adath's college students could be met.

1966–1967

In a September issue of the *Clarion* Rabbi Goodman addressed the issue of Vietnam and the Civil Rights movement, which had recently been the source of violence on Plymouth Avenue on the Near North Side. He also discussed the ever-increasing evidence of "Negro anti-Semitism."

"I pray that we shall utilize these Holy Days to reflect upon the many dimensions of Jewish life and to deepen our commitment to peace, to human dignity, to Israel and to the many values which are essential for the creation of a vital American Judaism."

Following a performance by the famed Israeli folksinger Geula Gill, Rabbi Goodman remarked that those who had heard her were especially touched by her moving rendition of "Eli, Eli," and her intense comments regarding her trip to the Soviet Union. "As she sang, even we who enjoy political freedom, social status and economic well being, sensed the fragility of Jewish life whenever our people have lived under terror and persecution. How this song must have plumbed the depth of the souls of her Jewish audiences in the Soviet Union!"

He went on to deride the anti-Semitism then prevalent in the Soviet Union, where synagogues had been systematically closed and the Jewish minority was under attack.

On December 25 Rabbi Goodman held a brunch for college students at his house and 74 men and women attended. Later that winter a large audience braved the bitter cold to attend a reading by Elie Weisel, inspiring Rabbi Goodman to remark that winter was perhaps just a "state of mind."

"The essential quality of life must be fervor," he later wrote of the event. "As artist and as human being, true life is a quest for fervor. Our feeble protests of Nazi excesses lacked fervor. We lack fervor today as we confront the spiritual oppression of Russian Jewry. In any and every way, we must raise our voices in a fervent plea and demand that the chains which shackle Soviet Jewry be broken."

Other stimulating and challenging issues Rabbi Goodman addressed that winter included the use and misuse of protest; "Can any good come from theological exchange?"; whether neo-Nazis had the right to free speech; and the role of religious leaders in the ongoing debate about Vietnam.

In March Dr. Markel and Charlotte Karlen presented a beautiful work of art to the synagogue by the contemporary Ukrainian Jewish artist Anatoli Kaplan, in honor of their son Bruce's Bar Mitzvah. The painting, depicting a scene from Sholom Aleichem's *The Enchanted Tailor*, was one of 23 in a series depicting a distraught Jew reciting the "Sh'ma Yisrael." A few weeks earlier Eve and Isadore Karon had presented a set of the Five Books of Moses to the Adath that were printed in 1863 in Russia and had been in Isadore's family ever since. In May of 1967 the Adath mounted an exhibit of Kaplan's paintings.

That winter a Jewish Archives of Greater Minneapolis was established by the Minneapolis Federation for Jewish Service in cooperation with the Minnesota Historical Society. Members of the Adath were asked to contribute published materials, personal memoirs, diaries, correspondence and pictures that might be of interest in preserving a history of the Jewish community of Minneapolis.

That spring a rabbinical court was established in the Twin Cities, and the well-known actor Howard De Silva spoke at the Adath's first annual Cultural Arts Series about Sholom Aleichem and the Yiddish language. Mr. De Silva's performance also, alas, exposed some glaring dead spots in the Adath sanctuary's speaker system. Before long the public address system was added to a list of needed improvements alongside a new bema and elevator. Inspired by De Silva's remarks about Yiddish, a few weeks later Cantor Amsel presented a medley of songs from the *shtetl*.

On a more contemporary theme, Rabbi Goodman spoke out that spring against the use of mind-altering drugs.

"Several of our teenagers and college students have asked me if there is a Jewish view concerning LSD or narcotics. It is my belief that while these drugs may have been unknown to our ancestors, they would nonetheless have damned anything that altered a man's ability to grapple with reality.

"The idea of taking a drug in order to 'liberate the mind' or to become 'high' is inconsistent with Judaism's view of the challenge of life. Just as the Kohanim had to approach their task with a zeal and a dedication which came from within, so must every Jew approach life (which is really service to God) by preparing himself through study, through meditation, through dedication. Artificial stimulants are simply that—artificial—and a true Jew has no business relying upon them."

That spring Rabbi Goodman was invited to offer the invocation at a luncheon at the University of Minnesota. The event was to commemorate the official acceptance of a gift given by Jay and Rose Phillips for the construction of a research laboratory in the University's projected medical center expansion. The gift was to be matched dollar for dollar by the federal government and it constituted a massive step forward in the medical research program of the University. "Our actions frequently have a far greater impact upon the community than we sometimes imagine," Rabbi Goodman later told the Adath congregation. "This is what the Bible would have us remember at all times! We in this congregation and in the entire Jewish community

Jay Phillips

have reason to be proud of Mr. and Mrs. Phillips. They have been blessed in life, but they have always demonstrated a willingness to help others. Yet they have never failed to come before the general community as identified and proud Jews, thereby bringing honor upon us in the eyes of all."

In May of that year Egypt's president, Gamel Abdel Nasser, expelled the UN Emergency Force from the Sinai Peninsula. It had been stationed there for more than a decade, following the Suez Crisis of 1956. As Egypt was amassing a thousand tanks and nearly a hundred thousand troops on the Israeli border, Israel launched a pre-emptive strike against Egypt's air force. Egypt's ally Jordan then attacked Jerusalem. By the time fighting had ceased six days later Israel had gained control of the Sinai Peninsula, the Gaza Strip, the West Bank, East Jerusalem, and the Golan Heights.

In the weeks that followed, Rabbi Goodman encouraged the congregation to give to Israel through the UJA Israel Emergency Fund. "Make no mistake about it: to the vast and overwhelming majority of American and world Jewry, Israel is not just another country. She is important to us, and her survival is essential for our well-being and our sense of self-respect. When you contribute to the UFA IEF, you are not only contributing to Israel—you are contributing to the future of the Jewish people."

The events reverberated through the summer months, and in September Rabbi Goodman wrote: "The year 5727 is the year when the Jewish world underwent deep and cataclysmic changes. As we gather in our synagogues and homes to usher in a new year, the events of June must be given priority in our mind and heart. The great victory of Israel was, in every sense, a victory of the Jewish people. In an era when it was fashionable to mourn declining Jewishness, we were overwhelmed by the large numbers of Jews who came to the aid of Israel—not only because they thought Israel was right, but because they were Jews. We were not at Sinai or in Jerusalem or in the Golan Hills when the battles took place and the victory was won. Yet this victory is ours—we share it personally because we, too, are Jews."

While earth-shattering events were taking place in the Middle East, a more modest transformation had also taken place at the Adath. The bema had been remodeled, the sanctuary had been redecorated and refurbished, an elevator had been installed, and the Esther Fink room had been furnished. Also that year, a post-confirmation class had been successfully organized. It was known as the Solomon Schechter Institute, and was open not only to Adath members, but also to youngsters from Beth El and B'nai Abraham synagogues. And 26 new families had joined the congregation.

Rabbi Richard Rubenstein, director of the Hillel Foundation at the University of Pittsburgh and a member of the university's philosophy department, was Scholar-in-Residence at the Adath for the pre-Selichot Kallah on September 29-31. He had been a classmate of Rabbi Goodman's at the Jewish Theological Seminary and also held degrees from the University of Cincinnati and Harvard. Rabbi Rubenstein was considered one of the outstanding young theologians of America and one of the most dynamic figures on the contemporary Jewish scene. His participation included Friday night services; Saturday afternoon with members of LTF, USY and Habonim, and a lecture at 9:00 p.m. Following his talk there was a question and answer period, social hour, and Selichot Service.

Rabbi Goodman and his wife Rae with tenor Richard Tucker (center) and accompanist.

1967-1968

During the High Holy Days that year, Rabbi Goodman focused attention on the recent Israeli victory in the Middle East. Ruth Brin prepared and published a pamphlet of readings for the Selichot services, designed and laid out by Sharon Lerner. More than 400 people attended. Following the services for the High Holy Days, Rabbi Goodman commended all those who had contributed to their beauty, including Buddy Guttman, "who chanted Shacharit so superbly," and the Torah readers, Kenneth Bob, Ariel Goodman, and Howard Schwartz.

The Sukkot celebration coincided with the Minnesota teachers' convention that year, which made it convenient for children to participate fully. Rabbi Goodman laid special emphasis on the lulav and etrog procession, and his Shabbat Eve sermon explored the ancient and modern significance of these dramatic rounds.

Later in October the Kallah Scholar-In-Residence, Rabbi Rubenstein, spoke on the subject of "Power, Barbarism and Sacrifice," arguing for the necessity that Jews embrace some aspects of barbarism. Rabbi Goodman did not entirely agree, as the comments in his column "From the Rabbi's Study" made plain: "Rabbi Richard Rubenstein's provocative talks, his controversial stands on Jewish power (he's for it) black power (he says it is anti-Semitic) and animal sacrifices (he favors its restoration in a rebuilt Temple—I don't) electrified and disturbed us. Yet he really gave us something to think about and to talk about."

The Ukrainian émigré Shmuel Agnon had recently been awarded the Nobel Prize in literature for his depictions of life in the shtetl and in Israel, and in November a noted authority on Agnon, Professor Arnold Band of UCLA, delivered the second annual Goldenberg Lecture at the Adath. The book *Our Crowd*, about wealthy Jewish families of New York during the late 19th century, was also a topic of widespread conversation.

Later in November Rabbi Goodman extended a familiar appeal to congregants, asking them to offer one day a week for a month to attend the morning minyan. "I hope that when Mr. Abrams contacts you, you will make every effort to commit yourself," he wrote. "...This is a far greater mitzvah than you might imagine..."

At mid-January services Rabbi Goodman reiterated the commitment of Twin City Conservative congregations to the equality of women in the synagogue, while raising the question of whether a limit should be set on this march toward equality. "If so, at what point?" he asked.

In February of 1968 Harry Golden, the author of the book *A Little Girl Is Dead*, spoke at the Adath Cultural Arts series. The book dealt with racial justice in the South. Later that month Rabbi Goodman drew some striking parallels between passages in Exodus and recent discussions that had taken place between President Lyndon Johnson and Prime Minister Levi Eshkol of Israel.

The Men's Club chose Sam Bender as Man of the Year that year. He was a past president of the organization, had been active for more than 20 years, and was currently serving on the national board of directors.

The Married Couples League sponsored a variety of excursions, including a square dance and a visit to Dudley Riggs Café Expresso.

Trials in the Soviet Union of dissidents, many of them Jewish, were a continuing preoccupation that spring. Some saw the trials as evidence of a thaw in Soviet repression, arguing that such dissent would have been ruthlessly stifled during Stalin's life. All the same, the continued persecution of the large Jewish minority in Russia was cause for grave concern.

In March Gladys Miller and Rae Goodman co-chaired a Torah Fund brunch at the Millers' Lake Minnetonka home, at which Mrs. Milton Lippitz spoke on the future needs of the Jewish Theological Seminary.

A pulpit dialogue also took place that spring on the pressing subject: "Should a Synagogue adopt an official policy on political and social issues?" with Jerome Fischbein and Sidney Rich delivering differing statements on the question. Mr. Rich argued that it wasn't enough for the synagogue to be in favor of virtue and goodness in the abstract, that it needed to make itself relevant to the concerns of congregants by fleshing out positions on questions of peace, open housing, anti-crime legislation and the like. Mr. Fischbein argued, on the contrary, that the synagogue should bring people together for prayer, camaraderie, and sociability. Its raison d'etre was to speak to the congregants' specific needs as Jews. Those who were really interested in making their position on such questions known could join appropriate groups or committees. And since unanimity was virtually impossible on any given issue, for the synagogue to take a public stance might very well weaken, divide and alienate members of the congregation.

At the question and answer period that followed, Elsie Cohen, a native of Germany, pointed out that the course of history might have been altered if the church had seen fit to speak out against Hitler and the German people in the 1930's.

At the end of March President Johnson made the announcement that he would not run for re-election, and a few days later Martin Luther King, Jr. was assassinated, adding further fuel to the political conflagration that was then sweeping the country. The following evening some 700 women and men gathered at the Adath to express their sorrow in a special tribute to the slain hero.

On May 4 and 5 the Adath USY-LTF Chapter presented *The Wall*, a play based on John Hersey's monumental chronicle of the destruction of Polish Jewry by the Nazis. It was the 25th anniversary of the Warsaw Ghetto uprising, and Rabbi Goodman later observed in his column, "During the Second World War, I was the age of our USY-LTF'ers who are putting on this play, and I remember the anguish of my parents and grandparents as the story of Nazi genocide began to unfold in all of its horrible details. European Jewry was destroyed, and who knew what the future of any Jewish community might be?

"The pain of the Six Million can never be totally dulled, and the memory of Auschwitz will continue to affect the manner in which we respond to external threats. Yet in the quarter-century since 'Warsaw' we have seen the creation of 'Medinat Yisrael' and a deepening of the roots of Jewish life here in America."

Not coincidentally, the dates of May 4 and 5 marked the 20th anniversary of the State of Israel. Other anniversary salutes to Israel took place throughout the summer.

The USY held a "Shul-In" that spring, bringing Jewish teenagers together in the synagogue for a night of discussion, an exciting movie with Jewish content, the opportunity to dance to a live band, and services the following morning. And on May 15, at the Family Dinner Finale, the Men's Club presented "A Jewish Laugh-In" produced by Syd Rich, profiling Jewish and Yiddish stories and anecdotes both modern and traditional. The Adath LTF group also presented an original script written by Rabbi Goodman, "The Torah According To Peanuts" based on a book by Christopher Short, *The Gospel According to Peanuts*.

At the annual meeting on May 26, the newly refurbished Sidney Goldish Memorial bema and the Esther Fink room were officially dedicated, and Robert W. Smith, the executive editor of the *Minneapolis Star*, spoke.

On June 5th Robert Kennedy was assassinated by Sirhan Sirhan, and Rabbi Goodman noted in the *Clarion* that Kennedy had been a supporter of Israel's right to exist, adding that "...Sirhan, an ardent Arab nationalist, obviously resented what he regarded as a betrayal of the Arab people and their cause. Like so many, he could see no other way to express his anger, his disagreement, and his hatred than through an act of terrorism."

1968-1969

Rabbi Goodman and his wife Rae returned from their summer visit to Israel full of enthusiasm for the experience, and also convinced of the need for Jews to be physically linked to their ancestral land. Ruth Brin's special Selichot Service, prepared the previous year, was once again put to use during that holiday. In fact, the service had drawn fine comments throughout the country and was being used or emulated in other congregations.

Inter-Congregational classes were set up for grades 3-6 in conjunction with Beth El, in order to establish larger classes and offer a more varied curriculum. The classes were to meet at Adath.

During his High Holy Day sermons, Rabbi Goodman compared world events to a theater of the absurd, with the Soviet invasion of Czechoslovakia and the humanitarian tragedy in Biafra adding to the sense of unreality. "It is then in a mood of despair and agony with which we approach our New Year 5729. With all mankind, we hope for an end to war—in Vietnam, in Africa, in the Middle East. We hope for an end to disarmament races and for the initiation of firm nuclear arms control. We hope for an end to the hostility between man and his fellows."

On October 13 a pre-Simchat Torah meeting was held at the Hillel House at the University. The program included a speaker and a film produced by the Jewish Chautauqua Society, *The Price of Silence*, in which Soviet anti-Semitism is put on trial, with Edward G. Robinson as prosecutor and prominent Americans as key witnesses. The film was followed by singing and dancing in front of the plaza outside of Northrop Auditorium.

On October 22, the first Jewish Holiday Home Tour was conducted at the Adath, with participants traveling from home to home. The chosen holiday themes and homes were the Sabbath (Rae Goodman); Chanukah (Ruth Brand); Passover (Ruth Stillman); and Jewish art (Charlotte Karlen). More than 120 women attended.

In his *Clarion* column Rabbi Goodman bemoaned the fact that the Simchat Torah festival was too often considered merely a children's event, and noted that in Russia "thousands upon thousands of Soviet Jews—especially the younger people and university students—spend the entire night of Simchat Torah in the square outside the Great Synagogue of Moscow. For them it is a vital affirmation of their Judaism and a way of asserting their oneness with us."

The following week the Adath commemorated the 25th anniversary of the rescue of Danish Jews by listening to an address given by Andrew N. Johnson, the Danish Consul General for the Northwest U.S. (Johnson was also president of the William Mitchell College of Law at the time). The third annual Cultural Arts Series opened when Sam Levinson, the author of *Everything But Money*, gave a very amusing presentation.

The Annual Israel Bond dinner honoree was Adath Vice President Jerry Fischbein, a tireless worker for Jewish education, synagogue welfare, and all humanitarian causes, and one of the most popular figures in the Adath and the overall Jewish community.

In February Rabbi Goodman made a quick trip to Israel to apprise the situation there first-hand. On his return he wrote a column in the *Clarion* expressing the need to lend further support to Israel through the Federation campaign.

"In the days gone by, each Jewish home had a *pushke*,

the metal container in which pennies, nickels and sometimes dimes were deposited, ultimately to be turned over to a favorite charity. Even the poorer Jew had a *pushke* and gave some *tzedakah*. It was a marvelous tradition among Jews.

"The need for *tzedakah* continues, but the *pushke* concept may no longer suffice. One of our major responsibilities is Israel, and you can't buy jets and maintain a defense budget of one billion dollars with nickels and dimes. That's what the Federation campaign is about."

Rabbi Goodman shared his impressions of the battlefields, the soldiers, and the deserts, but he also noted conditions and attitudes in the cities where, as he observed, life goes on as usual. "The people bear large tax burdens; they accept the inevitability of military service; they know that there will be incidents and injuries and deaths. They are also convinced that they are the wave of history and that their cause will triumph. Israel is armed to the teeth, and the possibility of war is discussed in the Knesset and coffee house alike. Yet, with it all, Israelis build for tomorrow when *shalom* will be a reality for them and the entire Middle East."

At the Men's Club-Sisterhood Dinner get-together on March12, *Star-Tribune* columnist Jim Klobuchar spoke on "How to be a Columnist and Survive," and USY presented excerpts from the play *Funny Girl*.

At the April 27 breakfast, Adath vice-president Moe Sabes gave an illustrated report of his tour behind the Iron Curtain as a member of Minnesota's "People to People Goodwill Delegation." The mission had been arranged by the Minnesota Department of Agriculture as part of a program established by President Eisenhower back in 1951 designed to help Americans learn more about their occupational counterparts behind the Iron Curtain. Moe had visited Brussels, Moscow, East and West Berlin, Prague, Luzerne, Berne and other cities during his trip the previous summer.

Also in the spring of 1969, in response to requests from congregants for a more participatory service, Rabbi Goodman introduced congregant participation, whereby a different worshipper presented a poem or reading of his or her choice each week. The selections chosen varied widely, ranging from original poetry to nature poems to readings from the Holocaust. At the same time, Cantor Amsel introduced the *nigun,* a wordless melody, which enabled even the non-Hebrew reader to participate in an authentic Jewish prayer mode. Little by little, the tone and mood of the *nigun* began to sink in, and the strangeness of

this new kind of worship experience began to dissipate.

Following similar lines, Ruth Brin agreed to develop new material for a modern Shabbat service. Through her efforts, special Israeli and oriental music was chosen and arranged by Aaron Sheffi, an Israeli who was the music director of the Jewish Community Center at the time. When it was completed the new service was printed in a special booklet with art cover by Theresa Berman and design layout by Howard Brin.

At the annual meeting Irving Brand stepped down from a two-year term as president and Melvin Orenstein succeeded him. A gigantic step forward had been taken by the synagogue in the twilight of Brand's tenure, when the Adath acquired the first 19 acres of land in the Village of Minnetonka, a suburb to the west of Minneapolis. The purchase of this land insured that the congregation would have a choice location for the site of a new synagogue complex, should there continue to be a shift of the synagogue's membership to the western suburbs, and should it be decided that the structure on Dupont Avenue could no longer meet the needs of the congregation. The purchase of land also provided the impetus for the congregation to develop a Century Fund to meet the synagogue's future physical needs.

Naturally many questions were raised about the purchase, and a few weeks later the incoming president, Melvin Orenstein, offered this synopsis of the event:

In the last few months, several members of the congregation have asked Rabbi Goodman, myself and other members of the board a number of questions concerning the land purchase by the synagogue in Minnetonka Township. In order that the corporation may be better informed, I am setting forth the information at which these questions seem to be directed.

The land, purchased on a five-year contract for deed, comprises approximately 26 acres. It is located on Hillside Lane, approximately three blocks east of Highway 73 and about ¾ of a mile west of Highway 18. Hillside Lane runs parallel to, and is approximately three blocks North of Cedar Lake Road and is approximately six blocks south of Highway 12.

The land is vacant and gently rolling in contour. It is bounded on the northeast corner by Windsor Lake and by homes on either side. There are three new schools (grade, junior and senior high) across Hillside Lane to the south of the property.

TRACING ADATH'S LONG SEARCH FOR LAND

In his annual report for 1969 Rabbi Goodman reviewed the long search for land:

"With the announcement that the congregation has purchased 19 acres of land as a possible future site for our congregation, our thoughts went back into the events of the last decade leading up to this purchase.

"There have been surveys in the congregation trying to determine what direction our Jewish community is moving as they migrate from the inner city. For a time it seemed that though a heavy trend was to move west to the St. Louis Park area, each year or two brought forth other trends. We found that there was a trend toward the Golden Valley area, then to the Edina area, then farther west toward Lake Minnetonka. Of recent years there is reported interest in the area of Plymouth township.

"As these reports came in, the search for land became more widespread and more intense by our committees. Various people have taken an interest in the search for land from time to time.

"Through the years, behind the scenes, Morris Besner has devoted more time and more effort to search out land with each and every report of a new move of the Jewish community that was moving from the core of the city. Morris has exerted every effort with the sincere desire to serve the needs of the congregation. All of this has been done beside his other responsibilities for the synagogue. He has served as chairman of the House Committee for nearly ten years, in maintaining the synagogue building as well as the other property of the congregation. He will soon be serving his 20th year as a member of the board of trustees of our congregation.

"In the recent search for land a number of parcels land were found, and it was determined that we select the site that we did. Our thanks to Sam G. Segal who directed us to this site. Thanks go also to the other members of the Executive Committee who were involved in searching out the details and making it possible to complete the arrrangements for this purchase. Melvin Orenstein, Jerome Fischbein, Sim Heller, Irving Brand, Moe Sabes, and Morris Besner handled the details for the congregation.

"The more we see of this site the better we like it. A really wise choice."

A land use committee has been appointed to plan best available use of the property in connection with the synagogue facilities ultimately to be constructed on the premises.

Three years ago, a long range planning committee appointed by the board recommended the purchase of land in the suburban area West of Minneapolis. The committee felt that the congregation could possibly meet its needs in the present area for approximately ten years. Now that the initial steps of the long range planning committee have been completed, it is imperative that sound financial policies with respect to a future facility be formulated. Careful consideration will be given by the board to the formulation of these policies in the immediate future.

I hope that you will take the time this spring or summer to view the property so that you may share in the excitement of the board and the staff which has been brought about by this important step for-ward in the congregation's long range plans.

An unusual fact about the property is that it was originally platted as part of the 'Palestine Addition' of Minnetonka Township. It makes one stop and think!

In a future Clarion we will show a map indicating the exact location of the future site of your Adath Jeshurun Congregation

Among the other significant achievements that Brand highlighted in his final speech as president was the establishment of a religious education evaluation committee which met frequently to take a long hard look at the Jewish educational programs available to children of the Adath, with the primary focus being the Talmud Torah Elementary Department.

U.S. Senator Walter F. Mondale was guest speaker for the evening, and he delivered an inspiring and informative address. A long-time friend of outgoing president Irving Brand and a law school classmate of incoming president

Mel Orenstein, Mondale devoted most of his remarks to the position he felt the administration should take with regard to Israel, calling for a positive and unequivocal statement not only regarding Israel's right to survive but on "her right to be treated equally as any other nation."

1969-1972

On July 20, Neil Armstrong and Buzz Aldrin became the first humans to land on the moon. The event was a source of amazement and pride for many Americans, and also fodder for pondering where the limits to human achievement might lie. During the High Holy Days Rabbi Goodman made use of the remarkable event to reflect on the lack of care that he felt was widespread within American society. He equated *teshuvah*—repentance—with re-entry, and suggested that "we, too, have collectively re-entered following a dizzying ascent on high... Will we turn our energies to easing human suffering in our midst? Will we carry with us the tablets of the Decalogue?"

At the Yom Kippur service his subject was "Woodstock and the Search for Integrity," and he made a special effort to thank all of those who had helped in various ways to make the High Holiday services so beautiful and meaningful, including Mark Rotenberg, Irving Guttman, Ariel Goodman, George Nudell, David Orenstein, Dr. Arthur Ballet, Ruth Brin, Jay Phillips, Gordon Savran, Dr. Harvey Gilbert, Sidney Scherling, Aaron Herman, Ed Grosmann, Al Davis, Shepley Backman and Albert Rosenfield, Al Meirovitz, and the entire office staff: (Mrs. Ben) Beats Auerbach, (Mrs. Ben) Hersh, (Mrs. Marvin) Myrtle Loe, and Paul Modell.

The second annual "Jewish Holiday-Art Home Tour" took place on October 7. The holidays and the homes were Sabbath and High Holidays (Maxine Lazar); Passover (Bonnie Bush); Sukkot (Rabbi and Rae Goodman); and Chanukah (Alvera Ackerberg). The programs narrators were Charlotte Karlen and Sabine Amsel, with Lorraine Shrell, Hinda Litman, Carolyn Abramson, Mitzi Diamond, and Betty Schnitzer also helping out.

That fall the Simchat Torah celebration was distinguished by the presence of a group of talented youngsters who went by the name of the Adath Jeshurunites. This group consisted of Larry Katz at the drums, David Orenstein on the trumpet, John Orenstein at the piano and Bruce Orkin on the guitar. They played the melodies associated with Simchat Torah, both new and old, as a background to the singing and dancing. Rabbi Goodman later expressed some misgivings about the use of this kind of instrumentation in the sanctuary. "It is, of course, a departure from traditionalism and every departure carries with it a bit of a risk." But he found reassurance in the words of the psalmist, "who called upon us to praise the Lord with cymbals and drums and strings, and reed instruments."

"I was glad that we had the opportunity to introduce this at our Simchat Torah Service, and I hope that we will now begin to develop a tradition whereby such instruments, properly used, will enable us to deepen and intensify our religious experiences. The fact is that all present came away with a feeling of sheer excitement with the *hakafot* and with the mood that was created in the synagogue."

On October 20, Adath philanthropist Jay Phillips received the B'nai Brith Anti-Defamation League's Humanitarian Award at the national committee dinner meeting held in the Radisson Hotel. Also in October, Star-Tribune columnist (and gourmet) Will Jones opened the Men's Club season by cooking his first kosher meal and delivering an off-the-cuff critique of recent movies and menus entitled, "After Last Night—Heartburn."

At the 46th Annual Histradrut Dinner on November 9 at the Sheraton-Ritz Hotel, Eli and Esther Rosenbloom received the Distinguished Service Award from Histradrut, whose Minneapolis campaign Eli had headed for 12 years. Esther Rosenbloom had served as musical director for Adath and was its organist for many years, and her cantatas helped make the synagogue's Shavuot services among the most beautiful in the nation. Allen M. Herman stated that evening, "For nearly half a century the Rosenblooms have been inspiring and outstanding communal leaders in various areas, especially those related to health services, vocational schools, youth, and cultural centers of Histradrut in Israel."

On December 17, as part of the Century Series (formerly the Cultural Arts Series) the famous child psychologist Dr. Haim Ginott spoke to a rapt audience. Dr. Burton and Carolyn Abramson hosted a reception at their home following the address.

A number of Adath ninth-graders attended the annual Midwest LTF Kallah in Lincoln, Nebraska on December 21-25, including Daniel Goodman, Bonnie Karlen, Maynard Katz, Mary Orenstein, and Amy Sadoff. Among the senior high students who attended a gathering in Rock Island, Illinois, were Melissa Cohen, Steven Elkin, Carol Fischbein, Buddy Guttman, Bruce Karlen, Nancy Miller, Jody Myers, Mark Rotenberg, and Roseanne Zaidenweber.

At the Tree of Life Donor Luncheon on January 20 members of the Sisterhood put on a musical production written and directed by Etta Fay Orkin called "Folkways & Fashions." Evelyn Siegel and a chorus of singers provided musical accompaniment for a parade of old-fashioned outfits from various eras. The models were Leah Blat, Carol Daniels, Rae Goodman, Arlis Grossman, Merle Kane, Barbara Mark, Cheri Morgan, Ruth Peilen, Avis Savitt, Sheila Segal, Lorraine Shrell, and Phyllis Sudit.

At Shabbat Service Friday evening, January 16, Rabbi Goodman continued his pulpit series on "The Issues Facing the Jewish Community in the 70's." Speaking on the subject of "Urban Affairs, Jewish Education and Federation," Rabbi Goodman affirmed the importance of the Jewish community having a "corporate" or "communal" presence in the inner city and involving itself in this critical area of our society. Rabbi Goodman stressed the point that the entire thrust of the Jewish tradition is that every man must regard another as his brother.

The Oneg Shabbat following the service was hosted by the Edwin and Sybil Neff and Burton and Annette Neff, in honor of their parents Herman and Sadye Neff, who were celebrating their 50th anniversary. Sadye had been active in the Sisterhood for many years, serving on the board and as a board hostess. Herman was elected as an Honorary Lifetime Board Member of the congregation, and was among the first recipients to receive the Shem Tov Award—true pillars of the congregation.

In February the Adath youth staged the musical *Oliver!* at Beth El auditorium under the guidance of youth director Al Finkelstein and advisor Vicki Gold. The cast numbered more than 70, and the production was deemed a "smashing success." Rabbi Goodman later remarked: "To those of us who are close to the youth program, the entire weekend was extremely gratifying. The overwhelming response of our congregation intensifies our conviction that as a synagogue, we must provide programs which offer our youth a creative outlet for their energies."

On March 13, USY presented a Shabbat Eve Rock Service, "The Edge of Freedom," sung by a 20-voice chorus under the direction of Marlys Fiterman and Morrie Katz with accompaniment provided by the Adath Jeshurunites, the musical group that had enlivened the Simchat Torah Service the previous fall. Rabbi Goodman later commented that the service was pleasing if somewhat controversial. He diplomatically added that "the sight of 25 teenagers participating in this Shabbat Service was heartening and most of us came away with a sense of Shabbat joy." He was later challenged by unhappy congregants to explain why he had allowed the service, and he replied that it demonstrated the "inner flexibility" of Jewish forms of worship.

"There are a variety of ways of singing *Sh'ma Yisrael*,

but what is really important is affirming the Oneness of God. There are a variety of ways of singing, 'Sing unto the Lord a new song,' but what is really important is that we strive to express unto God the sense of joy and wonder of life....it was simply a way of expressing the Shabbat in a different idiom."

On March 29 an enthralled and captivated audience sat for more than two hours under the magic spell of master folksinger and actor Theodore Bikel, as he sang melodies from many countries and in many languages. Adath congregants, their friends, and music lovers from all over the Twin Cities area jammed the main sanctuary and balcony to hear this consummate performer. He sang Hebrew and Yiddish songs, Russian, French-Canadian, Bolivian folk melodies and love lyrics, interspersing them with stories and asides in his warm and inimitable style.

On Earth Day, April 22, 1970, Rabbi Goodman compared the plagues suffered by the ancient Egyptians and modern environmental issues, and attributed both of them to hard-heartedness. "We, too, refuse to take the steps that are essential; we consistently find reasons for our lack of commitment. Some cite the right of private enterprise to do as it sees fit with its own property; others claim that technological difficulties are insurmountable. Yet the story of Egypt is that while the early plagues did not seriously affect Egyptian wealth or power; the distortion and imbalance of their national environment led to a breakdown of their society."

In an article a few weeks later, following the Kent State killings, he remarked that "college students are just too bright, the war [in Vietnam] is just too senseless and our leaders just too glib for them to be deluded." He concluded that "our society is now in the process of being torn apart."

At one Friday evening service that spring Lynn Ackerberg and Deborah Brin gave a special presentation based on a collection of poetry written by Jewish children in the Theresienstadt concentration camp. The pain and anguish—but also the hope and faith— made it a fitting reading for the Shabbat between Israel Independence Day and Yom HaShoah (the day set aside to commemorate the Holocaust.)

USY held their final picnic and installed a new slate of officers on May 31. An LTF farewell party was held two weeks later for all high school students "going to Israel, Ramah, Tavor, Herzl, anywhere—or nowhere" at the Goodmans: Mincha, Seudat Shlishi, Maariv, Havdalah, a cookout and dancing on the lawn.

On June 7, 1970, the Adath celebrated a double *simcha*, with the 86th annual dinner meeting and the celebration of Cantor Amsel's twenty-five years as *hazzan, shaliach tzibbur* and *ba'al tefillah*. Edward Grosmann gave the invocation, Joyce Orbuch offered a toast, and the blessing following the meal was delivered by Dr. Michael Yablonski. Esther Katz received a special Shem Tov Award presented by Jerome Fischbein. Special honors were given to Cantor Morris Amsel upon his completion of 25 years of service with the congregation. The choir paid a musical tribute to the cantor, and he and his wife were given a trip to Israel. Cantor Amsel accepted his gift and made brief remarks about his quarter-century at the synagogue. Rabbi Morris Gordon, former spiritual leader of the Adath, returned to Minneapolis to be the guest speaker for the evening.

That summer Rabbi Goodman departed for an extended period of study in Israel. During his absence the Adath enjoyed the leadership of several capable guest rabbis.

1972-1973

St. Paul Mayor Larry Cohen was the guest speaker at the Sisterhood's opening luncheon meeting on September 5, 1972. That year, during the High Holy Days, the congregation continued the recently re-established tradition of conducting the Tashlich ceremony on the east shore of Lake Calhoun, a few blocks west of the synagogue, in accordance with the words of the prophet Micah: "Thou wilt cast all their sins into the depths of the sea." More than 200 gathered at the pier that afternoon.

The synagogue engaged Rabbi Mark L. Shrager that fall to direct the youth and educational arms of synagogue life. He had recently returned from two years service as Jewish chaplain with the U.S. Air Force on the island of Okinawa, Japan. A Philadelphia native, he had been ordained in 1969.

In Gan Hayeled children studied the changes of the season with nature walks and discussions on how to get their homes ready for winter. They also took a field trip to the Bell Museum of Natural History to observe animals in their natural habitats and experience the Touch and See Room.

In September of 1972 a new Post-Bar Mitzvah adah was added to the Shabbat Morning Program (SMP), open to Adath members age 13 and older. The concept of dividing each age level of the SMP into an adah for intensified learning had been developed by Rabbi Goodman a few years earlier. Its special purpose was to give a large number of older students training in both subject matter and teaching methodology, followed by the opportunity to serve by passing on what they had learned to younger students. A sample of some of the courses or *chugim* (interest groups) being offered were: Israeli Dancing, Israeli Singing, Jewish Literature Through Drama, Torah Reading, Haftorah Reading, Haganot or Chazanut (cantorial chanting), Junior Choir, and Jewish Observance and Jewish Practices in Death and Mourning. During the year there were Kallot for each adah at Lyman Lodge.

On January 4, 1973, the Goodmans hosted an evening known as "Vacation Ventilation" with skating, sliding, and two films with very different themes: one documented a recent USY Pie-Eating Contest and the other captured highlights of the USY Russian-Israel trip filmed by Evan Miller, Maynard Katz and Mark Glotter.

In early May the Men's Club sponsored a dinner and the reading of the Broadway and Hollywood hit, *Cactus Flower*, with Syd Rich, Billy Aberman, Avis Savitt, Ann Dachis, Sam Abrams, Bea Rich, Dave Dachis and Zelmar Shrell in the cast. Later in the month USY put on an ambitious production of *The Sound of Music*, with Rebecca Bender, John, David and Robert Orenstein, Lynn Simon, Judy Tychman and Cynthia Friedman in the leading roles; the production was directed by Warren Magnuson, with musical direction by Allan Finkelstein.

President Jerome Fischbein was pleased to report at the annual meeting that plans were afoot to construct a kallah/retreat center on the Adath's Minnetonka property.

Rabbi Shrager, Rabbi Goodman, Jerry Fischbein, and Cantor Amsel at a Tashlich ceremony

The first Adath Bat Mitzvah at Masada, Susan Sigel.

"New young families with children must be attracted to join Adath Jeshurun," he told the congregation, "and the only way is to place a facility in their midst." But that was not the only reason the program made sense.

"Our own present programming for all age levels will be greatly enhanced with these structures. Rabbi Shrager will have a center that will insure the success of your youth activities and Rabbi Goodman will be able to strengthen our educational program to the adult congregation. Kallah/retreats nationwide have proven to be the greatest single stimulant to the enrichment of the Jewish way of life for all ages... Our congregation has always had a reputation for innovation and leadership in the Conservative movement. We cannot rest on our laurels. Constant improvement in our synagogue way of life will assure a better way of life for us all."

On Simchat Torah all the organizations within the synagogue participated in the *hakafot*. That year two processions were held simultaneously—one in the social hall, devoted to those under 30, and one in the main sanctuary for the rest of the congregation. Members of the Adath also joined other Twin City congregations in a special Simchat Torah outdoor celebration to coincide with Soviet Jews' observance. Each synagogue was assigned a "sister" community in Russia: the Adath adopted the Jews of Minsk. The celebration, organized by the Minnesota Action Committee, was held on 28th Street between Joppa and Monterey, which was temporarily renamed "Archipova Street." A Torah from each of the ten Twin City synagogues was carried aloft, and *hakafot*, dancing and singing to the Chassidic music of Jerry Mayeron commenced afterward.

In February, 2nd grade teacher Ruth Kirschner and assistant Barbara Sigel helped children write a group of delightful original prayers and assemble them into a book that was published under the title, *Our Prayer Book*. And in May the 7th grade of Adath religious school presented Sholom Aleichem's *A Pity for the Living* to the kindergarten and first grade. The cast included Leslie Segal, Jessica Rappaport, Helen Abrams, Melissa Herman, Linda Sachs, Debbie Segal, and Lou Ann Singer.

The theme of Adath's Holocaust commemoration that year was the 30th anniversary of the Warsaw Ghetto uprising. A "Living Memorial" digital clock was set up in the foyer of the main sanctuary and dedicated at Shabbat services on April 27 to remind everyone of the enormity and magnitude of the loss of Six Million Jews in the Holocaust. Jonathan Gross conceived and designed the clock, with Shirley Hansen providing the sculptural elements.

Rabbi Mark Shrager, who had served the congregation since the previous August, left in May to take a position as director of the Hillel Foundation at the University of Indiana in Bloomington. Eugene LeVee was hired to take his place as director of the Sunday Religious School, SMP and USY programs. A graduate of Yeshiva University, he had attended the Teachers' Institute for Men and completed his graduate work at Roosevelt University in 1972. He served as both Youth and Kallah leader.

Pesach, the Jewish festival of freedom, was observed for the 3,413th time, making it the oldest continually observed religious ceremony on record.

Rabbi Goodman and Cantor Amsel conducted a series of two Passover workshops that year, sponsored by the religious school and nursery school parents.

In May, Adath staged a play *The Mother of the Bride*, written by Audrey Efron and directed by Marlys Moscoe Fiterman.

On May 4, the congregation celebrated the 25th anniversary of Israel's independence. Leon Frankel, an Adath congregant who had served as a pilot in the Israeli air force in 1948, spoke on "The Israeli Air Force—25 Years Ago." All congregants who had visited Israel at any time in the past quarter century were honored.

On Sunday afternoon, May 27, a ground-breaking ceremony took place for the Kallah Center. Hundreds of trees were planted at the site that day.

Expanding on a program he had initiated before his visit to Israel, Rabbi Goodman sponsored an all-night Shavuot study session at his home, in an effort to symbolically reaffirm that every Jew continues to stand at the foot of Mt. Sinai. Rabbis Shrager and Moshe Lichtman, the associate director of the Hillel Foundation, joined Rabbi Goodman in teaching from the traditional *Tikkun*. The study session concluded at 5 a.m., followed by the morning service, a kiddush and breakfast. Regular Shavuot morning services were held.

The BBYO Minstrels, including Adath members Bruce Orkin, Mark Grossfield, Mark Cohen, Bruce Shapiro, Joe Weil, Art Shragg, Dorae Kaner, Wendy Kunin, and Carrie Trestman

1973-1974

Annual Selichot services began with a dialogue between Rabbi Goodman and Rabbi Moshe Lichtman, speaking on "New Dimensions of the Rosh Hashanah and Yom Kippur Liturgy."

High Holiday sermon topics included "Maimonides on Nixon," and "In the Year of Israel...Twenty Five Plus One."

On Yom Kippur war broke out once again in the Middle East, as Egyptian and Syrian troops crossed the cease-fire lines in the Sinai and Golan Heights, respectively, which had been captured by Israel in 1967 during the Six-Day War. The congregation, like the rest of the world, was shocked that the attack came on Yom Kippur.

Gan Hayeled held an open house on October 3. The Nursery School chairs at the time were Charlotte Berman and Dorothy Pink. Children had kiddush in the sukkah with Gene LeVee leading the service and explaining the etrog and lulav. The older classes took a field trip to the Woodlake Nature Reserve and observed birdlife in the area, went on short walks and collected fall leaves. Other field trips included the Bell Museum of Natural History and the Walker Art Center. The following month the children and their families had a seudah shlishit and havdalah service.

A "Parade of Sukkot" was held on Sunday, October 14, to the homes of Rabbi and Rae Goodman, Dr. Alan and Alice Briskin, Robert and Debby Wolk, Paul and Raleigh Kent, Dr. John and Rachel Levitt, Morris and Esther Katz, Leo and Fern Meltzer, Burton and Barbara Myers, Paul and Freddie Pink, and Alvin and Judy Goldstein. And Adah Gimel students built and decorated a congregational sukkah under the supervision of Laurie Mark and Jim Applebaum.

In November, at the United Synagogue's Biennial Convention, the Adath received the Solomon Schechter Award for its kallah retreat program. (The award is given to qualifying congregations who have distinguished themselves with outstanding programs in education, administration, and worship). At the time, the kallah retreat building was the only synagogue sponsored facility of its kind in the Upper Midwest to provide a traditional Jewish environment with sleeping accommodations for 50 children at a time.

For Thanksgiving the Sisterhood's "Gourmet Gals"—Shirley Backman, Beverly Skolnick, Goldie Wilensky, Betty Schnitzer, Freida Golden, Frances Grosmacht, Ann Goldstein and Mitzi Diamond—prepared their famed delicious potato knishes which they sold for $2.65 per dozen.

The Kallah Center under construction

The Sisterhood held an art auction a few weeks later, with all proceeds dedicated to the kallah retreat center. A call also went out for recipes to be included in a projected cookbook.

On December 16, as part of the 90th Anniversary celebration, "An Enchanted Evening" was held at the Adath. It featured Cantor Amsel and the Southwest High School Choir under the direction of Oscar Dahle performing an outstanding pre-Chanukah Concert of Jewish liturgical and folk music. Narrator Sabine Amsel dramatically set the stage for each number, and Coleen Fowler also added greatly to the enjoyment of the performance with her organ accompaniment. Nearly a thousand people attended and gave standing ovations to the cantor and choir. A social hour followed hosted by the Men's Club, chaired by Max Elkin and Martin Weinberger plus the committee of Carole Modell, Rose and David Sherman, Marlene and Sanford Goldberg, Nat and Reginald Werner, Goldie Wilensky, Beverly Skolnick, Anne Goldstein, Hinda Litman, Elsa Tolchiner, Sharon and Jeff Kivens, Bobbi Nemer, Gail and Steve Perlman, Barbara and Burton Myers.

In mid-January the second annual USY pie-eating contest took place. Scott Stein tried to defend his title but was defeated in the final round by Mike Perman, a new member.

Later that month members of the 4th grade religious school class wrote letters to Israeli soldiers who had taken part in the Yom Kippur War, and many of them received replies. An interesting one came from Benzy Cohn, a second year Israeli student at the Hebrew University of Jerusalem: "After being on the front for a month, I was happy to return home for a weekend and I was extremely pleased to find the letters from you and your students. I truly hope that within a number of days we will be able to return home for good. The important war, I hope, will now be fought in diplomatic circles and not on the battlefield. You have no idea how much we appreciate the help of American Jews. Their demonstrations of solidarity prove once again that Israel lives and that we are not alone. We also thank the American government for their help in supplying ammunition that allowed us to end the war quickly."

In February USY held its first kallah in the new center. The theme was "The Uniqueness of Jews." Rabbi Moshe Lichtman was the keynote speaker.

On February 19 the Men's Club sponsored a dinner featuring KMSP-TV host-moderator-producer Abraham "Dutch" Kastenbaum. He had been executive director and youth supervisor at Adath during the 1940s, but was now host of Senior Citizens Forum, a popular Sunday morning TV show featuring prominent guests discussing topics pertinent to the living patterns of older Americans. He spoke on the topic "The Upsurge, or the Age of the Elders," and in his address he called upon the *balabatim* of the synagogue to investigate areas of involvement that could be opened for older members and then to put these programs into effect as quickly as possible.

Later that month the Beth El and Adath Men's Clubs held a joint breakfast at which guest speaker Kyrill Khenkin, a former Russian journalist and news broadcaster on Moscow radio, discussed the plight of Soviet Jewry. This highly articulate spokesman for Jewish activists warned, "Don't be deceived by the fact that 80,000 Jews have left the USSR for Israel. It still does not mean any change in policy." He ended his address with the words "I suggest that you continue to denounce, yell, protest!"

On February 26, USY sponsored its annual giant Purim Carnival with booths, games, contests, prizes and a spaghetti luncheon. On Thursday, March 7, Adath parents and children gathered to hear portions of the *megillah* read followed by a special musical pantomime enacted and narrated by the assistant teachers in the SMP program. The costumed children took part in the Grand March led by Rabbi Goodman, followed by refreshments in the social hall. The next day the full reading of the *megillah* took place. In the religious school, the children made baskets, filled with sweets and homentashen and took *shaloach monot* to the Jewish residents of the Villa Apartments across the street from the Adath.

At the end of March, 1974, it was announced that a second Adath nursery school, Gan Hayeled, would open in September at the Heller Kallah Center under the direction of Pearl Pearlman. The nursery school on Dupont would continue under the direction of Marianne Wollstein. Both Gan Hayeled facilities operated as "open schools" with programming that included art, music, dramatic play, stories, language arts, science, math, games and large muscle activities, along with religious instruction at the child's level. Shabbat and Jewish holidays were celebrated in warm and enriching ways, enabling the children to enjoy and take pride in their Jewish heritage. Field trips and visiting resource people would continue to help broaden the children's experiences.

During the observance of Yom HaShoah on Friday evening, April 19, Eugene LeVee directed a dramatic reading of *I Never Saw Another Butterfly*, about the young inmates of the Terezin concentration camp in Theresienstadt, Czechoslovakia. James Applebaum, Melissa Cohen, Joni Kibort, Linda Levine, Robert Levinson, Howard Mark and Helene Share made up the cast.

On Shavuot that year, the choir performed the cantata *But a Moment of Holiness*. Adapted from a script written by Rabbi Goodman and Esther Rosenbloom, it celebrated the life cycle of the Jew. At the all-night Shavuot study session, Rabbi Marc Liebhaber taught Kabbalah.

An open house was held at the Kallah Center satellite preschool on June 4 to show parents the surroundings. Corinne Nierenstein had recently been appointed supervisory head teacher with "Miss Dolly" Rosenblum assisting. Pearl Pearlman, Ms. Nirenstein, Beverly Shapiro, Barbara Wilensky and Paula Verson were all present.

1974-1975

The two Adath Jeshurun nursery schools opened on September 4, one on 3400 Dupont Avenue South and the other at the Kallah Center in Minnetonka.

On September 3, the Sisterhood held a fashion show at their opening meeting with the theme "Dorothy Collins Home Show of Interior Design." Live models displayed the newest trends in home furnishings, each one serving as a "walking roomful" of decorating ideas. On the more serious side, the Sisterhood once again took up its collection of food and urged members to bring further contributions to emergency food shelf depots in Minneapolis.

At Selichot services Dr. Stephen Feinstein, a professor of Russian History at the University of Wisconsin, River Falls, brought the congregation up to date on the efforts of Jews to leave the Soviet Union and offered specific suggestions on what members could do to help. Mickey Bix and Sharon Lerner, Adath's Soviet Action Committee co-chairs, distributed special material.

During Rosh Hashanah and Yom Kippur the new "third service" was used, allowing for greater congregational participation by encouraging dialogue with the rabbi, having more congregational singing and extensive interpretive comments on the liturgy. The choir chanted the liturgy and John Orenstein taught and led the congregational melodies.

That year was the first complete year of kallah programming in the new Heller Kallah Retreat Center. The programs were geared to specific age groups (SMP, religious school students, confirmation class, USY, young marrieds and family groups) with special programming and activities, playtime, worship services, study-time and fellowship all conducted in a complete Jewish atmosphere.

In mid-September USY sponsored a progressive dinner during which attendees paid visits to the homes of the Shrells, Steins, Mandels and Englers. And on the last week of October, 38 8th graders participated in a four-day Kallah-On-Wheels to Winnipeg, Canada, meeting there with Kadimah members of Shaarey Zedek Synagogue.

Lisa Swaiman noted in the *Clarion* for October 22, 1975, that the Shabbat Morning Program was turning out many accomplished Torah readers. Irving Guttman had developed a department for Torah reading for the first time a few years earlier, and because the teachers were now better trained and active Torah readers, the number of students becoming involved in Torah reading was growing year by year. Even the Adah Aleph had initiated such a program for those who wanted to get a head start in Torah reading. George Orenstein had set up the program, called "Introduction to Torah Reading," in a semester course the previous year. The students studied the basics of Torah reading and got a broad overview of what Torah reading is all about, and those who showed special promise were put into a special advanced class in Adah Bet Torah Reading. "This year," Lisa noted, "all 39 Adah Betniks are enrolled in Torah reading."

Adah Gimel also advanced in its Torah reading program that year, with the number enrolled swelling from six to 16. Howard Mark and Judy Ribnick were the instructors.

On Thanksgiving weekend 35 USY members attended the Midwest region Kinnus at Arrowhead Lodge, Alexandria. Ruth and Norman Kirschner, Gene LeVee, Sue Schwaidelson and Sue Shrell were chaperones. Scott Stein was elected regional treasurer at the meeting.

In November yet another Adah was established for 9th graders, to be trained as SMP assistants. More than 20 youngsters met every other week with Rabbi Goodman to discuss news in the Israeli press. Following the Adah's own service, a Master Torah Reading class was held for those

Children at the Gan on Dupont during the mid-1970s

interested in being Torah reading teachers. The others participated in a discussion led by Cindy Herman and Larry Katz. On the intervening weeks, the Adah started out with a service of its own, followed by training sessions in group dynamics and leadership with Bob Wolk and Dr. Alan Briskin. Finally, the Master Class met while Rabbi James Michaels met with the other assistant teachers.

The plan was to work these assistants into normal classroom situations by the end of the year, though Adah Hey also arranged activities and planned for a kallah in the spring.

Meanwhile, two new educational ventures in Hebrew reading were started for adults. Morris Perman began teaching an elementary course in Hebrew reading on Saturdays designed for adults who had no knowledge of Hebrew but wanted to master the rudiments of the alphabet in order to be able to read the Siddur and to follow the Hebrew service; and Howard Mark initiated an adult Torah-reading class that met on Sundays.

Rosalind Horowitz became the new director of the religious school that year, and open houses held during November and December gave parents an opportunity to relate to their children's curriculum.

In October the Sisterhood Study Group began a new series. Rabbi Goodman taught a series of Monday morning classes on the *mitzvot* as developed by Maimonides; and Morris Perman, associate director of the Minneapolis Talmud Torah and one of the foremost Jewish educators on the national scene, spoke on the theme "The Quality of Jewish Education—Its Problems and its Hopes."

In December Ed Schwartz, a well-known Minneapolis personality, spoke to the Men's Club on the subject "An Affair of the Heart." Ed had had his Bar Mitzvah at the

Adath in 1916, and his father, Mayer Schwartz, had worked alongside Joseph Schanfeld, David Jeffrey and others to build the congregation and help newcomers from Europe learn English and find work.

On December 29 the Men's Club's guest of honor was Patrolman Harald Petterson, who had served the Adath for 20 years by regulating traffic on Sundays and holidays. Captains Tom Whelan and Jerry Shoemaker spoke on the various branches of the Minneapolis Police Department and how they coordinated their efforts with each other and with the state and federal agencies.

In January the Young Marrieds Study Group held a one-night retreat at the Kallah Center beginning with Havdalah, followed by a discussion on Jewish marriage and sex values. The couples then did some cross-country skiing across the still undeveloped countryside. The retreat concluded Sunday morning with services, breakfast and a discussion session. Bob and Sylvia Fine, and Hillary and Larry Freeman were in charge of the retreat, along with Rabbis Goodman and Woolf and their wives.

Later that month USY held a symposium to discuss Conservative Judaism. Adath USY members Brian Dworsky, Mark Meirovitz, John Orenstein, Scott Stein, Margie Stein and Jeff Upin were on the panel.

The Purim celebration that year included the performance of a "Purimspiel" written and directed by USY advisor Sue Schwaidelson, a graduate student in dramatics at the University of Minnesota, followed by an Oneg Purim in the "Shuk" of Shushan, with students of all ages manning the booths. Those who came in costume were allowed to play free-of-charge.

Israel's 27th anniversary was celebrated at Shabbat services on April 11 with Lt. Col. Yossi Ben Chanan as guest speaker. He was the brother of former Talmud Torah teacher Chaya Weingarten, and best remembered for the famous cover picture in *Life Magazine* showing him standing in the Suez Canal following the Six Day War. He had also fought in the Golan Heights during the Yom Kippur War the previous year, where he sustained serious leg injuries.

On the May 9 Shabbat, children honored all the preschool mothers by baking cookies, making corsages and presenting the mothers with a gift. They participated in blessing the candles, wine and challah, and sang *zmirot*. Rabbi Goodman was also a guest.

Early that spring Cantor Amsel had announced his retirement, and on May 2, Cantor Morton Kula, from Beth Shalom in Rosyln, New York, served as guest cantor. He had lived in Jerusalem and was associated with Hebrew

University Jewish Music Center and the United Synagogue Congregation in Israel.

The next week the Sisterhood presented "A Tribute to Cantor and Sabine," honoring the Amsels for their 30

Cantor and Sabine Amsel

years of service to Adath Jeshurun. Ann Dachis, Etta Fay Orkin and Ruben Miller wrote the script; Leon Lerner directed, and Larry Katz provided musical accompaniment. Barbara Mark and Arnold Aberman were the narrators and Lillian Kaplan hosted a reception following the performance.

In the summer of 1975, the Mishpacha program began its second season at the Kallah Center. The goal of the six-week program was to offer a multi-generational experience to members and friends of the congregation. Hence the name Mishpacha, which means "Family." The schedule also made it possible for youngsters to participate in the program without committing to a large block of time in advance.

1975-1976

Rabbi Goodman once again sent out an appeal for congregants to attend morning Shabbat services that year: "Shabbat Bereishit is an appropriate time to consider starting to come to Shabbat morning services. There is a special sense of warmth and sharing at the Adath on Shabbat mornings. The Torah Study Session and its emphasis upon development and exploring the meaning of Biblical and Rabbinic texts in the light of our contemporary situation is always stimulating and rewarding...Our synagogue

Dora Zaidenweber

Hinda Kibort

SHABBAT HASHOAH

On Shabbat HaShoah, the Shabbat preceding Yom HaShoah, congregants commemorated the 30th anniversary of the liberation of the death camps with a special pictorial display gathered by a noted Yiddish journalist and photographer, Bernard Ginsberg. At the service Ed Grosmann, Hinda and Leo Kibort, and Jules and Dora Zaidenweber, all of whom had survived the Nazi concentration camps, gave a pulpit presentation during which they related their experiences in the hours before and following their liberation from the camps in 1945.

At the first Holocaust Shabbat, held in 1971, Dora had said, "It is only natural that people should want to forget a terror filled past; that they should want to eliminate from their minds painful memories of the loss of near and dear ones and of suffering all but unbearable. A generation has now passed and the children of those of us who grew up in those days of the great tragedy, are now grown, many of them ignorant of what happened only so recently to their people. And what about their children? How will they know? We must keep the memory alive!

"The vast majority of those who perished left no survivors and there are no stones marking their graves; they are nameless and faceless. Yet they lived and loved and suffered and died, and, there has to be some way to perpetuate their *shem tov*—their good name!"

For the next ten years, Dora led the Holocaust Shabbat commemorations at the Adath Jeshurun with the help of her survivor friends and their families. The survivors were the spark that lit the fire of remembrance! Many became impasssioned speakers in the schools, churches and public forums.

on any given Shabbat is a very busy and full place. The Shabbat Morning Program for children ten years of age and up and the Shabbat Morning 'workshop' for children under ten add to a sense of excitement and movement."

On the first day of Rosh Hashanah, Rabbi Goodman issued the challenge to the congregation to organize an

Adath Jeshurun modern Jewish funeral society. The response was electrifying. For all life's occasions, including birth, Bar Mitzvah, marriages and wedding anniversaries, the synagogue offered its services directly. Now, for the first time, a complete traditional funeral would also be available for all members of the Adath at no cost. It would include the services of a funeral director, Chevra Kadisha (all Adath members), the *aron* (coffin), chapel, graveside services, and transportation for the *met* (deceased) and immediate family on the day of the funeral. This was to become one of Rabbi Goodman's greatest legacies.

On August 30 the Sisterhood sponsored a "Kabbalat Panim" coffee hour between the High Holiday workshop and the Selichot service to welcome both Cantor Morton Kula and Rabbi James Michaels, along with their wives Charlotte and Karen, into the Adath family. Beverly Skolnick and Goldie Wilensky were in charge of the refreshment committee with special help from Shirley Backman. Judy Goldstein and Carol Sue Greene arranged the Oneg Shabbat and kiddush.

During Selichot services Cantor Kula, the Adath's new cantor, led music workshops to teach the High Holiday melodies, accompanied by his son, Aaron, a classical accordionist, and organist Colleen Fowler. Rabbis Michaels and Goodman commented on the theological content of the liturgical selections.

New that year for Rosh Hashanah, the choir had raised seats in their section on the side, enabling all to see and hear them as never before. On Yom Kippur Jay Phillips celebrated the 40th anniversary of his chanting of the haftorah.

Rabbi Goodman wrote: "The Neilah service, which terminates Yom Kippur, has its own charm. This 'dusk' service has become one of our most beloved religious experiences of the Jews. There is real drama as the sanctuary slowly fills up as families return to the sanctuary for the sounding of the shofar which signals the end of the fast."

In late September Adath USY held a sukkah party at the Kallah Center with many attending dressed up as fruits and vegetables of the season. It was one of the funniest programs ever! A few days later the same group held its own *hakafah* at Simchat Torah services.

The Simchat Torah celebration was heightened by a Simchat Torah Combo comprised of Larry Katz on drums, Aaron Kula, accordion, and David Orenstein, trumpet. It was a singing, swinging, Chassidic and "pop" Simchat Torah. The combo played during the *hakafot* and celebration in Schanfeld Hall and continuing out onto Dupont Avenue as part of an expression of solidarity with world and Russian Jewry.

The following week the Sisterhood held its annual kallah under the guidance of co-chairs, Jennie Siegel and Lisa Greene. The theme was "The Role of Jewish Women" and the weekend event concluded with the group attending a dance at Beth El Synagogue.

In October a new dimension was introduced at the Adath when a "Shabbat Seder" was held, which concluded with singing and *Birkat Hamazon*, followed by Friday evening Shabbat services. This new line of events was based on a tradition among Jews that regardless of where you start your meal, you can recite the *Birkat Hamazon* (the Grace after Meals) where you complete it. It was hoped that the first Shabbat Seder would prove to be instructive for those who would like to spend part of the Shabbat learning some of the familiar and traditional facets of Shabbat singing and Shabbat observance.

Another innovation that year was that boys and girls began to read Torah and chanted Havdalah on the Shabbat before their Bar or Bat Mitzvah.

SISTERHOOD SHABBAT

On Friday evening, October 24, Rabbi Goodman spoke on the subject "Eshet Chayil: Woman of Valor, Then and Now." He said:

"*Eshet chayil*, a term used in Proverbs 31, describes the role of the woman as it was understood in antiquity. The *eshet chayil* passage which served as a model for Jewish womanhood throughout the ages, is challenged today by the Feminist movement. How valid is *eshet chayil* as a model? What are the implications of the rejection of the *eshet chayil* model for the survival of the Jewish family, of Jewish life, and of the Jewish community?"

That same evening Cantor Kula presented "A Suite for Eshet Chayil."

On Shabbat Morning, October 25, 1975, Adath Jeshurun held its first adult B'not Mitzvah, with 10 Sisterhood women participating—Marlene Goldberg, Freida Golden, Rhoda Jaffe, Sue Kaufman, Leah Myers, Bettina Schultz, Muriel Swerdlick, Joan Weinstein, Ardis Wexler and Nat Werner. The women chanted the haftarah and led the congregation in brief *Divrei Torah* (liturgical portions). They had studied during the previous year with Rabbis Goodman and Michaels, Cantor Kula and Joe King. Their curriculum included Hebrew, chanting of the service, and a study of basic theological concepts of the Jewish tradition.

Rabbi Goodman later described the service as "one of the most exciting events in the long history of the Adath Jeshurun... Their presence in the synagogue was an affirmation of their desire to grow as Jews through the study of our tradition. As each woman ascended the pulpit to recite the *haftorah*, as the entire group chanted the *brachot*. They again ascended individually to receive their gift from the congregation and the Sisterhood, all of us present were overcome with a deep feeling of joy.

"...The Bat Mitzvah of these 10 women is but one instance of people realizing their potential for growth. Their Bat Mitzvah is also consistent with the finest examples of our tradition. It should be viewed in the context of Rabbi Akiba, who began studying Torah at age 40; or in the context of a Ben-Gurion, who started studying Greek in his 60s; or in the context of our tradition that continually reminds us that the Torah is the heritage of every Jew, young and old alike.

(Back row from left) Nat Werner, Leah Myers, Marlene Goldberg, Rhoda Jaffe, Helen Vinitsky, Sue Kaufman and Freida Golden. (Front row from left) Joan Weinstein, Muriel Swerdlick, Bettina Schultz and Ardis Wexler, the first adult B'not Mitzvah.

"These B'not Mitzvah have, by their example reaffirmed that the study of Hebrew, the attempt to gain meaning from our traditional sources, and the desire to learn more about our heritage are not privileges to be afforded only to the young but are opportunities awaiting every person who wants to learn more about our heritage."

A second adult Bat Mitzvah class was formed that year.

An exciting and challenging program was announced for Gan Hayeled that year. It included cooking, scientific experiments, field trips, playground activities, and enjoying Shabbat activities on Fridays with a different special guest each week. Staff that year included Sydney Cohen, Paula Verson, and Barbara Wilensky. Beverly Shapiro directed an accelerated group and Linda Soderstrom was in charge of the creative movement program, under the direction of the Choreagram Dance Group. Cecil Kiperstin also joined the teaching staff.

In November there was a special Dads' Night with 100% attendance—a huge success! The children themselves prepared the Thanksgiving feast of turkey, soup, cranberries and cornmeal muffins.

Adath hosted a Thanksgiving Eve celebration that fall with St. Paul's Episcopal Church, Lake of the Isles Lutheran Church, Trinity Community Church and Grace Presbyterian Church. The event was an opportunity for Jews and Christians to gather with one another and to express a sense of gratitude for the freedoms and blessings of American life. In the past Adath had been part of an ecumenical Thanksgiving service but had not participated in recent years. A new minister, Reverend Ernsberger from Grace Presbyterian Church, encouraged the Adath to renew the custom, and Rabbi Goodman, in turn, invited Sister Catherine Litecky, the chairperson of the Theology Department of the College of St. Catherine, to present a scriptural message in honor of the International Year of the Woman. Bruce Orkin, Jody Winger and Roger Brooks brought along their guitars and joined in the singing of traditional Thanksgiving music. All attending were asked to bring an "offering" of canned goods to be donated to the Neighborhood Involvement Program, and two truck-loads of canned goods were collected for distribution to needy families. A mood of celebration and joy prevailed.

During Chanukah Rabbi Goodman spoke out against recent events at the United Nations:

"We celebrate Chanukah, this year, in a context of anger and resolve. We are angry at the unfair and unbelievably obscene UN resolution equating Zionism and racism. We have perceived - and correctly - that the target is not only the State of Israel, but also the Jewish people. We have expressed our anger at rallies, in newspaper columns, in letters to our political leadership. We have stated our resolve to proclaim to the world that Zionism is a form of Judaism and that both are colorblind...

"The *halacha* (Jewish law) insists that when we light the Chanukah candles, we are to place them in a window facing the street for all to see. This is an affirmation of our Jewishness; it is an act of self-definition. The *halacha*, by leading us to such acts of self-determination, created the raw material out of which Zionism was nurtured and the State of Israel ultimately formed even after close to two thousand years of exile.

"We now live during difficult and cloudy times. The traditional observance of Chanukah, of lighting the menorah and putting it where it can be seen by all, takes on added meaning as a proclamation of our Jewishness."

For the Gan Chanukah party and luncheon in December the children made clay menorahs and the rooms were decorated with a Chanukah motif. They learned about the Pilgrims, Indians and Maccabees. That December the chil-

(Above) Art Brand. (Above right) Adath picnic, circa 1980

dren also took a field trip to Children's Hospital to gain firsthand knowledge of what a trip to that facility would be like, should anyone ever need to go there. One of the tour guides, Donna Koppelman, later wrote to Mrs. Pearlman: "Your children were by far my most attentive group. Their alertness, interest and beautiful behavior were overwhelming. But as I watched you and your marvelous teachers, I could immediately see why. Your guidance, love and supervision were so far superior to any other school group I have taken through."

In December USY staged *Joseph and the Amazing Technicolor Dreamcoat*, featuring an original script by local playwright Joel Bassin; it was directed by Deborah Kafitz with a huge cast and musical direction by Mark Bloom.

On December 29, the city of Minneapolis hosted more than 80 members of the Leadership Training Fellowship at a regional kallah. Participants from as far afield as Texas, Ohio, and New York enjoyed a weekend of study, fun and friendship. Rabbi Goodman later wrote: "I have enjoyed coordinating this kallah on the local level. All three Conservative congregations from Minneapolis are anticipating the arrival of the LTF-ers and planning to extend a hearty *beruchim haba-im shalom aleichem*!"

Two different programs were held during the four-day kallah—one for 9th graders and one for 10th and 11th graders. The theme of the first kallah was "The Golden Age in Spain and the Spanish Inquisition," while the second kallah studied "The *Akeidah* (The Binding of Isaac) as reflected in Literature." When not studying, the attendees toured

Minneapolis, participated in winter activities, and attended a play at the Guthrie Theater.

Barb Pink, Teresa Miller, Saralee Shrell, Jacqueline Rivkin, Bobby Levinson and George Orenstein attended from the Adath, and Louis Miller and Rosanne Zaidenweber served on the staff.

At the annual "Tree of Life" Sisterhood meeting in January, Beverly Fine became chair of the Tree of Life Donor project, which raised financial support for the religious school and Gan Hayeled. The program was held in the evening and was open to husbands and friends. The Women's Liberation Movement and its implications for wives, mothers and Jews was the topic of formal discussion by a panel consisting of Irving Nudell, executive director of the Jewish Family and Children's Service; Byron Schneider, principal of Southwest High School; Roberta Levy, attorney; Rosanne Zaidenweber, recent Univery of Minnesota graduate; and Rabbi Goodman.

In February the Gan children visited the Lincoln Del to learn how bagels are made.

The Shabbat Shalom Chavurah started with Rabbi Michaels as advisor. He also began to teach a new class devoted to the study of Mishnah, Chavurah Mishnaiot. It met one hour before mincha services.

Cantor Kula and Rabbis Goodman and Michaels prepared a series of booklets that year, "Oneg Shabbat - Family Shabbat Observance," which brought together theoretical and practical guides to the traditional observance of Shabbat in the home.

A Walk for Israel was staged on Sunday, May 9, coordinated by the youth of Adath Jeshurun, B'nai B'rith Youth Organization, B'nai Emet, Beth El, Habonim, the Hillel House at the University of Minnesota, JCC, Kenesseth Israel, Temple Israel, Torah Academy and the Minneapolis Federation. The walk began and ended at Loring Park.

In 1976 Marsha Golob became Mispacha's new director, with Mark Burns, Andrea Magy, and Evan Goldstein (the official gardener) on the staff. That year the program really blossomed, doubling the attendance of the previous year to more than 1600.

1976-1977

Adath's Long Range Planning Committee submitted a report on September 16, 1976, following a 12-month study of the synagogue's future needs. Based on this recommendation, the Board of Trustees charged the Long Range Planning Committee, under the chairpersonship of Barry Krelitz, to develop remodeling plans. A sub-committee under Fred Berdass designated the architectural firm, J.J. Liebenberg and Associates (the original architect of the Adath) as the choice of the committee.

Rachel Levitt became the new director of the religious school. It was during this period that it became mandatory for children to attend Talmud Torah from grades three through eight. The extended day a week at Gan Hayeled, instituted the previous year, had been so successful that it was expanded to two days a week. Cecil Kiperstin was appointed the new pre-school director.

Gan Hayeled Pre-School began its third year at the Heller Kallah Center. All units were programmed by the director, Cecil Kiperstin, drawing on the talents of Paula Verson, talented in music and drama, and Beverly Shapiro, who was proficient in Hebrew, folk dancing and creative arts, and had worked with children for the better part of 18 years.

A pre-Selichot special program was held for young people who had visited Israel during the summer, including Brian Dworsky, Terri Orbuch, Judy Ribnick, Paula Rutman, David and Karen Siegel, and Todd Werner. Rabbi Goodman moderated the panel. The program included personal impressions of Israel and a slide presentation integrated with special music chosen and led by Cantor Kula.

The High Holidays once again included a Tashlich service at Lake Calhoun, which had grown in popularity year by year.

Chevra Kavod Hamet (the Society to Honor the Dead) began officially that year. It was formally announced the first morning of Rosh Hashanah. The revolutionary program made a simple, dignified funeral available to members of the congregation in time of grief and bereavement, at no cost to them. It was heralded by the rabbi as an extraordinary example of our congregation overcoming the inertia of many decades in dealing with death. He indicated that the work of the Chevra had been one of the most significant projects he had been involved with during his 25 years in the rabbinate, and he lauded the work of Dr. Alan Briskin, the chairperson, and the many members of the group "who had undertaken a variety of responsibilities which would

Choir director Marlys Fiterman directs the Adath choir in rehearsal. Cantor Kula is at far left.

On April 14, 1978, the Adath received an award for selling Israel Bonds. Rubin Miller, Charlotte and Irving Nudell, and Jerry Fischbein accept the plaque.

enable us to serve one another in time of great grief."

That fall Cantor Morton Kula introduced a new cultural program known as TAMID (an acronym for Theatre, Arts, Music, Israel, Dance.) It was designed to bring Jewish art and music to the congregation at minimal cost. Three events had been planned. Cantor Kula also organized a youth choir that year.

During Chanukah Rabbi Goodman was interviewed on the holiday on the "Boone & Erickson Show" on WCCO radio.

In January Rabbi Goodman wrote a column on *kavod horim*—honor of parents—and the next month Sisterhood president Rhoda Jaffe announced that the group was forming a Mitzvah Committee headed by Marlene Rutman to contact hospitals, write letters, make phone calls, provide transportation and visitor elderly congregants.

On Purim the largest corps of Megilla readers in the congregation's history was assembled. They ranged in age from 13 to 88 years, and read at three different services. A family evening service was held, followed by the annual "Shushan Shuk" carnival organized by USY, co-chaired by Sandy Kibort, Barb Pink and Saralee Shrell, with Aaron Kula and his combo supplying the music. Everyone was encouraged to dress up in costumes.

The 6th Shabbat HaShoah Observance focused on the "Art of the Holocaust" with a special display in Schanfeld Hall. Dora Zaidenweber read poetry interspersed with music of the Holocaust.

In May President Jules Levin revealed the Adath's new remodeling plans:

"Based on economics, we shall remain in the present location for a period of at least 10 years and should make the necessary changes to accommodate the needs of the congregation within that time frame."

And Rabbi Goodman wrote: "The Adath board of directors has voted to improve our congregational home: an extension to Schanfeld Hall to serve as a kiddush room; relocating the youth lounge in the school building; a new chapel; corridors of the school building will be turned into galleries and the administrative offices to be expanded; stained glass windows, in the social hall. I am personally pleased that at this point we are staying put. A new facility would involve abandoning the city of Minneapolis and I believe the city of Minneapolis should not be without a Conservative congregation."

The all-night Shavuot study session focused on the Book of Ruth, which was read by Marty Abramson, Mark Appelbaum, Jodi Bell, Sheryl Cohen, John Dworsky, Simma Gershenson, Mark Gittleman, Heidi Goldfine, Debbie Litman, Barb Nemer, Debbie Orbuch, Jay Perlman, David Pink, Howard Stillman, Joanne Trangle, and Rachel Wolk.

1977-1978

In 1977 Carol Glass became program planner and coordinator of both youth activities and SMP. She arrived with a master's degree in Jewish education from the Jewish Theological Seminary's Teachers Institute. Among her many responsibilities were to supervise staff for USY/Kadima,

Kallah Program, and SMP, co-teach the confirmation class with Rabbi Goodman and serve as a resource person for the Gan and religious school; develop study groups, visit hospitals, conduct shiva minyanim and worked with adults and senior citizens

At a pre-Selichot program Dora Zaidenweber shared her perceptions of a recent visit to Poland. Dora had survived the war in Poland along with her husband Jules, and since that time she had emerged as one of the interpreters of the significance of the Holocaust in Minnesota. The previous spring she had traveled to Poland with her daughter, Rosanne, revisiting many of the places she remembered from childhood, to see if anything remained of the vibrant Jewish culture of her youth. In her talk Dora shared her impressions of pre and post-war Polish life.

One focus during Rosh Hashanah was the *halacha* which governs the process of conversion. This had become a subject of special interest due to the efforts of the religious parties in Israel to amend Israel's Law of Return so that automatic citizenship would be granted only to those converts to Judaism who had been converted "according to *halacha*." Halachic conversion was also set within the context of Jewish-Gentile relations and the tensions surrounding interfaith marriages.

Rabbi Goodman was honored nationally midway in his 11th year as one of the three participants in the Jewish Theological Seminary "Sermon Seminar." The other participants were Ben Kreitzman, vice president of the United Synagogue of America, and Rabbi Stanley Rabinowitz, president of the Rabbinical Assembly.

On November 15, the Adath received a Solomon Schechter Special Award in Worship and Ritual for its Chevra Kavod Hamet at the United Synagogue Biennial Convention in New York.

The "Parade of Sukkot" that year included the homes of Debbie and Robert Wolk, Raleigh Kent, Dr. John and Rachel Levitt, Howard and Elaine Rutman, Amos and Reva Rosenbloom, and Cantor Mort and Charlotte Kula.

On December 8 a city-wide Chanukah luncheon for all women's organizations was held to celebrate Israel's 30th Anniversary, with Geri and Burton Joseph, who had recently returned from Israel, as guest speakers.

At the Torah Fund Luncheon on February 12, Gertie Abrams was honored. She had attended the first Torah Fund Luncheon 38 years earlier in 1940.

Later that month the Men's Club sponsored a Candlelight Dinner with brisket catered by Le Papillon. Entertainment was provided by the Renanim Dances and Singers, a

group formed in 1974 to enhance the enjoyment of Israeli and Jewish traditional culture. They performed a suite of dances and music from Chassidic, Yemenite, Arabic and Druze cultures of the ancient Middle East as well as modern Israeli pieces.

At the Sisterhood's Tree of Life Luncheon on April 4, local restaurateur and philanthropist Mama D gave a talk on "Recipes for Lunch, Life and Laughter."

In 1978 Larry Wechsler became the new kallah director. Ellen Daniels, Rachel Wolk, Mike Danovsky, Barry Mark, and Debbie Orbuch were on the staff that year.

In his Purim *Clarion* column, Rabbi Goodman praised the unique Purim celebration that had evolved at the Adath, with its tradition of costumes, the game booths of the Shushan Shuk and the meals provided by the Shushan Deli. "At the service the Adah Vatikim students read the Megilla to the accompaniment of groggers, cheers, etc., whenever certain names are sounded. Following the hour-long service, we returned to the Shuk to continue playing the games, to purchase *nashes* from the Sisterhood Shushan Bake Shoppe, and danced to the live music of Aaron Kula's combo."

NBC's TV mini-series *The Holocaust*, which had recently aired, was the pulpit subject on the first day of Pesach. The next day Larry Brown, Lisa Briskin, Peggy Orenstein, Laurie Mark, Saralee Shrell, Carol Glass, Louise Miller and Judy Ribnick chanted "Shir Hashirim," The Song of Songs.

On Israel's 30th Anniversary, at a special congregational Shabbat evening service, Daniel O. Newberry, director of the Egyptian Affairs Desk at the State Department, spoke on US policy in the Middle East.

On May 5 the Amsels were in town, and Cantor Kula invited Cantor Amsel to join him on the bema. At the May 7 TAMID concert Cantors Amsel and Kula sang solos and duets.

In his column at the end of May, Rabbi Goodman drew attention to a milestone in the Adaths's history:

"This weekend we celebrate pleasant and significant events in our congregation's history. It is our 94th anniversary, but it is also the year when we made the decision to reinvest our energies and our funds within the city of Minneapolis.

"In 1966 following a demographic survey of the congregation, a decision was made to modernize the sanctuary and pulpit at the cost of $100,000. The consensus was that within 10 years the congregation would relocate and the modernization cost would be but $10,000 a year.

"Though there had been talk of relocation to the Minnetonka site, the time was not right. Partially in response to the energy crisis, partially in response to the number of people who were making their own decision to live in the city, partially in response to the inordinate cost of building a new facility, we made the decision to remain, in the foreseeable future, on Dupont Avenue.

"We have invested $450,000 to renovate Schanfeld Hall, to add to a new kiddush room, to build a new chapel, to create a new youth lounge, to redesign our foyers, and to restructure our offices. All in all, we have made our synagogue more habitable and more beautiful.

"The response to our new look has been that of delight. We are happy with the facilities we now have. There is an air of excitement within the Adath Jeshurun today. There is excitement about the congregation's goals and achievements…There is the excitement of being part of a congregation that exercises leadership responsibly and forthrightly."

Esther Katz, Cantor Morton Kula, and Dolly Brandwein with the Solomon Schechter Award the Adath received in 1979 for their Shabbat Morning Program.

1978-1979

The 11 past presidents of the Sisterhood were welcomed at a September 5 meeting—a span of 42 years from 1935 to 1977. Anna Daskovsky, Ruth Libman, Dena Pink, Ruth Stillman, Sybil Katz, Lillian Gross, Ruth Dechter, Pam Brin, Jeanne Share, Polly Braunstein, and Rhoda Jaffe made an appearance. Lillian Kaplan, Rose Zimmerman and Maxine Lazar-Moss were unable to attend. The women told of their respective terms and recollections of the rabbi that they served under.

An unusual pre-Selichot program that year featured Lynn Gottlieb performing a biblical interpretation of Miriam in mime and dance. Ms. Gottlieb was a founder of the Bat Kol Players, a group of young women who devoted themselves to presenting stories of Jewish women in life and history through voice, dance and song. Gottlieb was also preparing herself for the rabbinate at the time, taking rabbinic courses at the Jewish Theological Seminary. She later served as rabbi at Temple Beth Or, the Congregation for the Deaf, in Manhattan. She was one of the few people who could teach classes for children and adults in both English and Hebrew sign language.

In December the Adath hosted the annual city-wide luncheon for Minneapolis Jewish women's organizations, with Professor Allen Pollack speaking on the plight of the Jews in the Soviet Union. Also in December, the ABC documentary *A Plain Pine Box*, exploring the work of the Adath Jeshurun Chevra Kovod Hamet, was shown at the International USY convention in Philadelphia. Phil Rosenbloom, David Orbuch, and Shira Goodman attended from the Adath.

The Phineas Phoke Combo (Bruce Orkin, Neil Alexander, Steve Waller and Brian Casement) furnished the music for the Purim dance. Rabbi Goodman noted in his column that the Purim story takes place in what is now Iran, expressing concern that "the Jews in today's Shushan are found in Tehran, Shiraz and in many other communities of Iran. Eighty-thousand Jews in Iran are now under the rule of the Ayatollah Khomeini."

On the brighter side, Israel and Egypt were at that moment on the verge of signing a peace agreement. And at Pesach that year a special Shabbat service was held celebrating the treaty. Rabbi Goodman and Rae were invited to the White House for the treaty signing with President Sadat, President Begin, President Carter and Vice-President Mondale.

Upon his return Rabbi Goodman reported:

"Receiving an invitation to be at the Peace Treaty signing and for the dinner which followed was like

THE ADATH JESHURUN CULTURAL
ARTS COMMITTEE PRESENTS

AN EVENING
WITH
ISAAC
BASHEVIS
SINGER
NOBEL PRIZE WINNER FOR LITERATURE

DR. DAVID FELDSHUH
DOING READINGS & RECOLLECTIONS

MUSIC BY
SANFORD MARGOLIS

DIALOGUE BY
RUTH BRIN

SUNDAY, NOV. 4th, 1979, 8 PM
GUTHRIE THEATER
MINNEAPOLIS, MINNESOTA

On November 4, 1979, under the auspices of its TAMID program, the Adath was honored to host Nobel Laureate Isaac Bashevis Singer as part of a program of music, readings, and dialogue.

winning a sweepstake. It was wondrously exciting to be in Washington that Monday. Rae and I regarded ourselves as representatives of the Adath Jeshurun at this momentous event....Hard to find the words to express the emotion at being there when Messrs. Carter, Begin and Sadat came out of the White House to take their places on the platform. The mood was that of a political rally; the excitement that precedes a championship game. The Marine Band playing the Egyptian anthem... once I heard 'Hatikva,' the enormity of the event was borne home. Like many other Jews there, my eyes began to tear and there was a lump in my throat."

At the annual dinner meeting Esther Katz became the Adath's first woman congregation president. Jules Levin and Joyce Orbuch co-chaired the dinner, and Jules Levin received the Shem Tov award. Two other Adath women were also elected to leadership positions at about that time: Judge Roberta Levy as the first woman Talmud Torah president (1976-78) and Theresa Berman (in 1979) as the first woman president of the Minneapolis Jewish Federation.

During Yom HaShoah observances Rabbi Goodman noted that President Carter had created a Presidential Commission on the Holocaust with Eli Wiesel as chairman; its main task would be to develop a program for a National Holocaust Memorial. Rabbi Bernard Raskas was appoint-

ed the local representative.

"We welcome the establishment of the National Commission on Holocaust observance," Rabbi Goodman wrote, "and the selection of the Twin Cities as the first site along with Washington, D.C. for a community-wide commemorative event which was held on April 23, 1979 at Temple Israel. At the Adath Jeshuran we established a tradition in 1970 of a Shabbat eve service devoted to the memory of the heroes and martyrs of the Destruction of European Jewry. We were the first congregation in this area to introduce this pioneering tradition." The Shabbat evening service on April 27 honored the women of the Holocaust.

On June 1, at the late Shabbat and Shavuot service, four couples—Esther and Morris Katz, Evelyn and Dr. Sidney Nerenberg, Etta Fay and Dr. Milton Orkin, and Betty and Sheldon Schnitzer—commemorated their Silver Wedding Anniversaries. The couples hosted an Oneg Shabbat after the service.

1979-1980

A highlight of the annual Selichot evening of study and service was the special Havdalah Cantata presented by Cantor Kula and the choir, celebrating the uniqueness of the community of Israel.

At the April 15 Tree of Life Luncheon, a new "Tree of Life" sculpture was unveiled and the year's donors were honored. Dr. Marilyn Chiat, a specialist in Jewish art and architecture, spoke on "The Significance of the Etz Chaim in Jewish Art and Religion."

The new "Tree of Life" had many facets and symbols, according to Marshall Ferster and Claude Reidel, the artists who had collaborated on it. The Star of David adorned the top of the glass case, and symbolic leaves surrounded the Tree, both in glass and interwoven bronze metals. The concept of the Tree of Life itself is represented by the tree and the multiplied reflections in the glass case. The names at the base of the tree are removable—new ones could be added yearly. Those names represented the symbolic roots of wisdom, made available for Adath young people by contributions from Sisterhood members.

The theme of the tenth annual Yom HaShoah was "The Holocaust from the Christian Perspective" with Professor Robert Willis of Hamline University as guest speaker.

TAMID sponsored a Lag B'Omer concert of Yiddish art songs, with Cantor Kula and Holly Callen performing along with conductor Marlys Fiterman and members of the Minnesota Orchestra.

On December 7, 1980, the Adath held a benefit at the Guthrie Theater with Tovah Feldshuh, the Broadway star of *Yentl*, in a one-woman performance.

1980-1981

In a September program on Jewish divorce and child custody issues, attendees watched the film *Kramer vs. Kramer* and then listened to a panel discussion by Rabbi Goodman; David Gordon, director of therapy services at the Minneapolis Jewish Family and Children's Services; and Judge Roberta Levy, a Hennepin County Municipal Court Judge.

The pre-Selichot service was a "Town Hall" open forum moderated by Dr. Arnold Kanarick on the subject of how members of Adath Jeshurun viewed the role of the synagogue in their lives and how they imagined that role would change in 20 years' time. A new feature of the High Holidays was the prayer supplement booklet prepared by Phil Snyder.

The Yom HaShoah Shabbat theme was "Righteous Gentile." A special presentation was prepared by Dora Zaidenweber: a walk through the "Avenues of the Righteous Gentile," the "street" on the grounds of Yad Vashem, lined with trees, each planted for a man or a woman designated as a "Righteous Gentile." Each tree represented heroic acts. Some of the stories were told.

Israel's 33 anniversary Shabbat was celebrated with Senator Rudy Boschwitz as guest speaker.

At the annual meeting on May 27, outgoing president Esther Katz announced that Rabbi Goodman's book, *A Plain Pine Box: A Return to Simple Jewish Funerals and Eternal Traditions* had just been published. The book told the story of the synagogue's own Chevra Kovod Hamet, "its conception, its birth, its growing pains, and its maturity."

At the Congregational Dinner the merger of the Chesed Shel Emes-Hertzl Memorial Park Cemetery was approved, and Norman Pink became the new president. It was the first time that the son of a previous Adath president had been elected to that office.

1981-1982

In the minds of many Adath leaders, the prospect of building a new synagogue on the property in Minnetonka had become a serious practical consideration as early as 1980. "The neighborhood was changing," recalled Norm Pink, "and we thought perhaps we should consider moving to where our congregants were moving—Minnetonka and Hopkins. It was a broad step to take, since at that time there were a lot of people who had spent their lives in South Minneapolis."

Among the many questions that remained to be answered, two stood out: how would the congregation react to the idea of moving, and where would it find the money to do so?

"There was plenty of skepticism, but a group of us felt we needed to look ahead," said Norm. "Jeff Schachtman was one of the more vocal among us who said we needed to do this. A lot of wealthy members were in their 70s and 80s. The classroom facilities on Dupont—behind the balcony or in the social hall with folding walls—were not conducive to learning. We owned the property in Minnetonka for the Gan, day camp, and weekend retreats. The new Hopkins High School was built across the road, so we knew the population was growing there. But a lot of people didn't want to move and interest rates were high."

The situation was complicated by the fact that Rabbi

Goodman and his family were *shomer Shabbat*. Because they lived in St. Louis Park, on Friday afternoon Rabbi Goodman and Rae would pack up clothes and move to a duplex on Dupont owned by the synagogue. Rabbi Goodman suggested that the Adath might want to replace the duplex with a house so he and Rae could make it their permanent home.

Many of the congregants who were opposed to the move to the suburbs supported the idea of expanding and remodeling the duplex for use not only by Rabbi Goodman and his family but also by the guests of other members who didn't drive on Shabbat. In the end the congregation voted not to remodel or replace the duplex.

Once the idea of remodeling had been laid to rest, it remained to be determined whether the congregation really wanted to move away from South Minneapolis. The board followed a strict protocol, using a parlor meeting model to answer people's questions. Sketches were circulated. Then, when every effort had been made to inform the congregation, a vote was taken. "It was all very legal," Norm later remarked, "No one could say it was skewed." And the congregation voted to proceed with the move.

It was a turbulent time for the congregation. Various controversies erupted in the course of the year involving the prospective move to a new location, mortuaries, and Rabbi Goodman's new plan for burial services. Economically it was a period of inflation and recession, Ronald Reagan was president and conservatism was on the rise. There was even talk of instituting prayer in the schools. Yet synagogue life went on as always, with a full array of services and community events.

On September 8, author Vicki Lansky and fashion coordinator Harmony Kaplan shared their experiences on the road from housewife and "peanut butter sandwich maker" to *PM Magazine* fame.

Pre-Selichot attendees watched a film, *Image Before Our Eyes*, produced by the Yiddish Scientific Institute (YIVO) on Polish Jewry between World War I and World War II.

Cantor Kula rendered the Yom Kippur Service with the aid of the choir conducted by Marlys Fiterman. The excitement of the Neila service climaxed with Havdalah, chanted by B'nai and B'not Mitzvah for the year 5742. Cantor Kula taught the students and Mitch Balk and Sheila Radman handled the technical arrangements. David and Mel Orenstein and Dr. Mel Sigel sounded the shofar, and for the first time a community break-the-fast was held with juice, coffee, tea, and cake.

"Art is Alive at Adath" was the theme of the art auction on November 1. The pieces were carefully chosen by Sharon Zweigbaum and her committee and the auctioneering was adeptly handled by Bill Aberman and Fred Traub. A week later the congregation was thrilled by the virtuosity of the Klezmer clarinetist Giori Feidman and his trio.

Rabbi Goodman was excited to be in New York later that month at the United Synagogue Biennial Convention, where he would serve as the scholar-in-residence and participate in several sessions.

"The most exciting event for me," he wrote, in anticipation of the trip, "will be in representing the congregation in accepting the Solomon Schechter Award for our Gan Shelanu. Gan Shelanu has a come a long way since we made the decision to move to the Heller Kallah Center. The level of Hebrew and music is extraordinarily high. The natural setting of Windsor Lake creates a lovely rural experience. The child development program ranks with all other pre-schools in the community. We're proud of this achievement, Susie Tatarka, her staff, the chairpeople and all the committee members who have given of their time and effort to make Gan Shelanu the pre-school that it is."

A Centennial Oral History project was getting underway, with Etta Fay Orkin as chairperson. The project's goal was to document the Adath Jeshurun's 100-year history. A committee had been formed and interviews of senior members of the congregation were in progress. The entire congregation was asked to contribute photos, programs, documents, and letters pertaining to the synagogue's history.

During Pesach the annual second seder was held, and the new haggadah published by the Rabbinical Assembly was discussed.

Rabbi Goodman was at that time vice president of the Rabbinical Assembly, an international organization of 1200 Conservative rabbis serving Jewish communities in North America, South America, Europe and Israel, and he had been formally nominated to be its next president. He was duly elected to that post at the annual convention on April 25. On May 22 the formal presentation of a special Torah mantle was made at Shabbat services by Rabbi Silberschein on behalf of the Rabbinical Association and accepted by Norman Pink. It was on loan to the congregation during the term of Rabbi Goodman's presidency as a sign of gratitude from the Assembly.

In May three Adath congregants were ordained from the Jewish Theological Seminary: Irwin Kula, son of Cantor Morton and Charlotte Kula; George Nudell, son of

Irving and Charlotte Nudell; and Neil Sandler, son of Hy and Betty Sandler. In a letter to Rabbi Goodman, Seminary chancellor Dr. Gerson Cohen noted: "It is a rare occasion when three young men from the same congregation have earned the coveted Jewish honor of ordination: It is a tribute to the Adath Jeshurun, to the Minneapolis Jewish community and to you as the rabbi of the congregation."

Rabbi Goodman (far left) Morton Kula, (far right) and three newly ordained rabbis, all raised at Adath: Neil Sandler, George Nudell, and Irwin Kula.

In honor of this occasion, Rabbi Goodman was invited to participate in the ordination ceremonies and was present in New York for the *simcha*. Cantor Kula, a graduate of the Cantorial Institute, joined the academic procession.

On July 13, 1982, Rabbi Goodman tendered his resignation from the Adath Jeshurun, effective September 1. He and Rae had decided to move on to warmer climes in Atlanta, Georgia. On August 12, the Goodmans hosted a *Sheva Brachot* evening in celebration of the marriage of their son, Ariel, to Dr. Tziporit Pryvas of Tel Aviv, in Schanfield Hall. And on September 2, a farewell program and reception was held honoring the Goodmans prior to their departure for Atlanta.

Rabbi Goodman left behind a liberal, egalitarian congregation, though during his 16 years as its spiritual leader, he had fashioned it in a more traditional mode than had his Reconstructionist predecessor.

He also left a legacy of an educated congregation with one of the largest contingents of Torah readers in the country. The many young people and adults he helped to educate and inspire are now proficient adults and parents, professionals and for the most part very knowledgeable and involved Jews. Many are leaders in their communities and synagogues throughout the country and abroad.

In the synagogue's 99th year, Cantor Mort Kula became the "captain" of the ship of Adath Jeshurun. President Norman Pink, the other officers, and the board of trustees, all pitched in to do their jobs. With the cantor's usual buoyancy, he helped to organize and plan the upcoming 100th anniversary celebration along with Chairperson Joyce Orbuch and a fantastic committee.

The Adath had recently hired an associate rabbi, Clifford Miller, and his wife, Debbie, had been put in charge of the Sabbat Morning Program and other educational programs.

In the Sept. 1, 1982 *Clarion*, Norm wrote in his president's Rosh Hashanah message to the congregation:

The past 14 months have been difficult ones for all of us involved in the functions of the synagogue. Many words have been said in the heat of passion, so to speak. These words can be compared to dust in the winds that will blow away in time....

I ask each of you to respect one another's opinions, feelings and decisions. I ask that each of you support the board's decision once you know the facts on which the decision was made. I ask that you come to board meetings, not with the intent of challenging, but with the intent to work and develop. Our board does not represent factions and parties. We are not a political committee. This is not a parliamentary platform. We represent a family—a congregation—that has been praying together for nearly 100 years.

A Rabbinic Search Committee headed by former president Judge Irving Brand worked diligently to find a new rabbi. They did their job well and on the weekend of January 28-29, 1983, Rabbi Barry Cytron was the guest rabbi. At the board of trustees meeting on February 20th, the board unanimously voted to accept the recommendation of the Rabbinic Search Committee and the Executive Committee to engage Rabbi Cytron as the rabbi of the Adath Jeshurun.

Top: USYers in the play "Damn Yankees," 1990, directed by Steve Barberio
Bottom right: (Left to right) Adath members Hedy Levy, Charlotte Nudell, Dina Elkin, Marlys Moscoe
Bottom left: Rabbi Barry Cytron

10
THE RABBI CYTRON YEARS
(1983 – 1996)

The years following the departure of Rabbi Goodman benefitted from the firm, steady guidance of Rabbi Cytron. They were filled with memorable events, including a year-long celebration of the synagogue's 100th anniversary in 1983-84. This period also marked the arrival of Rabbi Kravitz, who was to have an immediate and profound effect on the synagogue's social action programs. The era took on a new dimension in 1992 with the momentous decision to relocate the synagogue to Minnetonka.

THE ARRIVAL OF RABBI CYTRON

When Rabbi Goodman announced that he had accepted a pulpit in Atlanta, the congregation formed a search committee to look for a new rabbi. The committee was most interested in a candidate then serving as spiritual leader of Tifereth Israel in Des Moines, Iowa—Rabbi Barry Cytron.

As Jules Levin later described the course of events in his memoir:

In the spring of 1983, Rose and I, along with Martin and Esther Miller and Greg and Francie Corwin, traveled to Des Moines to meet with Rabbi Cytron and attend the Friday evening and Saturday morning services. Prior to the Friday night service we were the guests of the Cytrons for dinner with their family.

We were very impressed with Rabbi Cytron and many congregants we visited with had very positive things to say about him. One of the charges to the search committee was that our new spiritual leader be a "mensch." We felt that he personified that definition. His congregation did not want to lose him, but they agreed it was the right thing for him to be given the opportunity to advance his career by moving to a

larger community and head a larger congregation.

On Sunday morning of that weekend, I met with Rabbi Cytron at Embers, just as I had so many times with Rabbi Goodman, only this time it was the Des Moines Embers. We negotiated the financial terms of his employment and later that week I submitted our committee's recommendation to the board to hire Rabbi Cytron. The board approved and Rabbi Cytron became our new rabbi.

According to Norm Pink, "We looked for a rabbi who could bring us *shalom bayit*, who would be Minnesota-nice, available to all the congregants. Rabbi Cytron was well-loved by his congregants. But he was the person we needed. He was apolitical. He was friendly, he didn't speak down. He did say that if we wanted a fund-raiser, he was not the right man for the job—but in fact he was an excellent fund-raiser, because people loved him."

Rabbi Cytron, a native mid-westerner, was born and grew up in St. Louis. He graduated from Columbia University with a BS in Philosophy and received his ordination from the Jewish Theological Seminary in 1970. He served for two years with the JTS on rabbinic student recruitment. Since August, 1972 he had been the rabbi of Tifereth Israel. Rabbi Cytron received his PhD in 1981, writing his thesis on "Jewish-Christian Dialogue."

In 1969 Rabbi Cytron had married Phyllis Weinstein of Kansas City. They are the parents of Joseph, Davida, and Naomi.

Rabbi Cytron's synagogue in Des Moines definitely didn't want to lose him. According to Norm, the congregation would have given him almost anything he asked for to induce him to stay. But Rabbi Cytron had his own reasons for wanting to move—religious opportunities for his children.

"I had been in Des Moines for 11 wonderful years," recalled Rabbi Cytron. "It was a critical juncture for our children, then aged 6 through 12, to be in a larger Jewish community. I had considered a couple of different possibilities, but had pulled away from them in the end. Searches are done quite differently today; back then, it was a much more controlled, paternalistic system. We knew Adath by reputation and a bit through our kids, who had been at camp with children from the Twin Cities."

So Rabbi Cytron, his wife, Phyllis, a Jewish educator, and their children arrived in Minneapolis in the summer of 1983. He knew he was moving to a large city with a vibrant, engaged, and philanthropic Jewish community. What he didn't know, although the congregation had made an effort to explain the situation, was the state of the congregation to which he was moving. "The divisiveness was shocking to me when I arrived," Rabbi Cytron recalled. He notes that these days, people have "gotten smarter" about how to handle such transitions. Reform and Conservative congregations have now adopted a Protestant model in which an interim rabbi is hired—one who cannot be part of the search.

"It puts distance between now and the past, and allows everyone to calm down," Rabbi Cytron explained. "But it wasn't part of what people did then.

"I didn't realize the depth of anguish in the congregation. So I did a series of parlor meetings. I met with every congregant by dividing the congregation into groups of 30. I had maybe 40 different meetings. It was a nifty idea, but so hard—to be a pastor and just listen to people."

But listen he did. And gradually, he and the congregation worked through the process. Since the assistant rabbi, Rabbi Miller, had departed almost immediately after Rabbi Goodman left, Rabbi Cytron did the work alone, without other rabbinic support, for approximately four years.

As the congregation healed, it began to regain its former vibrancy. And—not surprisingly—to change.

"I was on some level returning the congregation back to its more progressive roots," Rabbi Cytron later said. "Rabbi Goodman had a history of being a little more conservative, both religiously and politically. Under Rabbis Rabinowitz and Lipnick, it had been more Reconstructionist. I was returning it, religiously and politically, more to the left of center."

When asked that first year if he would sermonize on politics or topical issues, Rabbi Cytron replied: "The last thing I need to do is make waves or create controversy. This congregation needs time to heal. There are still many people hurting."

Yet during his first months at the Adath, Rabbi Cytron made it clear that he was willing to speak out on politically sensitive issues. "South Minneapolis included a lot of academics. People were attracted to our intellectual orientation, and we held lots of serious conversations from the pulpit. Adath had a town/gown amalgam, a certain *panache*. The congregation wanted to be engaged and stimulated, and Adath was an interesting place intellectually and Jewishly. And Shabbat was hopping."

In the area of liturgy, Rabbi Cytron introduced new prayer book materials, including a new machzor by Jules Harlow that had been in print for a number of years. He introduced the *Sim Shalom* Shabbat prayer book as well, and Cantor Kula donated the old prayer books to congregations in Israel.

Rabbi Cytron was a runner, and he introduced the "Rosh Hashanah Run" in 1884. The 1987 *Clarion* just prior to the High Holy Days included a full page sheet for congregants to use to join the 4th annual run, signing the covenant: "I promise to get in shape, and keep up the exercise after the run, thereby remembering the Rosh Hashanah message: Choose Life!"

Sally Appelbaum

The Appelbaum family joined Adath to provide a preschool opportunity for their children. Sally Appelbaum went on to become board president from 1983 to 1985, serving during a decade that saw the departure of Rabbi Goodman, the arrival of Rabbis Cytron and Kravitz, and the celebration of Adath's 100th anniversary. Though the synagogue has maintained a focus on families and children, Sally worked to heighten

(above) The artist Mordecai Rosenstein with Joyce Orbuch in front of the water-color serigraph he created in honor of the synagogue's centennial. The original was donated by Dr. David and Dena Pink in honor of their 50th anniversary.

(left) Sharon Zweigbaum at the opening of the exhibit, "Judaic Needlework: The Continuing Legacy," at the Minneapolis Jewish Community Center. Sharon chaired the event, which ran from October 13 through December 22, 1983.

(below) One of the exquisite weavings from the needlework show.

awareness of and attention to other dues-paying members of the congregation—the ill, the elderly, singles, divorced, widowed, and gay and lesbian members.

In 1985, Sally and her husband, Ken, founded the Ken and Sally Appelbaum Family Life Education Fund (later renamed the Ken and Sally Appelbaum Keruv Fund). Twenty-five years later it continues to support the needs of Adath's diverse community with a specific focus on outreach to under-served populations.

Ken's motto was "People make miracles happen" and was among the first to meet with Rabbi Cytron to discuss moving the facility to Minnetonka.

Rabbi Kravitz remembered the issue of gay and lesbian inclusion as an evolving one; it was even discussed during his initial interview at Adath. He felt it was important that both he and Rabbi Cytron be involved in defining the congregation's place in the conversation. "What did people want from us?" he said. "Did they want commitment ceremonies? Conversion of partners?"

At a forum on the high holidays Rabbi Cytron chose to focus on the question. After that, some people thought the subject had been appropriately dealt with, but in fact it was far from resolved. Today, the Conservative movement has revised its position, and the congregation's newly invigorated Keruv committee is reaching out to gay and lesbian congregants in an effort to be as inclusive as possible.

❧ *The Centennial Celebration* ❧

The year 1983-1984 marked the 100th anniversary of Adath Jeshurun, and events took place throughout the year to mark the occasion. Joyce Dechter Orbuch was asked to chair a committee to plan and carry out the programs, and with the help of many talented volunteers, fundraisers, and marketing specialists, she devised a calendar of activities and events for each month of the centennial year. Melvin Orenstein, Bill Aberman and Sam Kaplan made visits and calls to congregants who were interested in supporting the effort financially, while Joyce and Cantor Morton Kula visited community leaders, financial institutions and foundations in search of additional funding.

Among the highlights of the year-long celebration:

• In September the Pink family, in honor of Dr. David and Dena Pink on their 50th Anniversary, presented a gold and watercolor serigraph of Hebrew calligraphic abstractions by Mordecai Rosenstein to the congregation depicting Adath's 100 years of life. The work was presented during the Bat Mitzvah ceremony of Janet Pink, daughter of Norman and Dorothy Pink. A limited edition of 175 prints were also sold.

Dr. David and Dena Pink

• Rabbi Barry Cytron gave a kick-off sermon on Rosh Hashanah, September 8, 1983, with the just the right amount of history and nostalgia.

• The first community-wide artistic event of the centennial year was titled "Judaic Needlework: The Continuing Legacy." The exhibition ran October 13 through December 22, 1983 at the Minneapolis Jewish Community Center. It was the first international exhibition of Judaic needlework ever shown in the Midwest. Guest curator Ita Aber, of Yonkers, New York, selected 85 works by artists from around the world, with about 20 percent coming from local and regional artists. Sharon Zweigbaum, an art historian and exhibition coordinator, chaired the event.

• In conjunction with the needlework exhibit, a number of Torah mantles were dedicated at the Chanukah Shabbat service on December 2, 1983. Using designs based on the themes of Psalm 100, needlework artist Alice Nussbaum created fabric covers to adorn the Torahs. Sixty Adath men and women helped needlepoint the covers, passing them from hand to hand and allowing people to complete small or large sections. Elaine Rutman and Priscilla Dworsky chaired this project.

• On November 4 and 5, 1983, as part of a scholar-in-residence weekend, Neil Gillman of the Jewish Theological Seminary spoke on the theme "The Shapers of Conservative Judaism." Gerald and Susan Weisberg were in charge of this weekend. That same weekend Lorraine Shrell chaired a Scholarship Sports Night for all ages at the Northwest Health and Fitness Club.

• In March 1984, Cantor Kula led a group of Adath members on a trip to Israel. The group focused their attention on Jewish arts, but also found time to dedicate a grove of 100 trees purchased by congregants to commemorate the Adath centennial. That same spring congregants in Minneapolis gave a gift of trees to the city with the assistance of chair Judith Tennebaum. Because of this gift, the City of Minneapolis proclaimed April 18, 1984 "Adath Day."

• That spring Bill Shragg, local Jewish photographer and media expert, produced a multi-media presentation traversing Adath Jeshurun's long history, with Bill Aberman and Harmony Kaplan providing the narration, music by the Adath Choir, and historical pictures from Sam Bender. Ricki Herling and Syd Rich were in charge of the production.

• On May 20, 1984 Adath presented the world premiere of *Hallel, Psalms of Celebration* by Yehezkiel Braun, who was also the Shabbat pulpit guest on May 18. Sandy Marrinson, Cantor Kula, Carol Bromer and Dorothy Pink chaired the event. The piece was commissioned by the Gary and Marsha Tankenoff family and dedicated in loving memory of Dr. David Gaviser. Under the direction of Marlys Fiterman, Cantor Kula performed as soloist with The Braun Centennial Chorus and members of the Minnesota Orchestra.

• A selection of Adath music, titled "From Strength to Strength" and directed by choir director Marlys Fiterman, was recorded and sold to congregants and community members. Chaired by Al Sasson, the recording included Jewish liturgical selections featuring Cantor Kula, the Adath Choir and a selection by Adath Cantor Emeritus Morris Amsel. The Minneapolis Jewish Federation gave Adath a grant to develop a library of Jewish music for young choirs all over the country, insuring the availability and continuance of Jewish music. The grant also made possible the creation of a youth choir comprised of children ages 11 and 12, to perform every month on Rosh Chodesh at Shabbat morning services.

• Jerry Fischbein was in charge of an activity during the year honoring past presidents. Hy Sandler organized a special Shabbat during which Cantor Amsel visited as Cantor Emeritus, and Alex Meirovitz was honored for his 25 years of service as executive director of the congregation. There were youth Shabbat weekends, chaired by Sheila Davis and Joan Weinstein, honoring Adath graduates, USY and Bar/Bat Mitzvah students. Marlys Fiterman was also honored at a Shabbat service for her 20 years as choir director.

• Robert Wolk and Dr. Jonathan Paradise moderated a Friday evening Shabbat program during which Adath honored its graduates who had become national rabbinic leaders: Rabbis Neil Sandler, Theodore Gordon, Miles Cohen, Ronald Shapiro, George Nudell, Stanley Gerstein, Bruce Younger, Steve Bob, Mendel Abrams, Howard Mark and Irwin Kula. The weekend, which included the Bar Mitzvah of Jed Kaufman, was organized by Reva Rosenbloom, together with Joan Weinstein and Sheila Davis.

Cantor Kula, choir director Marlys Fiterman, and Cantor Amsel, enjoy the anniversary festivities.

• Phyllis Sudit was in charge of a multi-generational Shabbat dinner and service honoring families who had been in the congregation for three generations or more. A "Carob Committee" was created to work with seniors and purchase large-print prayer books and a new sound system for the hearing-impaired. Additional committee chairs included Charlotte Kula, Roz Marks, Raleigh Brand, Fredda Norm, Jay Hoffman, and Jeff Schachtman.

The culminating weekend on June 3, 1984 was the "Birthday Party of the Century," chaired by Annetta Krelitz and held at L'Hotel Sofitel. The party included a brunch and annual synagogue meeting, with a beautiful advertising book of contributors, pictures, and Adath memorabilia, as well as an oral history presentation by Etta Fay Orkin. Annetta Krelitz welcomed the guests, Charlotte Kula provided the invocation, Martin Miller led motzi, and Rabbi Morris Gordon offered a benediction.

At this final event, committee chair Joyce Orbuch found it difficult to adequately thank everyone or even list the names of the hundreds of people who had contributed their time, effort and creativity to help make the event a success. But she later wrote: "Those months taught us that a dream which began a century ago was more alive than ever, and that the torch was being passed on to the next generation and to generations yet to come. We had spent an entire year honoring our congregation's past, knowing that the real purpose was not so much to remember the past as to vigorously step forward into the future."

1985–1987

Judy Goldstein became president of the Adath in 1985. One of the goals she set for herself was to introduce a new level of transparency into the operations of the board of trustees. "It was personally important to me," Judy recalled. "There was a perception that things were too closed

Judy Goldstein

off to the rest of the congregation." She had the executive committee minutes read at board meetings, and made sure to inform the Adath membership of the board's work via articles in the *Clarion*.

Judy also established a long-range planning committee chaired by Mel Goldberg that made recommendations in all areas of synagogue life. The board developed policy, office procedure and personnel manuals.

During Judy's tenure, Adath counted 1155 family units among its members. A demographic survey submitted to the congregation received close to 900 responses, which revealed that more than half of the Adath's members lived in the western suburbs. Specifically, 420 family units lived in zip codes 55416 and 55426, while 114 units lived in 55345. Movement toward the northern suburbs had not yet begun.

In 1985 the congregation received several accolades. As Judy explained in the *Clarion*: "Our congregation was honored at the recent United Synagogue convention as one of about a dozen congregations who are over 100 years old. We will be receiving a beautifully hand-calligraphied certificate to commemorate the occasion. We also received two Solomon Schechter Awards." One was an award for year-round programming around the Centennial celebration and the other was an honorable mention for music.

Other events that occurred during Judy's term of office included a presentation from the bema by a college professor who spoke about farm issues from the Jewish perspective—his name was Paul Wellstone; Cantor Kula was given tenure; the congregation inscribed a prayer book in memory of each congregant who died; in October, 1986 the downtown study group was formed; and the first adult Bat Torah class, with seven women, was formed.

Judy was particularly interested in supporting Israel, including support for the Masorti (Conservative) movement there. During her term, the board voted to establish a

policy that the congregation make an annual contribution of $500 per year to the Masorti movement.

In 1986, a much-beloved young man named Howie Stillman passed away. His friends, both Adath members and others, decided to establish the Howie Stillman Young Leadership Fund to honor his memory. A 1986 *Clarion* article read in part:

"The Fund will be a permanent memorial to a friend who touched the lives of many people with his warmth and optimism. Interest earned from the fund will be used to promote two important aspects of Howie's life, young leadership and journalism."

The first Howie Stillman Memorial lecturer was Judith Viorst, author of the highly acclaimed best seller, *Necessary Losses*. The second was Michael Medved; the third was Bob Greene, author and columnist for the *Chicago Tribune*. The fund continues to bring nationally renowned speakers to the Adath each year.

Also that year, the Adath welcomed two new staff members who continue in their roles to this day: Nina Samuels and Gisell Wien.

Also in 1986, Susie Tatarka (now Chalom) was made Director of Education, overseeing the Gan, Day Care, Sunday Religious School, Mishpacha and the Saturday Morning Program (SMP). Susie had joined the Gan in 1978 as director, where under her leadership it tripled in size and received a Solomon Schechter Award. She went on to serve

Susie Chalom sings with the kids at the Gan Mother's Day program, 1994

Adath for 27 years as a devoted teacher to students of all ages, from babies to grandparents.

Susie was born in the Philippines where her family was part of the Sephardic Jewish Community. In 1960, the family made aliyah. Susie graduated from Tel Aviv University with degrees in literature and linguistics with a specialty in English as a Second Language. She came to the U.S. in 1970 and continued her studies at the University of Minnesota, first in speech pathology and then transferring to education. She soon began teaching and taught at Talmud Torah for 11 years, initiating the Mechina program for the youngest students.

Marcia Golob, Gisell Wien, and Lil Goltzman

At the Gan, Susie developed new curricula that included the use of learning centers, training teachers in Judaic subjects, and introducing Shabbat and Havdalah rituals for the children. Her curricula were presented at CAJE conferences and imitated by other preschools. Many of her ideas were incorporated into the design for the education wing of the new Adath building. Susie has been influential in the larger Jewish community as well, serving as president of the Jewish Educators of Minnesota.

One program especially dear to her heart was the Tuesday Torah Study Group that she and Rabbi Kravitz started during "the move" as a way to study and keep in touch. Over the years, it's become a pot luck lunchtime Torah study with rotating leaders, including Rabbi Brusso and even some of the congregants serving as teachers.

"Adath is a unique congregation that has always had outstanding leadership, gifted clergy, and creative and Jewishly-educated congregants," said Susie. "They all give of their time and talent to make our educational programs the best that they can be. Many of the outstanding teachers in SMP started out as Bar/Bat Mitzvah students and continued on into adulthood to become teachers of the next generation—and now are the synagogue leadership."

Congregant Julie Kozberg, like many others, recalled seeking out Susie for answers to her many questions when her children were at the Gan. Julie noted the insight and wealth of information she received from Susie over the years.

Susie retired from Adath in 2006 to become executive director of the Minneapolis Talmud Torah.

Nina Samuels joined the staff in 1986 as Coordinator of Adult Programs. A native of Duluth, she has a master's degree in Adult and Continuing Education from the University of Michigan in Ann Arbor.

One of Nina's initial tasks was to assist Rabbi Cytron with administering study groups. There were already a number of Torah groups in place, including "Beersheva," led by Cantor Kula. Among Nina's current tasks are coordinating the Adath Bar and Bat Torah and Hebrew language programs and collaborating on programs with others in the community, such as the University of Minnesota's Center for Jewish Studies and the Jay Phillips Center for Jewish-Christian Learning. Through the latter, she works with Rabbi Amy Eilberg on interfaith dialogue between Jewish, Christian and Muslim believers in an "Interfaith Conversation Project."

Nina has served as chair of the Minneapolis Conservative Consortium (now the Twin Cities Conservative Consortium), which fosters adult Jewish learning among local Conservative congregations.

She is responsible for overseeing Synaplex, the annual Sampler of Jewish Culture, an international cooking series, and the Summer Sampler. She also coordinates annual events sponsored by funds in the synagogue's foundation, such as weekend scholar-in-residence programs. Last, but by no means least, she is editor of Adath's newsletter, the *Clarion*.

Gisell Wien was hired in 1986 as Rabbi Cytron's personal secretary (she is now the "rabbis' assistant"). As she puts it, she as been the assistant to the rabbis "longer than the rabbis have been at the synagogue." "I live and breathe this place," Gisell said. After Gisell leaves the office, each day she checks her phone and email messages, even taking synagogue-related calls from home. "If someone wants something done," she said, "they call Gisell."

At the 102nd Annual Congregational Dinner and Meeting in June, 1986, Al Meirovitz was honored for 25 years of service to the congregation. Originally from the business world, Al served with three rabbis, two cantors and 13 presidents. During his affiliation with Adath, he saw the congregation double in size as it expanded its programs to meet the needs of its membership.

During his tenure, the congregation undertook two major remodeling projects and the Heller Kallah Center in Minnetonka was constructed. Al was actively involved with the National Association of Synagogue Administrators. His professional service to the Adath went far beyond the standard confines of an executive director. "Call Al" was a phrase often used when all else failed. Through his administrative duties and his personal love and warmth, Al nurtured a generation at Adath.

In May of 1987 the Adath hosted a benefit for the Cantors Assembly of America's 40th Anniversary titled "Night of the Golden Voices." Participant cantors came from Kansas, Iowa, and around the Twin Cities. Even Cantor Kula's son, Cantor Mark Kula, traveled all the way from his congregation in New York City to be part of the celebrated event.

RABBI KRAVITZ COMES TO ADATH

In September, 1987, Adath welcomed its first assistant rabbi in a number of years, Rabbi Harold J. Kravitz, who came with his wife, Cindy Reich, and their infant son Gabe. (Their daugthers, Talia and Elana, were born in

Rabbi Kravitz and his wife, Cindy Reich, at the dedication of the new building.

Minneapolis.) A native of Philadelphia, Rabbi Kravitz completed his BA in History at Temple University in 1981. He did graduate studies at the University of Judaism in Los Angeles (now the American Jewish University), Hebrew University, and was ordained and received an MA in Jewish Studies at the Jewish Theological Seminary of America.

While Rabbi Kravitz was offered other positions, he found himself pleasantly surprised by Minneapolis during his visit here for an interview. "Irv Nudell and Hy Sandler hosted me and took me around the city," he recalled. "I only spent one day here, but I came away so impressed. I said to Cindy, 'This is a special place with *menchlich* people.' Initially, we had a hard time explaining to our families how we could have chosen to be in Minneapolis. When our families eventually visited they appreciated the choice we had made."

When Rabbi Kravitz arrived, Rabbi Cytron had been

leading the congregation for four years. Remarking on the peace Rabbi Cytron had brought to the once-fractured synagogue, Rabbi Kravitz said, "You could already see the healing taking place. People were looking for a new way to connect to their rabbi, exploring the nature of the rabbi's role."

"I came to a wonderful congregation," he continued. "There was an extraordinary level of knowledge and depth. The people were very accomplished, very talented, and at the same time, both kind and patient. I recall Bruce Nemer saying to me, 'You don't have to tell us all you learned in rabbinical school in the first sermon.'

"Rabbi Cytron was very thoughtful, intellectual, a good role model," said Rabbi Kravitz. "We started a wonderful partnership. The other extraordinary thing was that he was willing to be a true partner, not just give me the jobs he didn't want. He asked me to teach the Introduction to Judaism class and the Bar and Bat Torah program.

"He was also willing to take risks and try new things. His model was: engage people in Jewish learning and that becomes the core of your leadership. So I asked myself, 'What will I contribute? I decided to push for a social action program.'"

Thus, in addition to his early initiatives to revive the 20s-30s social group and the Kallah retreat program, Rabbi Kravitz revived the Adath Social Action Committee under a new name—Hesed. The Hesed Committee provided opportunities for acts of justice and lovingkindness within the synagogue and also in the surrounding community. The committee served as a forum for discussing projects conceived by its members and lending its approval and support to those it considered worthy.

The first project proposed and approved by the board made the Adath a partner with MAZON: A Jewish Response to Hunger, an organization that mobilized the Jewish community's response to hunger among Jews and non-Jews in the U.S. and abroad. Adath encouraged members to support the cause by urging them to donate 3 percent of the cost of *simchas*, such as weddings and B'nai Mitzvah, to MAZON.

Some of Rabbi Kravitz's local and national contributions to social action have included long-time service on the board of directors and executive committee of MAZON: A Jewish Response to Hunger. He also served as president of MICAH - the Metropolitan Interfaith Council on Affordable Housing (1993-96), served on the boards of the Jewish Family and Children's Service of Minneapolis, and on the Joint Religious Legislative Coalition (1991-94). In 1991 he was honored for outstanding child advocacy by Congregations Concerned for Children. He also was an advisor to the McKnight Foundation in setting up the Volunteer Initiative that launched Avodah B'Yachad, a service project of the JCRC.

At the end of her board presidency in May 1987, Judy Goldstein noted in the *Clarion* that although the congregation was still financially solvent, costs continued to rise. "We must begin now to plan for the time when dues and our current level of contributions will no longer be enough," she said. "We have begun an Endowment Foundation to help fund future programming."

In September of 1985, the congregation had formed a Long Range Planning Committee, chaired by Mel Goldberg. The committee spent a year gathering information and proposing changes in all areas of congregational life.

One recommendation of the committee adopted by the board related to the synagogue's physical property. The board proposed that the Adath sanctuary remain on Dupont Avenue and the kallah center be renovated with classrooms, offices, and space for support staff. It recommended that the duplex be sold and proceeds used for the improvements at the kallah center. However, once the

The November 24, 1987 *Clarion* contained an announcement that on December 20, Tom Friedman would be speaking. Friedman had grown up at Adath. In 1987, he headed the *New York Times* Israel Bureau. He won a Pulitzer Prize as *New York Times* correspondent in Beirut for coverage of the Lebanon War in 1992. His topic for the Adath speech: Israel Today—and Prospects for Peace.

property committee started to investigate the Minnetonka improvements, they found costs to rehab the structure disproportionate to the value of the building.

With the passage of time, congregants continued to move west and north, and the building on Dupont Avenue and the kallah center continued to deteriorate. "In the nursery school, a light fixture broke off the ceiling and fell to the floor," recalled Rabbi Kravitz. "No one was injured, but a staff member wrote a letter to the board complaining about the conditions in the center."

The congregation slowly inched its way toward a decision. Paul Pink succeeded Judy Goldstein as Adath board president (1987-1989). Prior to that time, Paul had been vice president of the property committee for a number of years, and, as an architect, completed some early renderings to use in approaching congregants about funding for the new building. Paul was an early supporter and proponent of the move, at one point compiling a list of reasons why he believed the congregation should move to Minnetonka.

Paul Pink

Paul said: "The Dupont property was technically not in violation of city or state codes because its non-conforming code requirements were "grandfathered in"—that is, it met the existing code requirements when it was built. However, any extensive remodeling would require the entire building being brought up to the current code requirements, a costly undertaking. Its mechanical systems were inefficient by today's standards and nearing the end of their normal life span. The Gan and accommodations for youth and educational activities were desperately short of space. Wrapping the balcony along the sides of the sanctuary would destroy the aesthetics of the sanctuary without significantly increasing the seating capacity. The site was zoned for multi-family residential uses and surrounded by apartment buildings, making parking difficult and parking expansion economically unfeasible." The synagogue was no longer capable of meeting the needs of the congregation. The congregation had simply outgrown the property. The building was "landlocked" and not readily expandable. As unpopular as the idea of leaving the Dupont property was at that time, with its many memories as a home to the congregation, and after researching the possibilities for staying at its present location, Paul Pink strongly advised it was time to move on.

1989-1991

In 1989, Joyce Orbuch assumed the presidency of Adath's board of directors. In summing up her tenure, she later wrote:

"Besides the regular operations of the congregation during my presidency, the most difficult and challenging task was managing the discussion regarding the move. A series of open forums was held to allow as many congregants as possible to voice opinions and suggestions. It became clear that a majority felt that the survival and continued growth of Adath required making the difficult decision to move to our present location. A weekend congregational vote was held… The decision was made. A moderate amount of time was spent to ease the fears and concerns of the congregants who lived within walking distance of the old building. I am proud and pleased that the outcome of this very difficult decision is so positive."

THE MOVE BEGINS

For Jeff Schachtman, the move began one very cold evening as he sat in a meeting with Mike Fiterman and Danny Berdass in the old kallah center. The doors had not been designed for the season, and light—along with plenty of winter air—was leaking in. While Mike re-hung the doors, the men began to talk, and soon Jeff was touring the Dupont building with Sonny Miller and Paul Pink, looking at its condition. Paul suggested they make a "necessity list" and a "wish list." After completing this tour, they did the same at the kallah center.

Jeff then called synagogue president Joyce Orbuch and asked her to create a committee to look into the buildings' conditions and options for what to do. "The city would never allow us to tear down single family homes to increase our parking on Dupont," said Jeff. "We couldn't expand our building to fill the needs that people foresaw."

Together with Donna Roback, Jeff co-chaired the Adath Jeshurun Building and Expansion Committee, charged with making recommendations about the move. Jeff called it the most complicated undertaking he'd been involved in.

Impromptu meetings took place around the Adath community. One at the Schachtmans' house drew so many people that the fire alarm went off.

The committee set up five sub-committees to better handle the complex undertaking. The two facilities were thoroughly investigated to determine what needed fixing and how much it would cost. The community sub-group talked with municipal governments and the Minneapolis Jewish Federation. Another group looked into the possibility of a third site, including the Minneapolis JCC. The needs group surveyed the congregation's households, attempting to determine the attitudes, desires and emotions of the membership.

Nonetheless, the committee recognized that the emotional attachment of congregants to the Dupont synagogue remained a huge countervailing factor.

Donna Roback, co-chair of the committee, recalled hearing a variety of strong—and divergent—views from members of the congregation. But like many congregants, Donna came to the conclusion that the physical problems with the current synagogue were insurmountable. "There was no way to expand," she said. "It would have cost a fortune to bring the building up to code."

In the late summer of 1991, Jules Levin received a call from a very worried Esther Katz. She was concerned that the board was leaning toward staying on Dupont. "She felt that this would be a terrible mistake," Jules later wrote, "and assumed I would feel likewise. Would I help persuade the board the right tack was to opt for a new building?"

Jules offered to help. "Little did I realize then that I was about to set out on a project that for the next four years would entail a major part of my energy and subsequently reward me with as much pride and gratification as I have ever experienced in communal work."

Jules spoke to the board of trustees in September, emphasizing the futility of attempting to raise the necessary funds to upgrade the Dupont site and the long-range benefits of relocating. He moved that a fundraising campaign for building a new synagogue be established. The motion

Mel Goldberg

passed 21 to 11. Still, the congregation continued to debate the issue.

Many people remember President Mel Goldberg as playing a major role in helping the congregation reach a decision. His wife, Paula recalled, "Mel's greatest challenge, and most important accomplishment for Adath, was his involvement in the vote and ultimate move of the building from Dupont Avenue to Minnetonka. Mel was a wonderful mediator and calming influence. He was well suited to the challenge in that he had been a law professor and administrative law judge. He was fair, objective and wise."

Finally, on October 21, 1991, a congregational meeting was called and the various positions were explained once again to those who attended. The expansion committee delivered its report, and it was also announced that on the basis of unofficial inquiries, Dan Heilicher was sure that at least $1 million would be pledged from just a handful of members. A vote was taken. Close to 60 percent of the congregation favored the move to Minnetonka.

Following the decision, some congregants started resigning. "People would have their Bar Mitzvah on Saturday and send in their resignation letter on Monday," said Rabbi Cytron.

Many people whom Rabbi Kravitz was close to were leaving, and he admitted he thought about going himself. "In the end, we lost about 100 households but picked up about 250. And that was based on dreams alone—we didn't have a building," he said.

"Interestingly, we didn't lose as many members as we feared, and many came back," Judy Goldstein said.

Of those who left, some stayed in the city, going to Mayim Rabim in the Linden Hills neighborhood. Many who resigned ended up going to Beth Jacob in Mendota Heights or Beth El in St Louis Park.

Raising the money

"We had a significant lead gift from Sally and Ken Appelbaum. It felt like an important first step, and it was," said Rabbi Cytron. But after having assessed the square footage needs and cost per square foot, the committee concluded that they needed to raise $8 million (though the actual cost ended up being more.)

"People panicked," recalled Rabbi Cytron. "So we decided to hire a professional fundraiser to canvas the congregation. He came back and told us that the money wasn't there, that we couldn't do it." But Jules Levin and Danny Heilicher said 'Yes, we can.'"

"We were told it would be okay and it was," said Rabbi Cytron. "We raised over $8 million, most of it before we even opened the doors. It was phenomenal."

Said Norm Pink, "Anytime you build an $8 million building, you have a professional fundraiser. But Danny Heilicher and Jules Levin said, 'No, we know our congregation better than any professional outsider.' They set up a committee and did their job. For a congregation to raise $8 million dollars without a professional fundraiser was unheard of. But we did it!"

Jules Levin recalled the experience in his memoir:

When the results [of the vote] were known…Mel Goldberg approached me and asked me to become the campaign chair. I suggested that he ask Dan Heilicher, who already had done so much and "deserved" the opportunity. I told Mel that I would serve as co-chair, and by not becoming the titular head I would not have to spend as much time on actual solicitations and could organize and plan a step-by-step campaign, utilizing the experience I had gained as campaign chair of the just-completed Ackerberg Jewish Community Campus.

Our goal was 100 percent participation and to attain that goal we had to "harness the human spirit" and give the members a sense of ownership. The methodology I employed was not complex. Involve everybody but start with big gifts and work down.

Recognition is important, so we had to make it possible for even the smallest giver to be …recognized. We first established dedicatory and memorial opportunities plus an inscription on the "Wall of Honor" for the larger givers. Later, for a somewhat lesser amount, we announced an opportunity for family names to be inscribed on a "Scroll of Honor." After that we announced another opportunity that would be equitable for all. We called it "Chamesh v' Chamesh," Five by Five. Members who pledged five times their annual dues payable over five years would receive an inscription on the Five by Five plaque. The fact that all the names on the "Chamesh v Chamesh" wall are of equal size, regardless of the actual size of the contribution, was a source of widespread pride to the congregation.

At the very end of the campaign, a "Book of Life" was also established listing the names of those who had pledged at least two times their annual dues.

"We needed very effective communications, and we did this by way of educational parlor meetings and a special bulletin detailing the progress of the project," Jules said. "Melissa Cohen Silberman did a terrific job on the bulletin, called the *Clari-Flyer*, that was published at least monthly."

Mel Goldberg helped the fundraisers to understand that some donors would be attracted to bricks and mortar, others to personnel, and yet others to programming. The synagogue needed to have a way to appeal to all of them.

In a small community, one thing leads to the next. After swimming at Northwest Racquet Club, Jeff Schachtman went into the hot tub and saw Burt and Leonard Ribnick (past president of Beth El synagogue). Burt suggested the synagogue should have a model of the new building to answer questions and provide a concrete look at what the funds were for, and he went on to pay for the model. The first night people saw it, Adath received $350,000 in pledges. Jeff recalls fondly "schlepping that model all over town."

Other congregants began to respond, with the Phillips family playing crucial role.

The generosity of the Phillips family has always had a profound impact on Adath. The main sanctuary is named for them in recognition of their gift to the new building. The Rose and Jay Phillips Fund of the Adath Foundation was set up initially to support the synagogue's adult learning programs with another gift. Then, in 1992, Jay Phillips left a large bequest to the Adath Foundation which established the Phillips Family Foundation Fund to support the greatest needs that exist within the congregation. Since 2003 a portion of the interest earned from the Phillips Family Foundation Fund goes to educational programming. The other portion funds the Director of Development position (currently held by Jennifer Herman Spiller) that has since fostered additional giving within the congregation.

On a more personal note, many remember Jay Phillips reading Haftarah or Maftir Yonah each year on Yom Kippur for more than 40 years.

SELLING "DUPONT AVENUE"

Aside-drama to the move story involved the sale of the Dupont Avenue building. Some thought that a heavy investment would be required to make it saleable, or that it would be best simply to tear it down. Instead, the First Universalist Church, housed at 50th St. and Girard Avenue South, offered Adath its asking price of $1.5 million. The catch: they wanted the building right away. And the congregation, of course, had to find somewhere to go.

"It was a miraculous set of circumstances—that's the only word I can use," said Sally Appelbaum. "The Unitarian church needed a building, and they bought 34th and Dupont for a sum much higher than we expected. Then Shir Tikvah bought the former church."

According to Rabbi Cytron, the congregation decided it would sell the building only on the condition of raising $4 million, including the Dupont Avenue sale.

"Three of us went to see Bud Grossman," Rabbi Cytron recalled. "We made a couple of visits and told him how critical his gift was. He gave an extremely large gift, but on one condition. He called me one night and said, 'You've got to make me a promise. Take the building sale money and put it in an endowment to pay for maintenance on the new build-

ing.' It was a really brilliant idea."

The Grossman family made a significant commitment to the building campaign and the N. Bud Grossman Family Chapel bears their name. The final portion of their building pledge payment was placed in the Adath Foundation to establish the N. Bud and Beverly Grossman Foundation Fund to support enhancements to the chapel.

And because of Bud Grossman's vision, when the Dupont building was sold, the congregation placed the proceeds of $1.5 million into a separate fund held by the Adath Foundation. Named the Capital Repair and Replacement Fund, its purpose is to assure that the congregation will always have resources to maintain the building.

These gifts, plus the Appelbaums', marked the establishment of the Adath Foundation as it exists today.

Esther Katz was asked to take charge of accounts receivable. "Past presidents usually fade into the background," she said. "But they called me back. I did all the recording long hand. The first contribution was $36 from a very elderly man....I never had any complaints about billing."

By September, 1992, the congregation had received pledges of more than $4.5 million, above and beyond the proceeds from sale of the building.

THE COMMITTEES FOR THE MOVE

In the middle of her tenure as president, Joyce Orbuch approached Norm Pink and asked if he would consider being president again, because they were about to start the design of the new synagogue. "I said, 'Why me?' since they had never recycled a president before," Norm recalled.

Unsurprisingly, the answer was that Rabbi Cytron believed congregants greatly respected Norm and felt he could bring people together. Norm agreed to serve again, provided he had Lee Sudit as treasurer and Dick Sachs to serve with him on the board as legal consultant.

Norm said, "I had never in my life seen a congregation that came together so fast and efficiently as Adath did to build the building." There were myriad committees which had to decide everything from what was needed for the nursery school and the kitchen to the color of fabrics on the seats.

Sally Appelbaum became one of the steering committee co-chairs. "Mel Orenstein and I chaired probably the most unusual committee that ever served Adath," she said. "Of the people on the steering committee, many were past presidents. We were all used to making business and professional decisions. But we worked together to determine what would be in the best interest of the congregation.

(seated, l to r) Irene Barbush, Mel Goldberg, Esther Katz; (standing, l to r) Norman Pink, Rabbi Barry Cytron, Mel Orenstein, Danny Heilicher, Rabbi Harold Kravitz, Joyce Orbuch, Ralph Kirshbaum, Dick Sachs.

"Before looking for an architect, a series of meetings was held to define in detail what our members deemed important in a new building. At our first meeting with Architect Moe Finegold, we were prepared to present him with information defining a building to 'serve the Congregation from the cradle to the grave' (infant daycare through the Chevra Kavod Hamet).

"Irene Bartram and Scott Bader did an outstanding job as co-chairs of the building committee. The creation of a new building was a shining moment in the history of the synagogue. The fact that we began talking to the architect before we knew what we wanted was also unusual. I didn't realize how rare our success was until later."

In a bittersweet memory, Sally recalled that during the building process, her husband, Ken, died. During his Shloshim, the Kallah Center was demolished and the outline of the current building's footprint was staked out for our members to see.

Other committee chairs included: Jules Levin and Dan Heilicher, fundraising co-chairs; Harriet Newman and Phyllis Heilicher, dedication weekend co-chairs; Delores Sigel and Sheila Lieberman, August 13 co-chairs; Joyce Orbuch, communications; Esther Katz, finances; Richard Sacks, real estate; Norm Pink, transition. These are only a fraction of the congregants who contributed countless hours in what was truly a labor of love.

The Architect

The architect selection committee was composed of 17 members who were either experienced in some facet of the construction industry or architects themselves.

They prepared and mailed "requests for qualifications" to 65 architects nationwide. They received 45 responses, interviewed five candidates and selected three finalists. The finalists were invited to Minneapolis for further interviews and committee members visited a number of their completed projects.

The selection committee and the steering committee met and recommended Finegold Alexander and Associates of Boston, whose principal, Maurice N. Finegold, FAIA, was a Harvard-trained architect. Among the firm's previous projects were several synagogues and the Ellis Island Restoration Project. Finegold had also worked on the U.S. Holocaust Memorial Museum.

"Moe Finegold I think was a great choice," said Rabbi Cytron. "He listened to everything we wanted. He was a practicing Jew, and he understood Jewish life. The congregation wanted an intimate setting that seated 1000."

On Sunday, August 30, 1992, the congregation held an all-day family picnic on the grounds of the new property. Titled "We're on the Move," the day-long event for all ages included a 5K walk/run/roll, games galore, races, pie-eating contest, and plenty of food.

A highlight of the warm, sunny afternoon was the appearance of Adath's very own "Swami," aka Rabbi Cytron, with his lovely assistant Etta Fay Orkin, in a "Stump the Swami" event. The picnic was a huge success, judging by the participation of more than 500 adults and kids—who managed to eat more than 800 hot dogs.

On a more serious note, at noon the congregation voted to approve the sale of the Dupont Avenue property to the First Universalist Church of Minneapolis for approximately $1,425,000.

THE NEWMAN LEGACY

In 1992, when the synagogue was facing financial challenges with the construction of the new building, Charles Newman decided to step up to the plate. His father had passed away in 1990. Charles, his wife, Phyllis, and his mother, Gert, strongly believed it was important that the synagogue have high quality professional staff and strong programming. To do this, they believed the synagogue needed long term funding. They wanted to provide a gift that would last in perpetuity and, after meeting with Rabbi Cytron, decided to create the Max Newman Family Chair in Rabbinics. (Gert passed away in December, 2005.)

According to Rabbi Cytron, "In three hours, we created an opportunity to fund this rabbinic chair— one of the first in the country. It was such an energizing experience."

Establishing the Chair in 1992 was a catalyst to move other endowments forward. Charles, Phyllis, and Gert felt it was important to support the Foundation's mission, endowing the congregation to secure its well-being for this and future generations.

"It's important for everyone to be a part of the synagogue community. We need to reach out to everyone regardless of their financial ability," Charles said.

Charles wants Adath, its staff and programs to be a model in the community. "That's my legacy. I want to give the synagogue a greater status. Dues can only pay so much. You need to bring in outside money, foundations and endowments for the synagogue to grow.

"I'm fortunate to enjoy seeing the benefits of excellent staff and innovative programming, rather than put it in my will, as many do," said Charles. "And I enjoy seeing where we've come from." Although Charles and Phyllis now live in Arizona, they continue to have a close relationship with Adath. Charles has been a member for nearly 60 years, attending nursery school, becoming Bar Mitzvah, being confirmed and marrying Phyllis in the synagogue.

Charles' father, Max J. Newman, came to this country with only "a nickel in his pocket," according to Charles. The synagogue was always a part of his parents' lives. "My parents went to services every Friday night," he recalled. Through the years, Max Newman gave to Jewish causes and talked about establishing a foundation, but never did so. Charles and Phyllis made Max's dream a reality.

After creating the Chair, Charles and Phyllis went on to become major supporters of the TAMID program.

Annual family picnic with the theme "We're on the Move," August 30, 1992 on the new property in Minnetonka.

On April 26, 1993, architect Maurice Finegold spoke to a standing-room-only crowd of congregants who had gathered for a first glimpse of the preliminary plans. Along with a large architectural model, Finegold provided sketches and drawings. The congregation was overwhelmingly enthusiastic about the beautiful, flowing lines of the building, harmonizing with the peaceful natural setting.

On July 11, 1993, the first in a series of "moving" historic events occurred when the congregation officially said goodbye to the Dupont Avenue building and handed over the keys to the new owners, the First Universalist Church. Synagogue presidents, past and present, accepted a final aliyah and then carried the Torah scrolls outside, where they were ceremoniously carried away in a "sacred" minivan. The congregation then celebrated a groundbreaking at the new Minnetonka site.

CONGREGATION WITHOUT WALLS

From July, 1993 to August, 1995 Adath was literally a congregation without walls.

The two rabbis and their staff came to work each day at a scrap metal business: office space generously donated by Kal Abrams and his family in their family business at 1109 Zane Avenue North in Golden Valley. "You could smell the propane from the forklifts," recalled Norm Pink.

During the transition period, Shabbat and holiday services, B'nai Mitzvah, SMP and Religious School, adult education, youth programs and daily minyan were held at the Minneapolis Jewish Community Center in St. Louis Park. Gan Shelanu and Camp Mishpacha conducted their programs at the Minneapolis Talmud Torah.

Ralph Kirshbaum, Adath's executive director since 1989, recalled:. "The transition years, when we met at the Jewish Community Center, were difficult ones, but every-

one came together. It took a lot of coordination, but we worked as a community. Rabbi Cytron and Rabbi Kravitz had a lot to do with how people felt."

Originally from San Francisco, Ralph's family had moved to the Twin Cities when he was eight. Prior to Adath, he worked at Temple of Aaron synagogue, and subsequently at Concordia College as vice president of finance.

Though the interim period was challenging, it produced a few unexpected benefits. The JCC provided plenty of parking for members and Adath's rental payments provided them with financial support. For those holding B'nai Mitzvah, it was an opportunity for the synagogue to establish a pattern of modest Shabbat luncheons.

Other Conservative congregations opened their doors to Adath members, providing space for weddings and funerals. "The community could not have been more generous, especially Beth El," recalled Rabbi Cytron. "It spoke to a real sense of unity."

The High Holy Days, of course, provided a special challenge, but again, with a silver lining. In 1993, services were held in the Minneapolis Convention Center, enabling the entire congregation to worship together in one service for the first time in 44 years. The hall was cavernous—a setting anything but intimate. But the sight of 2,500 members singing, rising, sitting, praying together was truly awesome. It was a never-to-be repeated experience.

The next year's High Holy Days services took place at Earle Brown Heritage Center in Brooklyn Park, a pleasant, casual, retreat-like facility but without a space large enough for the entire congregation to sit together at once.

All during this time, Ed Agranoff served as technical wizard. "Whenever we had logistics questions or problems, from the sound system at Earle Brown Center to getting set up at the JCC, to moving the Ark and the Torahs to the

The Torah-mobile

convention center, he was our one-man committee," said Norm.

Ed recalled the excitement of the Convention Center High Holy Days as well: "Everyone was together at one time. I heard people saying, 'I didn't know you belong here,' because we had previously never all been in the same building at once."

Ed emphasized that during the two years of transition, "everything really remained cohesive. If ever there was a time to unravel, that was it, and it didn't."

And the hard work paid off. "The dedication weekend was such a thrill," Ed recalled. "Now, years later, I still get a real thrill when I walk into the building."

An article from the November 1992 *Clari-Flyer* suggests just how mind-boggling the logistics of the move were:

> *Imagine living in the same house for 65 years where you've raised three generations of your family. Next imagine moving your family and all of its cherished belongings—an abundant accummulation over the years—to a new home. But, there's just one hitch. Your new home isn't ready and your transitional living space is very limited.*
>
> *You have a precious few months to sort through all of your possessions and divide everything into three categories: what you absolutely need, what can be stored but needs to remain accessible, and what can be stored and must remain totally inaccessible for a two-year period.*

One of the most difficult decisions the congregation faced was what to do with the stained glass windows in the sanctuary of the old building. Many expressed the hope that the synagogue would be able to take them, but concerns about their fragility and the high cost of moving them led the building committee to conclude that this was not a viable alternative. It was finally decided to take up the suggestion of Judith Brin Ingber, and maintain continuity of the precious windows through the creation of an artistic display. Architectural photographs of the windows were turned into transparencies by Ann Hofkin and Maria and Dennis Saari, and Judith worked with Jerry Zweigbaum to create the Window Wall. It now graces the Archives Wall donated by Al and Helen Kagin in honor of their family to memorialize the Dupont building here on Hillside Lane.

THE BUILDING TAKES SHAPE

On March 22, 1994, the walls of the kallah center finally came tumbling down. The sadness of watching that era end was balanced by the excitement of walking around the site of the new building, where on the grass, Irene Bartram had placed colorful balloons to mark the location of the sanctuary, the doors, and the Gan.

The May 1994 *Clari-Flyer* announced that a contractor had been hired—Adolfson & Peterson. Construction began in earnest, and gradually, the edifice began to take shape.

"Whatever is in that building right now was designed by a committee," said Norm. "The process was not without bumps, but everyone realized it was for the good of the congregation and the bumps smoothed out. It was challenging, but a good time."

"The most influential figure contributing to the appearance of the synagogue was architecture and building chair Irene Bartram," said Mel Orenstein. "She said, more or less, 'I will do all the work if you keep everyone off my back.'"

A brochure titled "Next Year in Minnetonka" provided a room-by-room tour of the new building. In the introduction Irene described the essence of the spiritual spaces: "We've attempted to duplicate the sense of 'timelessness' from our Dupont building," she said.

"After studying the spatial relationships we were accustomed to, we believe we've created a similar mood and feeling. We've retained the sense of intimacy, while achieving our goal of increasing our seating capacity."

"I had seen the plans, but when I saw it going up, I thought, 'Oh my, it must be miles from one end to another,'" said Mel. "The Mankato-Kasota stone behind the bema came up on a flat bed truck and required a crane to lift it off and put it in place. I worried that it wouldn't hold—but it did."

Mel might well have worried. The stone, quarried from the Oneota formation, dates back to the Paleozoic age and weighs 8.5 tons! It required a 100-ton crane to hoist it into place.

The ten chapel windows are of special note. They were designed by stained-glass artist Ellen Mandelbaum of New York to represent the minyan. Fringes of a tallis hang in the glass, lending the impression that tallitot are hanging down, protecting the chapel. The Ark in the chapel was designed by Laurie Gross.

Said Norm, "If only there was a way to fully describe the exuberance of the congregation—the willingness to pitch in and do. There was such a spirit of unity. This experience wiped out all the trials and tribulations of my first presidency. It was so satisfying to see a congregation divided 10 years before renewed as a forward-looking congregation."

The New Building Takes Shape

In the July, 1995 *Clari-Flyer*, Norman Pink described a solitary walk through the nearly finished new building, seeing in his mind's eye both the past and the future of the congregation. He wrote:

I swept off some plaster dust and sat down. The geese were quiet and the plastic wrap no longer flapping. I realized that I did not leave anything behind on Dupont Avenue. I had everything with me that was important. Along with memories, I had visions of the future. A future that will soon be in the hands of the SMP students who will be studying in the sunlit carpeted area that they themselves helped design. All too soon the Gan children will take their place as they become SMP students. I looked up at the bema, devoid of any décor. I envisaged past leaders of our congregations as they held the Torahs as is the custom for Kol Nidre. They were smiling; for it was good.

THE DEDICATION CEREMONY

Rabbi Kravitz recalled that one particularly enjoyable aspect of the move was preparing for the dedication ceremony. "I worked with a committee and we planned a whole weekend of activities," he said. "I asked Renanah Halpern to create a *ketubah* that picked up the theme of dedication of new building—a dedication to values and tradition upon which this congregation stands."

Rabbi Cytron's address to the congregation was a renewal of the covenant. "My message was that our congregation is about the fulfillment of the covenant—not about power and might, but about being a blessing from God. It was a wonderful, wonderful experience."

At 10 AM on Sunday, August 13, 1995, the doors opened at the Adath Jeshurun's new home in Minnetonka to the sound of a blaring trumpet fanfare. More than 1,000 congregants, dignitaries, and special guests attended the celebration. Among the attendees were Rabbi Joel Meyers, Executive Vice President of the Rabbinical Assembly, who was guest speaker; architect Moe Finegold; Senator Paul Wellstone; and Representative Jim Ramstad.

"Words cannot express the emotions that each and every one felt at the Dedication Ceremony," Jules Levin later remarked. "From the opening trumpet fanfare to the presentation of colors and singing of the 'Star Spangled Banner' and 'Hatikva' to the mezuzah ceremony; the Torah processions with past Adath presidents accompanied by *frailach* music of the Adath Klezmer Orchestra; the stirring Adath choir renditions of 'Hallelujah' and 'Sim Shalom'; and finally the ribbon cutting, the lighting of the *Ner Tamid*

(Eternal Light), and blowing of the shofar—it was one of the most emotional and moving experiences that I have ever been a part of."

Scott Bader can still vividly remember walking into the newly completed synagogue. "The building was done and the sound system contractor was testing the sound system. I happened to walk into the sanctuary just as *Phantom of the Opera* was playing at a volume so loud that the entire space was filled with music. My eyes welled up as I looked around this vast beautiful space and realized what we had all accomplished."

"Adath holds a special place in my heart," Scott's wife Kerry said, "mainly because of my family's history with the synagogue. My grandparents belonged here, my parents belonged here, and my brothers and I were consecrated, Bar and Bat Mitzvahed, and confirmed at the Adath. Scott and I were married at Adath and all of our kids went through the same "life cycle" events as we did growing up here. We always laugh, though, when we remember that our first son's Bar Mitzvah was held in the building on Dupont, our second son's Bar Mitzvah was held at the JCC (our temporary home while the "new" building was under construction) and our daughter's Bat Mitzvah was held in the current building, which Scott worked so hard to create as associate chair of the building committee!"

Jeff Schachtman says that to this day, he feels a sense of joy when he sees kids run through the entrance hall. "To have a congregation, you really have to bring people in," he said. "We wanted to create a community, and we needed a building to do it."

Top (Left) Adath past-presidents on Dedication Day. (Right) Adath Board on Dedication Day.
Middle: (Left) At the Adath groundbreaking.: Rabbi Cytron, Norman Pink, Cantor Kula, Irene Bartram and Bill Aberman.
(Right) President Norman Pink and President-Elect Carol Bromer. Bottom: (Left) Fundraising Chair Danny and Phyllis Heilicher with
"dedication ketubah" by artist and Adath member Rani Halpern. (Right) Stephen Lieberman chatting with Sabine Amsel.

Top left: President Mel Goldberg
Top right: Past presidents carry the Torahs

Top left: Andy Weiner; Middle: Joyce Orbuch; Right: Tom Grossman
Bottom: Dedication Day Committee, August 1995

Top left: (Left to right) Rani Halpern and Anat Bar-Cohen; Top right: Adath's Klezmer Orchestra plays a lively tune
Middle left: Raleigh and Scott Kaminsky with a friend; Middle right: (Left to right) Sabine Amsel, Barbara and Burt Myers
Bottom left: Mrs. Louis Kitsis with Senator Paul Wellstone; Bottom right: Bud and Beverly Grossman and family

Top left: (Left to right) Rabbi Kravitz, Hazzan Buckner, and Rabbi Cytron lead the processional into the new sanctuary
Top right: Irene Bartram and Jeffrey Schachtman
Middle left: Hazzan Buckner and Rabbi Kravitz; Middle: Dan Heilicher and Jules Levin; Middle right: Rabbi Kravitz affixes the mezuzah
Bottom left: At the dedication. Bottom right: Rabbi Cytron with architect Moe Finegold

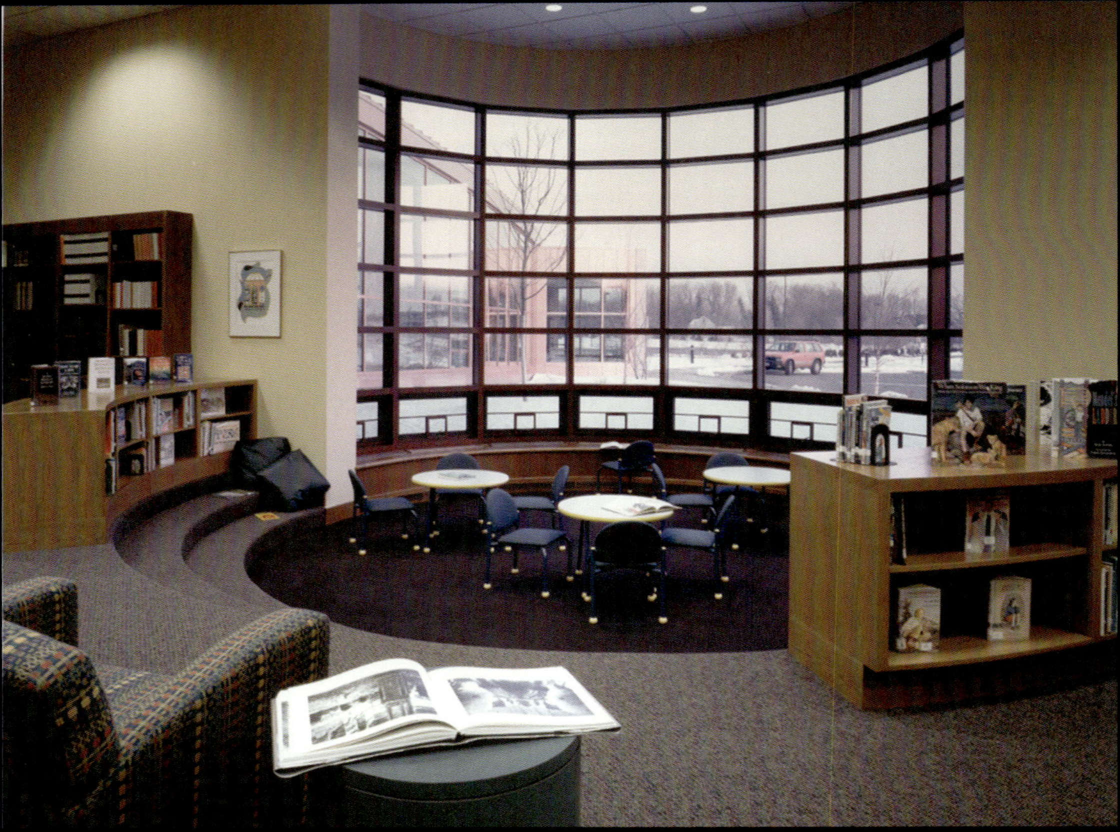

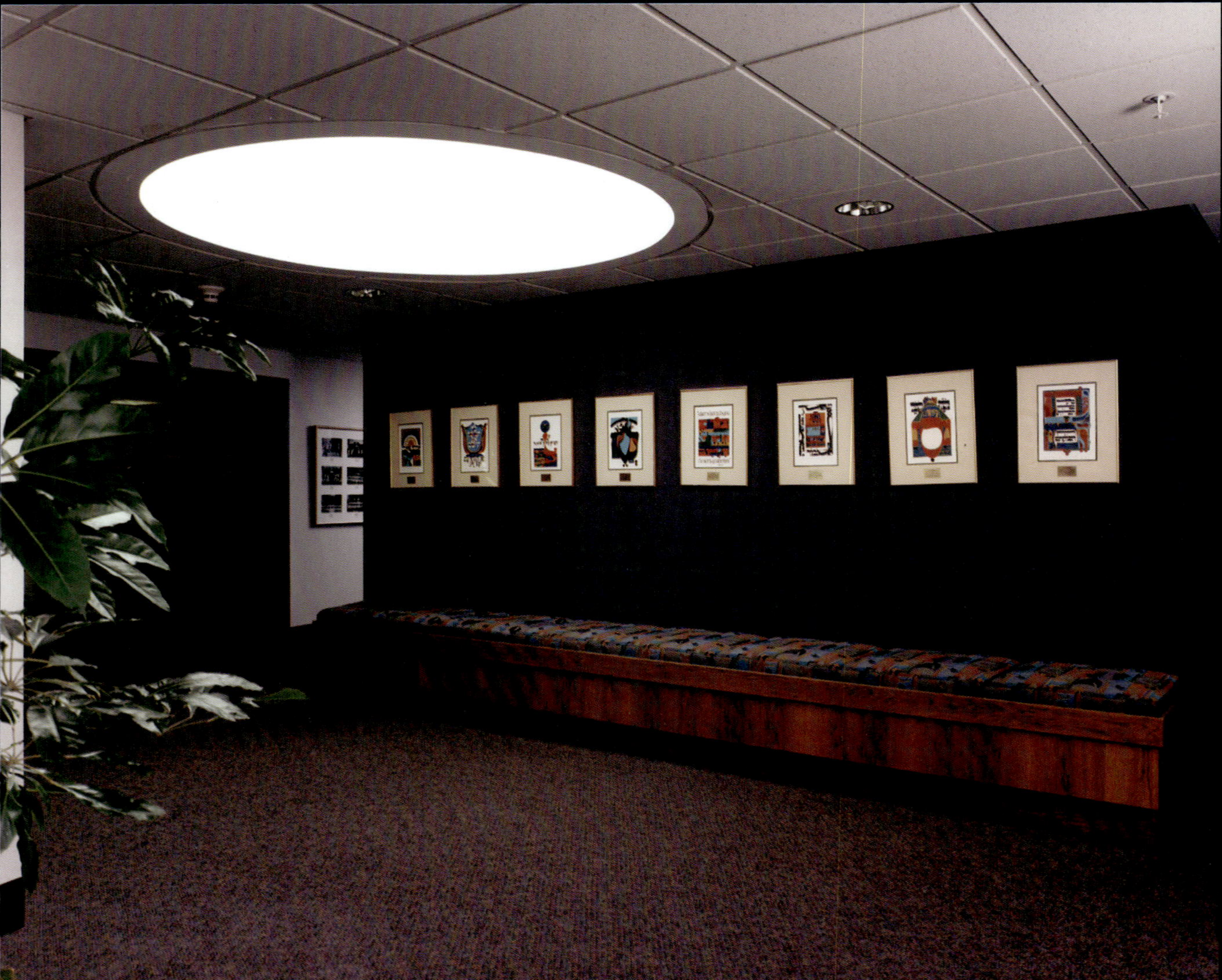

After the Adath moved to its present location, there was concern about the fate of the stained glass windows in the old building, which the new owners wished to remove. In 2002 Etta Fay Orkin went to Evan Maurer, the director of the Minneapolis Institute of Arts, for advice. He immediately called Adath member (and MIA board member) Beverly Grossman, who gave him funds for the removal of three of the windows. Etta Fay raised other funds by giving money herself and soliciting contributions from Jon Rappaport, Harry Lerner, Theresa Berman, Iric Nathanson and his brother James. John Salisbury of Gaytee Glass Co. (on the ladder, right) removed, restored, and replaced six of the windows in several locations in Minneapolis, including the MIA, the Jewish Historical Society, the Minneapolis Jewish Day School, and the new Adath Jeshurun library, with the help of funds from the MIA, the Leo & Lillian Gross Family Fund, the Jay & Rose Phillips Foundation, and Etta Fay's friends and family. It was a labor of love pursued by Etta Fay, Iric Nathanson, and Norman Pink, and its success ensures that future generations will continue to enjoy the beauty of these windows.

For descriptions see page 217

IN HONOR OF
OUR GRANDDAUGHTER
AMY BETH RODICH
MARCH 1 1991
BY GRANDPARENTS
ELAINE & HAROLD DORN

For descriptions see page 217

Top: The Adath choir directed by Marlys Fiterman
Bottom: (Left to right) Three generations of shofar blowers: David, Harry and Mel Orenstein

Top left: (Left to right) Tom and Liba Stillman,
Lee and Phyllis Sudit
Top right: Julie Sherman and children
Middle left: Marcy Buckner and children
Middle right: Chris Bez, center,
with son Nick and Avis Savitt
Bottom left: Reva Lear
Bottom right: Sylvia Schwartz

Happy Days at Adath

Thanks to donations by generous congregants over the years, Adath Jeshurun has developed a notable collection of Jewish art. Sharon Zweigbaum, Adath's curator, has provided the following descriptions of the artworks and ceremonial objects reproduced on pages 218-221.

Page 210

Megillah, silver, scroll on single roller. Donated in honor of Mr. & Mrs. Herman H. Neff's 45th wedding anniversary – January 18, 1965, by their friends. Relates events from the Book of Esther, which is read on the joyous festival of Purim.

Yad, silver, a Torah pointer. Donated in 1961 by Mr. and Mrs. Isadore Wolk in honor of their 50th anniversary. The Yad is used when reading the Torah and is fashioned as a hand with a thrust forefinger on a rod. One should not touch the Torah page with an actual finger.

Marriage Ring, pewter, 18th or 19th century. Donated in 1973 by family, in honor of Mr. and Mrs. Morris Besner's 40th Anniversary. Ages ago, an elaborate communal Jewish wedding ring was often rented and then returned after the service. In its place the bride would then receive a plain gold band from her husband. The house symbol is dominant: a couple marries under the chuppah, which represents the future home of the bride and groom.

Chanukiah, silver and gilt. An 8-branched oil lamp with shamash (servant light). Symbols are lions, crowns, 10 Commandments, etc. Used during Chanukah, the Festival of Lights, celebrating the victory of the Maccabees over Syrian Greeks.

Page 211

Kiddush Cup, silver. Decorated with grapes and organic patterns. After kindling the Sabbath lights, a Kiddush (sanctification) over a cup of wine is recited. Kiddush cups are created in a variety of styles.

Etrog Holder, silver. Donated in 1981 by Elaine and Harold Rubin in honor of granddaughter, Beth Rodich. Oval-shaped container to hold an unblemished etrog, or citron, for Sukkot.

Bronze ark doors, designed by California artist Laurie Gross. Characterized by embossed and applied Hebrew letters and six winding tendrils on each door, suggesting *tzitzit* and the 12 passageways through the sea. The specific Hebrew text interprets *Shirat Hayam* (the Song of Moses) as Moses and Miriam fled Egypt and crossed the Red Sea. Torahs are revealed through the open doors. The parchment scrolls contain the Five Books of Moses, sacred to all Jews. They have varied fabric, stitched and metal mantels (covers). Also pictured are several silver *rimmonim*, adornments for the wooden Torah rods and a *keter*, or Torah Crown.

Page 212

Sylvia Mangold, "Nut Trees," oil on canvas, 1985. This work by the noted contemporary artist was donated in 1996 by Bud and Beverly Grossman for the Grossman Chapel. The lines in the nature subject matter echo patterns in the chapel's stained glass windows and relate to the woodsy setting beyond. Mangold's work is included in the Museum of Modern Art, NY; Whitney Museum of American Art; Museum of Fine Arts, Boston; and other museums.

William Saltzman, "Eretz Yisrael" ("Pioneer"), a large oil painting, 1956. Donated in 1956 by the Mirviss Family. This high-quality work is by the deceased former Macalaster College Professor of Art and noted public artist.

Ben Shahn, "Decalogue" a hand-watercolored silkscreen with applied gold leaf. The famous American artist indicates here his love of letters, particularly Hebrew script. Donated in 1996 by Kentucky resident Paul Schwartz in memory of family members, Goldie and Meyer Gilbert.

Page 213

Vitkinofsky (the probable artist), "Chaim Weitzman," oil on paper. About 1950s. Memorial to Harry Glickman. In 1948 Weitzman became the first President of Israel.

Yaacov Agam, "Newborn Star," Agamograph, 1990s. Donated in 1996 by friends in honor of Margo and Fred Berdass's 50th Anniversary. This kinetic, holographic art work is ever-changing, depending on one's position.

Tallitot, prayer shawls available for congregational use. The tallit is a garment worn like a shawl or scarf during daytime services and is a highly respected Jewish ritual object. Wearing a tallit is a public declaration of one's love, respect, and devotion to Judaism. The tallit has fringes (Heb.: tzitzit) attached to its corners, consisting of eight dangling threads, or more accurately, four threads doubled over and wound and knotted in a symbolic manner. Tallitot are made of wool, cotton, or silk and may be white or colored, often with striped black or blue patterns.

Top: from left, Andrea Segal, Cantor Buckner, Nina Samuels,
Rabbi Kravitz, Malcolm Katz, Rabbi Matsa, and Susie Chalom.
Above left: Howard and Gail Milstein with baby Sophie
and grandparents Mort and Merle Kane.
Above right: the Over the Hillside group

11
THE RABBI KRAVITZ YEARS
(1996 –)

In the nearly 15 years that have elapsed since the congregation moved from South Minneapolis, synagogue life has bloomed anew in Minnetonka. The building of the new synagogue was a cathartic experience—a monumental task that required vision, dedication, cooperation, and a huge amount of hard work. Following the departure of Rabbi Cytron, Rabbi Kravitz was installed as Adath's Senior Rabbi, assuming the Max Newman Family Chair in Rabbinics. With warmth, intelligence, steadfast leadership and a *haimish* spirit, he has guided Adath into the 21st century, embodying its dedication to Torah (learning and tradition), Avodah (prayer and spirituality), and Gemilut Hasadim (acts of kindness).

Since the Adath Jeshurun congregation moved to Minnetonka, there have been challenges, but no major upheavals. The membership has swelled to more than 1200 households and financial stability has increased to the point that the budget has been balanced since 2002. The rejuvenation and phenomenal growth of the Adath Foundation, the arrivals of Cantor Buckner, Rabbis Matsa and Brusso, and other clergy and staff, and a proliferation of new programs, services, committees, and *havurot*, are among the highlights of the past 15 years.

CANTOR BUCKNER ARRIVES

Following Cantor Morton Kula's retirement in 1994, Cantor Scott Buckner came from Boston to join Adath along with his wife, Marcy, and their children Heather, Ethan and Matthew. (Their fourth child, Rachel, was born in Minnesota.) A graduate of the Cantors Institute of the Jewish Theological Seminary, Cantor Buckner has an outstanding lyrical tenor voice. He has studied in the Cantorial program of the Institute for Jewish Spirituality, and has introduced sacred chanting to the congregation, using the style and music of Rabbi Shefa Gold along with his own

compositions. Cantor Buckner serves on the ethics committee of the Cantors Assembly.

Cantor Buckner says he was immediately attracted to Adath by the warmth of the community—despite the minus 12 degree February weather he faced on his first visit. "I also was attracted by the vibrancy of the congregation," said Cantor Buckner. "I saw youth who were very involved. The congregation asked thoughtful questions, and they were open to creativity and ideas for new music I wanted to bring. They were willing to experiment and try things out—and are always looking to grow and add new dimensions."

Cantor Buckner was also impressed by the professionalism and experience of the staff.

The cantor quickly became involved with TAMID, working with Ron Butwin, who was chair at the time. Among the many high points of TAMID, one program featured Cantor Buckner and two of his colleagues who flew in to perform together as the Three Jewish Tenors. The cantor also recalls fondly the night he was given the opportunity to sing the finale with guest artist Marvin Hamlisch.

Ongoing highlights of congregational life for Cantor Buckner include the Neilah service on Yom Kippur, when he sees a "packed house" of congregants who are familiar with and can participate in the entire service. "The singing is incredible," he said. "At a time when I should be exhausted, the energy of the congregation reenergizes me."

Cantor Buckner recalled the excitement of dedicating the new building and the gratification of being a part of people's simchas—weddings, births, B'nai Mitzvah—as well as celebrating his own family's simchas (four B'nai Mitzvah) at Adath. He is glad to be present for congregants in their times of need, and appreciates the support he and his family have received from congregants during difficult times.

"What the congregation did for us has left a lasting impression," he said. "It solidified their place in our hearts."

Cantor Buckner performs with Theodore Bikel

RABBI KRAVITZ BECOMES SENIOR RABBI

Scarcely was the new *Ner Tamid* kindled when Rabbi Cytron announced his resignation. He later remarked, looking back on the event, "It's not unusual in religious life in America—in fact, it's kind of standard—for a clergy member to walk in the front door of a new building and right out a side door. There aren't any good answers as to why that happens. In my case, the move had been exhausting. I hadn't had any training for fundraising and I was exhausted."

Yet Rabbi Cytron's success in raising funds, both for the new building and for the Foundation, was far better than these remarks would suggest, and it's likely that the enticement of what lay ahead also spurred his departure. Rabbi Cytron had given a presentation to Eddie Phillips as part of the new building's fundraising, and less than a year later Phillips approached the rabbi with a proposal to assume directorship of the newly created Jay Phillips Center for Jewish-Christian Learning, and to occupy the Jay Phillips Chair in Jewish Studies at St. John's University in Collegeville, Minnesota. The Center had been established to promote education and improve relations between Jews and Christians.

"I never really had a chance to enjoy the building and it would have been nice to spend some good times there," Rabbi Cytron said. "It was hard to say goodbye to the Adath and to realize that I had left a piece of myself behind... But life is about losses. And teaching has been wonderful and fulfilling."

Sally Appelbaum noted: "When Rabbi Cytron decided to leave—God bless the congregation in its wisdom. They realized Rabbi Kravitz was right here. Rabbi Cytron was

unusual in that he looked at Rabbi Kravitz as a colleague, not an assistant. There was not the typical clash of egos between rabbis—nor has there been since."

So it was that in June, 1996, outgoing board president Norm Pink reported on several significant changes in personnel that had occurred during his three-year tenure. Cantor Kula and Executive Director Ralph Kirshbaum had retired, and the congregation had welcomed Cantor Buckner. Malcom Katz was hired in Ralph's place. Rabbi Cytron was asked to serve as Adath's first Senior Scholar. Rabbi Kravitz was chosen to serve as Senior Rabbi, assuming the Max Newman Family Chair in Rabbinics, and Rabbi Myrna Matsa joined Adath as assistant rabbi.

Malcom Katz came to Adath in 1996 from Congregation Sharei Tzedek, a 2,100 family-member congregation in Detroit, where he served as synagogue administrator. He previously worked in residential real estate and for IBM. Originally from Detroit, Malcom graduated from Wayne State, lived in Denmark, and served in the Peace Corps.

Also in 1996, the congregation engaged Rabbi Myrna Matsa, a 1995 graduate of JTS, as assistant rabbi. Following graduation, Rabbi Matsa was involved in hospital and hospice work, specializing in bereavement issues and studying to become a certified chaplain. Prior to her rabbinic studies, she graduated from the University of California, Berkeley, moved to New York and worked in the computer field. After celebrating an adult Bat Mitzvah in 1981, she began studying, experiencing and teaching Judaism. Rabbi Matsa worked to put herself through the Jewish Theological Seminary by teaching Hebrew school, adult education, and serving as a scholar-in-residence for various programs.

On September 6, 1996, the congregation gathered to celebrate Rabbi Cytron's installation as Senior Scholar and express appreciation for his contributions to Adath and the community. His scholarship, intellectual breadth and gifted teaching were noted, as well as his numerous contributions to both the congregation and the larger community.

In his new position as Senior Scholar at Adath, Rabbi Cytron would continue to participate in the life of the synagogue. Among his responsibilities would be to teach adults and speak from the pulpit on several Shabbatot each year.

On Oct. 11, 1996 Rabbi Kravitz was installed as Senior Rabbi, Max Newman Family Chair in Rabbinics.

In addition to his many activities in the realm of social action on behalf of MAZON and MICAH, Rabbi Kravitz served two terms as co-chair of the Minnesota Rabbinical Association. He served on the board of Jewish Family and Children's Service and on the board of the Joint Religious Legislative Coalition.

Rabbi Kravitz is also devoted to the cause of the Israeli Masorti (Conservative) Movement, and Adath's involvement with the Masorti movement has strengthened over the years. In February 2005, Rabbi Kravitz led a group of 27 congregants to Magen Avraham in Omer, Israel, our sister congregation. That relationship was established in the 70s with the congregation's first rabbi, Michael Graetz.

The trip was Rabbi Kravitz' third since 1999. Rabbi Brusso has also led several trips to Omer, Israel. The teenagers from Magen Avraham visited Adath in the summers of 2005 and 2008. Rabbi Graetz made visits to Adath as scholar-in-residence, and the current rabbi, Gil Nativ, was a scholar-in-residence in March of 2009.

Long Range Planning and Task Forces

The move to Minnetonka, an anticipated change in membership, and the evolving needs of the Jewish community made this an opportune time for congregation-wide dialogue and self-examination. Therefore, a Long Range Planning Committee was set up and given the task of formulating a mission statement for the congregation as it entered a new century in a new home. The committee reviewed reports from a wide array of groups including the Adult Education Committee, By-Laws, Chevra, Dues, Finance, Fund Raising, Hesed, Membership, New Americans, Personnel, Primary Education, Public Relations, Ritual, Secondary Education, Singles (Age 40-plus), and Youth Commission. In October, 1996, the committee issued its report.

It made recommendations in the areas of Information Gathering and Sharing, T'filot (Prayers and Ritual), Education, and Congregational Life Issues. These recommendations ranged from the specific—"bridge programming between second and fifth grades"—to the general—"develop a community of youth that is invested in their Jewish education and exhibits leadership." The committee suggested that the board, which is so often absorbed in the nuts and bolts of running a large congregation, should set aside a time each year "for discussion and reflection of issues that affect the vision and long term future of the congregation."

To address ongoing issues in the synagogue, Rabbi Kravitz implemented a task force model to address congregational concerns one at a time. To involve individuals who would never have agreed to join a standing committee, Rabbi Kravitz proposed that a limit of 12 to 18 months' commitment be placed on those who agreed to participate. The task force model was well received and a number of contentious issues were addressed via the process.

The task force first tackled the issue of High Holy Days services. It was determined in 1997 that the Gimel service needed to be redone to make it truly a family service, geared toward those with elementary-aged children. The task force also concluded that it was important to balance the needs of many who appreciated the choir during High Holy Days with those who wanted a simpler service. On the second day of Rosh Hashanah, two services would be offered concurrently. Everyone would begin Shacharit together in the social hall. Those who preferred a service with straight davening, congregational responses and songs for the Torah service and Musaf would remain, while those who preferred more elaborate music with hazzan and choir would move into the sanctuary.

The content of the sanctuary services would be altered somewhat to increase congregational singing and participation. Hazzan Buckner also proposed to change the style and quality of the music for both choir and congregation to heighten its spirituality.

Following the success of the High Holy Days task force, Rabbi Kravitz convened a second task force in 1998 to address Shabbat morning services. Every effort was made to ensure that the group reflected the diverse needs and interests of the entire congregation.

One issue facing the committee was whether the social hall should be reserved for private Kiddush luncheons or opened up to the entire congregation following services. It was finally decided that congregants could have a private luncheon in one half of the room. The other half would remain available for a congregational Kiddush.

These days, most Shabbat mornings at Adath see large crowds—the Bar or Bat Mitzvah family and their guests mingling with the "regulars" of all ages, "SMP families," and dozens of SMP students, many of whom make a bee-line for the best "sweet table" in town.

While today such arrangements are taken for grant-ed, they were once considered controversial, and Carol Bromer, who was president at the time, recalled, "We ta-bled board discussion for a year to give people time to get used to the idea."

At Adath, the B'nai Mitzvah celebration is part of the Shabbat morning service, not the other way around. "Rab-bi Kravitz talked about the Adath being one community," Carol said. "There are people who are here every week. How do we create community? If the child is demonstrat-ing his/her ability to be a good adult Jew, you need the congregation to witness and welcome the child."

Carol also noted that parent speeches have changed. They no longer consist merely of a recitation of their child's accomplishments, but usually reflect on the week's *parsha* as well. And the child's ability to deliver a *d'var torah* has also grown; now they often find profound meaning in the text.

A third task force, Derekh Eretz (proper conduct or re-spectful behavior), arose out of concerns about the behavior of congregants—especially children—during Shabbat.

The synagogue wanted to offer a warm and welcom-ing environment, but expected appropriate behavior on the part of children, as well as adherence to the laws of Shab-bat governing picture taking, writing, cell phone use, etc. "We'd had some complaints," Rabbi Kravitz recalled.

In an open letter to the congregation printed in the *Clarion*, task force co-chair Dan Kohen wrote:

> Our children are our most precious resource—they are our future and we cherish them. In order to set reasonable expectations, guidelines and con-sequences, the Adath Board has authorized the for-mation of a Derekh Eretz task force.
>
> In the meantime, we ask our members of all ages to discuss these issues and take ownership of our behavior ....Please respectfully tell children who are misbehaving to stop. We are asking everyone to help set a proper example and demonstrate what is appropriate behavior in our synagogue. Parents, please be responsible for your children and be sure they are not unsupervised.

1996-1998

Carol Bromer was Rabbi Kravitz's "first board presi-dent." "One of the first things on my agenda," he re-called, "was to create a process for identifying leadership to avoid having a frantic search."

"In some ways, this is what I am proudest of," said Carol. "Leadership had typically come from kind of a closed group who all grew up together in Minneapolis." Carol herself was not a Minneapolis native. In her assess-ment, the congregation has opened up, and newcomers can now readily find a place at Adath. In addition, there is a real partnership between lay and professional leadership.

By 1996 the Bar/Bat Mitzvah student population had grown so large there were no longer enough Shabbatot for each child to have his or her own date. For the first time since the 1970s, Adath had to double up on dates. When her term as president ended, Rabbi Kravitz asked Carol to take on the project of Bar/Bat mitzvah assignments.

The situation was all the more challenging because that first year, only a few doubles were needed. "One of the doubles was my daughter Talia, with Aviva Goldblatt," said Rabbi Kravitz. "We thought the experience would be half as good—but instead, it was twice as good!"

In 1997, Adath held its first annual blood drive chaired by Joni Weinstein, who continues to organize the annual drives today.

Among other issues addressed during Carol's tenure was the updating of the synagogue's bylaws. For instance, updating the policies related to egalitarianism formalized the synagogue's commitment to those principles, aligning the bylaws with Adath's self-image as a progressive, egali-tarian community.

Carol also worked to open up the synagogue to the non-Jewish community as a program venue. Today, many visitors who have never set foot in a synagogue attend events at Adath, where they are universally impressed with its beauty and warmth. The Adath served for a number of years as the host of the Hennepin County Library Pen Pals lecture series, and writers as diverse as Tom Wolfe, Amy Tan, Richard Ford, and Khaled Hosseini have given presen-tations in the sanctuary.

1998-2000

Jerry Zweigbaum headed committees and served on the board for approximately 20 years before his death in 2001. His involvement included a role as property chair, a major role in acquiring and administering the Adath

INSPIRATION FOR AN AWARD-WINNING DESIGN

In November 1999, the congregation learned from Maurice Finegold, architect of the new building, that Adath had received a 2000 Design Award in the category of Liturgical/Interior Design from *Faith and Forum* magazine and the Interfaith Forum on Religion, Art, and Architecture. Finegold once described his conception in the following terms:

When I first visited the site, I was inspired by the strong bands of blue and green emanating from the lake, the land and the sky. They reminded me of the Talmudic text describing when morning prayers may be recited, viz. when one can discern between blue and green. Those colors inspired the chapel. The sanctuary, on the highest point of the land, was inspired by an historic space whose warmth and intimacy on a large scale, helped shape this principal space. And the contours of your land influenced the gentle curving shape of the social hall and educational wings as well as the soft lines of the library and chapel. A powerful historical image is evoked by the use of local masonry, literally rising out of the landscape.

A special idea emerged for the school concept as I observed past Bar/Bat Mitzvah students teaching the younger ones. I thought a comfortable and conducive space for kids to talk to one another would be the carpeted amphitheater and that became the inspiration for the organizing element of the school wing.

Chesed Shel Emes Cemetery, and serving as head of the Interiors initiative on the architectural committee for Adath's new building. In preparation for the 1995 move, Jerry coordinated the interior design in collaboration with architect Moe Finegold's team and Adath's Building Committee, including pew construction, textile and furniture selections, refining the *ner tamid*, installing the stone behind the bema, and other features.

Jerry served as board president from 1998 to 2000. Among the leadership challenges he faced were screening and hiring additional personnel for the new building and

conducting exit procedures for departing executive and clerical staff. He was also active in refining the maintenance and upkeep systems in the new building. Jerry was known as a gentle, helpful, yet firm mentor.

During his tenure as president, the congregation purchased the new *Siddur Sim Shalom*. Rabbi Kravitz wrote in a 1999 *Clarion,*

The Siddur, which guides us in prayer, is made up of prose and poetry from biblical, rabbinic, medieval and modern literature. Throughout the ages some

Jerry and Sharon Zweigbaum

of the most important insights of our people have been incorporated into its pages.

For this reason there is a need to revise our Siddur from time to time, to re-explain its contents, to translate anew, to add contemporary poetry to help make prayer more meaningful to a new generation. It is in this spirit that the Conservative movement has recently published a new edition of our prayerbook, Siddur Sim Shalom, for Shabbat and Festivals. This new Siddur includes new translations and more explanation. It is more gender-sensitive in the language it uses to describe God. Another innovation is to provide egalitarian wording in the Amidah which includes the Matriarchs, as has been the custom of our congregation for several years. It contains additional liturgical poetry including a number of elegant prayers by our member Ruth Brin, who was consulted in the creation of this Siddur.

There is another Adath connection to this new Siddur. The chair of the editorial committee for this edition was Rabbi Leonard S. Cahan of Potomac, Maryland, whose wife, Elizabeth, and brother, Bruce, grew up at the Adath. Her mother, Ruth Peilen, along with family and friends, have made a generous gift of the new Siddur to our congregation in memory of their husband and father, Ellis Peilen, who served as president of the Adath from 1955 to 1958.

In 1999, Bernie Goldblatt became executive director of Adath. Bernie and his wife, Leslie, have been Adath congregants for 25 years. They have named their daughters, Talia, Aviva, and Leora, celebrated their B'not Mitzvah, and soon will be seeing their eldest daughter married in the synagogue.

"In conjunction with the Minneapolis Jewish Day

School, Adath has had the most profound effect on my family of all the organizations to which we've belonged," Bernie said. "Our children have learned what it means to be Jewish at the Gan, SMP, in services, and at Kiddush luncheons."

"Both personally and a professionally," said Bernie, "the Adath community is probably the nicest group of people with which I have been associated." As an executive director, Bernie has had the opportunity to talk with and visit numerous congregations nationwide. "We are among the most fortunate congregations," he said. "We have very high-functioning lay leadership, clergy, and staff. People take for granted that other synagogues run like ours—but they don't!"

2000-2002

It may be a well-kept secret that when Rabbi Aaron Brusso was looking for the right match to begin his pulpit career, he and his wife, Hana Gruenberg, turned down a congregation in lovely, temperate, Palo Alto, California. Why did they make what might be regarded as an unusual choice?

Rabbi Aaron Brusso, his wife Hana Gruenberg, and their children Sari, Zoe and Ilan at Camp Ramah in Wisconsin.

"We chose Adath for many reasons," said Rabbi Brusso. "One was the opportunity to work with Rabbi Kravitz. I've learned from him what it is to be a rabbi. It was a smart decision—he's a wonderful teacher and mentor in so many ways, willing to allow you to do things that are of interest to you."

Tellingly, these words echo exactly those of Rabbi Kravitz about his decision to work with Rabbi Cytron many years ago.

"There were a number of people on the search committee who reflected different demographics and were proud to be a part of Adath," Rabbi Brusso continued. "They had a deep sense of the history of the place. There was stability and tradition here, and yet an openness to creativity and progressiveness.

"The people were warm and down to earth. They were interested in who we were. We didn't have kids when we came here—all three of our children were born here. It's been a wonderful place to have our kids."

Rabbi Brusso was ordained by the Jewish Theological Seminary in New York, where he also received a Masters degree in Jewish philosophy. Originally from Chicago, he was an active member of USY, attended Camp Ramah, and was a leader at the American University Hillel. Rabbi Brusso currently co-chairs the Minnesota Rabbinical Association, is co-chair of Koach: the Conservative Movement's presence on college campuses, and is a member of the ethics committee for Children's Hospital.

On Rabbi Brusso's agenda has been working with young adults, trying to get them involved in the congregation. "This age group tends not to be involved in Adath," he said. "We started meeting in people's homes and socializing, with the idea being that you don't have to be a member, but you need some association. It's a form of outreach."

"The 125th celebration is a big event coming up—it will be a chance to recruit the next group of 20s-30s," he said.

Rabbi Brusso has devoted a good deal of time to study groups, including Talmud study on Tuesday mornings and a Heschel reading group twice a month. And he's popular with the synagogue's young people of all ages. His youth, energy and enthusiasm, and sense of humor make the teenaged set gravitate toward him.

In fact, there was a time when he was mistaken for one of them. Hired when he was only 28, Rabbi Brusso tells the story of being stopped by an older woman on Shabbat as he carried the Torah through the sanctuary. She asked him, "Are you the Bar Mitzvah boy?" He's never been quite sure if she was serious, he admits.

One of his innovations was to initiate a staff kallah just for SMP teachers—kids of post-Bar and Bat Mitzvah age. "They needed their own prayer and learning space," he said.

Rabbi Brusso's sermons are another of his strengths. They're warm, sincere, thought-provoking and often punctuated with humor. They carry a message that resonates with the congregation.

Rabbi Brusso has also devoted significant energy to building up the Gimel Family Service as a place where multiple generations could pray and learn together. "I wanted to infuse the service with ruach, prayer, and learning that includes stories, music, and interactive conversation," he explained. "I started out on the High Holy Days with high school and college kids helping lead the service, but they kept graduating." So he tapped congregant Steve Mintz to work with him. In 2007, they created a *machzor* especially for the Gimel Family Service.

Leonard and Clara Savitt, who endowed the Youth Chair, with youth director Laura Condon Leventhal, the first to hold the endowed position.

In 2000, Leonard and Clara Savitt, members of Adath since 1947, gave a very generous endowment to the Adath Foundation to assure funding in perpetuity in support of the Youth Director position. Through the Leonard and Clara Savitt Youth Director Chair, the Savitt family name will be forever linked to the Adath Jeshurun Congregation.

Moe and Esther Sabes (above) were involved in affairs of the Jewish community for many years. In 2002 the family made a generous gift in their honor to Adath Jeshurun which allowed it to retire its mortgage.

Sadly for Adath, as this book went to press, Rabbi Brusso informed the congregation that he is seeking a position as senior rabbi of his own congregation; he and his family will be greatly missed.

"Norm Pink likes to tell everyone the story of the 'little girl' who went on to become synagogue president," said Raleigh Kaminsky. When her two children were very young, Raleigh organized the Noah's Ark program. "My first appearance ever before the board was in 1984 to ask for money to fund the program," she recalled.

Raleigh Kaminsky

Raleigh joined the board herself in 1985, assuming the presidency in 2000. Meanwhile, the Noah's Ark Shabbat Service—with a service, singing, and stories for families with young children—is still held on the first Friday night of every month, and remains as popular as ever. The participants use a prayer book dedicated to Raleigh's mother.

One issue during Raleigh's tenure was the large enrollment for nursery school, essentially a good news/bad news situation. When the interest in the preschool burgeoned, a lottery system of registration had to be put in place.

On Shabbat Bereshit in 2001, Adath began using a new chumash, *Etz Hayim.* It was developed with the editorial contributions of great Jewish scholars including Chaim Potok and Harold Kushner. In 2002, sofer Rabbi Moshe Druin visited to help maintain the synagogue's Torah scrolls. Plans were made to institute a new tradition on Simchat Torah to recognize two community members as *Hatan Torah* and *Hatan Beresheet* for their significant contributions.

One highlight of Raleigh's term was the retirement of the building mortgage. In 2000, the congregation still owed $1.2 million on the new building, Raleigh recalled, and was paying more than $6,000 in interest every month. In 2001, the New Building Fund changed its name to the Building Continuity Committee. Jules Levine and Danny Heilicher, who had been so successful with the initial building fundraising, along with Melvin Orenstein, once again came out of retirement to try to raise more funds.

They approached people who were newer members of the congregation, as well as people who either weren't able or weren't inclined to give the first time, Rabbi Kravitz recalled. "Then, Jules and I approached Bob Sabes and proposed a gift of a certain amount," Rabbi Kravitz said. "Instead, he offered a sum that would pay off the entire mortgage, as a way to honor his parents."

At the congregation's annual meeting on June 20, 2002, outgoing president Raleigh Kaminsky announced the gift by the Sabes Family Foundation. The synagogue site was renamed the "Moe and Esther Sabes Campus" in honor of the benefactor's family.

Moe and Esther Sabes were involved in the Jewish community for many years, not only contributing to the financial well being of the community but giving of their time with active participation as well.

Esther was a board member of the Women's League for many years, and also was active on the Education Committee. Moe, who died in 2000, was active in the congregation's Men's Club and was awarded its coveted "Bell Ringer" award for outstanding service. Moe was also a member of the Adath's Board of Trustees, and in the sixties served on the Long Range Planning Committee. Little could he have imagined in 1968, when the congregation purchased the property that the Adath is now a part of, that he was playing a major role in the acquisition of a site that now bears his and Esther's names.

The Sabes family was honored at the annual meeting, during which their gift was formally accepted. Rabbi Kravitz said, "The congregation is extremely grateful for the generosity of the Sabes family. The naming of the campus in honor of their beloved parents and grandparents will be a tribute to the family's love for the Adath and the long relationship they have had with the congregation."

2002–2004

Jim Sherman, Rabbis' Associate, moved to Minneapolis from Sioux City, Iowa, in 2002 with his wife, Estie. They wanted to be close to their son and daughter-in-law, David and Julie Sherman, and their four grandsons. With sons living in three different states, they chose the city that would represent the least "culture shock," Jim said.

In Sioux City, Jim described himself as Congregation Beth Shalom's "rabbi with a small 'r'." Although not ordained, Jim was able to serve as its spiritual leader. Under Iowa law, a lay minister can legally perform marriages if approved by the congregation. In addition, he officiated at funerals and ceremonies of *brit milah*. According to Jim, "Judaism is a lay religion. The people should be doing these things themselves. You do not need to turn it all over to the rabbi. The rabbi should be the teacher/preacher."

Jim and Estie Sherman

Jim and Estee arrived in Minneapolis just as Rabbi Kravitz was preparing for a six-month sabbatical. Because of Jim's experience on the pulpit, Rabbi Kravitz asked him for his assistance. Jim helped Rabbi Brusso with *divrei Torah* and the Bar and Bat Mitzvah kids' preparation. When Rabbi Kravitz returned, he asked Jim to stay on part time.

"I couldn't have asked for a nicer thing to happen," Jim said. "This is what I like to do." Jim now helps teach Judaism classes, serves as part of the rotation of *mincha* leaders, is staff liaison for the Yad Simah Tovah (Adath's Caring

Community program), leads Etzion (a senior adult study group) and various Torah studies, and more. His greatest joy, however, is "working with the clergy team in Bar/Bat Mitzvah preparation, helping the kids write their *divrei Torah*. I enjoy getting to know each kid."

Beyond his part-time employment with Adath, Jim works with Sholom Community Alliance, going to Menorah Plaza and leading small study groups with residents at Knollwood Place Apartments and Roitenberg Family Assisted Living Residence.

Judy Cook remembered carrying on the tradition of leadership development as a focus of her presidency. "It was one of the major things I worked on with Rabbi Kravitz," she said. "Adath has developed a lay leader-clergy relationship that we believe is unusually strong." Furthermore, the leadership is not selected based on financial contribution, but rather, on its talents, interests and a willingness to participate. "That says a lot for who we are," said Judy.

Of her experience growing up at Adath, Judy said, "I think when you grow up here you find it a place that is open and fair and encourages you to ask questions—and

Judy Cook

is there for you." Judy believes Adath prides itself on a culture of excellence. "We provide Jewish leaders to the Minneapolis and national communities," she said.

"We encourage adult education and glom on to you if you want to study," said Judy. "And we have a real culture of participating, of giving back. There are so many people who do so many little things for others. That's why I put my energy here—it's a really good community."

One challenge during her presidency was Rabbi Kravitz's sabbatical in Israel. "We worked very hard to set it up," she recalled. "We looked at the skill set of our leadership and matched it with the tasks at hand. We tried to prepare for any type of crisis and arranged for back-up help for Rabbi Brusso." As a result, the sabbatical went extremely smoothly.

"When I went on sabbatical in the spring of 2002, I felt the congregation was in a good place with Rabbi Brusso and the lay leadership. Everything went really well," agreed Rabbi Kravitz.

Like many former presidents, Judy has remained very

(Above) David and Renee Segal

(Right) Rabbi Kravitz with his wife, Cindy Reich, and their children Talia (left), Elana and Gabe

involved in congregational life. In 2007 she co-chaired the Educational Strategic Plan and in 2009 is helping work on the new strategic plan for the entire synagogue.

2004-2006

David Segal recalled a number of noteworthy events occurring during his board term. For example, inspired by Rabbi Eliot Dorf, a major thinker of the Conservative movement who served as that year's Numero-Steinfelt scholar, and by Rabbi Brusso's electrifying High Holiday *d'var Torah*, in 2004 Adath launched a Keruv ("bringing closer") committee. According to David, the congregation established the committee, chaired by Deborah Litman-Zelle, to make the gay and lesbian community feel more welcome. Discussions that started in the committee resulted in the Jewish community sponsoring a booth at Gay Pride weekend.

"The Keruv committee is about normalizing the gay and lesbian community," said Rabbi Brusso. "It's about recognizing a community need and filling it, especially given our mission as a progressive, egalitarian congregation."

Another "outreach" program was actually called "Inreach," explained David. Headed by Carol Bromer, a group of approximately two dozen congregants was trained and went out to visit hundreds of congregants in their homes. Its purpose was to create a friendlier congregation, build community, and identify concerns and interests of Adath members. The "visitors" shared their findings and insights with the staff and board.

Fall of 2004 saw the beginning of the L'chaim campaign,

replacing the annual Yom Kippur Appeal. Chaired by Heidi Schneider, it was a huge success. The campaign, now staffed by Bernie Goldblatt and Lauren Hoffman, and chaired by Scott Grossfield, is in its fifth year and has raised as much as $280,000 annually.

In September, 2005 Adath celebrated Rabbi Kravitz's 18th ("Chai") year as its rabbi. "The congregation decided to honor him with a Hesed Fair, knowing that was the kind of thing he would appreciate," said David. "The huge weekend celebration was very well received, with congregants as well as members of the wider Jewish and non-Jewish social action communities attending."

Rabbi Kravitz's friend and colleague, Rabbi Elie Spitz, served as scholar-in-residence. Eric Schockman, president of MAZON: A Jewish Response to Hunger, also attended, making a presentation to honor Rabbi Kravitz's years of service.

"Three Davids"—David Pink, David Orbuch, and David Segal—all sat on the executive committee. The Inreach project presented its findings. And a huge TAMID concert brought Itzhak Perlman to perform on the Adath bema.

"Another exciting event was the STAR foundation choosing Adath to participate in Synaplex, an initiative to bring Jews into synagogue on Shabbat by using creative programming," David Segal said.

Also during David's term, Susie Chalom retired to become executive director of Minneapolis Talmud Torah. While Adath began a strategic planning process to decide on educational needs and directions, Deborah Litman-Zelle took over at SMP and Janice Schachtman at the Gan.

Debby is a fourth generation Adath member who, like

ADATH CONGREGANTS

Ben and Reva Kibort

When Ben and Reva Kibort were looking for a synagogue to join in the mid 1950s, Reva wanted one she could walk to. Adath Jeshurun was a natural choice, because it was only a few blocks away from their home on 32nd Street and Irving Avenue. Holocaust survivors and struggling new Americans, Ben and Reva vowed that as soon as they were able, they would pay their full synagogue dues.

In 2008, with four generations of Kiborts at Adath—including two great-grandchildren at the Gan—Ben and Reva have been fortunate enough to create an endowment for children unable to afford Jewish camps, Israel programs or USY visits to Poland's concentration camps.

When their three children, Phillip, Pam and Gary, were young, Reva would take them Saturday mornings to the synagogue. Ben promised that when he no longer needed to work on Saturdays, he too would join them. Ben now attends Shabbat morning services weekly, still sitting in the same spot were the family has sat for approximately half a century. The building may have changed, but the relative location of their seats has not.

"We have always loved the Adath. It is a home away from home for us. Adath has been like a family for us," said Reva.

Ben and Reva Kibort

stint as the Adath's interim education director, Debby has served on and chaired numerous volunteer committees.

The congregation's education programs have always played a role in Debby's life. Among her teachers and mentors were the nursery school's "Miss Dolly" and Sunday school's Rachel Leavitt. When the opportunity arose, she felt it was her turn to give back to the "educational foundation" what she had received. And she hopes her daughters will continue to lead their communities, as have the generations before them.

During this period Adath also hired Lauren Hoffman to work as a part-time coordinator for L'Chaim and the fundraising arm of Tamid, freeing up Jennifer Spiller to devote her time to the Foundation.

2006-2008

When David Orbuch was chosen board president in 2006, he became half of the first-ever mother-son synagogue president duo. (His mother Joyce had served as president from 1989 to 1991.)

"I felt as president that it was an honor to lead the congregation and be able to support it in the way leaders did before me," David said. "There is the story of how a kid gets put on an adult's shoulders so that he can see the stage—that's what happened to me. I stood on the shoulders of previous Adath leaders and that gave me 125 years of a congregation that is one of the strongest in the U.S."

David had three goals he hoped to reach during his presidency. One was strengthening board leadership; a second was planning for the future by strengthening and deepening Adath's commitment to its clergy. The third was redefining the board's role to become more strategic, focusing on the spiritual and economic health of the congregation. "I spent a lot of time changing what the board did at meetings," David recalled. Under his new model, meetings became a forum for debating and discussing broad strategic issues, rather than for listening to committee reports.

As a result of an education strategic planning committee chaired by Mike Greenstein and Judy Cook, the board formed an education cabinet in 2007. "The board was intimately involved in setting objectives for how education played an integral role in our Adath community," David said. "We created a vision for education in our congregation and then aligned committee structures to meet our needs, creating program objectives."

"Because of the strength of clergy and the health of the congregation, there was no big crisis or issue during

the generations before her, was married and became Bat Mitzvah at the synagogue. Debby and her husband, Bob's, two daughters, Naomi and Alisha, also participated in SMP and became Bat Mitzvah at Adath. In additon to her

Education Strategic Planning Committee

In 2007 the Board created an education strategic planning committee to evaluate and re-envision Jewish learning. Chaired by Judy Cook and Mike Greenstein, the committee process included in-depth analysis of the synagogue's existing programs as well as discussions led by education consultants Dr. Rob Weinberg and Cindy Reich. In addition, nearly 100 congregants shared their thoughts on the role of education at Adath at a town hall forum.

In its final report, the committee presented a set of 15 recommendations that addressed specific programming needs. The committee recommended the creation of a Director of Jewish Learning position to oversee and coordinate all education programming throughout the congregation. Rabbi Lilly Kaufman was later hired for this position.

The committee also recommended a governance structure that would oversee and embrace the continuum of lifelong learning. To that end, the congregation was asked to amend the bylaws by replacing the Vice President of Ritual position with the newly created Vice President of Jewish Life and Learning, whose primary role would be to chair an education "cabinet." There are now four vice-presidents on the executive board with "education" as part of their portfolios.

The recommendation marked a significant change in Adath's board structure related to education and ritual, reflecting the growth of programming in those areas. As recently as 2003, one vice president member had chaired Secondary Education, the Youth Commission, and Adult Education. In 2004, a new vice president of Adult Learning position had been created.

my presidency," David continued. "It allowed me to focus on our strengths and to position the congregation for the future."

David enjoys having "hands-on" involvement with Adath. "I like the leadership role," he said, "but it's all about connecting with the congregation to learn from them." He likes working with youth and has been especially involved in the Gimel Family Service.

"I have been at Adath since my *bris*," David said. "Adath has given me so much and been so important in my life. It was where I hung out, made my friends, went to USY, acted in plays…Now it's where *my* kids went to the Gan, go to USY. My friendships, my education, my Judaism—it's all connected."

In his leadership role, David has been inspired by the example of Rabbi Kravitz. "Rabbi Kravitz's *neshama* is seen in everything he does, from his leadership on the bema to his work with our board of directors. He is fiercely dedicated to Adath Jeshurun and works extremely hard. During my time as president it often seemed that God gave him more than 24 hours in a day to ensure that we remain a dynamic and vibrant community that is spiritually and financially healthy. The Adath is a reflection of Rabbi Kravitz: strategic, compassionate and dedicated to *torah*, *avodah* and *gemilut hasadim*."

In 2006, Rabbi Kravitz became the Chairperson of the Rabbinical Assembly's Vaad HaKavod, the Committee for Professional Ethics which reviews cases of suspected misconduct and abuse among the rabbinate.

The Berman Family Chair in Jewish Learning

In the spring of 2008 Adath Jeshurun Congregation and the Adath Jeshurun Foundation announced the establishment of the Berman Family Chair in Jewish Learning, which assured the funding of a newly created Director of Jewish Learning position. Rabbi Lilly Kaufman was engaged to fill the new position, working with clergy, other educational professionals and lay people to oversee and coordinate Jewish learning at Adath Jeshurun across all ages.

Theresa Berman with Rabbi Lilly Kaufman

"The Berman Family Chair in Jewish Learning will bring us closer to realizing our educational vision for our congregation's future," said Rabbi Kravitz at the time of the endowment. "We feel blessed to have four generations of the Berman family in our congregation and for their lifelong commitment to Adath and our community. It is an honor to have our educational efforts linked to the Berman family name and thus ensure that what goes on inside the Nathan and Theresa Berman Family Education Center of the synagogue and beyond is maintained for the future at the highest possible level."

Over the years, Theresa Berman, her late husband Nathan Berman, and their family, showed their commitment to Jewish education in myriad ways. They were active participants in Adath's educational programs from the preschool level to adult learning opportunities. In 1983, they sponsored the Centennial Scholar-in-Residence, Rabbi Neil Gillman. In 1985 they endowed a Theresa and Nathan Berman Scholar-in-Residence Fund in the Adath Jeshurun Foundation to support visiting scholars to the congregation. Their generosity allowed Adath to welcome a multitude of outstanding scholars, including Rabbi Bradley Shavit Artson, Dr. Avivah Zornberg, and, in 2008, Noam Zion.

2008–

Six months into her presidency, Heidi Schneider reported she was excited by the events taking place at Adath.

One was the long term strategic plan on which the synagogue was embarking. "It's more of a re-visioning," Heidi said. "What is the future of the synagogue? We want to engage as many congregants as possible, hear what they think is important. It will be a very creative process. We have a lot of young, new members, and we want to make sure we meet their needs.

"One nice thing about being president is that I get to hear from people all the time. I hear them say we are warm and welcoming, and that they find Adath a place where they can fit in," she said.

"I myself was a transplant and also a Jew by choice," Heidi continued. "So this is very meaningful to me. It's about welcoming strangers and finding them a place to be involved, whether it's the Gan, or Hesed, or the Adult Learning Committee."

Heidi attributes that openness in large part to Adath's clergy. "They are completely committed to this. They are there for you and allow you to go as far as you will, to realize your potential," she said. Reflecting on Barak Obama's recent inauguration, Schneider said she would have laughed if someone had told her when she converted 17 years ago that she would one day become synagogue president.

Heidi is impressed with the talents of the Adath community. "I am continually amazed at the quality and depth of knowledge of our congregants, who are opinion leaders in the community at large," she said. "Another reason the synagogue is thriving is that our lay people are tapped by clergy on things such as financial and legal issues."

A highlight of Heidi's tenure thus far has been the arrival of Rabbi Lilly Kaufman in August, 2008.

Rabbi Lilly Kaufman

Rabbi Kaufman joined Adath as Director of Jewish Learning. She was also the first person to hold the newly endowed Berman Chair of Jewish Learning. A native New Yorker, she was ordained as a hazzan at Jewish Theological Seminary in 1998 and as a rabbi by the same institution in 2001. She has served as a pulpit rabbi at Congregation Tikvoh Chadoshoh in Bloomfield, Connecticut, for the past seven years. A graduate of Barnard College, Rabbi Kaufman worked in book publishing in New York for 16 years before returning to graduate school to become a cantor and then a rabbi.

Her special love is education for all ages. While at the seminary, she worked at a New York synagogue for five years helping to develop an adult learner's minyan on Shabbat mornings. In recent years Rabbi Kaufman enjoyed incorporating the arts into her teaching techniques at Tikvoh's Religious School. She takes special pleasure in seeing young people and adults develop their spiritual, critical, and ethical skills through the study of Torah, and converting ideals into action.

Rabbi Kaufman is a member of the Rabbinical Assembly and the Cantors Assembly of the Conservative Movement. She is a member of the Ethics Committees of both assemblies, and serves on the Publications Committee of the RA.

"As the newest staff person at Adath, " she said, "I am most impressed by the transmission of the values of decency, warmth, generosity of spirit, excellence, and lack of ostentation. In a synagogue as large as this one, it is rare to feel this combination of values in daily life, and at all levels of the institution.

"This is an energizing place, and it is part of my role here to help that energy grow! One only has to visit Gan Shelanu any weekday, stroll through 'the Pits' during the Shabbat Morning Program (SMP), borrow snacks from the USYers on Tuesday evenings, peek in on B'Yachad classrooms on Sunday mornings, observe our excellent Adult Ed offerings, note our many volunteer Torah readers, or sample the varied offerings of Synaplex and our Jewish Culture Sampler, to feel this positive energy. On this 125th anniversary of Adath, we know we will go *mihayil l'hayil*, from strength to strength!"

Top: Gan children on a field trip to the Minneapolis Public Library
Bottom left: Adath "Ruths" at the synagogue gather in the library for a photo after their *aliyah*
during the reading of the "Book of Ruth" on Shavuot. Everybody in this photo is named Ruth.
Bottom right: President Heidi Schneider with husband Joel Mintzer
and sons Asher and Isaac, on Asher's Bar Mitzvah

12
ADATH JESHURUN TODAY

From its roots in the bustling pioneer city of Minneapolis, Adath Jeshurun has grown to become one of the largest and most progressive Conservative congregations in the country, with more than 1200 households and a wide array of social groups, support services, and educational programs functioning alongside its deeply rooted ritual and spiritual practice. In addition to being welcome at minyan or Shabbat services, people are invited to participate in the myriad programs, classes and committees that together constitute "the Adath."

In the year 2009, Adath Jeshurun is a vibrant, thriving congregation. "We are more than a synagogue—we are a sacred community," said executive director Bernie Goldblatt. "I meet with every new congregant for an hour or more. I try to help them understand the value of being a member of our community, telling them about all the classes, the programs, the committees; about Hesed and Yad Sima Tova and the Chevra...They usually had no idea, and they are always amazed by the opportunities.

"I also tell them that when they invest their time and finances with us, that we bear a tremendous responsibility to value them and their resources. We try to provide recognition to both staff and congregants—that's what builds pride in community."

Bernie is quick to credit his staff: Rafina Larsen, finance director; Bob Simon, facilities director; Chris Yarger, office manager; and Beth Mayerich, food services director. "We're the 'back room,'" he said. "If we are successful, things run smoothly, and no one notices us. Satisfaction has to come from knowing that.

"Our staff members are people who innovate, and who mind the store," Bernie continued. "They make sure we are not spending more than we should and that we are bringing to bear the highest quality standards. If the finances and the facility are in good shape, then the clergy and teachers can concentrate on spirituality and community-building."

Current board president Heidi Schneider describes Bernie as the "behind-the-scenes guy who keeps our synagogue running smoothly." She credits him with in-

troducing new integrated software and data management tools to make the Adath office run more efficiently, and pursuing environmental initiatives that also save money. "Bernie takes greatest pride," Heidi added, "in his good relationships with our members and the synagogue staff. He makes sure the staff's day-to-day efforts are appreciated. He has devoted himself to enhancing Adath's communications with its congregants, including the increased use of digital technology and the design of Adath's beautiful website."

Bernie is a member of the board of governors of the North American Association of Synagogue Executives and in 2008 co-chaired its national conference.

THE ADATH FOUNDATION

Of all the accomplishments of the Board of Trustees under her presidency (1985-1987), the most important to Judy Goldstein was getting the Adath Foundation off the ground. In 1986, the board passed bylaws and articles of incorporation for the Foundation. Its mission is to endow the congregation to secure its well-being for this and future generations. But when the congregation set about raising funds for the new building, the Foundation essentially ended up on the back burner.

Tom Grossman served as the Foundation's president from January 1997 until May 1998. Under Grossman's leadership, the Foundation was rejuvenated. A minimum amount of $10,000 was established to open a new foundation account, foundation account record keeping was

Adath Foundation Board (Left to right) Front: Carolyn Abramson, Alan Gingold, Charles Newman, David Segal, Rabbi Kravitz, Carol Bromer. Middle: Herman Markowitz, Mike Greenstein, Rick Sieband, Doug Savitt, Mel Goldfein, Jennifer Herman Spiller. Back: Norman Pink, Joel Lifland, Bernie Goldblatt, Rabbi Brusso

improved, and several new accounts were established. Herman Markowitz took over the reins in 1998.

Each year, the Foundation grew. In July, 2003, the foundation hired Jennifer Herman Spiller as development director, and by 2004, there were more than 40 endowed funds and two endowed chairs, the Max Newman Family Chair in Rabbinics and the Leonard and Clara Savitt Youth Director Chair. Assets totaled $3,187,276. That year, Alan Gingold succeeded Herman Markowitz as Foundation president.

Roni and Alan Gingold have both been involved in a number of efforts to strengthen the programming as well as the financial backbone of the congregation. The couple met at a Bar Mitzvah at Adath and were married at the synagogue in 1997, while Alan was Foundation president. Along with Sue Oreck, Roni has also co-chaired the annual TAMID concert, with the goal of turning it into a major fundraiser.

"Growing up in Chicago and watching his family's synagogue cease to exist, Alan learned at a young age that no congregation's future is guaranteed," explained Roni. "We are both motivated to assist the Adath Foundation in its effort to assure the long-term future of our congregation. Participating in events at the synagogue and having our social life relate substantially to friends we met at Adath makes our congregation of central importance and a force for good in our life together."

On December 17, 2005, the Adath Foundation celebrated 18 years of commitment to our congregation's future by dedicating a Wall of Honor. The Foundation Wall of Honor was made possible through the generosity of Charles and Phyllis Newman in memory of his mother Gertrude Newman's 100th birthday.

By 2008 the Foundation had grown to more than $4 million. We now have 75 endowed funds and a total of three endowed chairs.

"The Foundation's success reflects an organization that is very healthy leadership-wise," said Rabbi Brusso. "People see it as backing a winner—we will do good things with it."

ADULT LEARNING COMMITTEE

Nina Samuels has been the staff member ably directing the Adult Learning programs since 1986. Says Paula Fox, an active committee member, "Nina's many years of experience as program director, combined with her great skill and effort, have greatly enhanced Adath's adult educational programming. Meetings of the Adult Learning Committee are fun; we take turns giving a *d'var Torah*, and the small group of 10 to 12 lends itself to interesting discussion. Members are very knowledgeable and address personal Jewish experiences as well as Torah.

"Nina discusses upcoming educational activities with

The Adath Chesed Shel Emes Cemetery in Crystal

Adath Jeshurun Congregation currently owns a cemetery located at 3800 Winnetka Avenue North, in Crystal, Minnesota. From its founding, the cemetery has been committed to providing a place for burial with dignity for Jewish families, regardless of their economic status.

This cemetery, originally known as the Independent Chesed Shel Emes Free Burial Society for the Poor, Inc., was incorporated on January 8, 1924. In 1924-25, Minneapolis suffered a diphtheria epidemic, and had the highest rate of this illness in the nation. The Jewish community was not immune. Among the earliest burials at the cemetery are children who died during these years. Their graves are near the back of the property. The first officers of the corporation were J. Shapiro, V. Finkelstein, A. Weisman, and S. Tolchinsky.

When the cemetery was incorporated, the location seemed distant from the Jewish community. Yet, the general location was selected by several Jewish burial societies to establish cemeteries. Thus, the cemetery's original property was next to other Jewish cemeteries, and over time these properties have combined.

In February 1967, the cemetery combined with Hertzl Memorial Park, and then changed its named to become the Chesed Shel Emes Hertzl Memorial Park.

The cemetery's property was also adjacent to the Workmen's Circle Cemetery Association. The Workmen's Circle was incorporated on July 15, 1933, and provided a means for laborers to make regular payments during their life in return for a right of burial. In June 1977, Chesed Shel Emes merged with the Workmen's Circle. The combined cemetery kept Chesed Shel Emes's name. At that time, Chesed Shel Emes was led by George Benowitz, and the Workmen's Circle by Samuel Bellman. Today, a sign designating the Workmen's Circle burial area remains on the property.

Perhaps because of its history, in recent years the Workmen's Circle area became a location of choice for the burial needs of the Jews who moved to Minneapolis from the former Soviet Union. Both the Workmen's Circle section, and now other parts of the cemetery, contain monuments written in Cyrillic, as well as in English and Hebrew.

Despite the recent merger between Chesed Shel Emes and the Workmen's Circle, the cemetery recognized its need to affiliate with a congregation. The cemetery's leadership was aging, and its Board of Directors believed that a congregational affiliation would ensure future leadership. On August 24, 1981, Chesed Shel Emes merged with the Adath Jeshurun Congregation. Harry Ostrow signed the merger agreement on behalf of the cemetery; and Norman Pink, then president of the synagogue, signed on behalf of Adath Jeshurun. While the cemetery has since been known as the Adath Chesed Shel Emes Cemetery, it has not been an independent entity since its merger with Adath Jeshurun.

The cemetery is presently adjacent to one other Jewish cemetery, the Beth El Memorial Park (which was incorporated on December 12, 1952). Beginning in 1987, the cemetery and Beth El agreed to work together in developing their properties, while also maintaining their separate status. As a result, the two cemeteries have adopted common development plans and removed a fence that once separated them. Jerry Zweigbaum, on behalf of the cemetery, provided this vision and leadership.

No history of the cemetery can be complete without also mentioning the decades of service by Samuel Bearmon. Sam led the cemetery for many years, provided legal advice, and emphasized the need to beautify the property. Today, the cemetery maintains a beautification fund in his honor. Hersh Berman has also provided decades of service, planning cemetery events and assisting families during times of memory. Following the merger, the cemetery has been under the successive leadership of Jerry Zweigbaum, Tom Wexler, Peter Cooper, Joel Mintzer, and Joe Lifland.

Today, the cemetery continues its commitment to provide a burial place for all members of the Jewish community, regardless of need. A recent significant gift by Robert Reznick has assured the cemetery's ability to provide indigent burials. In the last few years, the cemetery has added a new burial section and a large family burial area. It is in the process of re-grading the land, in order to accommodate future needs, and of planting more trees for the future beauty of the property.

the committee. The chair, currently Lon Rosenfeld, consults with Nina, and other members play more of a supportive role—brainstorming ideas, helping out at various events, baking refreshments for the Sampler, and more."

"Whenever we do adult learning," Nina said, "there is always a component of community-building. It's a chance to break down the big congregation into smaller groups where people can learn and connect face-to-face."

New adult study groups have continued to form. A downtown group meets weekly at lunchtime with Rabbi Kravitz. Rabbi Brusso leads a Heschel group. One group studying the weekly Torah portion started around 1996.

Another area that has continued in popularity is the Adult Bar and Bat Torah class. The class was developed to help congregants develop skills to be literate adult participants in the service. The year-long course helps members understand the parts of the service and prayers, and teaches basic Hebrew skills. Upon completion, the students celebrate becoming Bar and Bat Torah on Shavuot.

Other Hebrew language and culture classes include a Bible study group in Hebrew taught by congregant Sally Abrams, who teaches Hebrew at the Minneapolis Jewish Day School, and a modern Hebrew class, "Yanshufim," meaning "owl," taught by congregant Renana Schneller, a professor of Hebrew Studies at the University of Minnesota.

CHEVRA KAVOD HAMET

"In the balance of life, rarely are we given the opportunity to affect the life of another human being quite so deeply as at a time of their complete emotional vulnerability—the death of a loved one," said Bruce Nemer. "Performing the mitzvah of *shmira* (guarding the covered body before the funeral) for the Chevra Kavod Hamet of the Adath is one of those opportunities. I try to tell people that if they have not yet done so, they should not delay in putting their names on the Chevra list and volunteering the next time they are called.

"The often-repeated phrase is that you should join in the work of the Chevra because it is the mitzvah that no one can thank you for. However, this is just not so. I find that those few hours of mitzvah work is one of the times in your life that you will be, and feel, most thanked—aside from the birth of your children."

Jerry Zweigbaum was a charter member of the Chevra. He went on to become chair of the men's Chevra and participated in more than 80 *taharas* (ritual washing of the body). He conducted recruiting, training and public workshops on the important meaning of the Chevra service. To

THE ADATH YESHURUN CEMETERY IN EDINA

Adath Jeshurun Synagogue was incorporated in 1884 under the name A'Tas Yeshurun. At that time its founders deemed it necessary to establish a cemetery. Although there was a Jewish cemetery within the Minneapolis city limits (the Montifiore Cemetery), the city would not grant permission to establish another one. Land was therefore purchased on France Avenue, on the outskirts of Minneapolis. At that time the land was out in the country, though today it's in Edina.

In 1912 a separate corporation was established according to state guidelines and named the Adath Yeshurun Cemetery Association. Its funds were kept separate from those of the Adath Jeshurun Synagogue. It had its own officers and was managed independently of the synagogue. It had no legal association with the synagogue, and its bylaws did not allow it to mingle its funds with those of the congregation. Today it continues to operate as an independent entity, has no legal connection to our congregation, and still retains the original spelling Adath Yeshurun Cemetery. An interesting note is that a long-serving president of the Adath Yeshurun Cemetery, Morris Kantar, also served as president of the Adath Jeshurun Synagogue from 1932 to 1943.

the uninitiated, he explained the terminology and stressed the exceptionally holy nature of the acts performed by dedicated volunteers.

In a panel Jerry conducted on November 10, 1996, he spoke of the challenges he faced when he first became involved in the Chevra:

I was first approached about 20 years ago and was faced with fear about such intimacy with a deceased person. I agreed to be a shomer (guard) and six months

Clockwise from upper left: the Adath
championship baseball team, 1918;
the Maurice Kronick family;
Evelyn Cohen Siegel,
organist and choir member;
the Hershman children

later the new committee wanted me to do a tahara *with the team. I put my trust in the Chevra leaders and my fears were allayed. As a result of active involvement, I felt great personal gratification, knew a true religious experience, and participated in the ultimate mitzvah, because you can receive no thanks, as this is an anonymous act. I formed deep friendships and gained heightened respect for life and its fragility.*

Julie Kozberg is currently a Chevra volunteer. For 15 years she has been part of the Chevra on the first-call list for the women's *tahara*. "Participating in the *tahara* has had a huge impact on me," she said. "It is an amazing group of women."

These days, between six and 12 families a year use the services of the Chevra, which is co-chaired by Bruce Nemer and Cindy Dubansky. Bruce succeeded Max and Dinah Elkin, who chaired the Chevra with dedication for many years.

As for Enga, the Chevra's original partner, "like the new Pharaoh who arose and knew not Joseph, Enga was gobbled up by a conglomerate who did not know the Chevra," Nemer said. "We found a new connection with a family-owned mortuary, Washburn McReavy, who has treated us all with great respect and has been ever so marvelous in attending to our needs." Currently, a local cabinet maker constructs the *aronim*, or "plain pine box" caskets, according to the Chevra's design.

ETZ CHAYIM – ADATH'S ENVIRONMENTAL INITIATIVE

E tz Chayim, Adath's Environmental Initiative, was founded in 2007 in response to growing concerns about how we as a Jewish community should fulfill our responsibilities as stewards of God's world. In his Rosh Hashanah, 2006 sermon, Rabbi Kravitz presented several reasons Jews should make energy efficiency and the environment a much higher priority. Taking greater responsibility for the environment was a natural extension of a central Jewish theme celebrated on Rosh Hashanah—*Hayom Harat Olam*—that God is the creator of the world. Jews should also be motivated out of concern for the security and well-being of the State of Israel and the dangers to America posed by dependence on Middle Eastern oil.

Numerous members eagerly supported the formation of what is now called Etz Chayim—Adath's Environmental Initiative. Chaired by Carol Sarnat and Anne Trockman, the group's mission is to educate congregants about the Jewish tenets on environmental sustainability and stewardship. It provides the tools to help congregants evaluate and reduce

their energy consumption and waste generation. The organizers were pleased to see the extent to which Adath's Property Committee and staff had already been adopting environmentally friendly and cost-saving practices.

In December 2007, the Etz Chayim Initiative sponsored a Synaplex Weekend to raise environmental awareness and promote the use of CFL light bulbs as part of a campaign orchestrated by COEJL—The Coalition on the Environment and Jewish Life. The committee also held an educational event on the weekend before Tu B'shevat in February 2009. Encouraged by members Jonathan Shaver and Karen Yashar, this weekend was used to launch our synagogue's participation in Tuv Ha'Aretz, a program created by HAZON, an international Jewish environmental organization that fosters partnerships between Jewish congregations and community supported agriculture (CSA) farms to provide fresh local produce to members. Mike Jacobs, a Jewish farmer who manages Easy Bean Farm in Milan, Minn., delivered a *d'var Torah*, and at last count nearly a 100 Adath households have signed up for the program. This initiative also provides fresh produce to our neighborhood foodshelf, run by the Inter-Congregational Communities Association. The committee looks forward, through the effort of Debra Greenblatt, to having a bike rack installed at the synagogue to encourage alternatives to driving.

HEKHSHER TZEDEK

I t may have been Rabbi Kravitz's first YouTube appearance, but that didn't detract from the seriousness of the matter. In fact, it reflected a world-wide awareness of a pressing issue: the mistreatment of immigrant workers, as well as animals, at the Agriprocessors kosher meat plant in Postville, Iowa.

When Rabbi Kravitz spoke in front of Agriprocessors' gates in July 2008 as a representative of Hekhsher Tzedek, it was only the latest of his many efforts to extend social justice. "The *Forward* came out with an exposé, first of animal mistreatment, then of worker mistreatment. It was so scandalous," he said. "A group led by Rabbi Allen went to meet with the company, and were assured that the problems would be addressed." Rabbi Morris Allen urged the leadership of the Conservative movement to work with Jewish Community Action to create Hekhsher Tzedek, an initiative emphasizing the ethical dimension of Kashrut.

In May of that year the federal government raided Agriprocessors, arresting almost 400 undocumented workers. It was the largest immigrant roundup to date, and the

Music

first time such workers had been prosecuted rather than simply being deported. "It received enormous publicity," Rabbi Kravitz said. "After the raids, Cindy and I went down to Postville with Morris and our daughters. I wrote an e-mail about what we saw, and it went out around the world.

"The mission of Hekhsher Tzedek and the situation in Postville speaks to the values of our congregation," he said, "including our commitment to tradition and to being decent human beings."

Officially, the mission of the Adath Jeshurun Hekhsher Tzedek committee is to support and promote the principles and standards of the national Hekhsher Tzedek committee by increasing awareness of consumers and producers about Hekhsher Tzedek; encouraging kosher food producers to seek certification, now called Magen Tzedek; educating our congregation and encouraging its members to support these efforts; and participating on an inter-congregational committee to provide feedback and support on national initiatives.

The national organization is a shared effort between the Rabbinical Assembly and the United Synagogue of Concervative Judaism to display a seal on already-designated kosher foods that reflects production benchmarks consistent with Jewish ethical standards including wages and benefits; health, safety, and training; animal welfare and production; corporate transparency; and environmental impact. Hekhsher Tzedek also works with Minnesota's Jewish Community Action.

The seal ensures that not only are kosher products rooted in the proper Jewish methods of inspecting and slaughtering animals, but that the food is produced in a way that demonstrates concern for those human beings who are involved in its production.

HESED

"Lovingkindness endures forever." - Psalm 136:3

Since its inception in 1988, Adath Jeshurun's Hesed Committee has provided our congregation with dozens of programs exemplifying "grace" and "lovingkindness," common translations of the Hebrew word *hesed*. Involvement in the Hesed Committee is both within and beyond our congregation, and is seen not only as an obligation but also as an invaluable opportunity to rebuild community and repair our world.

The work of the Hesed Committee ranges from collect-

ADATH CONGREGANT

Marcia Cohodes

Adath has been a part of my life for as long as I can remember. I grew up at the building on Dupont Ave. where I attended pre-school, religious school and Talmud Torah. It was in this building that I was consecrated, had my Bat Mitzvah and was married. It was also through Adath that I mourned the loss of my parents and, through this experience, came to appreciate the sense of community our congregation offers.

My father died a few months after I had returned to Minneapolis in 1982 after living away for nine years. The synagogue was in transition, having lost Rabbi Goodman, and was in the process of interviewing for a new rabbi. I began attending the 7:20 morning *minyan*, where I prayed daily with the "regulars," many of whom had known my father through men's club and various committees at Adath.

After 11 months of daily *minyan*—including Father's Day, when my fellow morning *minyan* attendees all hugged me—Cantor Kula told me I was going to be honored with the first *aliyah* on Simchat Torah. I realized then how much that previous year had helped me through the grief process. I will always remember the support I received from the congregation.

Twenty-three years later, our children read from the Torah on Simchat Torah and the following Shabbat celebrated their B'nai Mitzvah—on my father's Yahrtzeit.

Marcia Cohodes, David Goldsteen and their children Aaron, Rebecca and Avi.

Clockwide from upper left: A celebration at the Adath; Earl Schwartz and Nina Samuels; Art Brand at a synagogue picnic; Adath congegants Roberta Hoffman, Linda Singer, and Estelle Kane; Martin and Esther Miller.

ing and donating items for food shelves to advocacy for the homeless, helping educate newly arrived Ethiopian Jews in Israel, and providing transitional housing for single mothers and their children in Minneapolis.

Under Rabbi Kravitz's leadership, in 1988 the congregation held a series of meetings to discuss the revival of the Adath Social Action Committee. The first decision was to broaden the goals of the committee and rename it the Hesed Committee. The committee embraced a mission that would "serve to coordinate and provide opportunities for acts of justice and lovingkindness within the synagogue and in our communities."

The group decided on a structure in which members would undertake specific projects based on their interests and on the group's perception of needs. The committee would serve as a forum for discussing and sponsoring those projects and would give its approval to those it considered worthy of Adath's support.

The first project proposed and approved by the board made the Adath a partner with MAZON: A Jewish Response to Hunger, an organization that mobilized the Jewish community's response to hunger among Jews and non-Jews, in the U.S. and abroad. Adath encouraged members to support the cause by urging them to donate 3 percent of the cost of simchas, such as weddings and B'nai Mitzvah.

The congregation also decided to support MAZON by charging an additional 3 percent at synagogue-sponsored events, such as congregational Shabbat dinners.

In 1989, a significant Hesed activity involved locating families to host newly arriving immigrants from the Former Soviet Union. The committee continued its involvement with STEP: St. Louis Park Emergency Program, collecting food and money for this organization which supplies groceries and services to those in need. STEP is the only area food shelf stocking kosher food.

The committee solidified a relationship with The Shelter Project at Our Savior's Lutheran Church, which continues to this day. Adath study groups, *havurot* and committees volunteer to prepare, deliver, and serve one meal a month at this shelter which serves about 30 people an evening.

The committee also decided to help provide meals to another food shelter, Loaves and Fishes Too, which involves serving dinner for 450 to 500 people.

In March, 1989, the committee added the Pushke Project, collecting money for a new beneficiary chosen each year. The first recipient was Passage Community. A specially designed *pushke* was made available to congregants to keep at home.

Over the years, the Hesed committee has formed liaisons with MICAH (Metropolitan Interfaith Council on Affordable Housing); Jewish Community Action; TOMER, a cultural identity center for Ethiopian Jews in Israel; Congregations Concerned for Children; Linda Weber Hesed Fund to Advocate for Families and Children at Risk; Nechama – Jewish Response to Disaster; West Metro Faith Communities in Action; and collaborations with JCRC on Avodah B'yachad projects.

One special Hesed project was collecting books from area synagogues to send to B'nai Israel Synagogue in California, which had lost thousands of library books to arson.

In 2001, Hesed had accumulated more than $10,000 in donations and decided to invest money in a local Community Investment Bank (CIB). These banks invest their money in local communities to improve living conditions and reinvigorate local economies. In May 2001, the Adath Foundation approved the establishment of a Hesed Endowment with the money to be invested in a local CIB. In 2002, $20,000 was invested in Franklin National Bank, primarily in the Whittier neighborhood of South Minneapolis. Half of the funds were provided by the Adath Foundation.

As of 2005, Hesed projects and alliances included Project Isaiah Food Drive on High Holidays, Minnesota Food Share Drive, Congregations Concerned for Children, Child Advocacy Network, Hesed Emergency Fund, JCRC Justice Squared, North American Conference on Ethiopian Jewry (NACOE), Joint Religious Legislative Coalition (JRLC), and Kehilat Yotzer Or (a Conservative community in an underprivileged neighborhood of Jeruselem). The committee also redesigned the Hesed brochure and created note cards to sell.

In 2006, new partners included Avenues for Homeless Youth in North Minneapolis and the Save Darfur Humanitarian Response.

In 2008, in the spirit of the Hesed committee, Rabbi Brusso began engaging the synagogue in an effort to generate concern about a livable minimum wage. "Clearly the current minimum wage does not meet basic needs," Rabbi Brusso said. "What do you need in the Twin Cities for food, housing, clothing, transportation, health care – just the basics, without savings or entertainment? It's closer to $12 an hour than the current $6.15. We decided we needed to look at that within the context of Adath workers, according to the principle of 'check out your own house before telling other people to check out theirs.'"

Hesed Committee chairs have included Harriet Kohen (first chair), Judi Tennebaum. Sheila Field, Steve Krikava, Barbara Rubin-Greenberg, Scott Grayson, Carol Bromer,

Weddings

ADATH CONGREGANT

Bruce Nemer

When I tell people I am a convert, I often get a surprised look, because my family is well known in the community to be Jewish. I then explain that I was born Jewish, but "converted to ritual." And I owe it to the atmosphere and culture of the Adath. Adath plays a role in my life as my true spiritual home.

I was raised in an intensely identified home, but not a ritually identified one. My maternal grandfather was one of those immigrants who rejected the ritual life of Poland but was a fervent Zionist. After my wife and family and I joined the Adath in the early 70s, we began our spiritual journey.

Without any knowledge of ritual whatsoever, I was very uneasy with the concept. However, the study groups we joined helped. The spiritual leaders of the Adath—rabbis and others—welcomed me without judgment and with open arms. The model I saw was one of people who were so comfortable with themselves and their Judaism that I wanted to become one of them.

The congregation itself was the last component. As I sat on the *bema* as a pulpit officer at our eldest daughter's Bat Mitzvah in 1976, I looked out over the congregation and noticed there were a lot of people who were "regulars" and whom I knew to be extremely nice people. On the way home that day, we decided that we wanted to know what they knew. So it happened that more than 30 years ago, we became "Shabbat regulars."

Ella Mogilevsky, and Paula Fox.

On November 12 and 13, 2008, Adath hosted a Minnesota anti-hunger summit initiated by MAZON and organized by the Legal Service Advocacy Project and other advocacy organizations. Eric Schockman, president of MAZON, addressed 110 hunger workers who attended from around the state.

Congregant Paula Fox said recently, "I became involved in the committee as a result of the Hesed Fair that was part of Rabbi Kravitz' 18th anniversary celebration. Since I work with children, I was interested in the Interfaith

Children's Advocacy Network (iCAN), at that time known as Congregations Concerned for Children.

"This committee is the special domain of Rabbi Kravitz, whose commitment to social action/social justice issues is commendable. Our major focus is on three areas—housing, hunger, and children. As part of the 125th anniversary activities, we hope to encourage more Adath members to participate in social action/social justice activities, giving of their time as well as their money."

INCLUSION COMMITTEE

Adath's Inclusion Committee began in February, 2003, chaired by Jeannie Gilfix, with Sharon Rosenberg-Sholl serving as staff liaison. The current chair is Marlee Kivens, and Rabbi Lilly Kaufman now serves as staff liaison.

Paula Fox has served on the committee since its beginning. "I have a dual interest, having a physical disability myself and working as a school psychologist with children with a wide range of disabilities," Paula said. "Shelly Christensen, program manager of the Jewish Community Inclusion Program for People with Disabilities, has met with our committee and shared her enthusiasm. She wrote a guidebook for evaluating the inclusiveness of organizations and institutions, and Adath was one of several congregations that piloted this manual. We considered both issues of building accessibility and program accessibility, as well as raising awareness and acceptance of people with disabilities."

The committee participated in the first National Disability Awareness month in February, 2009. Events included a community-wide film-showing and a *d'var Torah* relating to disability awareness.

"Working with Rabbi Kaufman has been a particular pleasure," said Paula. "In working with Marlee and me to discuss our *d'var Torah*, she engaged us in Torah study with great enthusiasm, drawing many relevant connections to disability issues."

INTERFAITH CONVERSATIONS PROJECT

The Interfaith Conversations Project (chaired at Adath by Harriet Kohen) is a program of the Jay Phillips Center for Jewish-Christian Learning in cooperation with Adath Jeshurun, Pax Christi Catholic Community of Eden Prairie and the Islamic Center of Minnesota in Fridley. The project was established in 2007 with the goal of learning about one another, building relationships, dispelling stereotypes and misunderstandings, and creating a strengthened sense of commonality among the three communities.

Top: Rabbi Morris Gordon and Adath Confirmation class of 1948.

Middle: (Left) Erwin Grossman and his family on his Bar Mitzvah; (Right) Merrily and Ronald Auerbach were the first twins to have a B'nai Mitzvah at the Adath, March 7, 1959.

Bottom: Norman Pink, Rabbi Kravitz, Rabbi Matsa and Dr. Howard Bach, *mohel*, at the *bris* of a Pink grandson Gabe.

Activities have included Sukkot dinners, learning sessions, visits to one another's places of worship, and living-room dialogue groups for ongoing sharing. At a joint service project hosted by Feed My Starving Children, a non-profit organization working to alleviate global hunger, an enthusiastic group of children and adults hand packed meals, which were then shipped to more than 50 countries.

In 2009 the name of the Jay Phillips Center for Jewish-Christian Learning was changed to the Jay Phillips Center for Interfaith Learning.

KEREN OR

Karen Siegel-Jacobs (1961-2001), daughter of Eileen and Jerry Siegel, grew up at the Adath. In 2001, at the age of 40, Karen died following knee surgery, leaving behind her husband, Matt, and two children, Allison and Zachary. To honor her memory, her parents established a permanent endowment in the Adath Foundation, the Karen Siegel-Jacobs Fund, and launched *Keren Or*.

Keren Or (Ray of Light) is an annual, refereed, creative arts forum to showcase the artistic talents of Jewish youth throughout Minnesota. Cash prizes, certificates, and publication in *The American Jewish World* are awarded in the categories of prose, poetry, and photography. At the conclusion of the contest, winners are recognized at an awards reception. Teens in grades 7-12 are encouraged to submit their entries for consideration each fall.

Through projects such as *Keren Or*, the Karen Siegel-Jacobs Fund preserves Karen's memory for a blessing and brightens the lives of others who follow in her creative path.

"When our daughter died unexpectedly, we felt that we had to find a way to channel our grief into something positive that would honor her memory," said Jerry and Eileen. "As a teenager, and even before, Karen had been a gifted writer, especially of poetry, and so we developed *Keren Or*, a creative arts contest for teenagers in our Minnesota Jewish community.

"Participation in the contest has grown each year and the awards banquet at the close of the contest has become a community event. We are deeply gratified to hear from the parents and students how affirming it is to have their creative efforts recognized and to know we are encouraging artistic activities that our daughter loved."

KERUV

The Keruv Committee's vision is to "bring close" individuals who feel they are on the margins of the Adath community. The committee focused initially on issues related to gays and lesbians within Adath, the Twin Cities and the Conservative movement.

The Keruv Committee has had a dual focus of education and action. Subjects have included the biblical and rabbinic sources regarding same-sex relationships, the importance of *halacha* in the Conservative movement, and the process of change in *halacha*.

One of Keruv's goals has been to help create a welcoming and comfortable space for gays and lesbians within the Adath community. For example, the congregation sponsored parlor meetings which offered gay congregants, their parents, siblings and friends the opportunity to talk about their experiences both at Adath and in the broader Jewish community.

The Adath rabbis have provided leadership and vision in the Twin Cities Conservative congregations by speaking openly of issues from the bema and in the community.

In 2008, the Keruv committee continued to work toward integrating and normalizing the synagogue experience for gays and lesbians within the Adath community. After the issuance of the *tshuvot* by the Conservative movement's Law Committee, Keruv invited members to meet with the rabbis and discuss the meaning and impact of the Committee's decisions. The movement decided that gays and lesbians are always welcomed as members, and it's up to each congregation to decide about commitment ceremonies. The committee asked the rabbis to continue the work they had begun to articulate a philosophy and policy regarding commitment ceremonies for same-sex couples.

In the future, Keruv hopes to consider other Adath constituencies who may feel marginalized, such as intermarrieds and the singles population.

PRIMARY EDUCATION COMMITTEE

The Primary Education Committee currently oversees all programming at Adath for families and children from birth through the 4th grade, according to committee Vice President Jeannie Gilfix. This includes the Gan (infant care through Pre-K classes); B'Yachad (Sunday school program for K through 2nd grade); and Havayah K'tana (for K through 4th grade families) run by Tamar Fenton. The latter is a special twice-a-month Shabbat

Congregational Life

learning program for children while their parents enjoy services in the sanctuary.

Noah's Ark Shabbat Service, where families with young children through age five are invited to a Shabbat worship service, takes place approximately one Friday night a month. This service is designed for the youngest family members with singing, stories and prayers of an appropriately short duration.

The Gimel Family Service is an interactive service with music for families on High Holidays and Synaplex Shabbatot. On major Holidays—Sukkot, Pesach, and Shavuot—grandparents or other special adults and young children are invited to attend L'Dor V'Dor programs.

Shabbat babysitting is also available.

In 2008, the Primary Education committee welcomed Rabbi Lilly Kaufman to oversee educational programming at Adath. Rabbi Kaufman also took on the directorship of the B'Yachad program while the Primary Education committee searched for a permanent program director.

"My family has been members of the Adath for over 60 years," said Jeannie, "and it is so rewarding to watch my children learn, grow and develop their own Jewish identities as they participate in and experience the same wonderful programs that I participated in as a child. I am honored to serve as VP of Primary Ed, and to oversee and support all the dedicated staff and volunteers who help to provide high-quality Jewish programming at the Adath.

"My profession is in the area of child and family mental health, and I am keenly aware of how important and formative a child's early years of development can be. It is highly motivating to me to participate in building a community that nurtures and supports families with young children, as they will be the future of our congregation, and of the Jewish community at large."

GAN SHELANU

Established in 1937 as the first Jewish nursery school in Minneapolis, the original Adath school was housed in the synagogue's building at 3400 Dupont Ave. In its early years the school worked closely with the University of Minnesota's Nursery School/Kindergarten/Primary Education Department, and won a number of awards as one of the top preschools in the area.

After the synagogue bought land in Minnetonka and built the Heller Kallah Center, the school was moved to the kallah center site. The new venue was more geographically convenient for the many young Adath families who lived in the Western suburbs. Although the kallah building was never constructed to house a preschool, nonetheless the program flourished. In 1979, the program became "Gan Shelanu (our garden) Preschool" —winning a coveted Solomon Schechter Award after its first year.

In its early years in Minnetonka, the school was open for morning classes and "extended day" childcare, closing by 3 p.m. every day. As more women entered the full-time workforce, the Adath Board of Directors eventually was convinced that Jewish childcare was a necessity, and the school day was extended to 5:45 p.m. Over the years, the school's registration grew dramatically, and five years after moving to Minnetonka, the school reached the building's capacity of 65 students.

In 1994, the Adath voted to build a new synagogue on the site of the Heller Kallah Center. The Gan relocated to the Talmud Torah building in St. Louis Park for two years, until the new building's completion. In August, 1996, the Gan moved to its present facility on Hillside Lane, with an increased capacity of more than 150 children. The new building afforded the Adath an opportunity to provide Jewish infant childcare beginning at six weeks of age—the only synagogue in the Twin Cities to offer this infant daycare.

Today the Gan has more than 125 children ages six weeks to five years old enrolled in its infant, toddler, preschool and childcare programs. During the summer, Camp Mishpacha is in full swing, with campers enjoying outdoor games, water play, nature activities, gardening projects and more.

At the Gan, children receive a variety of learning experiences within a Jewish context. The Gan's goal is to provide a first-rate early childhood program, compelling Jewish education, and identity-building programs. In addition, the school offers a series of parent education classes focused on Jewish topics. These programs encompass the latest knowledge from the early childhood education field, along with an added dimension – communicating Jewish values and attitudes to students and their families.

In 2007, the school launched a comprehensive family life education program to integrate the experiences of the students in the classrooms with their home and family observances. Taking a multi-generational approach, the material provides a "roadmap" for parents to build on their own family traditions and begin new ones.

Parents often describe how their child's first exposure to "formal" Jewish learning at the Gan inspired them to think about their own relationship to the Jewish community. The Gan provides families an opportunity to become "mini communities" that can endure long after their children graduate from the program.

Gan Shelanu

Janice Schachtman has been part of the Gan for more than 20 years. Her involvement at Adath Jeshurun began when, as a high school senior, she earned her first paycheck teaching Sunday school to first and fifth graders. Janice taught Sunday school through her college years and continued after her first child, Mindy, was born. She recalled teaching with a wonderful group of women, including "Miss Dolly" Rosenblum, Eileen Seigel and Sabine Amsel.

Janice Schachtman and friends at the Gan

Janice transitioned from being a Sunday school teacher to a "Gan mom." When Mindy was in kindergarten and her son, Michael, was three years old, Susie Chalom, Gan director at the time, asked Janice if she "would just help a few hours a week."

"I told her I would do it as long as Michael was in school," Janice recalled. "Michael is now 25!"

Janice became Gan director in 2008. "It's a labor of love," she said. "I'm passionate about the school, the synagogue and the wonderful people—staff and parents—I work with."

"It has been a wonderful staff over the years," she continued. "Many taught because it was a calling." Janice noted that the staff doesn't teach for the money, as there are better-paying jobs. You can have the nicest building in town but it doesn't mean much without the people," she said. "We try to create a community—not just with the kids, but with the families."

In addition to outside causes, "We try to enhance the continuity between what we are teaching about Judaism at the Gan and what the kids are doing and can do at home," Janice said. "What I learn from the kids every day is the greatest reward of all."

Rosh Hodesh: It's A Girl Thing!

"Rosh Hodesh: It's A Girl Thing!" is a program begun in 2001 by a national organization, Moving Traditions. The program is an informal, monthly celebration of the ancient New Moon (Rosh Hodesh) holiday. Established to build self-esteem, Jewish identity and leadership skills at an age when girls need empowerment skills, the program helps them to navigate the wider culture's risky messages.

"Rosh Hodesh: It's A Girl Thing!" started at Adath in 2004 with a group of 16 7th grade girls. Hana Gruenberg and Helaine Bolter served as group facilitators and continued with that first group through the girls' 11th grade year. Every year since, a group of 7th grade girls from the synagogue has created a new, ongoing Rosh Hodesh group.

Jewish institutions of all affiliations currently offer nearly 300 Rosh Hodesh groups across North America. Leaders participate in training sessions, receive manuals with program information and suggestions, as well as participate in monthly conference calls with other group leaders around the country. The Adath group typically meets once a month from September through May.

"We repeat the months every year, but we always look at it in a new way. We relate women in the Torah to our lives now. The group discussions and activities are fun and give us good strategies to use in our lives," said Alexis Fishman, who participated in the first Adath group.

Secondary Education Committee

In 2006, the Secondary Education Committee created a mission statement for the Shabbat Morning Program (SMP): to prepare our children for a lifelong commitment to Judaism and to reinforce positive Jewish identity through learning and service to the Jewish Community.

Todd Werner currently serves as vice president of Secondary Education. Among Todd's numerous contributions to ritual and learning at Adath are the years he has spent teaching Torah trope to adult congregants.

As it has done since its creation, SMP continues to prepare children, beginning in the fifth grade, for their B'nai Mitzvah through classes in ethics, prayer, Torah trope, individual tutoring and community building. The eighth grade teachers-in-training study ethics, leadership development, prayer and Torah skill building, and practical teaching skills. Teens in grades nine through 12 act as tutors. A weekly youth service provides students and tutors with

Top row: (Left) Arnold and Honi Cohen. (Right) Betty Kohn, Leslie and Bernie Goldblatt. Middle row: (Left) Mike and Sally Abrams and family. (Right) Dr. Tom and Liba Stillman, Amy Stillman and children. Bottom row (Left) Elaine and Ralph Kirshbaum, former Adath executive director. (Right) Ella Mogilevsky, Cantor Mort Kula and Etta Fay Orkin.

Top : Steve Schachtman, Irv Nudell, Mike Fiterman, and Ron Zamansky
at morning minyan during Chanukah.
Middle (Left) Adath tour to Israel (Right) Dancing the hora.
Bottom (Left) Adath tour to Israel visiting an underground cistern at Tel Sheva in 2005.
(Right) Adam Lurie at his Bar Mitzvah in Israel.

opportunities for leadership and skills development.

In the mid-2000s, Susie Chalom created a new SMP manual for the teen teachers. Popular annual programs and classes have included a Learner's Minyan for parents, a barbeque at the rabbis' homes, the fifth grade kallah, the sixth grade family kallah, and the teen staff kallah.

Mike Greenstein, who currently serves in the newly created role of vice president of Jewish Life and Learning, grew up at Adath and attended SMP as a child. He has taught in the program for more than 25 years, along with other congregants such as Risa Kessler, who has served for years as an administrator in the education department and tutored many of our B'nai Mitzvah.

"SMP is unique in that it's kids teaching kids," said Mike.

The layout of the Berman education wing is designed with kids in mind, with classrooms on the second floor surrounding the "pits." On Shabbat morning, kids spill out from the classrooms onto the steps of the pits, where teens tutor the younger children in prayers and Torah trope.

Despite having to tear down the kallah center to build the current synagogue, the Secondary Education Committee remains committed to kallot as a way for youngsters to share the Shabbat experience as a community.

About ten years ago, Joel Green implemented an ethics class as part of SMP. The "Trial of Abraham" was a popular annual event in his class. "These classes help make SMP more than just a Bar and Bat Mitzvah program," Mike said.

Also contributing to young peoples' religious training has been Don Masler. A recipient of the synagogue's Shem Tov award, Don has given unstintingly to youth education, in addition to leading services and helping out wherever needed.

In addition to SMP, the Secondary Education Committee oversees USY (there is also a Youth Commission), "Rosh Hodesh: It's a Girl Thing!," confirmation, and the kallah program.

SYNAPLEX

In the fall of 2005, Adath Jeshurun was invited to participate in a new and exciting program call Synaplex developed by STAR (Synagogue, Transformation and Renewal) a privately funded non-profit organization. Its objective is to "enable contemporary Jewish individuals and families to celebrate Jewish life through a menu of innovative options in the realms of prayer, study, social and cultural programs during Shabbat in the synagogue." Synaplex brings them together in Jewish "prime time" at the grassroots organization of the Jewish community that is in the synagogue on Shabbat.

The program was designed for a high-functioning, healthy congregation whose members may not be attending Shabbat services but who desire community and care deeply about choice, freedom to express themselves spiritually, and in joyful celebration.

Historically, the synagogue has been a Beit Tefilah, a house of prayer; Beit Knesset, a house of meeting; and Beit Midrash, a house of study. Synaplex revitalizes that tradition for the 21st century by emphasizing all of these meanings concurrently. Even though the Adath had already started innovative Saturday programs, Synaplex provided support material to "help us do what we were already doing—only doing it better," said Nina Samuels. The Synaplex model provided the venue for worship, gathering and learning with coordination shared by Rabbi Kravitz, Rabbi Brusso, Nina Samuels, and a number of visionary co-chairs.

Planning for this program began in the winter of 2006, and the first Synaplex Shabbat took place 18 months later, in the fall of 2007. Ellen Sue Parker and Chris Bez, along with their committee and a myriad of volunteers, ran six very successful programs through the spring of 2008.

Jill Orbuch was then hired as the Synaplex coordinator. Chris Kellogg and Carrie Lifland became co-chairs and continue to work with Rabbi Brusso, Nina Samuels and other staff and weekend co-chairs, to develop new and stimulating ideas for this highly successful concept.

Nina said, "To me the most satisfying result of this program is seeing new leadership emerge. I now realize the depth of talented, enthusiastic, creative individuals that we have in our congregation." A result of this new program is that congregants are forming new bonds with other congregants that they may not have known before. Whether one participates in a literary discussion, a gourmet experience, a mind/body/wellness

Ellen Sue Parker, first Synaplex co-chair

session, a bible study group, or by attending the Shabbat service in the sanctuary, Synaplex is revitalizing our Shabbat for the 21st century. "Ellen Sue Parker's vision is still a large part of Synaplex. She is the motivator, the visionary—the one with a special flair who, along with Chris

Top: Rabbi Kravitz inducts Adath Board members
Middle: (Left) Adath Sisterhood Tree of Life artwork;
(Right)Adath staff members Rafina Larsen, Nina Samuels, Lauren Hoffman (seated), Chris Yarger, Tobi Cooper, Bernie Goldblatt.
Bottom: (Left) Food Services staff Heather Tipper and Beth Mayerich; (Right) Facilities staff: Bob Simon, Joan Ehlers, Ed Ramires,
Cathy Parmalee , Gregg Parmelee, Scott Jacobson, Mauricio Cortes

Bez and our professional staff, have set high standards for the Adath," said Nina.

"With innovative programs such as Synaplex, we will continue to be regarded as one of the outstanding Conservative congregations in the United States."

In 2009 Synaplex continued to explore new themes and be responsive to the congregation's interests. Most popular emerging "new traditions" include the Gimel Family Service, Spiritual Yoga, and the Coffee House.

TAMID

TAMID is an acronym for Theater Arts Music Israel Dance. It has continued to flourish under the leadership of Hazzan Buckner. The program was aided by a major contribution from Charles Newman, who saw it as an "opportunity to bring in money and to put the synagogue on the highest possible pedestal." The musical program, which has showcased such noted artists as Yitzhak Perlman and Art Garfunkel, has enhanced the synagogue's standing both in the Twin Cities and nationally, raising funds for the congregation and providing entertainment for the wider community.

Another significant concert was "Three Jewish Tenors": Alberto "Abe" Mizrahi, Jacob "Jackie" Mendelson, and Scott Buckner. They were accompanied by Linda Hall Gerson, assistant conductor of the Metropolitan Opera, in a concert of Jewish and classical music in the style of "The Italian Tenors." Other recent concerts have included "Mandy Patinkin in *Mamaloshen*," "An Evening with Marvin Hamlisch," and "A Magical Evening on Broadway" featuring Mike Burstyn.

In 2007 the congregation implemented a new structure—a general TAMID committee and a TAMID Annual Benefit Committee, which plans and coordinates the main concert/event of the year. Recent TAMID chairs include Ron Usem, Barbara Parks, and Roni Gingold.

THE ADATH WEBSITE

Adath established a website at www.adathjeshurun.org in 2000. Overseen by "webmaven" Matt Gilfix, the site received a Solomon Schechter Gold Award at the 2002 United Synagogue Biennial Convention. In 2008, under the leadersip of Bernie Goldblatt, the congregation redesigned the website with consultant Heidi Dibble. Weekly e-mail blasts provide members with quick access to "breaking" news at Adath.

YAD SIMA TOVA

In 2003 Rabbis Harold Kravitz and Aaron Brusso asked Susan Himmelman Shapiro and Julie Kozberg to co-chair a committee to develop new ways to reach out to the older adult members of the Adath Jeshurun community. No name was given to this committee: organizers decided to wait until the true focus was determined. The two chairwomen, with the assistance and guidance of Jim Sherman, Rabbis' Associate at Adath, developed several new programs of outreach and readied a plan.

Tragically, Susan Himmelman Shapiro was killed in a car accident during the summer, and the visionary, committed, creative ideas she brought to the table were taken away from us. To continue the work, Julie Kozberg asked Fay Kaye to become her co-chair, and planning moved forward.

Knowing how important this work was to Susan, the committee decided to honor her memory by naming it after her. Taking her Hebrew name, Sima Tova, the official name became Yad Sima Tova: Adath's Caring Community. Since the word *yad* means both hand and monument or memorial, it feels as though the "hand of Susan Himmelman Shapiro" is truly invested in this work, serving as a fitting memorial. "It's a reminder to me of Sue's vision," Julie said.

Today Susan's vision is healthy and strong, and a valuable asset to the Adath community. A recent development has been the Congregational Nurse Program staffed by Deborah Jewett through Yad Sima Tova, with funding assistance from JFCS, NORC, and most recently, the Mt. Sinai Community Foundation.

Yad Sima Tova now provides transportation to Adath services and synagogue events. Volunteers visit homebound congregants, enabling them to stay connected to our community. An annual Chanukah Party and a monthly Ma'ariv service and program are provided for the residents of Knollwood Place Apartments. A volunteer for Yad Sima Tova arranges for leaders of monthly Kabbalat Shabbat services at Jones-Harrison Residence and Sholom Home West. Meals are made available when desired to those who are ill or returning home from the hospital.

The synagogue suggests that families celebrating a sim-cha add a donation to their catering costs to allow Yad Sima Tova to purchase a kosher dinner. Grief support through personal contacts is available to those who have lost a loved one, and a healing service is available upon request, providing comfort and prayer for those recovering from an illness.

Paula Fox recently said, "What stands out in my memory of Adath is the personal connections and sup-port, both in happy times and sad. For instance, when we had a baby naming for our daughter in 1982, Rabbi Goodman and others commented on how beautiful she was. More recently, during my severe illness, my hus-band and I got so much support from Adath—visits from clergy and friends, a healing service, meals from Yad Sima Tova. I truly had the feeling that this was my family, and they cared."

YOUTH DEPARTMENT

Youth group programming for children and teens in grades 5-12 falls under the purview of the Youth De-partment. The largest component is USY (United Synagogue Youth), for high school students in grades 9-12. USY was started in three Twin Cities Conservative synagogues more than 60 years ago with a few dozen high school students. Today it has more than 440 chapters spread across all of North America. Adath is a member of Emtza Region USY, which extends from Winnipeg to Denver and St. Louis, covering 11 states and one Canadian province. Each year, USY holds three major regional conventions and one inter-national convention. Adath historically has sent the largest delegation from Emtza Region to each event.

USY and its feeder programs—Kadima (grades 7-8) and Maccabees (grades 5-6)—provide the opportunity for young Adath congregants to participate in synagogue life and the larger Conservative movement. Teens can take ad-vantage of programming at the chapter and Twin Cities levels, as well as at regional/international events includ-ing summer programming in the U.S., Europe and Israel. For many teens, the USY Pilgrimage programs provide an initial trip to Israel, forging a lifelong spiritual and emo-tional connection.

Weekly programs planned by an Executive Board of 10 USYers, under the supervision of our full-time Youth Director, support the overall goals of informal education as well as Israel awareness, social action, and, of course, lots of socializing to build our community of teens. Over

ADATH CONGREGANT
Sara Chelstrom

Sara Chelstrom has been a member of the Adath community all her life. To Sara, Adath is a "place of belonging." "Adath has always been there for me, and sometimes I've needed it more than other times," says Sara. This was especially true 14 years ago, when Sara and her husband, Marty, had a baby girl who died at birth. Rabbi Cytron's words of comfort "had an impact not just for me," said Sara, "but for Marty, who was not born into the Jewish faith."

Sara describes Adath as a place that connects her to her roots. "I have ties to Adath and it has sentimen-tal value because I'm a fourth generation 'Adathee,'" she says. Sara recalls going into the Adath kitchen with her grandmother, Ruth Stillman. She remembers what an honor it was for women to be asked to pour tea at onegs. She also has fond memories of the Shabbat Morning Program, the Purim carnivals, and High Holi-day services. She wants to establish this sense of be-longing and comfort for her own children, Carly, Grant, and Macey. Sara enjoys seeing the continuity of the next generation connecting to Adath. "Now my mom knows all of the women in the kitchen," she said. "And now my kids go back there with their grandma."

the years, Adath USY has been recognized within the re-gion for outstanding social action programming, member-ship levels and the most creative scrapbook. Through all of our programming, we strive to meet the larger objectives of giving the kids a comfortable home in the synagogue as well as preparing them to take an active role in the Jew-ish community as adults. For those who wish, leadership opportunities abound. Adath USY has always had strong representation on regional and international executive and general boards.

Within the congregation, the Youth Department is most visible through two events that serve both as fundraisers and highly popular programs for the Adath community: the annual musical and the Purim Carnival. More than 50 young people are involved in each of these events, carrying on longstanding Adath traditions in which many of their parents were involved as teens. Many USYers are also involved in the weekly SMP program, tutoring younger children in synagogue skills, just as they were tutored themselves. It is through these relationships, as well as through participation in Maccabees and Kadima, that younger children become involved, anticipating the day when they will become USYers. It is *L'dor va Dor* in action.

The Youth Commission, which typically has about 15 members from the congregation, advises the Youth Director and helps execute the larger events during the year. We have served as a model for other synagogues with our hands-on involvement.

In the larger Jewish community, Adath USYers have been visible through their volunteer efforts, such as Super Sunday, leading services at Sholom home, and volunteering at Jewish Family and Children's Services and helping out at their annual benefit.

When USYers come together to celebrate Shabbat, an indescribable energy fills the space. During those services, as well as regional events hosted by Adath, the community is offered a glimpse into the spirituality of these teens when

PRESIDENT HEIDI SCHNEIDER
ON RABBI KRAVITZ

"I agreed to serve as president because of Rabbi Harold Kravitz. Many of us in leadership positions at Adath jump at the chance to work closely with him. He is a *mensch* and a great mentor. He has a special ability to identify future leadership in the congregation and to teach lay leaders how to take on important roles on committees and in synagogue governance. Rabbi Kravitz has a strong vision for Adath—one rooted in Jewish values, a deference to Adath's history and culture, and strategic insight into the best ways to embrace change. His dedication to *tikkun olam* through social action and to love of Israel are values he models for the entire congregation.

"Rabbi Kravitz has a national reputation as a rabbinic leader. I had the pleasure of visiting the Jewish Theological Seminary with him and the co-chairs of the rabbinic search committee. There we heard again and again from both students and Rabbinical Assembly leadership that they also turn to Rabbi Kravitz as their mentor, esteemed advisor, visionary leader, and ethical compass. I was immensely proud to hear how much Rabbi Kravitz is valued by his peers, as well as his congregants."

they hear hundreds of voices praying together, singing *z'mirot*, and "*benching*" Birkat HaMazon, along with the accompanying hand motions which have been developed over the years.

A duck has served as our mascot for so long that we cannot recall when he came "on board." Our Chapter song ("Adath, Adath, that's our cry....") is typically followed by a rousing rendition of "Oh, when the Ducks come marching in...." The smiles on their faces as they sing and tell jokes that only USYers would find funny (maybe because only they would understand them) indicate the sense of belonging and community-building that we strive to achieve.

We see the fruits of our labor and the long-term positive effects of Youth Department programming year after year as USY alums return "home to Adath" during college breaks and after they are married, participating in Shabbat services, attending synagogue events, serving on the Board of Trustees and in committees, and simply enjoying each others' company. It is not unusual to see groups of adults paging through old scrapbooks in the Youth Lounge, recalling with fondness their days in Adath USY.

Philip Sherman has been a member of Adath for 15 years. Currently a rabbinical student, Philip was president of Adath USY in 2000-2001 and Emtza regional president in 2001-2002.

According to Philip, the synagogue, and particularly USY, provided him with a Jewish community on a daily basis. His involvement helped establish friendships, provided the opportunity to take on leadership roles, and made it financially easier to attend summer camp and visit Israel. "Adath allowed me to see the best in Conservative Judaism," he says. "Wherever I go with my life and future family, it will be modeled in light of the Adath."

Andrea Lear was an active member of Adath USY throughout her high school years. She held many positions, from communications vice president to president. "My involvement with USY allowed me to explore my Judaism in creative ways. It also gave me the opportunity to develop leadership skills in a positive environment," Andrea said.

As a result of her experience in USY, Andrea continues to be involved as a USY staff member and has decided to pursue a career in informal Jewish education as the Programming and Development Coordinator at Herzl Camp. "Adath served as my foundation by providing me with spiritual, educational and social outlets for exploring my Judaism," Andrea said. "I want to make sure the young members of our community have these opportunities as well. This is why I continue to do what I do."

WOMEN'S LEAGUE

Since 1882 (before the founding of the Adath itself!) women's organizations have made significant contributions to the Adath community. In 2009, the Women's League celebrates 90 years of affiliation with the National Women's League for Conservative Judaism. A highlight of the Women's League is baking and selling hamentaschen for Purim each year. The group also publishes the annual congregational calendar and provides Kiddush cups and candlesticks to the Bar/Bat Mitzvah children.

The League continues to support the synagogue with a variety of activities, typically making annual gifts to the Torah Fund, Jewish Theological Seminary, Jewish Braille Institute, American Red Cross Disaster Fund, Hillel, MAZON, Howie Stillman Fund, JFCS Hanukkah Fund, STEP, Emtza Region USY, and

Women's League past presidents including: (front row, left to right) Polly Braunstein, Rose Zimmerman, Grace Besner, Dena Pink, Ruth Bender, Lil Gross; (back row) Rhoda Jaffe, Pam Brin, Harriet Sherman, Ardis Wexler, Raleigh Brand.

Gan Shelanu (Tree of Life event).

Book clubs, *mikvah* visits, and an annual bingo party for seniors at Menorah Plaza are a few of the other ongoing activities of this active group.

From its origins in the pioneer community of Minneapolis, Adath Jeshurun has become one of the preeminent Conservative congregations in the United States. Its character has been shaped by the personalities of its rabbis, its strong lay leadership, the ethos of the region in which it developed, and the countless initiatives and events that make up the fabric of its history, a few of which are chronicled in the pages of this book. Adath Jeshurun has transformed itself more than once in response to new challenges and circumstances, searching for new and more effective ways to sustain the values of a progressive, egalitarian and sacred community, dedicated to *Torah, Avodah,* and *Gemilut Hasadim.*

As Adath Jeshurun Congregation completes its 125th year, there is a sense of continuing vitality and participation. "The Conservative movement is said to be aging," Rabbi Kravitz said recently. "But at Adath, the age of the congregation has gone down significantly. We have half the student body of Talmud Torah."

"We are a nice size—there are so many opportunities for people to find a group," said current president Heidi Schneider. "We have a great staff, ideas from congregants are always welcomed—it's a very creative place to be. Our values are in the right places. It makes me proud to be the president—we are a highly functional organization and that bodes well for the changes we are likely to make. I am excited to be president during the 125th anniversary celebration, so that I can help focus a portion of it on looking toward the Adath of the future. I am very optimistic about where we will go."

Top row (Left): Saul, Lena, Melvin and Louis Sinykin. (Middle): Sally G. Neff. (Right): Max and Lena Graceman
Middle row (Left): Stillman Family. (Right): Ruth Libman and Zelda Epstein
Bottom row (Left): Sophie Burnstein. (Right): U. S. Vice President Walter Mondale, Bill Aberman, and Jules Levin

Top left: Rabbi Goodman and Cantor Amsel, Confirmation class in 1970s
Top right: Dr. Milton Orkin and daughter Aimee
Bottom: The sanctuary at 3400 Dupont Ave. during a wedding

Top: The Orbuch family including two Adath presidents, Joyce Orbuch (front row center) and son David Orbuch (second from left, top row)
Bottom left: Neal Gendler and Margie Wasserman and sons Jason and Aaron on Jason's Bar Mitzvah
Bottom right: Cindy Goldfine with daughter Ellie, grandson, and mother Harriet Davis

Top Left: Adath's first annual "Hat Day" honoring congregant Ella Chester, who always wore hats to shul.
(Back row, left to right) Daughter Perci Chester, Fay Kaye, Sarah Moscovice, Ella Mogilevsky, Ann Hofkin, Sylvia Fine, Kari Chester, Ruth Elias, Anat Bar-Cohen, Judi Tennebaum, daughter-in-law Lili Chester. (Front row) Rani Halpern, Carol Bromer, Edja Latarus, grandson Marty Chester, honoree Ella Chester, Naomi Oken.
Top Right: Four generations of Kane family: Dorothy, Merle, Gail, and Sophie
Middle Left: Three generations of Davis women. Grace Davis, Grace Besner, Sheila B. Davis
Middle Right: The Dorothy and Norman Pink Family
Bottom Right: The Abramson family: Carolyn Abramson, Mayer and Rae Blicker, Paula, Burt, Jody and Marty Abramson

PEOPLE INTERVIEWED FOR THE FIRST 100 YEARS SECTION BY ETTA FAY ORKIN

Beatrice Cohen Abrams, Gertie Abrams, Cantor Morris & Sabine Amsel (video), Rabbi David & Bertha Friedman Aronson, Phyllis Beskin Bearman, Sam & Ruth Bender, Dr. William Bernstein, Stella Gordon Birnberg, Howard Brin, Raleigh Gross Cable, Harold Chucker, Ruth Davis, Harriette Friend Fingerman, Leo Frisch, Julius & Ethel Goldman, Louis & Ann Goldstein, Rabbi Arnold M. Goodman (video), Bernice Cowl Gordon, Dorothy Davis Gordon, Rabbi Morris Gordon, Rabbi Theodore H. Gordon, Leo & Lillian Gross, Maurice & Margie Grossman, Dr. Samuel & Josephine Hechter, Gazella Kanter, Lillian Krelitz Kaplan, Thomas & Etta Miller Kaplan, Jacob J. Liebenberg, Joan Lipnick Abelson, Hiram & Josephine Sinaiko Mendow, Gerald "Sonny" Miller, Dr. David & Dena Marcus Pink, Norman Pink, Rabbi Stanley Rabinowitz, Esther Schanfield Rosenbloom, Dr. Sidney Scherling, Eddie Schwartz, Charles Shapira, Harriet Sherman, Evelyn Siegel, Sophia Singer, Reva Ziff Stern, Ruth Brockman Stillman, Helen Grouse Winer, Rabbi David Younger, Rose Selcer Zimmerman.

OTHER INTERVIEWEES AND THE INTERVIEWERS

Beatrice Auerbach, Morris Besner, & Stanley Kronick (interviewed by Goldie Wilensky); Harold Bernstein (by Francis Stesin); Irving Brand, Louis Cohen, Jerome Fischbein, Saul Meyers, and Ellis Peilen (by Ruth Peilen); Sim Heller (by Charlotte Scher Kula); Rhoda Neimark Jaffe, Esther Katz, and Pearl Pearlman (by Naomi Rotenberg); Cantor Morton Kula and Al Meirowitz (by Nancy Brown); Jules Levin and Irving Nudell (by Harriet Kohen); Jacob Mirviss (by Carmi Pollock); Rabbi Stanley Rabinowitz (by Dr. Sidney & Jeanette Naftalin Scherling); Linda Grossman Schibel (by Margie Grossman); and Emma Wolfson (by Gail Wolfson Goldstein).

THOSE WHO CONTRIBUTED WRITTEN MEMOS, PHOTOS AND ADDITIONAL INFORMATION

Arnold "Bill" Aberman, Rabbi Mendel Abrams, Dr. Burton and Carolyn Blicker Abramson, Ruth Bank Abramson, Ruth Hodroff Abry, Sophie Album, Betty Farkas Ansel, Sally L. Appelbaum, Genevieve Goldblum Barnett, Helen Kanter Beaubaire, Daniel Berdass, Fred & Margo Berdass, Jeff Berdass, Rhea Gass Berman, Shirley Zimmerman Beugen, Sue Rosenbloom Black, Shirley Bob, Rabbi Steven Bob, Arthur & Raleigh Brand, Polly Braunstein, Ruth Firestone Brin, Pam Brin, Fanny Burnstein, Harriette Goldstein Burstein, Elizabeth Peilen Cahane, Audrey Capman, Rudy & Miriam Charney, Burton Cohen, Pauline Weise Cohen, Rabbi Barry Cytron, Sheila Besner Davis, Dr. Burton Diamond, Norman Dockman, Zola Dockman, Dr. Evan Ellison, Beverly Wexler Himmelman Fink, Israel D. & Paulette Fink, Barbara Pink Fishman, Edythe Fleisher, Judy Sigel Freeman, Charles Frisch, Rabbi Stanley Gerstein, Blanche Goldberg, Louis Goldenberg, Gail Wolfson Goldstein, Etheldoris Stein Grais, Jill Sigel Greer, Sanford "Bud" Gruenberg, Erwin Grossman, Rose Rosenfield Hecker, Frank & Eva Herschman, Judith Brin Ingber, Betty Gross Jonas, Lois Josewich, Dorae Kaner, Dr. Bruce Kanter, Harmony Slater Kaplan, June Schwartz Kauffman, Marilyn Karasov, Raleigh Grossman Karatz, Dr. Markel & Charlotte Karlen, Abraham & Naomi Berman Kastenbaum, Eric A. King-Smith, Cecil Rosen Kiperstin, Norman & Ruth Brin Kirschner, Valerie Pink Evans, Betty Jane Kremen, Kathie Kremen, Jean Olesky Ladin, Shirley Mae Epstein Lane, Reva Segal Lear, Mort Levinson, Rachel Gross Levitt, Rhoda Greene Lewin, Adelle Lieberman, Hinda Litman, Michael Loring/Sam Mirviss, Francelyne Oppert Lurie, Mark Luther, Sandra Fink Mandel, Sybil Wolk Marbestone, Rabbi Howard Mark, Rabbi Herschel Matt, Rabbi Clifford Miller, Martin Miller, Rabbi Abraham E. Millgram, Sally Kirschner Minsberg, Cheri Rappaport Morgan, Ella Mogilevsky, Betty Kozberg Rappaport Nathanson, Florence Nathanson, Maxine Siegel Nathanson, Burton & Annette Herschman Neff, Alan Neuwirth, Daniel Neuwirth, Joyce Dechter Orbuch, Dr. Bruce A. Orkin, Sandra Lieberman Okinow, Edward Orenstein, Melvin Orenstein, Catherine Orkin Oskow, Marjorie Ellison Papermaster, Ruth Peilen, Jay Phillips, Jessica Rappaport-Hattis, Julie Rappaport-Liberman, Golde Rappaport, Belle Woolpy Rauch, Gertrude Zimmerman Ravitz, Judith Ribnick, Renee Jacobs Ribnick, Sydney & Bea Rich, Shirley Smiler Rivkin, Sybil Robinson, Dr. David & Joyce Sklamberg Rosenbaum, Amos Rosenbloom, Judge Noah Rosenbloom, Phyllis Fruchtman Rosenfield, Sue Rubel, Lois Hechter Rutman, John Salisbury, Marlene Berkman Salkin, Hy Sandler, Rose Schwartz, Russell & Sylvia Harris Schwartz, Dr. Sheldon Segal, Sophie Herschman Segal, Maurice Selcer, Ruth Seltz, Marion Stillman Shapiro, Dr. Stanley Shapiro, Louis Shore, Lorraine Segal Shrell, Saralee Shrell-Fox, Sue Shrell-Leon, Dr. Melvin & Delores Kaner Sigel, Susan Sigel-Teboul, Maxine Goldie Smiley, Samuel Smilow, Lena Singer Sinykin, Louis S. Sinykin, Dr. Melvin B. & Julianne Harris Sinykin, Mary Spector, Rosalind Engler Steinfeldt, Dr. Thomas Stillman, Phyllis Stillman Sudit, Peter Sussman, Marsha Gaviser Tankenoff, Sophie Teener, Rodney Schanfeld Wallace, Dorothy Weiner, Connie Grossman Wilensky, Marjorie Cohen Zats, Jerry & Sharon Chernoff.

Anne Orenstein

Dorothy Gordon

Barry Krelitz

Bea Adams

Bill Saltzman

Arnold and James Grais

Edith Linoff Edelman

Charles Shapira

Lillian Krelitz Kaplan

Harold Chucker

Millie Stillman

Sidney Sherling

Josie Hechter

Dr. Sam Hechter

Harriet Sherman

Jeanette Sherling

Jack Liebenberg

Judith Rachel Gordon

Leo Frisch

Raleigh Cable

Jacob Mirviss

Ruth Davis

Ruth Abry

Russ Schwartz

Syd Rich

Stella Gordon Birnberg

Sonny Gerald Miller

Margie Grossman

Morrie Grossman

Ruth Kronick

Leo Gross

Lil Gross

Howard Brin

Stanley Kronick

Sam and Gertie Abrams

Adath Jeshurun Leadership

Senior Rabbis

1884-93	Aaron Herman Sinai	1912-27	Rabbi C. David Matt
1887-88	Michael Jeffrey	1927-29	Rabbi Jesse Schwartz
1894-96	Rabbi Samuel Marks	1930-46	Rabbi Albert Gordon
1897-1903	Rabbi Aaron H. Sinai	1946-52	Rabbi Morris Gordon
1903-05	Rabbi S. Silber, Dr. I. Agat	1953-60	Rabbi Stanley Rabinowitz
1905-07	Rev. Mordecai Rivkin	1960-65	Rabbi Jerome Lipnick
1906	Rev. Dr. Solomon Roubin	1966-82	Rabbi Arnold Goodman
1906-1955	Meyer D. Mirviss	1983-96	Rabbi Barry Cytron
1908	Rev. Paul Segall	1996-present	Rabbi Harold J. Kravitz
1910-11	Rabbi Joseph Silver		

Presidents

1884	Nathan Gumbiner	1950-52	Samuel Libman	1983-85	Sally Appelbaum
1890s	Michael Jeffrey, Marx Harris, Charles Kronick	1952-55	Maurice Grossman	1985-87	Judy Goldstein
		1955-58	Ellis Peilen	1987-89	Paul Pink
1900	William Weisman	1958-62	Sim Heller	1989-91	Joyce Orbuch
1903	Isador Cohen	1962-63	Sidney Goldish	1991-93	Melvin Goldberg
1904	J. Frudenfield	1964-67	David Gordon	1993-96	Norman Pink
1909-32	Joseph Schanfeld	1967-69	Irving Brand	1996-98	Carol Bromer
1932-35	Louis B. Schwartz	1969-71	Melvin Orenstein	1998-2000	Jerry Zweigbaum
1935-43	Morris Kantar	1971-73	Jerome Fischbein	2000-02	Raleigh Kaminsky
1943-46	Dr. David Pink	1973-75	Irving Nudell	2003-04	Judy Cook
1946-47	George Stillman	1975-77	Jules Levin	2004-06	David Segal
1947-48	Arthur Figen	1977-79	Gerald Miller	2006-08	David Orbuch
1948-50	Louis M. Cohen	1979-81	Esther Katz	2008-	Heidi Schneider
		1981-83	Norman Pink		

Shem Tov Award

The Shem Tov (Good Name) Award is given to individuals who have contributed substantially to congregational activity and have had significant impact on the life of the synagogue community. Each year, several months prior to the annual meeting, a committee, composed solely of previous award recipients, meets to select an individual who best meets these criteria.

1959 Sam Abrams	1978 Morris Besner	1993 Jeffrey Schachtman
1960 Hemlan Neff	1979 Jules Levin	1996 Daniel Heilicher
1961 Aaron Herman	1980 Irving Nudell	1997 Edwin Agranoff
1962 Ellis Peilen	1981 Judy Goldstein	1998 Norman Pink
1963 Sim Heller	1982 Max & Dinah Elkin	1999 Charlotte Nudell
1964 Sidney Goldish	1983 Sydney Rich	2000 Carol Bromer
1965 Sheldon Gensler	1984 Joyce Orbuch	2001 Martin Bush & Ben Kibort
1967 David Gordon	1985 Martin Miller	2002 Jerry Zweigbaum
1970 Esther Katz	1986 Maurice Selcer	2003 Bruce Nemer
1972 Melvin Orenstein	1987 Goldie Wilensky	2004 Barbara Parks
1975 Gerald (Sonny) Miller	1989 Donald Masler	2006 Julie Kozberg
1976 Jerome Fischbein	1990 Raleigh Brand	2007 Mike Greenstein
1977 David Sherman	1991 Sally Appelbaum	2008 Ellen Sue Parker

MEN'S CLUB PRESIDENTS

1927-30: Louis B. Schwartz

1931-32: Dr. Harold Cooperman

1932-34: 0scar Friend

1934-36: Dr. David Axi1rod

1937-38: David Goldbeig

1936-J9: Nat E. Winston

1939-41: Irving M. Naiditch

1941-43: Edward Sokol

1943-45: Davld Spivak

1945-47: Archie Miller

1947-48: Sam H. Libman

1948-49: Barney J. Rubel

1949-50: Herbert J. Bitton

1950-51: Bernard Gale

1 951-52: Joseph Gitlin

1952-53: Max Kantor - Cecil Krelitz

1953-55: Samuel Bender

1955-57: Henry Kane

1957-59: David Gordon

1959-61: Sydney Rich

1961-62: Sy Friedman

1962-63: Sam Bender

1963-64: Sam Bender - Sydney Rich

1964-66: David Sherman

1966-67: Herman Jolosky

1967-68: Herbert Freedland

1968-70: Arthur Brand

1970-71: Jules Levin

1971-72: Max Elkin

1972-73: HowardAppleman

1973-74: Leonard Levine

1974-76: Martin Weinberger

1976-78: Julius Goldman

1978-80: Bernard Dinner

1980-82: Mort Levenson

1982-84: Otto Dube

1984-2002: Volunteers

2002-06: Charles Savitt

2006-09: Ivan Bonk

WOMEN'S GROUPS PRESIDENTS

1882 - Mrs. Nathan Gumbiner (Founded as Sisters of Peace)

1906 - Mrs. Charles Sternberg (then Ladies' Aid Society)

1914-15 Rose Weisman (Isadore)

1915-16 Jennie Gross (A.Morris) (then Ladies Auxiliary)

1916-18 Tillie Zekman (Arthur)

1918   Mathilde Schechter founds National Women's League, (Adath Jeshurun was 1 of 4 founding members)

1918-20 Susan Gruenberg (Jake H.)

1920-23 Gussie Zimmerman (Louis)

1923-24 Lena Matt (C.David)

1924-29 Josephine Mendow (Hyman Z.) (became Women's League)

1929-32 Jennie Gross (A.Morris)

1932-33 Sarah Engler (Morris)

1933-36 Mayme Breslow (Joseph)

1936-39 Anna Daskovsky (Morris)

1939-41 Ruth Stillman (George)

1941-42 Ruth Libman (Sam)

1942-43 Dena Pink (David)

1943-45 Helen Winer (Louis)

1945-46 Lea Sokol (Edward)

1946-47 Marian Figen (Arthur)

1947-49 Freda Kantor (Max)

1949-53 Lillian Krelitz (David)

1953-55 Rose Zimmerman (Harry)

1955-57 Sybil Kotz (J.J.)

1957-59 Lillian Gross (Leon)

1959- 61 Shirley Solomon (Harry)

1961- 63 Ruth Dechter (Louis) (became Sisterhood of Adath Jeshurun)

1963-65 Eve Freund (Martin) (became Adath JeshurunWomen's League)

1965-67 Maxine Lazar (Alec)

1967-79 Pam Brin (Robert)

1969-70 Audrey Efron (Irving)

1970-72 Jean Share (Leonard)

1973-75 Polly Bruanstein (Louis)

1975-77 Rhoda Jaffe (Paul)

1977-79 Beverlee Fine (Ralph)

1979-80 Ruth Bender (Sam)

1981-82 Ardis Wexler (Thomas)

1982-83 Harriet Sherman (Alan)

1983-86 Elaine Weber (Irving)

1986-87 Adina Goldstein

1987-89 Elaine Weber (Irving)

1989-92 Judy Goldstein (Alvin)

1992-94 Sharlene Schwartz

1994-96 Connie Sandler

1996-98 Past Presidents' Council

1998-99 Faye Stillman

1999-2001 Raleigh Brand

2001-04 Arlene Ben Shalom & Laura Weber

2005-06 Arlene Ben Shalom

2006-08 Ardis Wexler & Marilyn Sudit

2008-10 Sherri Steinman

Adath Jeshurun
Congregation Households

As of January 1, 2009

Aberman, Arnold
Abraham, Andrew & Erica, Danielle,
    Rachel
Abrams, Kalman & Riva Gould
Abrams, Michael & Sally, Leigh, Daniel,
    Brett, Howard
Abrams, Ronald & Joanne Rogin-
    Abrams, Benjamin, Alexander
Abramson, Carolyn
Abramson, Kevin & Nina, Jacob,
    Adam, Annie
Ackerberg, Stuart & Romy, Morgan,
    Romy, Jordyn, Bennett, Reina
Adelman, Floyd & Andrea, Barbara
Agranoff, Edwin & Marjorie
Aharoni, Menacham & Carol, Yosef,
    Avraham
Aleynikova, Semon & Rimma
Alkalai, Jacqueline & Harel, Alon,
    Andrea
Alter, David & Jodi, Zachary, Jonathan,
    Rachel
Altman, Robert & Robin, Benji,
    Shoshana
Ansel, Darrell & Loni
Ansel, Richard & Amy, Madeleine,
    Grace, Abigail
Antonoff, Michael & Mara, Eliana
Appelbaum, Phyllis
Appelbaum, Sally & Robert Miller
Appelman, Avery & Cindi, Lillianna,
    Branson
Apple, Fred & Jan, Elizabeth, Molly
Appleman, Jack & Terry
Arenson, Ivan & Diane, Michael,
    Gregory, Haley
Armel, Roberta, Jonathan, Elizabeth,
    Benjamin
Aronauer, Glenn & Lisa, Ashley, Logan
Aronson, Robert & Roberta

Babushkina, Svetlana
Bacaner Ganz, Nina & Eric Ganz, Ariel,
    Lily

Bader, Kristi & Gary Swartz, Lindsay,
    Adam, Zachary
Bader, Scott & Kerry, Jon, Jacey
Bader, Sidney & Molly
Badiner, Tom & Patti, Alisa
Badower, Mike & Sarah, Ben, Eli
Bahar, Phillip & Keri, Zachary, Chana,
    Talia
Bailey, Abbie & Bill, Tillery, Kelsey
Baines, Barry & Sandra, Alisha, Hannah
Bakal, Barbara, Jeffrey, Michael, Sarah
Baratz, Stanford & Amy, Blake, Justin,
    Courtney
Barberio, Sharline
Baron, Gary & Sandra, Mara, Avi
Barry, Michael & Etta, Alexandra,
    Benjamin, Jacob
Barry, Ronald & Shari, Mark, Jordan
Bartram, Irene, Vanessa
Basman, Neville & Michelle, Craig,
    Kali, Jenna
Bass, Lawrence & Marlene
Bassin, Irving
Baumel, A. Samuel & Elizabeth,
    Jennifer, Daniel
Bayer, David & Fran, Mitchell, Jeremy,
    Eileen
Bearman, Barbara
Bearmon, Jeanne
Beaubaire, Susan, Alanna, Lauren
Beck, Maureen
Becker, Susan, Melissa, Joshua
Belenky, Fima & Anya
Bell, Martin & Ginger
Bemel, Robert & Randi Livon, Danielle,
    Arianna, Louis
Bender, Alan & Abby
Bender, Brian, Samantha
Bender, Mitchell & Priscilla Chester,
    Alexander
Bender, Rebecca, Lincoln
Benditt, David & MaryAnn
Bennett, Lisa
Benowitz, Stephen & Jane, David
Berc, Jeffrey & Yvonne, Aaron, Hannah
Berdass, Daniel & Pearl, David, Joshua

Berdass, Margo, David
Berde, Michael & Carol
Berg, Richard & Carol, Traci, Justin
Berger, Brian & Gail, Sarah, Jaclyn,
    Alexander
Bergman, Minnie
Berkowitz, Benjamin
Berkowitz, Jerome & Sharon, Minna,
    Michelle, Sara
Berman, Bradley & Erica, Cade, Payton,
    Dylan, Kenzie, Taylor, Michael
Berman, Lyle
Berman, Michael & Judith, Oren, Noah
Berman, Richard & Charlotte
Berman, Theresa
Bernick, Saul & Maureen
Bernstein, Burton & Sara, Hannah
Bernstein, Donald & Etta, Elizabeth,
    Jacob
Bernstein, Ralph & Stephanie Sargent,
    Jacob
Berris, Barbara
Berris, Ellen & Stan, Hannah, Andrew
Bershow, Harold & Aileen
Bersten, Alex & Raisa, Gene, Melani, Alan
Besikof, Darrel & Rochelle, Daniel,
    Alison
Besikof, Justin & Meira, Madelyn, Ivy
Bez, Christine
Binder, Glenn & Dorae, Jessica,
    Matthew
Binenstock, Stuart & Meagan, Coby
Birman, Michael, Glen, Maria
Birnbaum, Gary & Bonnie
Bix, Milton
Blatt, Arnold & Sura-Fraida
Bloch, Anthony & Alyssa, Rebecca
Bloom, Matthew & Michelle, Maia,
    Joah, Ethan
Bloom, Michael & Mary, Corey
Bloom, Morton
Bloom, Paul & Kristina, Braden,
    Lauryn, Makenna
Boderman, Bradley & Yelena, Alexa,
    Zachary

Bonk, Ivan & Jill, Corey, Jamie
Bookin, Marvin & Sharon
Borenstein, Neil & Sue Freeman,
    Alexandra, Jacob, Benjamin
Borken, Philip & Jennifer, Gabriel,
    Hannah, Leah
Borkon, Edward
Borkon, Marilyn
Boroditsky, Shane
Brand, Idelle
Brand, Jethra
Brand, Joel
Brand, Lea & Cory Goddard, Jackson,
    Winona
Brand, Raleigh & Harlan
Brand, Ruth
Brelje, Robert & Joyce
Brendzel, Avrom & Ida Dreyfus, Sarah,
    Tamar
Brin, Robert & Pam
Brin, Ruth
Brodskiy, Roman & Irena Levina
Bromer, Michael & Carol
Broms, Myron
Broms, Timothy & Marilyn, Adam,
    Ross
Brown, David & Sandra
Brown, Harold (Chip) & Robin
    Chosid-Brown, Katelyn, Jason,
    Harrison
Brusso, Aaron & Hana Gruenberg, Sari,
    Zoe, Ilan
Buckner, Scott & Marcy, Heather,
    Ethan, Matthew, Rachel
Budda, Jeremy & Jenna
Burstein, Jefferey & Trudy, Miya
Burstein, Steven & Anne, Zachary,
    Jacob
Burton, Ron & Elaine
Busch, Nathan & Deborah Coen
Bush, Martin & Bonnie
Butwin, Ronald & Lois, Andrew, Rachel

Chalom, Suzanne
Chargo, Mitch & Susan, Elan, Abby, Ari
Charney, Rudolph & Meriam
Chelstrom, Sara & Martin, Carly,
    Grant, Macey
Cherner, Roman & Galina, Margarita
Chesen, Edward & Debra, Daniel,
    Geoffrey
Chester, Martin & Haley Schaffer, Ella,
    Sophie

Chester, Sheldon & Lili, Kari
Coen, Edward
Cohen, Arvin & Paula
Cohen, David & Amy, Jeffrey, Grant
Cohen, Deborah
Cohen, Ethel (Eddy)
Cohen, Gary & Margaret Macneale
Cohen, Isaac & Jamie, Marcel, Estelle
Cohen, Joe & Fredell
Cohen, Leah
Cohen, Martha
Cohen, Matthew & Dina, Halle, Cecelia
Cohen, Richard
Cohen, Richard & Diane
Cohen, Sheryl
Cohen, Stuart & Margery
Cohn, Barbara
Condon, Scott & Laura, Zachary,
    Maya, Alex
Cook, Richard & Judy, Andrew, Brian
Cooper, Gary & Tobi, Amy
Cooper, Peter & Gloria, Seth
Cooper, Scott & Debbie, Laura,
    Stephanie
Cooperman, Andrew & Dyanne,
    Madeline, Nina, Samuel
Cooperman, Bruce, Yona, Aviv, Chase
Cooperman, Elena, Yona, Aviv
Cooperman, Rodney & Judith
Corey, Brian & Diane, Ariel, Riva
Corwin, Gregg & Frances, Mitchell,
    David
Covin, Mark & Janie, Steven, Anthony,
    Marissa
Cowle, Beatrice
Crohn, Aaron & Mona, Amie, Scott,
    Paulette
Crohn, Estelle
Cuellar, Janet, Scott, Jacqueline
Curry, Sheree, Jared, Joshua
Curtis, Laurie, Rebecca, Jonathan
Cytron, Barry & Phyllis
Cytron, Todd & Amy, Hanah, Dara, Mia

Dachis, Bruce & Toni, Adam, Ali
Dachis, David & Anne
Dachis, Gary & Elaine, Louis, Marnie
Daitzchman, Luciano & Rena, Gabriel,
    Isaac
Daniels, Jeffrey & Elizabeth, Lucy, Josie
Danovsky, Burt & Micki
Davidson, Robert & Shellie Specter,
    Alan, Marc

Davis, Beatrice
Davis, Charles & Sheila, Mara
Davis, Fran
Davis, Gregory & Maureen, Stephanie
Davis, Harriet
Davis, Harry & Adella
Davis, Ruth
Desnick, Evelyn
Devin, David & Wendy, Laini
Diamond, Cynthia, Melissa, Michaela
Diamond, Lawrence
Diamond, Mitzi
Dickstein, Mel & Linda Foreman,
    Thomas
Dickstein, Sidney & Ann
Diker, Ronald & Alexis, Joshua, Marnie
Dobrin, Daniel & Andrea, Hailey
Dobrin, Steven & Cecilia
Dorfman, Jay & Elisa, Michael, Alexis
Dotterweich, Alecia & Gus, David
Douglas, Harold
Dresner, Harley & Elyse Scheuer,
    Daphne, Zachary
Dubansky, Cindy
Dworsky, David & Debra, Anna,
    Robert, Meredith
Dworsky, Mischa
Dworsky, Natalie
Dworsky, Peretz
Dworsky, Richard & Linda, Dylan

Efron, Irving & Jean
Eichen, Erwin & Natalie
Einisman, Alan & Karen, Eli, Jonah
Eisenberg, Jay & Gabriela
Eisenstadt, Betty
Elias, Allan & Judith
Elias, Walter & Ruth, Liora, Daniel
Elkin, Max
Ellis, Gerald & Claire
Emmons, Michael & Judith
Engel, Harry & Sari, Jamie, Shana
Engel, Randy & Wendy, Emily
Engelson, Steven & Robin, Daniel,
    Shoshana
Engler, Harold
Epstein, Eugene & Carole
Esensten, Jeremy & Amy
Estrin, David & Linda
Ettedgui, Avraham & Linda
Ettedgui, Daniel & Henni, Graham,
    Nova, Aviv

Ezrilov, David & Julie, Allie, Carly,
Ezrilov, Richard & Jennifer, Samantha,
    Benjamin
Ezrilov, Robert & Vivian

Farkas, Juanita
Feder, Marilyn
Fefercorn, Rosella
Feingold, Jody
Feldberg, Michael & Rachel, Victor
Feldman, Daniel & Shelly, Isabella,
    Lindsay
Feldman, Joseph & Ellen, Evelyn, Kira
Feldman, Marlene, Sara
Feldman, Noah & Aimee, Allison,
    Chloe
Fern, Gary & Helen, Andrew, Elizabeth
Feynberg, Mikhail & Ivgenia Sagalchik
Fine, Michael & Catherine, Lauren,
    Alexis, Alison
Fine, Rich & Judy
Fineberg, Geraldine
Fink, Dr. Paul & Lucy
Fink, James & Beth, Joshua, Elyssa,
    Deanna
Fink, Jeffrey & Vivian, Alexander, Alana
Fink, Neil & Nancy, Josh
Fink, Richard & Beverly
Finkelstein, Steven & Stacy, Robb, Eli,
    Zoe
Finn, Mark & Sharon
Fischbein, Howard & Marilyn
Fischbein, Irving & Dina
Fischbein, Jerome & Bernice
Fischer, Mark & Lucy Rose Fischer
Fischman, Kenneth
Fisher, Alex & Daniella, Aviva
Fishman, Andrew & Barbara, Alexis,
    Michael, Gabriel, Elizabeth
Fishman, Mordechai & Cindy, Jacob
Fishman, William & Beverly, Evan,
    Rena, Ross
Fiterman, Michael & Linda, Debra
Flam, Darryl & Janet
Fleisher, Edith
Flom, Harvey & Evelyn
Floum, Sonya
Fogel, Richard & Nina, Ariella, Sasha,
    Ian
Fogelson, Joshua & Shelley, Jonathan,
    Michelle, Danielle
Fortune, Donna & Lamont, Aaron
Fox, Norman & Paula, Shira

Fraher, David & Rebecca Biderman
Frank, Bradley & Deborah, Gavin,
    Sydney
Frank, Bradley & Emily, Tessa
Frank, Daniel & Barbara, Lisa, Robyn
Frank, Peter & Connie, Daniel, Andrea
Frankel, Leon & Ruth
Frankel, Mark & Karen, Jacob, Rebecca
Frankel Hayes, Rita & John Hayes,
    Kelly, Elizabeth
Frankman, Leland & Marles
Fredkove, Joseph & Gloria
Freeman, John & Beth, David, Andrew
Freeman, Mark & Jennifer, Annie,
    Joshua, Isabel
Freeman, Michael & Patricia, Joseph
Freeman, Richard & Linda, Benjamin,
    Matthew
Freeman, Wayne & Sandra
Friedman, David & Susan, Marc,
    Deborah
Friedman, Edward & Margery
Friedman, Evelyn
Friedman, Jerome
Frisch, Charles
Frisch, Janet
Frisch, Melvin & Patti
Frisch, Suzy & Steven Swenson,
    Madeline, Grace, Evelyn
Fromstein, Richard & Raleigh Shapiro
    Fromstein, Mari, Elisha, Julia
Fuerstneau, Glen & Carol, Brian, Becky,
    Jacob
Furman, Michael & Revital, Eliana

Gabor, Beth Anne & Tony, Jaime,
    Jonah
Gagnelius, Wesley & Veronica Sirotin
Gale, Estelle
Galinson, Aaron & Teresa, Sydney,
    Noah
Galinson, Michael & Rochelle
Galinson, Mitchell & Tracey, Samantha,
    Emma
Galinson, Robert & Pamela
Gapany, Markus & Sabina
Garber, William & Sharon, Adam,
    Lillian
Garden-Bell, Debra, Jennifer, Tom
Garon, Lynne, Jacqueline, Daniel
Garon, Sherman & Lorraine
Garvie, Julie
Garvis, Allan & Idy

Gasiorowicz, Hilde & Stephen
Gaviser, James & Judy
Gedan, Joel & Kimberly, Alicia, Stefanie
Gelfman, Mark, Daniel
Gelfman, Michael & Allison, Mira,
    Rachel
Geller, Cary & Inna, Rachel, Alexandra
Geller, Daniel & Heidi, Andrew, Jordan
Geller, Elaine
Gelperin, Aaron & Kimberly, Sidney,
    Louis
Gendler, Nancy & Craig Hinderks, Jack
Gendler, Neal & Marjorie Wasserman,
    Jason, Aaron
Gensler, Mitchell & Debra, Elliot,
    Jessica
Gensler, Steven & Peni, Marc, Brent
Gerstein Atkin, Natalie
Geskina, Raisa
Gesundheit, Sim & Suzanne Singer
Getzkin, Jeffrey & Nancy, David,
    Adam,
Getzkin, Michael & Helen, Shari,
    Melissa,
Gewolb, David & Melissa, Todd, Barry
Gilbert, Esther
Gilbert, Neil & Joanne, Adam, Scott,
    Charles
Gilfix, Linda
Gilfix, Steve & Jeannie, Zachary,
    Hannah
Gillett, Neal & Pamela, Sarah, Gabriel,
    Aaron, Rebecca
Gillman, Stanford & Barbara
Gingold, Alan & Roni, Lauren, Danielle
Gingold, Bernard
Ginsberg, Joel & Sara, Samuel, Joshua
Gittleman, Melvin & Rochelle
Glatzer, Seymour & Gail
Gleeman, Mitchell & Jacqueline,
    Marissa, Bradley
Glikin, Igor & Yana, Michael
Glotter, Joel & Joanne
Glotter, Mark & Debra, David, Rachel,
    Michael
Gold, Michael & Deborah, Maxwell,
    Zoey
Goldberg, Barbara
Goldberg, Jonathan & Kristen
Goldberg, Matthew, Alexander, Elijah
Goldberg, Paula
Goldberg, Rachael Solomon, Alexander,
    Elijah
Goldberg, Rose

Goldberg, Sanford & Marlene
Goldblatt, Bernard & Leslie, Talia,
    Aviva, Leora
Goldenberg, Chad & Debra, Ruth, Rose
Goldenberg, Jacob & Linda, Rachel,
    Ann
Goldenberg, Jeffrey & Karen Yashar,
    Sarah, Adam
Goldenberg, Louis & Diane
Goldenberg, William & Susan
Goldfarb, Bette
Goldfein, Melvin & Judith
Goldfine, Harold & Cynthia, Sara
Goldman, Glen & Davida, Anya, Isaac
Goldman, Joshua & Jessica, Noah, Sam
Goldman Cherwitz, Linda, Kevin
Goldsmith, Edward, Susan, Neil
Goldsmith, Elon & Ilyse, Hannah
Goldsteen, David & Marcia Cohodes,
    Avi, Aaron, Rebecca
Goldsteen, Rose
Goldstein, Adina, Daniel
Goldstein, Alvin & Judy
Goldstein, Gail
Goldstein, Riva
Goldstein, Sheila
Golob, Brian & Sandra, Mark, Laura,
    Scott
Golob (Chernoff), Marsha
Golos, Ellery & Lila
Goltzman, Lillian
Goodman, Michael & Miriam, Daniel,
    Elizabeth, Lauren, Jacob
Goodman, Rose, Philip
Gordon, Avron & Bari
Gordon, Jillian
Gordon, Scott & Terri, Ilan, Batia
Gordon, Stephen & Nancy, Samantha
Gotlieb, David, Elly, Asa, Zoey
Gotlieb, Paul & Leslie, Nate, Marlene,
    Rachael, Isaac
Gottlieb, Steven & Jill, Sydney
Gould, Adeline
Gould, Jay & Sherri, Ross, Marc, Liza
Gould, Richard & Marsha
Grais, Carol, Tammi
Grais, Etheldoris
Grais, James
Grais, Jason & Jacy
Granote, Joshua & Paula, Aleeza, Shira,
    Gabriela
Gray, I. Benjamin & Melanie
Gray, Jeffery & Rebecca, Talia, Sophie
Gray, Norton & Susan

Gray, Scott & Terri, Lily, Julia
Grayson, Scott & Debra, Shira, Mark,
    Daniel
Green, Joel & Renanah Halpern, Tamar,
    Elan
Greenberg, Barry & Barbara Rubin-
    Greenberg, Nathaniel, Blair, Ethan
Greenberg, Douglas & Susan
Greenberg, June
Greenberg, Norman & Beth Silverwater
Greenberg, Rita
Greenberg, Tina, Ezra, Eli, Avi
Greenblatt, Paul & Debra, Samuel
Greene, Leonard & Carole
Greenfield, Ida
Greenstein, Gerald & Betty
Greenstein, Mark & Kimberlee, Joshua
Greenstein, Michael & Teri, Allison,
    Matthew
Greenstien, Karen, Jared, Zachary
Greller, Barry & Suellen, Jason
Grichener, Yakov & Klaudya
Gringauz, Lazar & Raisa
Grone, Daniel & Debbie, Lauren,
    Andrew
Grosnacht, Joseph & Frances
Gross, Eva & Ella Weiss
Gross, Jeanne
Gross, Jonathan, Alexander
Gross, Peter & Susan, Benjamin,
    Joshua, Jacklyn
Grossfeld, Abraham & Lillian, Nora
Grossfeld, Scott & Michele, Rachel,
    Marissa
Grossfield, Marc & Debra, Jaclyn,
    Adam
Grossfield, Stuart & Joan
Grossman, Barbara
Grossman, Erwin & Arlis
Grossman, N. Bud & Beverly
Grossman, Stephanie, Alene, Noah
Gruenberg, Karyn
Gudmundson, Hans & Felicia, Roselyn
Guttman, Matthew & Deborah, Alexa,
    Zachary

Habermann, Mike & Minda Gralnek,
    Audrey, Lila
Halper, Andrew & Judy, Abby, Mollie
Hammer, Bruce & Susan, Daniel, Laura,
    Rebecca
Hampel, Mark & Barbara, Erica,
    Stephanie, Morgan

Harold, Nancy
Harris, Ruth & Marcy
Hartman, Robert & Nancy, Benjamin,
    Michael, Joey
Hasko, Joshua & Laurie, Gabrielle,
    Rachel
Hausman, Eric & Debra Altschuler,
    Emma
Heilicher, Ira & Jackie, Hannah
Heilicher, Matthew & Zehorit, Ethan,
    Leeyah, Mickela, Orielle
Heilicher, Phyllis
Heilicher, Todd & Beverly, Justin,
    Breanna,
Held, Howard & Susan, Stephanie,
    Justin, Marni Beth
Held, Jerome
Helms, Wayne, Virginia
Herman, Bradley & Barbara
Herman, Gerri
Herman, Irving & Frances
Herman, Ross & Kimberly, Daniel,
    Alexis, Aidan
Hersk, David & Nancy
Herstig, Brian & Laurie, Gabriel, Zoe
Hill, Daniel & Shari, Hannah
Hill, Earl & Shirley
Hill, Mercer & Geraldine
Himmelman, David & Ruth Hampton
Hirsch, Alan
Hjulberg, Carol
Hoffman, Earl & Barbara, Deborah,
    Howard
Hoffman, Edward & Lauren, Maxwell,
    Tessa
Hoffman, Jay & Roberta, David
Hofkin, Michael & Ann, Benjamin
Hofman, Margot & Judy Santos
Hollischer, Jack & Ruth
Horowitz, Jack & Reva
Horowitz, Steven & Susan, Rachelle
Horwitz, Gregory & Stacy, Shayna
Hubert, Elisabeth
Husney, Betty

Ingber, Jerome & Judith, Shai, Noah
Izek, David & Patricia, Aaron, Isabel,
    Emma

Jackson, Elaine
Jacobs, Harlan & Linda
Jaffe, Manuel & Gloria

Jasco, Duane & Beth, Felicia, Hailey
Jernell, Betty, Chantell, Tara,
Jewett, Theodore & Deborah Bearman
    Jewett, Ethan, David
Joffee, Neal & Tanya Joffee Feldberg
Johnson, Jerry & Sandra
Johnson, Rick & Wendy, Rachel, Daniel,
Jolson, Brad & Diane, Melanie,
    Benjamin
Jonas, Miriam
Jonas, Peter & Betty
Juntilla, Tamara & Charles, James,
    Alyssa

Kadet, Kenneth & Sharon, Ethan,
    Ryan, Justin
Kafka, Thomas & Susan
Kagan, Emiliya
Kaganovich, David & Nadia, Boris, Ilya,
    Jacob
Kaganovich, Moris & Valentina
Kagin, Al
Kagin, Stanley & Jeanne, Ryan, Gillian,
    Alexander, Zachary
Kahn, Michael & Rita
Kahn, Richard, Carly, Robert, Thomas
Kahn, Ross & Nancy Krawetz, Noah,
    Asher
Kalin, Dick & Nancy Kleeman
Kaminsky, Randall & Raleigh
Kampel, Salomon & Margarete
Kane, Bruce & Sue, Matthew, Steven,
    Michael
Kane, Joseph & Estelle
Kane, Morton & Merle
Kane, Rosalie & Robert
Kane, Terry & Mitzi
Kaner, Robert
Kanevskiy, Alexander & Lyudmila,
    James, Jonathan
Kantar, Stanley & Sheila
Kanter, Brad & Amy, Tyler, Ashley
Kaplan, Daniel & Lauren, Bradley,
    Noah, Shayna
Kaplan, David & Marci, Shelby, Cassie
Kaplan, Eve & Lawrence McDonough,
    Megan, Roxana
Kaplan, Fred & Rosalind
Kaplan, Harvey & Suzanne, David,
    Michael
Kaplan, Joel & Harmony
Kaplan, Manuel

Kaplan, Sheldon & Rivia
Karasik, Mark & Violet, Tatiana
Karasov, Marilyn
Karon, Mark & Janice, Mollie, Jennifer
Katz, Gail
Katz, Larry & Lori, Adam, Molly
Katz, Morris & Esther
Kaufman, Hal & Julie Berman, Leo,
    Nathan
Kaufman, Lilly
Kaufman, Suellen
Kaufmann, Allen & Sharon, Jacob,
    Jessica, Benjamin
Kaufmann, Farley & Karen, Jason, Evan
Kaye, Keith & Valda, Jessica, Deborah,
    Maxine
Kaye, Mitchell & Fay, Jennifer, Aaron
Kellogg, Christine & Jack Leveille,
    Sarah, Miriam
Kelner, Barry & Nancy Bender-Kelner,
    Marshall, Malcolm, Sage, Jackson
Kern, Abraham & Rebecca
Kessler, Jerrold & Rhella
Kessler, Steve & Risa, Alexis, Leah
Ketover, Scott & Linda, Jason, Alyssa,
Khabie, Nissim & Wendy, David, Jacob,
    Tobias
Kibort, Ben & Reva
Kibort, Charles & Andrea, Beth,
    Michael, Samantha, Max
Kibort, Gary & Stacy, Raleigh, Grace
Kibort, Jesse & Cymbol, Julia, Audrey
Kieffer, Leroy & Miriam
King-Smith, Eric & Roxie
King-Smith, Ruth
Kiperstin, Alec
Kiperstin, Frank
Kirschbaum, Bess
Kirschner, Abby
Kirschner, Ruth
Kirshbaum, Ralph & Elaine
Kirzon, Roza, Irena
Kitsis, Arlen & Tybelle
Kitsis, Mary, Robert, Kevin
Kitsis, Steven
Kivens, Jeffrey & Sharon
Kivens, Marlene
Klaiman, David & Amy, Max, Jacob,
    Zak, Ethan
Kleiman, Ansel & Beth
Kleineman, George
Kleineman, Steven & Reesa, Daniel, Beth
Kleiner, Morris & Sally

Kline, Barie & Laurie Goldman, Jeanette,
    Benjamin
Kogen, Walter
Kohen, Daniel & Harriet
Kohler, Gary & Deborah, Sarah, Anna
Kohn, David & Eileen, Dana, Shira
Kohn, Mary
Korsh, Anthony & Carrie
Korsh, Doris
Korsh, Howard & Diane
Korsh, Leslie & Jill, Michael, Shayna
Kotlarz, Corey & Lisa, Abby, Eli
Kozberg, Marc & Julie, Joshua, Rachel
Kozberg, Martin & Lois
Kozberg, Steven & Jill, Mollie, Abby,
    Ellie, Sarah
Kramer, Matthew & Heather, Ari
Krantz, Belle
Krasnik, Jacob & Mary
Kravitz, Harold & Cindy Reich, Gabriel,
    Talia, Elana
Krawetz, Debra
Krelitz, Barry & Annetta
Krelitz, Steven, Lillian, Benjamin
Kremen, Zenith & Merle Anne
Krichmar, Richard & Vicki, Brooks
Krikava, Steven & Linda Singer
Krivolapova, Serafima
Kronick, Ruth
Krupp, Mayer
Kuhl, Michelle & John, Jordan
Kuperman, Allen & Diane, Sandy, Lisa,
    Michael
Kuretsky, Peter & Jodi, Alexa, Seth
Kuretsky, William & Janis, Amy

Labofsky, Arnold & Charlotte, Joshua
Labofsky, Barbara
Lamain, Bette & Gerrit
Lampert, Lorene
Landy, Bryan & Robin, Barry, Erin
Langer, Elaine
Lapidus, Neil & June Cook-Lapidus
Lapkin, Catherine, Elliott, Hannah,
    Sophie
Lapp, William & Linda
Larson, Elizabeth, Amy, Lauren
Latts, Shirley
Laurie, Sadie & Edythe
Lavenda, Robert & Emily Schultz,
    Daniel, Rachel
Lavin, Jerome & Bonnie Ross, Joseph

Lazar, Raymond & Judith Mares Lazar, Whitney

Lazar, Steve & Bonnie, Alexander, Elliot, Talia, Mollie

Lazar, Susan

Leafman, Lillian

Lear, Reva

Lear, Sandra, Catie Jo, Jacquelyn, Ariel

Lear, Steven & Sheri, Andrea, Kimberly, Cassie, Daniel, Rebekah

Lebewitz, Jon & Kathryn, Sam, Sophie

Leder, Mark & Susan, Max, Ross

Lederer, Howard & Lisa, Elyse, Brian

Lederfine, Darren

Lefkow, Edward & Stephanie, Aaron, Shoshana, Ella

Lefty, Dianne

Lehman, Jeffrey & Diane, Alexander, Austin

Lehrman, Brad & Karee, Alec, Ryan

Lent, Michael & Lynne, Tommy, Aaron, Daniel

Lent, Morton

Leonard, Todd & Beth, Daniel, Zachary, Eli

Lerman, Gregory & Rose Kendall Lerman

Lerner, Donald & Harriet

Lerner, Ethel

Lerner, Harry & Sandra

Lerner, Leon & Elaine

Leventhal, Steven & Laura, Noah, Samuel

Levey, Daniel & Suzanne Weinstein, Emma

Levin, Irene

Levin, Jules & Rose

Levin, Myles & Michele, Jeremy, Shaun

Levin, Nettie

Levin, Sophia

Levin (Deceased), Robert

Levine, Edward & Noreen, Bradley, Andrew

Levine, Jerrold & Ruth

Levine, Lois

Levine, Robert & Joan, Michael, Ross

Levinger, Harold & Sheila Field

Levinsohn, Alys

Levinson, Chernie

Levitan, Jay & Linda, Mitchell, Suzanne

Levitt, Alan & Beverly Pilcher, Margo, Noah, Samuel

Levitt, Daniel & Suzanne, Charles, Joseph

Levitt, John & Rachel

Levitt, Kenneth & Christina, Rebecca, Hannah, Sarah

Levitt, Merle & Marla

Levitt, Murray & Shari, Adam, Joshua

Levy, David

Levy, Jeffrey

Levy, Jonathan & Beth Virnig, Jacob, Zachary

Levy, Matthew & Deborah, Joshua, Zachary

Levy, Robert & Roberta

Lewis, David & Teena

Liberman, Miriam

Liberman, Ziv & Tal, Ron, Danielle, David

Lichten, Erwin & Lois

Lieberman, Daniel & Suzanne Fenton, Emet, Charles, Leo

Lieberman, Stephen & Sheila

Liebo, Jack & Rhoda, Max, Greta, Samuel

Lifland, Joseph & Carrie, Tara, Adam

Lifson, Marshall & Marjorie

Lifson, Todd & Jane, Andrew, Jeffrey

Lipets, Helen

Lipnik, Alex & Polina Gerber

Lipschultz, Brian & Sari, Robyn

Lipshutz, Martin & Laura, Sara, Michael

Liss, Lois

Litman, Amy, Alexandra

Litman, Dana & Lindsay, Ethan

Litman, Thomas & Hinda

Litow, Micah

Litton, Jeremy & Michele, Joseph, Elizabeth

Locketz, Miles & Sandra

Lodge, Susanna & Timothy, Hannah, Samuel

Lokpez, Ederick

Londer, Howard & Vicki, Amie, Anthony

Londer, Jason & Aryel, Eliana, Jacob

London, Jonathan & Alison, Matthew

London, Michael

London, Michael & Susan

Long, DeeDee & Harry, Elise, Lindsey

Lorberbaum, Anne

Low, Ari & Courtney, Ethan, Alexandra

Lui, David & Amy Rosenblatt Lui, Yonatan

Lurie, Richard & Francelyne

Lurie Mars, Linda & Stephen Mars, Jacob, Maxwell, Samuel

Luther, Mark & Deborah, Avital, Noah

MacKinnon, Pamela & James, Brett, Judd

Madigan, Rebecca & Michael, Elizabeth, Joshua

Malinsky, Debra

Malinsky, Florence

Mandel, Jeffrey

Mandel, Sandra

Marcovitch, Ben & Rollie

Marcus, Bruce & Hilary Bearmon Marcus, Loren, Allison

Marcus, Irving & Sylvia

Margoles, Alan & Cheryl Speeter Margoles, Sarah, Daniel, Michelle

Margolis, Irving & Clara

Margolis, Jeffrey & Krista, Ruben, Bret

Mark, Charles

Markowitz, Herman & Nancy

Marks, Edward

Marmet, Jordan & Marnie, Zachary, Sage, Gabriella

Marofsky, David & Debra, Laura, Stacee

Marx, Jason & Michelle, Brandon, Elyssa

Masler, Donald

Masler, Gary & Toni, Jonathan, Daniel

Mastbaum, David & Amy, Alexandra, Grant

Matas, Arthur & Sandy, Aaron

Maul, Naomi & Warren

Meirovitz, Sara

Meisler, Seth & Michele, Ilana, Ethan, Abigail

Mekler, Gregg, Joshua

Mekler, Vi

Mekler, Wendy, Joshua

Melnick, Bradley & Susan, Joshua

Melzer, Leo & Fern

Merriman, Beth, Danielle, Sydnie

Metchnek, James

Metchnek, Rose

Meyer, Neil & Gail

Meyers, Marion

Milavetz, Richard

Miller, Alan & Roberta

Miller, Esther

Miller, Julie, Cali, Zachary

Miller, Michael, Cali, Zachary

Miller, Todd & Ann, Joshua, Eve

Milstein, Howard & Gail, Samuel, Nathan, Sophie

Mintz, Steven & Patricia, Molly, Sophie,
Heidi, Jack
Mintzer, Joel & Heidi Schneider, Asher,
Isaac, Rachel
Mirviss, Jeffrey & Jill, Sydney, Zachary
Mirviss, Joel & Danna, Sophie, Hannah,
Michelle
Mirviss, Paul & Sandra Klein-Mirviss,
Zoe, Carly
Misheev, Efrem & Natella, Ross, Anna-
Mariya
Mitchell, Frances
Mogilevsky, Ann, Joshua, Jenna
Mogilevsky, Ella
Moldo, Marc, Danielle
Molnar, Andrew & Jennifer, Robbin,
Matthew, Ruby
Morton, Jill & Rick, Max, Jack
Moscovice, Ira & Sarah, Anya
Moscowitz, James & Amy Taswell, Tali,
Kira, Dori
Mosow, Jack & Bernadine
Mulmed, Lawrence & Mitzi
Myers, Barbara

Nabedrick, Jack & Annette
Nabedrick, Joseph & Stacie, Lucy,
Cassidy
Naiman, Polina
Nassauer, Fred & Shirley
Nathanson, Debbye
Neff, Burton
Neff, Daniel & Cindy, Jason
Neff, Edwin & Cibbi
Nemer, Bruce & Roberta
Nemer, Dana, Jessica, Alexa
Nerenberg, Evelyn
Nerenberg, Lex & Leslie, Mark, Marissa
Neuman, Richard & Judith
Neuman, Robert & Corinne
Neuwirth, Gerardo & Esther
Newman, Barry & Amy, Allisa, Paige
Newman, Charles & Phyllis
Newman, Gayle
Newman, Larry & Roberta, Jerad,
Randy
Niedorf, Mark & Marcia, Samuel
Nilva, Samuel
Notkin, Michael & Rimma, Gary, Eli
Nudell, Irving & Charlotte
Nudler, Gennadiy & Anna, Svetlana,
Jonathan

Oken, Martin & Naomi
Orbuch, David & Jill, Sarah, Elana,
Rachel
Orbuch, Martin & Joyce
Oreck, Michael & Susan, Stephanie,
Allison,
Orenstein, David & Leslie, Julie Ann,
Lucy, Harry
Orenstein, David & Suanne, Maxwell
Orenstein, Melvin & Beatrice
Orenstein, Norman & Lillian
Orkin, Etta Fay
Oskow, Craig & Catherine, Noah, Aviva
Ostfield, Benjamin & Joan
Ostrowsky, Alex

Papermaster, Theodore & Dorothy
Parish, David & Gabrielle, Joshua,
Reuben, Simon
Parker, Aaron, Sarah, Naomi, Simone
Parker, Enrique & Libby, Noa, Tali
Parker, Jonathan & Ellen Sue, Adam,
Betsy, Danielle
Parker, Leonard
Parks, Lawrence & Barbara
Paul, Stephanie, Jessica, Collin,
Payton, James & Abbe, Sydney, Eli
Peilen, S. Bruce & Lisa, Elizabeth,
Edward
Peilte, Joseph & Nancy
Pekurovsky, Ilya & Elena, Elizabeth,
Daniel
Pelleg, Shimon & Adrienne Trangle-
Pelleg, Amir, Maia, Ayla
Peltz, Paul & Henrietta
Pentelovitch, William & Vivian Fischer,
Norman, Tovah, Noah, Ari, Miriam
Perecman, Jack & Cheryl, Laurie, Ben
Perepelitsyn, Ilya & Lioudmila Sitnikova,
Sophia, Gregory
Perl, Justin & Lynn, Alexandra, Phillip
Perlman, Michael, Jackie, Benjamin
Peterson, Carole, Danica, Shane
Pfaffinger, Michael & Janet, Joseph, Jack
Phillips, Bart & Lynn, Freddie, Samantha
Phillips, Laureen
Phillips, Lawrence & (Sharon) Tamara,
Allie, Jacob
Pilcher, Ben & Lil
Pine, Steven & Arlene, Joshua
Pink, David & Tamar Fenton, Aiden,
Asher, Ronen, Liel

Pink, Joelle
Pink, Michael & Amy, Madeline,
Maverick, Isabelle
Pink, Norman & Dorothy
Pink, Paul & Fredda
Pistner, Paul & Margaret
Pogorelsky, Dmitry & Emiliya, Bryan
Pollitz, Ilana & Michael, Jacob, Morgan
Pomerantz, Roselyn
Portner, Lana
Posada, Raul & Mia, Nathan, Jesse
Povolotskiy, Larry & Svetlana
Sinelnikova, Anya, Gabriella
Price, Joseph & Louise, Julie
Price, Linda, Zachary, Faith
Price, Martin & Mildred
Proman, Richard & Susan
Przetycki, Lejzor & Klaudia, Molly
Ptaszek, Steven & Sharon Lehrman,
Jessica, Justin

Rabinovitz, Jeffrey & Jill, Sig
Raff, Kevin & Merit, Alexander
Raison, Jeffrey & Marilyn Reiter, Eva
Randy-Larsen, Rochelle & Gary Larsen,
Heather, Hilary
Rappaport, Jon & Diane, Naomi, Shira,
Fred
Rauch, Vivian
Ravine, Charley
Raymond, Michael & Aimee Orkin-
Raymond,Rachel, Abraham, Ora,
Leila
Rayzman, Khana
Resnick, Marilyn
Resnick, Michael & Susan, Rebecca,
Rachel, Alyssa, Samuel
Ribnick, Renee
Ribnick, William & Gail, Justin, Leslie,
Lauren
Richter, Shirley
Richter, Ted
Riger, Norman & Grace
Ring, Harold
Rivas, Dennis & Vicki, David
Roback, Stacy & Donna
Robbins, Donna
Robin, David & Jeanne, Philip
Robin, Sandra
Robinow, Avrom & Nancy, Mark
Robinow, Lewis & Marla Lurie,
Harrison

Robitz, Gerald
Rochlin, Harvey & Harriett
Rodich, Daniel & Beth, Talia, Sari
Rodich, Michael & Dona, Jessica
Roether, Geoffrey & Susan, Max, Ella
Rose, Jason & Lindsey, Ari, Spencer
Rosen, Sandra, Neil
Rosenbaum, David & Joyce
Rosenbaum, Harold & Louise
Rosenbaum, Martin & Tema, Gail,
    Steven, Emily
Rosenberg, Betty
Rosenberg, Lesli
Rosenberg, William & Demmie,
    Rebecca, Jennifer, Matthew
Rosenberg-Scholl, Sharon & Tina, Ian
Rosenbloom, Amos & Marsha
    Mc Donald
Rosenbloom, Reva
Rosenfeld, William & Jody Winger
Rosenfield, Lon & Barbara Friedman,
    Michelle, Philip, Sari
Rosenthal, Harold
Rosenthal, Jules & Gay
Rosenzweig, Jean
Rosoff, Eleanor
Rosoff, Scott & Sheri, Jack, Annie
Rotenberg, Richard & Lisa, Jordan,
    Emily, Jason
Roth, Aaron & Sheila, Hannah, Sarah
Roth-Laube, Lydia & Herbert Laube,
    Jason, Justin
Rozen, Douglas & Lisa, Alexis, Jacob
Rubel, Alan
Rubenstein, Joseph & Deborah Shatin
Rubenstein, Oren & Jan, Matthew,
    Rachel
Rubin, Harold & Elaine
Rubin, Scott & Jodi, Jack, Julia
Rubin, Stuart & Carol, Jaclyn, Madeline
Rudin, Jeffrey & Vivian Pearlman, Lisa,
    Daniel, Madeline
Rudin, Pearly
Rudin, William
Rudnitsky, Barry & Vicki, Tracy, Jody
Rudoy, Irving
Rusakov, Leah, Adina, Miriam
Rush, Steven & Nancy, Samuel
Rutman, Marlene

Saadi, Deborah, Yonaton
Sabes, Esther

Sabes, Jon & Kristine, Morgan, Jackson,
    Brooke
Sabes, Robert & Janet
Sabes, Steven & Amy, Lauren, Natalie
Sachs, Richard & Geneva Middleton
Sacks, Alexei & Wendy Kivens, Eitan
Saferstein, Michael & Sara, Sophia,
    Isabella
Salita, Dean & Rebecca, Jonah, Aubrey,
    Celia
Salita, Jack & Sarah, Julia, Oliver, Henry
Salsberg, Sandra
Sandler, David & Elizabeth, Kerah, Ebin,
    Asher
Sandler, Gerald & Connie, Jay, Todd,
    Lee, Amy
Sandler, Hy & Betty
Sandler, Joy, Danielle
Sandler, Noah & Stacy, Maxwell, Sophia
Sandler, Reid & Judith, Michelle
Sandler, Victor & Annette Malinsky
    Sandler, Rebecca, Amy
Satz, Mark & Gail, Seth, David,
    Herschel
Satz, Sandra
Savitt, Burton
Savitt, Charles & Kori, Danielle, Maia,
    Jessica
Savitt, Douglas & Joanne
Savitt, Gregg & Debra, Adam, Jonathan,
    Madeline
Savitt, Leonard
Savitt, Steven & Gloria Kumagai, Joshua
Savitz, Steven & Jana, Joshua, Zachary,
    Jacob
Savran, Laurie
Schachtman, Jeffrey & Janice, Mindy,
    Michael
Schachtman, Steven & Nancy
Schachtman, Todd & Nicole, Samuel,
    Oliver, Louis
Schaffer, Ian & Sandra, Candice
Schechter, Herbert & Marta
Schept, Robert & Edith
Schlussman, Rona
Schmieg, Laura & Jeffrey, Jonah, Eliza
Schneck, Paul & Susan, Lauren, Emily
Schneider, Byron & Barbara, Laura,
    Andrew
Schneider, Gary & Lynne
Schneller, Amos & Renana, Netta, Gily
Schraber, Paul & Shari, Erika
Schulman, Joshua & Sara, Charlie

Schultz, Leonard & Michele, Jennifer,
    Joseph, Michael, Natalie
Schumeister, Steven & Judith, Stacey,
    Andrew
Schwartz, Charlene, Rena, Ian,
Schwartz, Howard & Jeannie, Abigail
Schwartz, Raleigh
Schwartz, Robert, Ian
Schwartz, Sylvia
Schwartzfield, Sidney & Lorraine
Segal, David & Renee, Benjamin, Leah
Segal, Faye
Segal, Harold
Segal, James & Tamra, Zachary, Evan,
    Cole
Segal, Leonard & Susan, Nathaniel,
    Andrew, Talia
Segal, Raley
Segal, Robert & Lucinda Cummings,
    Isaac, Samuel
Segal, Robert & Norma, Spenser
Segal, Saul & Beth Ann
Segal, Sheldon & Carol
Segal, Stephen & Sharon, Aliza, Gabriel
Segal, Sylvia
Segal, Veta & Richard Frost
Segall, Miriam
Segelbaum, Martin & Lauren, Dani, Ben,
Sela, Paz & Jan Nemer Sela, Joy, Amy,
    Dory
Selcer-Frankman, Rolle Sue
Sell, Neil & Katherine Wilson
Selnick, Michael & Maureen, Lauren,
    Allison
Selnick, Sylvia
Seltz, Lewis & Beverly, Phillip, Stewart
Seltz, Ruth
Serfaty, Meir & Karen, Yoni, Elan
Serrell, Judith
Shamblott, Richard & Kathy, Jessica,
    Zachary, Jacob
Shanedling, Esther
Shapiro, Allan, Dana, Evan,
Shapiro, Bonni
Shapiro, Freida
Shapiro, Howard & Mimi Winger,
    Lindsay
Shapiro, Merle
Shapiro, Neal & Judith, Marc, Daniel
Shapiro, Peter, Michelle, Talia, Leah
Shapiro, Tillie
Share, H., Peter
Shark, Marjorie

Sharon, Ilan & Cindy, Ofir, Eliyah
Shaver, Jonathan & Iris Tzafrir, Avraham, Ariel, Amital
Shaw, Jeffrey & Cari, Daniel, Jessica, Carly
Shaw, Maurice, Barbara
Shaw, Peter & Michelle Chez-Shaw, Aaron, Marissa, Eli, Avi
Shear, James & Wendy, Jordan, Zachary
Sherayzen, Sofiya
Sherling, Glenn & Sheri, Ryan, Joseph
Sherman, Alan & Harriet
Sherman, David & Julie, Philip, Jeremy, Ian, Caleb
Sherman, James & Estelle
Shifman, Mikhail & Margarita, Julia, Anya
Shkolnik, Gennady & Yevgeniya, Alexander, Anna
Shmidov, Boris & Rachel
Sholler, Lawrence & Alice
Shom, Anne, Beverly
Shpayher, Norma
Shrell, Zelmar
Shteyman, Boris & Ida
Shurslep, Alex & Lina, Sabina
Siedband, Rick & Carol Sarnat, Elan, Kyla
Siegel, Gerald & Eileen
Siegel, Joshua
Siegel, Paul & Melissa, Jacquelyn, Jason, Jonah, Vanessa
Sigel, Melvin & Delores
Sigel, Steven & Sheila, Rachel
Sikora, Abraham & Marjorie
Silberman, Sheldon & Melissa
Silberstein, Marshall, Joshua
Silver, Dee
Silver, Melvin
Silver, Sarene & Jack Jagoda, Lawrence
Silverman, Ellen & John Lee, Madeline
Silverman, Jeanne
Silverman, Joel & Anne, Maya, Ethan
Silverman, Sherwin
Silverman, Stephen & Dianne
Silverstein, Andrew & Patti, Sydney, Jacob
Simenson, Steven & Wendy, Forrest
Simes, Joel & Roberta, Michael, Lauren
Simon, Anna, Zachary
Simon, Elaine
Simon, Jesse & Stacy, William, Jack
Simon, Mark & Ricki Roberts

Singer, Charles & Ann, Daniel, Ethan, Jason
Sirotin, Ilya & Karin Vineretsky, Angelica, Jonathan
Skolnick, William & Fran
Slutsker, Ilya & Debra, Mandy, Benjamin
Smith, Corey & Debrah, Drew, Aylah
Smith, Howard & Clarice
Smith, Robert & Deborah, Jacob, William
Smith, Steve & Janis, Jennifer, Jeffrey
Smolen, Howard & Robin, Aidan, Darion, Ari
Snyder, Herman & Betty
Snyder, Jaye & Kenneth Brimmer, Graham, Camille, Lucia, Tess
Snyder, M. Philip & Sharon, Laura
Snyderman, Arnold & Myra
Somers, Bette
Sondell, Jason & Sandra, Aidan, Caleb
Specktor, Sharon
Spencer, Craig & Debra, Andrew, Abby
Spencer, Jack & Marlene, Lindsay
Spicer, Paul & Sharon, Natalie, Michael
Spielberg, Stephen
Spiller, Daniel & Jennifer, Tobin, Abbott
Spira, Florence
Star, Leon & Rimma, Sonya, Vitaly, Miriam
Stein, Andrea & Nicholas, Senna
Stein, Andrew & Zohari, Neil, Brit,
Stein, Mark & Vicky, Jack, Elliott, Jody
Stein, Sanford & Cheryl, Ariel, Brianna
Stein, Steven & Lori, Samuel, Alexander, Nathaniel
Steinman, Ellen, Maury, Shelby, Dana
Steinman, Gerald & Carol
Steinman, Leslie, David, Jeremy, Rebecca
Steinman, Randall, David, Jeremy, Rebecca
Steinman, Sharyn
Stern, Allen & Cheryl Chimenti, Amy
Stern, Michael
Stern, Sigrid
Stern, Virginia
Stern, Wayne & Deborah, Jeff, Jessica, Michael
Stesin, Mark & Heather, Marlee, Kenneth
Stillman, Andrew & Cassandra, Alexandra
Stillman, Beverly
Stillman, Bruce & Naime Berge, Max, Grace

Stillman, Craig & Nancy, Madeline, Chloe
Stillman, David & Sharon, Ellie, Jonah, Sadie
Stillman, Faye
Stillman, M. Thomas & Liba
Stillman, Martin & Amy Susman-Stillman, Jacob, Ruby, Zachary
Stillman, Norton
Stillman, Ralph & Faye
Stillman, Scott & Susan, Noah, Ari
Stolz, Howard & Maria, Liliapua
Stone, Jon & Linda, Dahlia, Isaac, Amira
Strauss, Andrew & Cara, Emerson
Striker, Todd & Barbara, Eli, Samuel
Stropes, Christopher & Cindy, Elizabeth, Ellie
Sudit, Lee & Phyllis
Sudit, Marilyn
Sudit, Michael & Cheri, Geoffrey, Samantha
Sugerman, Deborah, Noah, Jacob
Sugerman, Jeff
Sussman, Alan & Vicki, Emily, Noah
Sussman, Lloyd & Marjorie
Sussman, Peter & Joanna, Mia, Zachary
Sutin, Jack & Rochelle
Swaiman, Jerrold & Barbara, Isaac, Ethan, Danielle
Swartz, Daniel & Laura, Mira, Isaac, Eden
Swartz, Steve & Harriet
Swerdlick, Willard & Muriel

Taback, Jean
Tankenoff, Gary & Marsha
Tankenoff, Scott & Helene, Daniel, Samantha, Mollie
Tapper, JR & Helene, Ari, Natan, Talya
Taragan, Barbara, Maayan, Afek, Yamit
Taran, Barry & Susan, Jess, Matthew
Taran, Eva
Taran, Jess & Elizabeth, Max
Tarkow, Howard & Janet, Lynn, Mara
Tarshish, Jonathan & Cindy, Gabriel, Evan, Adam
Tatarka, Zvi
Tennebaum, Bruce & Judith, Daniel
Teplinsky, Scott & Kim, Talia, Isaac
Thaler, David & Natalie, Alex
Thaler, Sharon, Jacob, Samuel, Abraham
Thiegs, Lisa & Joseph, Jacob, Eleanor, Samantha

Tilsner, Joel & Gail, Daniel, Laura,
Toberman, Howard & Deborah, Sari,
Amy,
Toberman, Marian G.
Toberman, Marion
Trach, Elisabeth & Terrence Goblirsch,
Hannah, Tyler, Madelyn Jo
Trach, Laurie
Trach, Ronald
Trestman, Jerry & Sharon
Trimble Hart, Andrea, Sebastian
Trockman, Daniel & Anne, Isaac,
Hayley
Troup, Rollie, Samuel
Tuvman, Kenneth & Helen, Adam,
Isaac

Ugorets, Olga, Angela, Aaron,
Nathan,
Nicole
Usem, Jeffrey & Stacie, Joshua,
Benjamin
Usem, Madalyne
Usem, Ron & Mary Tambornino

Velick, Sally
Vinitsky, Harvey & Helenlois
Vlosky, Bernard & Junghee
Volkert, Sherryl & Paul, Spencer, Maya

Wachs, Stuart & Janette, Leah, Jonah
Wallack, Max & Pearl
Walonick, Bruce, Jeff
Walonick, Charlotte
Walters, Barbara, Melissa, Justin,
Courtney
Warshawsky, Robert & Joyce
Washko, Nannette & Leonard, Grace,
Sarah, Elizabeth
Wasserman, Luis & Laura, Alana
Wasserman, Pavel & Ada
Weber, Elaine
Weber, Herbert & Barbara

Weil, Joseph & Robbi, Kathryn, Brian,
Jessica, Jacob
Weinberg, Jody, Paige, Haley
Weinberg, Ted & Eileen
Weiner, Andrew & Marci, Halley
Weiner, Gertrude
Weiner, Richard & Marla, Emily,
Jacqueline, Eva
Weinrib, Richard & Estee, Laura
Weinstein, Martin & Lora, Max,
Molly
Weinstein, Sheldon & Joan
Weisman, Gerald & Dorothea, Lisa
Weisman, Herbert & Dori
Weiss, Daniel & Amy, Jacob, Eliana
Weitz, Lillian
Werner, George & Lillian
Werner, Reginald & Natasha
Werner, Robert & Gayle, Michael,
Jeremy
Werner, Todd & Naomi King-Smith,
David, Arielle, Jonathan
Wertheim, Larry & Alice Okrent, Joel,
Ira
Wexler, Thomas & Ardis
Wieker, Miriam, Alexander
Wilensky, Howard & Alaine, Andrea,
Dana
Winer, Edward & Michelle
Winger, Eileen
Winnick, Lorraine
Winnick, Stephen & Arlene, Beth,
Robert
Winthrop, Reva
Winthrop, Stephen & Sonia, Edward
Wippman, Gertrude
Wirpel, Eleanor
Witebsky, Alan & Sandra, Jon,
Michael, Sarah
Wittcoff, Harold & Dorothy
Wittcoff, Theodore & Cynthia
Wittenberg, Jeffrey & Bonnie, Adam,
Michael
Wolchansky, Daniel & Melissa
Wolfe, Brent & Deborah, Maxwell,
Nathan

Wolfe, Jeff & Susan, Samuel, Benjamin,
Rebecca
Wolfe, Rustin & Allison Kaplan, Oscar
Wolfish, Barry & Randi, Jonathan,
Robyn
Wolfson, Margaret
Wolfson, Samuel & Randee, Bailee,
Jeffrey
Wolk, Carl & Marlene, Matthew
Wolk, Mark & Debra, Ariel, Justin
Wolk, Robert & S. Debby
Wolpert, Stephen & Jill
Woodman, Heidi & Stewart, Isaac,
Aaron

Yurko-Graney, Esther

Zacks, Jeremy & Jennifer, Yoni
Zaidenweber, Dora
Zamanskaya, Ninel & Ilya Paller
Zamansky, Ron & Lynn, Rory, Drew
Zames, Jonathan & Karen, Justin
Zaroff, David & Amy, Jordan, Noah
Zelle, Robert & Deborah Litman-
Zelle, Naomi,
Alisha
Zeman, Edward & Jane, Rachel,
Matthew
Zevelev, Lyubov & Alexandr, Eugene,
Marina
Ziessman, Scot & Julie, Emily, Zoe
Zimmerman, Manly
Zipkin, Heidi & David, Alexis,
Zachary, Ellie
Zipkin, Jill, Asher
Zoss, Barry & Teri
Zoss, Jeffrey & Stefanie, Marley
Zouber, Daniel & Dawn, Nathan, Levi
Zweigbaum, Larry & Barbara, Marlee
Zweigbaum, Michael & Elissa, Jacob,
Adin, Benjamin
Zweigbaum, Nate & Minnie
Zweigbaum, Sharon